# The Strategic Implications of
# European Union Enlargement

**Center for Transatlantic Relations**
**The Paul H. Nitze School of Advanced International Studies**
**The Johns Hopkins University**
1717 Massachusetts Avenue, N.W., Suite 525
Washington, D.C. 20036
Tel. (202) 663-5880
Fax (202) 663-5879
Email: transatlantic@jhu.edu
http://transatlantic.sais-jhu.edu

ISBN 0-9753325-8-9

# Table of Contents

# Acknowledgements

The idea for this book was launched in 2003 shortly after the European Union had decided to take on ten new countries and when the Convention was preparing a draft text for a Constitutional Treaty to accommodate decision-making in the EU. The project was expanded in 2004 during an authors' meeting in Washington to capture the breadth of the topic including both thematic and regional issues. We would like to thank the Thyssen Foundation for their generous support of a conference held on October 25, 2004, cohosted by the German Marshall Fund of the United States, in Brussels. We would also like to thank our colleagues at the Center for Transatlantic Relations, Katrien Maes, Philip Van der Celen, and especially Jeanette Murphy, for their careful work on the manuscript and their help planning the authors' meeting in Washington, and Marianne Viehfeger at the Department of Political Science, University of Erlangen, for her help administering the conference in Brussels. The Centre for European Policy Studies (CEPS), the Belgian Royal Institute for International Relations and the German Marshall Fund organized a presentation of the book in Brussels. We would like to thank Daniel Gros, Marco Incerti and Sven Biscop for their support. Last but not least we thank the authors for their energy and enthusiasm. Each author writes in his or her personal capacity, the views expressed are those of the authors and not their institutions.

*Esther Brimmer*
*Stefan Fröhlich*

# Introduction

With the 2004 enlargement, the nature of the European Union changed profoundly. The repercussions will be felt for years to come. The institutions of European integration have expanded several times before.[1] However, the 2004 enlargement brought in ten new countries raising the EU population's to over 450 million people.[2] In an historic move, Eastern and Western Europe were reunited in a regime of peace and stability. This book examines whether and how the enlargement affects the European Union as a strategic actor in international affairs.

Combining supranational and inter-governmental elements, the European Union is unlike any other organization on the current international scene. It is like a living organism that grows and changes over time. The 2004 enlargement ended one period of development and opened another. It reunited Europe and bridged the Cold War cleavages, but also extended the Union farther east and south. This process would continue in 2007 when Bulgaria and Romania are expected to join. In 2004, the European Council promised to open accession negotiations with Turkey in October 2005. The weight of the EU is no longer centered on Western Europe; therefore, enlargement may change what interests are advanced and who is heard in the policymaking fora of the Union. It certainly has affected the public's views in existing Member States. Concern about enlargement's effects on the European Union was one of the reasons voters in France and the Netherlands rejected the European constitutional treaty in referenda on May 29 and June 1, 2005, respectively.

This book examines the impact of the enlargement from a variety of perspectives. Initially one might assume that the EU would gain more power from an increase in size and population; but the new states are

---

[1] The original six signatories of the 1957 Treaty of Rome were Belgium, France, the Federal Republic of Germany, Italy, Luxembourg and the Netherlands. Successive enlargements brought in Denmark, Ireland, and the United Kingdom in 1973, Greece in 1981, Portugal and Spain in 1986, and Austria, Finland, and Sweden in 1995.

[2] The ten new members are Cyprus, the Czech Republic, Estonia, Hungary, Latvia, Lithuania, Malta, Poland, Slovakia, and Slovenia. See Delegation of the Commission of the European Union, "More Facts and Figures on the European Union and the United States." Available at http://www.eurunion.org/profile/EUUSStats.htm

poorer than the fifteen older members. However, there are many different kinds of power in the complex international society of the twenty-first century. An enlarged EU may wield some kinds of power and lose others. Therefore, the impact could be quite diverse and diffuse. Most authors in this volume do not argue that the EU's strategic engagement changes solely because of its increased size. Instead they highlight the effects of bringing in countries with geostrategic interests different from the previous members or the latest enlargement changing the basic nature of the EU itself—and, thereby, making it behave differently.

This is not a consensus text. Authors express varying opinions and different conceptions of Europe. The editors endeavored to respect these views by retaining the authors' own choices about capitalization of words with geographical and thematic significance such as "Eastern Europe."

Part one concentrates on the EU members themselves; part two addresses the region; and part three broadens the perspective to consider transatlantic and transnational issues. Thus, parts one and two look at the strategic impact in a geographic context, whereas part three takes a thematic approach. Stefan Fröhlich's opening chapter sets the stage explaining the EU after "the big bang." In chapter two, Hanna Ojanen and Kristi Raik discuss the most recent enlargement and Northern Europe, whose states joined in the immediately previous enlargement. In chapter three, Ulrike Guérot looks at how enlargement has affected existing member states, especially the founding states who have seen their EU change dramatically over the years. László Kiss's chapter four presents the effects of enlargement on the strategic outlook of new members in Central and Eastern Europe.

The authors in part two consider the EU's neighbors. Opening the section, Michael Leigh's chapter delineates the Union's new Neighborhood Policy and how it differs from accession policy. In chapter six, Henri Barkey and Anne-Marie Le Gloannec explain the impact of the most recent enlargement on aspirant Turkey. Timofei Bordachev considers the Russian perspective in chapter eight. Lothar Rühl concludes the section with an analysis of enlargement and relations between Europe, the Mediterranean and the greater Middle East.

In the third part, authors analyze transnational issues. In chapter ten, Esther Brimmer considers the impact of the most recent enlargement on transatlantic relations and the EU's strategic emphasis. In chapter eleven, Chantal de Jonge Oudraat presents a "euro-pragmatist" view of enlargement and the EU's role at the United Nations. In the following chapter, Daniel Gros notes that the enlargement did not add significantly to the already wealthy EU's global economic role, but does raise the possibility of more policy coordination in international institutions if members so choose. In chapter thirteen, Patrick Cronin and Muriel Asseraf elucidate EU and US policies on development aid and show that better transatlantic cooperation is not only a question of money. In chapter fourteen, Antonio Missiroli addresses strategic perspectives in an enlarged EU towards the use of force and the European Security and Defense Policy. In chapter fifteen, Peter Wehrheim explains agricultural policy and the latest enlargement. In chapter sixteen, David Michel discusses global environmental policy and the EU's enlargement to countries with their own ecological problems.

At the outset of the project in 2003, we wanted to understand whether the latest round of enlargement would have a geostrategic impact. The chapters present analyses of complex and diverse aspects of the EU's strategic presence. Most of the chapters were completed in late 2004 or early 2005. The defeat of national referenda in both France and the Netherlands on the EU's constitutional treaty in mid-2005 reinforces the importance of understanding the impact of enlargement. This book begins the exploration of how the enlarged EU and reactions to it are reshaping international affairs.

# The Strategic Impact of Enlargement within the EU

# Chapter 1

# The EU After the Big Bang

Stefan Fröhlich

## Introduction

On May 1 2004, ten new members joined the European Union (EU). This is by far the largest group that has been admitted to the EU at one go and it is a landmark achievement as it seals the end of the division of the continent. Only a few weeks later, on June 18, the European Heads of States and Government agreed on a new constitutional foundation for the enlarged Union trying to bring the EU to a higher level of integration and tie the member states together more closely.[1] Supporters of both would argue that this is another proof that widening and deepening have always gone hand in hand.[2] Enlargement is part of the success story of the EU and has been a key driver of and a triggering factor for further integration efforts. Nevertheless, all the joy should not distract from the fact that the differences in per capita income between old members and new members have never been so large before, implying that the difficulties of integration have also never been so large before. This begins with the common Constitution to which the members of the EU will have to agree. It is far from certain that the public will accept the proposal if referenda are held as planned in a number of countries, including Belgium, Denmark, Ireland and the United Kingdom (UK), and probably also France, Luxembourg, the Netherlands, Poland, Portugal and Spain. In the UK in particular, such a referendum could lead to quite an embarrassing result. It is unlikely that the EU could then simply follow the Irish example and keep voting until the desired result is produced. At this point, it is not clear how the EU could deal with such a blow.

---

[1] Conference of the Representatives of the Governments of the Member States. Provisional consolidated version of the draft Treaty establishing a Constitution for Europe. Brussels, June 25, 2004 (OR.fr). CIG. 86/04 2003.

[2] Christoph Heusgen, Jutta Edthofer, Issue 12—"Towards the "Big European House"?, in: *Challenge Europe Online Journal* (September 13, 2004). European Policy Centre, Brussels.

Apart from this fundamental question, it not only remains to be seen what concrete progress the Constitutional Treaty (CT) actually entails but also whether the enlarged EU can successfully tackle the list of unresolved issues. Though the institutional changes envisaged by the CT are the farthest reaching in the Union's history, the EU still needs to find a way to an efficient policy- and decision-making process, including, first of all, the reduction of the number of Commissioners to a workable level, clarification of the division of labor between the new President of the European Council (EC), the Commission President and the new EU Foreign Minister, and consequent implementation of the possibilities for flexible integration. As the number of actors has increased, the complexity of the Union's decision-making processes will rise unless member states develop a new culture of consensus and compromise or a fundamental overhaul of the institutional scaffolding takes place. It is doubtful that those mitigating developments will occur. Rather new and old members will tend to push for their own interests in a more articulate way than before making the Constitutional Treaty's most important goal—a more efficient decision-making—almost untenable.

Beyond these institutional adjustments, there are at least three sources of conflict which have to be addressed in an enlarged EU: the *economic disparity* with all its consequences for financial redistribution, especially regional policy schemes, in the EU; the *new competition between old and new members*, which let some observers speak of a "race to the bottom" supposedly been touched off by the new members, others of a healthy pressure for some of the old members like Germany and France to finally implement the reforms necessary to fulfill the "Lisbon agenda"; last but not least the *geographic scope* letting the EU outreach to regions of real or possible instability—with tremendous implications for Common Foreign and Security Policy (CFSP)/ European Security and Defense Policy (ESDP). One could easily add another one—though it will not be addressed in this paper—, that is the *structural diversity* reinforcing the differences between "heavy-weights" and "lightweights" in terms of population, society and economy impeding the development of a collective identity.

This list of unresolved conflicts is of no small order. What is disturbing is the fact that the EU has not been able in recent years to implement even some of the necessary changes before enlargement.

After enlargement, all the problems have only become more difficult. More members with a veto power in certain policy fields will make a decision more difficult to reach and strengthen the tendency to reach minimalist decisions. And more members mean more possibilities for coalition building and pork barreling, further hindering reform.

## The new Constitutional Treaty: an answer to the institutional repercussions of enlargement?

The new Constitutional Treaty basically contains three central innovations.[3] First of all, the appointment of an elected President of the EC and the creation of the post of a European Foreign Minister contribute to the consolidation of political leadership in the enlarged EU. Second, by strengthening the European Parliament's (EP) rights of co-decision and its budgetary powers, the Union's institutional framework comes closer to a two-chamber legislative system. Third, the new constitutional foundation strengthens the EU's ability to evolve dynamically in the future by the extension of the possibilities for flexible integration and the establishment of simplified procedures for the reform of decision-making and many EU internal policies.

Though these are important steps in the integration process, the question remains of what concrete progress the Constitutional Treaty actually entails in terms of efficiency and political leadership. The power to take action in a Union of twenty-five or more states will largely depend on the ability of the political leadership to define goals and to push for their implementation in day-to-day politics. The executive must have the authority to take the initiative and co-ordinate the actions of the member states. But any proposal to change had to be pragmatic to avoid transposing solutions from other bodies that would be meaningless in the EU's unique institutional framework.

In other words, one could not simply follow the letter of Montesquieu's separation of powers but one had to adopt its spirit in clarifying legislative and executive responsibilities. There was no other way then to live up to the EU's reality of both its Community and intergovernmental strands. That is why, on the plus side, in the future

---

[3] Conference of the Representatives of the Governments of the Member States, Provisional consolidated version of the draft Treaty establishing a Constitution for Europe. Brussels, June 23, 2004 (OR.fr), CIG 86 04 2003.

the EP will be stronger (sharing decision-making control over some 70 areas, including agriculture and the structural funds; with vital control over the often opaque decisions of the Commission and the Council of Ministers) and national parliaments will have a new role in limiting EU legislation, the Constitution will make the EC a fully fledged EU institution, so its decisions can be challenged in the European Court, and why the European Commission will have executive power by right and not merely on the decision of the Council of Ministers—all measures which should create greater clarity and accountability. And this, of course, is also the reason why on the negative side, there are new complexities like the dual presidency (a rather confusing innovation); the future foreign minister, who will wear two hats (as a Commissioner and as a servant of the member states) and must share his or her representative role with the Council President; the old rotation principle regarding the chair of the different ministerial councils between all twenty-five; or the assurance of the "one vote per state" principle in an enlarged Commission.

In the enlarged EU, reform of both the directly elected EP and the bureaucracy in the Commission of course is relatively straightforward. Their numbers must be kept manageable but their structures do not have to change dramatically. Regarding the Commission's effectiveness, the decision of the Intergovernmental Conference to reduce the number of Commissioners is a positive result. The formula laid down in the Constitution provides the number to be set at two-thirds of the number of member states. In an EU-27, this would mean that the Commission would comprise 18 members, including the President and the EU Foreign Minister. Even more praiseworthy is the decision that the distinction between "European Commissioner" and "Commissioner" without voting rights proposed in the Convention's draft, was not taken up in the Constitution.[4] The problem however is that the reduction of the Commission's size will only take place from 2014 onwards, and not in 2009, as the Convention's model for the Commission had proposed. There is no doubt that until that point the negotiations and the political bargaining climate will become harsher in the Commission despite the extension of the Commission President's powers for determining the internal division of labor in the Commission.

---

[4] Consolidated version of the draft Treaty, Art. I-25.

It would be also wrong to expect the differences in the EP to be only mathematical. Fundamental changes will appear in its political dynamics. The most important change will be the creation of new alliances, some "holier" than others. In its constitutive session mid-July, the EP returned to the traditional partnership of center-right European Peoples' Party (EPP-ED) and European Socialists (PSE), which is a clear change to the past parliamentary term when the axis of power spanned between EPP-ED and Liberals. Though enlargement did not polarize EPP-ED and PSE but rather united them in a number of key areas and in the goal to uphold and even expand the influence and position of the EP in the institutional triangle, one shouldn't underestimate the possibilities of important alterations in the relationship between the largest national delegations in different parties.[5]

Certainly the most fundamental implications caused by enlargement will be related to the Council of Ministers, where all the member states are represented, and the European Council above it, where heads of state and government meet every three months. They are the most powerful set of institutions of the EU, sharing both executive and legislative power. And they were/are most urgently in need of reform. That is where the Convention and the final Constitution have only achieved a mixed record—blocked by the member states themselves.

The introduction of a President of the EC, elected for a period of two and a half years, certainly is a positive feature of the new Constitution. The potential influence of the EC is high, as it is supposed to give guidance to and establish all other Council formations. As a consequence of the new continuity in the chair of the EC, the relative institutional influence and decision-making capability vis-à-vis the Council and the Commission might also be enhanced. However, the real power of this new office will depend on what its president makes of it and how he/she manages the rather vague division of labor between him/her and the new Foreign Minister. In CFSP matters there will be considerable disagreement on questions of competence between the two offices, and between them and the Commission President.[6]

---

[5] Pija-Noora Kauppi, Issue 12—"Towards the "Big European House," in: *Challenge Europe Online Journal* (September 13 2004).

[6] Draft Treaty, Art. I-21, par. 2.

The creation of the EU Foreign Minister in this context could also strengthen the Union's foreign policy profile and improve the coherence of EU external relations.[7] Apart from the ambiguities regarding the division of tasks, the effectiveness and influence of the Foreign Minister will also be limited by the inadequate extension of majority decision-making in CFSP. Another critical issue is the Foreign Minister's hybrid role between the Commission and the EC. One can expect his/her loyalty rather to lean towards the interests of the EC thus weakening the Commission. In any case, for the enlarged EU to maintain coherence of its actions and to increasingly assume responsibility as a global player, the EC and the new Foreign Minister will have to take on a substantial leadership role.

Regarding the new voting system in the Council and the extension of majority voting, the record of the new Constitution is an ambivalent one. Even during the negotiating process fears of domination felt by applicant countries had to contend with fears among some existing members that deeper integration was at risk. The most prominent example was the split of the member states on a fault-line dividing the old members from the new—founder states (France and Germany) at one extreme and latecomers (Spain and Poland) at the other. France and Germany, joined by the UK, were accused of trying to form a new directoire in the Council of Ministers, to counter the more integrated European Commission and the Parliament, by instinct and composition more sympathetic to the smaller states. Against severe pressures from Poland and Spain, who tried to preserve their Nice-status as "almost bigs and equals," the thresholds of the future voting procedure in the Council laid down in the Constitution were increased by 5 percent compared to the Convention's draft thus decreasing the enlarged Union's effectiveness. The Intergovernmental Conference raised the quorum of states necessary for a qualified majority from 50 to 55 percent, and the population quorum from 60 to 65 percent. Above that, a blocking minority in the Council must now include at least four member states. The idea behind this additional criterion is to limit the weight of the most populous countries, most particularly France, Germany and the UK.

---

[7] Draft Treaty, Art. I-27.

Compared with the system of triple-majority set down in the Nice Treaty, the voting procedure laid down in the Constitution is a success. Compared with the Convention's draft, however, the increase of the thresholds of the future voting procedure and the introduction of supplementary conditions will make it more difficult to shape majorities and easier to form blocking minorities.

In the case of the extension of majority decision-making in the Council, there is no need to mention that this is the decisive instrument for more efficiency in the enlarged EU. The need to be flexible in this regard is also implicitly recognized in the draft Treaty, as it states the possibility of extending majority voting without having to renegotiate the whole treaty via the so-called "passerelle clause"—albeit by unanimous decision. Nevertheless, there are areas—like some areas in justice and home affairs, CFSP/ESDP (mostly defense-related), tax harmonization, questions of social security, some areas of trade in services and intellectual property, some in environmental policy—where unanimous decision-making will most likely continue in the medium term. The prospect of further enlargement may also decrease the political will to cede unanimity in these fields—considering also the fact that the new "emergency brake" clause in the Constitution provides the possibility of a de facto veto for every member state in a number of sensitive areas. In this context, given the possible conflicts over the division of funds in the enlarged EU (chapter III), it may also turn out to be one of the biggest failings that the Constitution retained the principle of unanimity for setting up a multi-year financial framework beyond 2013.

Fortunately, such tendencies may be compensated by more flexibility in different policies. As the EU expands, "enhanced co-operation" (as it already exists under the framework of opt-outs in main policy areas such as the euro, Schengen, and defense) is likely to continue in main policy fields at a more pronounced level. Most probably, this enhanced co-operation will increasingly include the second and the third pillars. With the growing number of member states the possibilities of forming different sets of alliances will also increase. Recent power struggles in the EU already indicated that there are no natural allies any longer, not even among the smaller or larger member states. Even for the Franco-German axis, which seemed to get new momentum because of the Iraq war, there is no guarantee of an ever-lasting relationship in the enlarged EU as different interests regarding the EU's budgetary reform and the Common Agricultural Policy (CAP) have demonstrated. It is therefore probable that on a number of issues member states will engage in temporary and pragmatic ad hoc pacts. This will certainly enhance the multi-speed Europe approach and could strengthen the Union as long as these pacts are organized in an EU framework.

Political leadership in the Union will become a very ambivalent and delicate issue in the enlarged EU. It can either give Europe fresh impetus, or just deepen its divisions as the trilateral summit of the "big three" in Berlin in February 2004 demonstrated when, in spite of frantic lobbying, only a few countries (Belgium, the Czech Republic, Greece and Hungary) were interested in following the invitation to assemble a "pioneer group" of countries that would press ahead with deeper integration in vaguely defined new policy areas; the majority instead, looked at it as an avant-garde initiative that could be a means of coercing other member states.[8] But there is simply no alternative to more flexibility. More members and a greater diversity in an enlarged Union will otherwise put a strain on current structures and endless debates will emerge on the practicalities of making EU politics. For example, is it really imaginable that every government minister takes the floor on every agenda point? It would make the traditional tour de table unbearable for even the most enthusiastic federalists. The same is true with regard to the principle of unanimity, which in the future EU will have the capacity to paralyze it like never before. But progress in individual policy areas will also slow down even under qualified majority voting if we do not use more "enhanced co-operation" and let the 'willing and able' go ahead in specific areas.

## The Agenda 2007 Proposals: a real paradigm shift?

On February 10, 2004 the Commission published its proposal for the "financial perspective 2007-2013." The new financial framework contains proposals for regulations on Europe's future cohesion, structural and agricultural policy, two proposals on the reform of the European own resources system, and a draft version of a reformed

---

[8] *Financial Times*, February 16, 2004, p.9.

inter-institutional agreement between the Council, Parliament and the Commission.[9] A week later the Commission adopted the third report on economic and social cohesion.[10] These two documents form the basis of the so-called "Agenda 2007" reforms. Finally, on July 14, 2004 the Commission presented a package of detailed draft legislation specifying the communications published in February 2004 on the key issues of the future and the financial basis of the Union's policies. The new package will determine the financial basis for EU policy-making until the middle of the next decade. The ambitious goals of the Commission's proposals are to generate value for money by structural operations, and to focus funds on projects, which generate added value at a European level. Overall, they try to balance, on the one hand, solidarity for the new members and weak regions in the old member states with, on the other hand, investments in future tasks.

Moreover, according to Brussels, the CAP will, for the first time, not be the dominant expenditure category. The unwillingness to increase transfers to Brussels on the one hand and the increase in the number of farmers, caused by enlargement, on the other, cannot be reconciled without structural changes to the CAP.[11] However, since the financial framework for CAP was defined by the compromise reached in this field in October 2002 and valid until 2013, greater efforts for savings had to focus on the second largest part of the EU budget, namely the EU's structural and cohesion policy. Yet it is in this policy field, where old recipients are unwilling to give up transfers in order to benefit new members with a greater need for financial support while at the same time having to follow Brussels' ambitious spending plans.

The Commission is sticking to a total budget of €336.1 billion, whereby 78.54 percent of this amount is to be set aside for the primary objective "Convergence," the highest support category. For the

---

[9] European Commission, *Building our Common Future: Policy Challenges and budgetary means of the Enlarged Union 2007-2013*, COM(2004), 101 final, Brussels, February 10, 2004.

[10] European Commission, *A new partnership for cohesion. Convergence competitiveness cooperation. Third Report on economic and social cohesion (Cohesion Report)*, Brussels, February 18, 2004.

[11] Apart from that, the ongoing negotiations in the Doha Round of the World Trade Organisation, and the required changes to the system of agricultural support for European farmers that will have to follow if those negotiations are really to be a successful round, will certainly result in tremendous political problems within the EU. The modest proposal that Commissioners Pascal Lamy and Franz Fischler presented was already vigorously rejected by France.

two other objectives, "Competitiveness and employment" and "Territorial cohesion," the Commission estimates that respectively €57.9 billion (17.2 per cent), €13.2 billion (3.9 per cent) will be required.[12] Net payers are calling for a drastic reduction of these totals and a concentration of resources on the highest support category, i.e. the EU's least-developed regions. On the other hand, the UK and Germany support the Commission's proposal regarding the attribution of a special status to those regions, which for statistical reasons following the accession of the eight poorer new members in Central and Eastern Europe exceed the limit of 75 percent of EU-gross national income (GNI) set for the highest support category. In both countries regions are affected by this proposal.

Another contentious issue in this context is the Commission's idea to tie the European structural and cohesion funds to the objectives set out in the Lisbon Strategy. The Commission holds that economic growth and cohesion are complementary tasks and that European cohesion policy should be an integral part of the Lisbon Strategy. The net payers, however, reject this re-orientation of the objectives and claim that the way the funds are spent should be determined according to the aim set out in Art. 158 of the EC Treaty: to reduce existing differences in structural development between various regions by promoting the most disadvantaged regions. The instruments for implementing the Lisbon Strategy, they argue, are instead at the national level's disposal. Apart from that, there would be no need for any additional spending programs at the European level. Rather there should be a constant exchange of information and competition, following the Commission's "open method of co-ordination," to attain the Lisbon objectives.

Anyway, the reallocation of funds will certainly lead to more tensions given the demographic changes Europe faces in the coming decades. An aging population means that social expenditures will increase significantly in every member state. Taking this implicit public debt into account, Germany's debt is estimated to stand at some 270 percent of Gross Domestic Product (GDP), and the situation in

---

[12] EU Commission, *Third Cohesion Report*, op. cit.

[13] Carsten Hefeker, "Europe after Enlargement: What's next?," in: *Intereconomics* (May/June 2004), 114-115.

other member states is not much better.[13] This will not only have tremendous implications for domestic policy; this is why the Stability Pact should remain restrictive—not for the sake of a common currency but for the sake of pending pension obligations.[14] It will also imply that redistribution between member states will become less possible politically and financially at a time when the socio-economic gap is higher than ever before in the history of the Union. The call for restraint with the ambitious €1,025 billion EU spending plan by the six main paymasters—Austria, UK, France, Germany, the Netherlands and Sweden—sounds the opening shot in what can be expected to be a fierce battle over the size of the future EU budget, which is likely to last for years. The net payers emphasized that they did not favor an EU budget close to the current budget ceiling of 1.24 percent of the EU's GNI, a measure of gross domestic product used for public expenditure, and on December 2003 urged the Commission to make "painful" choices and to cap spending at its current level of 1 percent of GNI.[15]

The group of net payers, which also includes Denmark and Finland, which were not signatories of the December letter, has been strongly opposed by the group of "cohesion countries," including Greece, Portugal and Spain that reject any drastic constraint to the 1 percent margin and instead call for a rise in allocated resources close to the Commission's proposed financing scheme. A third group, gathering around Belgium, Luxembourg and Italy, does not seem to have a firm view on the budget ceiling. Last but not least, the new members agree on two objectives: rejecting the 1 percent ceiling and weakening the upper limit of 4 percent of national GDP for payments made to them out of the EU budget.

Though the net payers are not calling into question the budget ceiling of 1.24 percent of EU-GNI in general, they wish both authori-

---

[14] The other side of the fiscal coin certainly is that Europe has to decide what to do with the Stability and Growth Pact, which is continuously, and quite openly and aggressively, violated by the larger governments such as France, Germany and Italy. The issue here again is not only the credibility of the Pact but the general need to come to fiscal terms with the structural changes in ageing societies. The Pact is an indicator of whether governments are able to respond to these challenges or not. If not, debt crises and financial problems will also affect the core of the international financial system.

[15] *Financial Times*, February 11, 2004, p.6.

zation and payment appropriations to remain clearly below this level—especially as actual payments total some 0.98 percent of EU-GNI. The Commission wants to pledge significantly more funds, i.e. higher authorization, so that appropriations for payments average 1.14 percent of EU-GNI in total.[16] Compared with the proposal by the net payers, the Commission's proposal would make a difference of more than €113 billion in payment appropriations, and almost €210 billion, if appropriations for commitments are considered for the overall period. Put another way, this would be the amount of savings for the net payers compared with the Commission's approach. According to calculations of the German Institute for International and Security Affairs, given Germany's present share of 22.6 percent of the funds provided, the alternative would save €47.44 billion over the entire period whereas if the Commission's levels are used, Germany would only save €22.67 billion.[17]

One should add that the Commission starts from the assumption of an average growth of 2.3 percent in EU-GNI over the next seven years, which is quite an optimistic forecast. If growth rates turn out to be lower and payments will get closer to the 1.24 percent budget ceiling, the net payers' financial burden would even increase. For this reason, they still reject the Commission's proposal as a starting point for negotiations. The UK has already indicated that it would not allow a reconsideration of its special status with regard to its refund that keeps its contribution at a net balance—a debate that has been rekindled by the Agenda—, and France will certainly not give up the interests of the French farmers. Germany has evoked additional potential for disintegration among the net contributors by insisting that the EU structural funds should primarily be spent on helping the least-developed regions of the enlarged EU—a proposal that will of course find grateful allies among its new neighbors. If, however, the implementation of the Agenda is to begin early in 2006—as the Commission has scheduled—the member states have to reach an agreement by June 2005 at the latest.

---

[16] Commission tables detailed proposals for Community spending 2007-2013. Reference: IP/04/910 (July 14 2004). http://europa.eu.int/rapid/pressReleasesAction.do/reference

[17] Peter Becker, "Agenda 2007," *SWP Comments 20* (August 2004), p.4.

## Economic competition in the enlarged EU: "race to the bottom" or chance for structural reforms?

This analysis reveals another source of conflict. Negotiations on the next financial framework for the enlarged EU is not just a one-way concern with the old members worried about much of EU funding shifting towards new member states such as Poland, the Czech Republic and the Baltic States. It is a process of mutual dependence, with pressures and incentives and thus bargaining between old and new members as these negotiations will almost certainly also bring more pressure to bear on the older members to reform in terms of tax harmonization, competition among localities and job exports (outsourcing). Governments in the large euro zone economies already worry about painful reforms in welfare states to make their countries more competitive and attractive as investment locations by reducing their high tax burdens and real unit labor costs. If the new members realize that the current system will not be tenable for much longer, they may be able to force "old Europe" to accept change and find ways to deal with those challenges.[18]

The problem with the current enlargement round is that it takes place in the middle of a period when hopes are rising that the euro zone economy is at a turning-point, but when the EU still seems to be far away from its Lisbon target to catch up with the American economy by 2010. Though European politicians praise the Union's huge economic advantages—its stability, social cohesion, investments in infrastructure, a skilled workforce, and the promise and as-yet-unfulfilled potential of the world's biggest market—, European growth has been too low for years, averaging 1.7 percent annually since 2000.[19] While there have been four quarters of growth in the US since the fourth quarter of 2003 with clearer signs of recovery, in Europe, it has been quite the reverse: when economic growth started to go up in the US, it started to go down in Europe.

In part, this reflects Europe's traditional position lagging behind the US in the economic cycle. But there are signs that the forces pow-

---

[18] Ognian N. Hishow, "Pressure from the East European Member States, German Institute for International and Security Affairs." *SWP Comments 24* (September 2004).

[19] Gordon Brown, Nicolas Sarkozy, Hans Eichel, "Europe must reform if it wants to speed up growth," in: *Financial Times*, May 21, 2004, p. 13.

ering the current upturn are weaker in Europe. The reasons for this are manifold and well-known: lower level of employment; lower productivity as Europe has not been able to take advantage of the benefits the US has reaped from new information and communications technologies in the 1990s; inflexible labor markets due to the high ratio of social insurance contributions to wages; the average tax burden in the EU; less flexible monetary and fiscal policy; less responsiveness to economic and financial changes, to mention the most prominent ones.[20] Thus, the key questions are: will enlargement further contribute to the already existing gap in terms of European competitiveness? From the internal prospective, how much pressure will the new members put on the EU to reform the social welfare state on the one hand, and how much will costs to the West increase in the form of higher transfers on the other hand?

Optimists hold that in the long run, the EU growth rate would catch up with that of the US as productivity will be boosted from integration of the new members' low-wage labor forces and the results of a number of domestic reform efforts (already taking place in the UK, the Netherlands, Ireland, and some Scandinavian countries) in core European economies such as France and Germany following the upcoming election circles. Skeptics tell us that, despite some ambitious economic reform steps in Western Europe, and hopes that the new members will provide a growth spark to the rest of Europe, expectations would be likely exaggerated.[21] The only way for income levels to converge across the expanded EU is for productivity in the new members to rise towards western levels which requires huge investment in and turnover of both human and physical capital in those countries. Though there has been some of that in terms of useful infrastructure, retraining and education projects, there is still a long way to go given the initial gap in productivity levels and GDP per head in most countries (respectively 40 and 46 percent of the EU-15 level).[22] To catch up with the per capita income of the EU-15 will

---

[20] Stefan Fröhlich, "Globalization and the Future of Transatlantic Relations," Working Paper 106/2003, Konrad-Adenauer Foundation, Sankt Augustin (April 2003).

[21] For a discussion on this question see Adam Posen, Fleeting Equality: *The relative size of the US and EU economies to 2020*, US-Europe Analysis Series (September 2004). The Brookings Institution, Washington.

[22] *Economist Global Agenda*, "A May Day milestone. April 30th, 2004," October 8, 2004. http://www.economist.com/agenda/displayStory.cfm?story_id

require growth rates at least 3 percentage points above the long run average of the old members.

However, as the biggest adjustment steps took place shortly after the collapse of the planned economy in the early 1990s, the largest gains in form of increased merchandise trade and direct investment in these countries have already occurred.[23] It was in this period that labor and savings have been released from inefficient uses, market incentives were adopted and the needed infrastructure was provided, that capital moved to the most promising investment opportunities, and new technologies were introduced. In other words, recent growth rates have already provided a very contradictory picture: immediately after giving up the planned system the economies of the new members started to expand at a rate up to 6 percent a year. But as of the end of the nineties the pace slowed significantly to less than 2 percentage points above the EU-15 growth rate. This reflects again the diffi-culties of the catch-up process for these countries.

Moreover, one shouldn't overestimate the new member countries' overall economic size relative to the EU-15. Even growth rates a few percentage points higher on average in those countries translate into little added demand or capacity for the old members. However, this means also, that the degree to which the domestic economies of the old members could be hurt by the future capital outflows to these countries (without significant net returns) is often overstated. As in the German case, gross direct investment in the former accession can-didates ranged around some 45 billion Euros between 1990 and 2003, that is 1.5 percent of the overall German gross capital invest-ment.[24]

This leads to the second aspect of the issue—the internal one. It is an exaggeration to blame the current domestic problems in countries like France and Germany on the pressure from the new countries. Of course direct investment created jobs in the East—sometimes even at the expense of the German or (certainly to a lesser extent) the French labor markets. Yet it is also true that investment in these countries will create income in the form of net profit and other return to capital, not

---

[23] Ognian Hishow, "EU Extension to the East and Exporting jobs," *SWP Comments 8*, Berlin (May 2004).

[24] Ibid

to mention the fact that outsourcing in the 1990s rescued many companies, which otherwise would have gone bankrupt.

Basically, the discussion is dominated by two assertions: the EU-15 is too expensive as an investment location due to its high tax burden and jobs are threatened from low wages in the new members (outsourcing). Again, one has to take into account that the peak in terms of job exports was reached in 2003 and of course reforms introduced in countries like Germany and France are not solely in response to enlargement but basically the result of increased competition in a global world. Nevertheless, enlargement has spurred reforms in the EU-15, not so much because of the alleged tax competition in terms of the burden on labor. Of course, corporate tax rates in the new members are far lower than in Germany, or other western economies, ranging from 28 percent in the Czech Republic at the high end to 15 percent in Estonia at the low end. Slovakia recently introduced a unified corporate, personal income, and value added tax rate of just 19 percent. However, taking the high ratio of social insurance contributions to tax revenue, work in the new members has also become more expensive during the 1990s. By 2002, in countries like the Czech Republic, Poland or Hungary, the percentage of social insurance contributions in the total tax revenue was similar to that of Germany (all ranging between 33 and 39 percent).[25] The real 'problem' for the old members in the short run is with the low cost of capital in these countries, which attracts direct investments in production forms that are both capital and technologically intensive and improves the quality in the capital stock in the new members.[26] In the long run, however, as investments promote the quality of human capital and the convergence of productivity and hourly wage rate in the new members, the effects will be the creation of fewer jobs and the loss of their cost advantage.[27] The effect of this will be that the new members will gradually lose their competitive edge as an investment location with cheap labor.

Efforts in the EU-15, especially in France and Germany, to reduce the cost of labor by lowering non-wage costs, as a first step to reduce

---

[25] UN Economic Commission for Europe, Economic Survey of Europe, 2004, No. 1, Geneva 2004, 136.

[26] Hishow, "Pressure from the East European Member States", p.2.

[27] European Commission, European Economy (No. 4, 2003), Brussels 2004, 11 ff.

the public sector share of GNP, and at the same time to modernize the tax systems is the right answer to domestic problems. This option is better than calls for tax harmonization, which is likely to reduce growth rates in the new member states and thus increase the cost to the EU-15, in form of higher transfers.

## Implications of enlarging CFSP/ESDP

A third source of conflict will certainly be the ambivalent relationship that the new members have with the Euro-Atlantic institutions. Currently, they all have an absolute preference to entrust security in Europe, and even beyond, to NATO under American leadership. All of them worry that ESDP could become a way to exclude the US from Europe and all hope that it does not. This deliberate pro-American choice goes hand in hand with a clear analysis of developments in the US. However, if Washington were to change its relationship with NATO fundamentally, the Union's ESDP would remain as a fall-back position—an alternative institutionalization of defense that would avoid the worst of all scenarios: a general re-nationalization of defense.[28]

Moreover, continuing unrest in Iraq is leading even the so-called "new" European countries to pull their troops out of the country. The perception that Iraq is a troubled enterprise, or indeed a failing venture, has increased the political costs for those European leaders who have supported Bush and boosted the electoral returns for those that criticized US policy. Hungary has already announced its intention to withdraw its troops from Iraq and Poland would like to do the same after the Iraqi elections. Despite all fears of a German-French *directoire* in CFSP/ESDP matters, joined by the United Kingdom from time to time, there is now a greater consensus between "old" and "new" Europe on helping especially the political process in Iraq.

There is a link between the EU's geographic enlargement and the widening of its strategic awareness. The new members will give priority to relations with the eastern part of the continent, and they will try

---

[28] Stefan Fröhlich, "Euro-Atlantic Enlargement and its implications for ESDP," in: A. Maurer/K-O Lang, E. Whitlock (Eds.), *New Stimulus or Integration Backlash? EU Enlargement and Transatlantic Relations*, SWP, Berlin (July 2004), 29-35.

to convince old members in the EU to develop CFSP and ESDP in that direction. The prospective inclusion of candidates from Southeastern Europe will have a similar effect, extending the EU's future strategic vision and interests automatically to the fringes of the Middle East and Asia. Expanding the EU simply means that it faces an enlarged periphery and comes in touch with regions of uncertainty. The 2004 enlargement round makes the Union a direct neighbor of the Ukraine (a country with a pro-Western foreign policy rhetoric, but rising political and economic dependence on Russia), Belarus (Europe's last dictatorship), Moldova (Europe's poor house, haunted by the Transnistria conflict), Russia (along the whole Eastern Baltic Sea region, including Kaliningrad with all its soft security risks), and of course the fragile post-Yugoslavia. The permeability and safety of the new eastern borders thus will become vital interests of the new members and presumably shape their approach to CFSP/ESDP and other relevant issues such as national minorities, illegal migration, cross-border trade or visa regulations.[29]

In this context, Russia is the key country in the region with a tremendous impact on EU interests in its new periphery. Brussels wants to support further democratic development to benefit from Russia's vast economic resources and potential as a major trade and economic partner while at the same time secure Russia's continued collaboration in the "war on terrorism" and other relevant security issues. With regard to the wider Europe, the EU will face the challenge of demanding from Moscow that it respect the sovereignty and territorial integrity of its neighbors by arguing that good relations with Moscow and integration into the EU are not incompatible goals for these countries. This is the only way to prevent Russia from reasserting a dominant role in Eastern Europe—currently a potential threat in Russian foreign policy.

While it will be difficult to reconcile the conflicting priorities of strengthening CFSP/ESDP and reorienting it further east, it will, at the same time, be impossible to perpetuate what is currently one of the CFSP's biggest problems: the EU's (geo)strategic introversion. The new members are, theoretically at least, better suited to take radical steps towards making ESDP more responsive to the EU's new

---

[29] Roland Dannreuther (Ed.), *European Union Foreign and Security Policy: Towards a Neighbourhood Strategy*, London/New York: Routledge, 2004.

periphery and to pooling military capabilities—with an emphasis on specialization, multinational complementarity of forces and joint procurement projects—though they recognize that they still need to develop specific capabilities that are essential for meeting new threats, specifically focusing on counter-terrorism. In recent years, they have done everything possible to cooperate with the military alliance, participating in peacekeeping missions in Bosnia, Kosovo and even Afghanistan. That is why at the 2002 Prague Summit the US welcomed the accession of Romania and Bulgaria to NATO and why they would also like to see them being members of the EU. Bulgaria closes the land bridge between Hungary and Turkey, letting NATO and—once Turkey has become member—also the EU reach out into the Black Sea and Caspian basin. In addition, Romania has become an important ally in Afghanistan with a strategic base in the Black Sea.

Diverging historic experiences and the peculiarities of geographic location will certainly evoke a wider range of foreign and security policy interests in the future EU. Nonetheless, after enlargement the EU more than ever needs clarification on its geostrategic ambitions. It is almost certain that the new members will automatically force the EU to define more clearly its vital zones of interest within an enlarged EU given their unstable periphery. Closely related to this aspect are two issues:

1. *The question of the geographic scope of the EU: "how wide and how deep."* The EU's success in transforming and integrating new members, in turn, has been contrasted with its long running inability to develop strategic approaches to countries and regions that cannot and should not be offered membership for the near future. The Commission's new design of a policy, first known as "wider Europe," now the "European Neighbourhood Policy," is a first step in that direction trying to "export" stability to and create incentives for political and economic reform in neighboring countries without an offer of membership.[30] The "Copenhagen criteria" in effect, define an institutionalized Europe in civic terms rather than delimiting enlarge-

---

[30] Commission of the European Communities COM(2003) 104 final, „Communication from the Commission to the Council and the European Parliament: "Wider Europe—Neighbourhood: A new Framework for Relations with our Eastern and Southern Neighbours," Brussels, March 11, 2003. http://europa.eu.int/comm/world/enp/pdf/com03_104_en.pdf

ment on geographical grounds. Even the new Constitutional Treaty does not clarify the criteria for Union membership. It vaguely states that such membership "shall be open to all European States which respect the values referred to in Article I-2, and are committed to promoting them together."[31] If the slightest consensus on the limits of 'Europe' existed, it would be easier for the EU to agree on its response to the lengthening queue of applicants—and vice versa insofar as the ability of potential applicants to assess their own suitability for membership.

2. *The question of setting priorities for the type of force-projection operation to which the EU members wish to be able to contribute.* This is one of those areas in which the beginnings of an answer have been provided by ESDP's "Headline Goal" without openly raising the question of what the European capability should be primarily tailored to do. In 2002, European countries sent military forces to intervene to restore and maintain peace in Afghanistan, Rwanda, Sierra Leone, Ivory Coast, Kuwait, Iraq, Georgia, Tajikistan, Bosnia, Kosovo, and Macedonia. In 2003, significant deployments were dispatched individually in Congo. A total of nearly 100,000 troops from European countries are deployed abroad. Yet, in a majority of cases, these deployments have been dependent on external sources for transport, support, and protection. The capacity for autonomous action remains severely constrained. Progress has been made on capabilities and infrastructure but the process has encountered structural obstacles, the first and best known being the level of military expenditure.

The EU's new ambition also has serious implications at the operational level. Implicit planning assumptions envisage a virtual geographical radius for EU military crisis management up to approximately 2,500 miles from Brussels. With an enlarged Union, the potential radius stretches as far as 6,200 miles from Brussels. This has consequences in terms of projecting and sustaining forces. The EU security strategy provides the EU with a new framework that demands more rapid deployability, more flexible units, and more combined joint forces.

---

[31] Conference of the Representatives of the Governments of Member States, Brussels, August 6 2004 (OR.fr) CIG 87/04. Treaty establishing a Constitution for Europe. Title IX, Article I-58, 1.

This implies the transformation of European military forces. The revolution in military technologies has dramatically changed the way American forces now operate; the effects of this transformation have been obvious in the recent conflicts in Afghanistan and Iraq. Europe cannot rival the scale and speed of these developments and for the most part, reform efforts remain painfully slow and disordered but the transformation of its own forces is nonetheless a precondition to an effective European Security Strategy.

Last but not least, the EU's willingness to become more autonomous and more responsible not only needs clarification in terms of the unnecessary difficulties with Washington but also with regard to the delicate balance between flexibility and legitimacy when it comes to decision-making. Waiting for the lowest-common-denominator decision in a Union of twenty-five members could lead to paralysis and inaction. On the other hand, further "communitarisation" of CFSP/ESDP seems completely unrealistic in the medium term given the fact that especially the new members, together with the UK, have a clear preference for a "Europeanized" NATO (making a more independent ESDP counterproductive) and thus an intergovernmental approach to the organization of European Foreign and Security policy. This explains why Europeans already have agreed that a group of countries could deepen their cooperation in defense after a qualified majority vote of the European Council. Permanent structured cooperation opens the way for role specialization, asset pooling, common procurements, and ultimately an effective rationalization of defense efforts throughout the Union. If Europeans develop this common will, there should be also the possibility of implementing horizontal specialization among members whereby respective niche capabilities could become collective assets for the EU—a point closely related to the issue of transatlantic command structures.

## Conclusion

There are basically two scenarios for the future development of the EU after enlargement. The one is that Europe continues to try to solve the structural challenges by making slight changes to the current system which are acceptable to everyone and thus mostly ineffective. This is a very likely scenario given the fact that also under the new provisions of the Constitutional Treaty the EU system continues to be a mix of compromise-based supranationalism and intergovern-mentalism, characterized by makeshift solutions that turn out to be quite persistent. Powers will remain diffused in a mist between member states and the EU institutions. This could lead to a new type of "Eurosclerosis" in the sense that the enlarged EU will lose its ability to make decisions and to deal with its internal problems and its increasing external problems, such as security policy, its relations with the US, its policy towards neighbor and developing countries, and the terrorist challenge. This will ultimately lead to the exemption of countries from certain policy areas/measures, to opt-outs of some CFSP fields, and—in the worst case—even to leaving the Union using the exit option that the new Constitution contains.

In the second scenario, Europe can adjust to the fundamentals of its policy. It realizes that more harmonization cannot be the answer to more competition within and between the countries of the Union. It is able to reach clear political decisions as to which policy fields should be common ones (excluding agriculture), and how much solidarity or redistribution there should be between members states. It gives the countries the power to decide in which areas they want to cooperate according to the "method of open coordination" instead of increasing the "aquis" ever more. The provisions regarding the instrument of enhanced cooperation are now combined in a more plausible manner. Moreover, two new instruments of differentiation have been introduced in the field of common defense policy—"structured cooperation" for member states with higher military capabilities, and "closer cooperation" in the field of mutual defense. Thus, change is possible. Member States that want to go beyond what already exists can do so by means of special treaties between them, whether bi-, tri-, or multilateral. The resulting Community will more closely resemble the "multi-speed-Europe" than the formally structured arrangements referred to as the "Europe of variable geometry." In such a Community *mutual recognition* is the basic principle instead of harmonizing everything in an ever-growing Union along the traditional community method.[32]

While the second scenario is more desirable, and a condition if Europe is really to be able to fulfill the "Lisbon agenda," it remains to be seen whether the EU will go down this path. It has missed the

---

[32] Stefan Fröhlich, *The Difficulties of EU Governance*, (Frankfurt: Peter Lang, 2004), 157-164.

opportunity to do so when it was comparatively easy, though this does not mean it is impossible now. Hopefully, new members will bring more pressure for reform to bear on the older members and force the larger EU to recognize the challenges and address them soon and comprehensively.

*Chapter 2*

# The Strategic Impact for Northern Europe and the Baltics

Hanna Ojanen and Kristi Raik

## Introduction

The Nordic-Baltic region is tied together by centuries-old historical bonds. The Swedish empire stretched over a large part of the area up to the early 20th century. For example, the Estonians know the 17th century as "the good old Swedish time" when the University of Tartu (one of the oldest universities in the region) was established by the Swedish king. The Norwegians, for their part, celebrated their 100 years of independence from Sweden in 2005. The Cold War implied a dramatic division and a halt to normal relations between the countries separated by the Iron Curtain, but since the late 1980s, cooperation has been strengthening again. The five Nordic and the three Baltic states have among themselves, and sometimes also comprising other Baltic Sea region countries, dense networks of common organizations, governmental and non-governmental, public and private. Of the five Nordic countries, three are members of the European Union: Denmark, Finland and Sweden, while Norway and Iceland are linked to the Union through the European Economic Area.

Having supported the independence of the Baltic countries, Estonia, Latvia and Lithuania, the Nordics worked actively for their membership in the Union. The main reason for this was the expected positive effect of enlargement on regional security and stability. In this chapter, the implications of enlargement for these countries are examined. The chapter discusses the importance of centripetal and centrifugal forces at play in the region, locating similar views and dividing lines between the countries. It considers the possibilities for instrumental coalition-building within the EU and whether the increasing centrality of the Union for the Nordic countries might together with the Baltic countries' membership lead to a "reunion" of the region, also increasing pressure on Norway and Iceland to join.

## The Nordic and Baltic states in the EU

*Different Nordic membership profiles*

The five Nordic countries considerably vary among themselves both as to their relations with the Union and as to their membership profile. When Sweden and Finland joined the EU in 1995, it was predicted that they would become "top-of-the-class members," in contrast to Denmark whose profile in the Union had become that of a "naughty boy."[1] Denmark had opted out from the most advanced federalist features of the European Union as a result of the negative vote in the referendum on the Maastricht Treaty in 1992. The opt-outs, also called the Edinburgh exemptions, include common defense, or preparation and implementation of actions with defense implications, EU citizenship,[2] parts of Justice and Home Affairs that are not intergovernmental in character, and the third phase of the Economic and Monetary Union (EMU). Yet, Sweden came rather to share the Danish skepticism on the Union, explained to some degree by the skeptical public opinion and political parties that are very critical of the EU.[3]

Finland, however, did become a "model pupil" at least as far as the first years of its membership were concerned. Finland is the only one of these countries to be member of the Economic and Monetary Union (EMU).[4] Finnish public opinion has been relatively stable in favoring the Union, some 40% being in favor, some 30% against, yet not necessarily as critical as to aim at leaving the Union. There is, however, disinterest towards the EU that is shown by the low turnouts in EP elections (31% in 1999, 41.1% in 2004).[5]

---

[1] See Hans Mouritzen, "The Two Musterknaben and the Naughty Boy: Sweden, Finland and Denmark in the Process of European Integration," *Cooperation and Conflict* 28:4 (1993), pp. 373-402.

[2] Union citizenship can only be seen as a supplement to national citizenship, not as a replacement.

[3] The Danish EU-critical *Junibevægelsen* and *Folkebevægelsen mod EU* are now joined at the European Parliament by Swedish representatives from the equally critical *Junilistan*.

[4] Denmark voted 'no' to Euro in September 2000 by 53.7%, Sweden in September 2003 by 55.9%.

[5] Tapio Raunio and Teija Tiilikainen, *Finland in the European Union*. (London: Frank Cass, 2003), pp. 37-38.

Security political affiliations are another main difference between the five: Norway, Iceland and Denmark are members of NATO, while Finland and Sweden are militarily non-aligned. Yet, this has not impeded them from cooperating with each other in security and defense. In addition to traditional UN peacekeeping cooperation, one example is NORDCAPS (Nordic Co-ordinated Arrangement for Military Peace Support), military cooperation between the five with regard to military peace support operations that includes a Nordic Pool of Forces Register[6] with some 12,000 personnel. There is also defense materiel cooperation among them.[7] Cooperation within the Union in these matters is complicated not only by the fact that not all are members, but also by the Danish defense opt-out.

Although Iceland and Norway are not EU members, they are in the European Economic Area, and also part of the Schengen agreement that was exceptionally extended to them in order to safeguard the pre-existing Nordic Passport Union. Nordic cooperation functions in a sense as their link to the Union. They also share the other Nordic countries' concern for the Baltic Sea region. Moreover, as EEA members, they contribute financially to the new member states. Through the EEA Financial Mechanism, Norway will pay €113 million per year to the 10 new EU members between 2004-2009 in return for the access to the internal market of the enlarged EU.[8] Similarly, Iceland pays about €1 million to the new members annually.

For Iceland, fisheries have been the main reason for keeping out of the EU. Iceland's security policy is based on a bilateral relationship with the USA in addition to NATO membership. Iceland's participation in Nordic security political cooperation has been very limited, and in the context of Nordic cooperation in general, it has been somewhat critical of Nordic cooperation being too concentrated on the Baltic Sea region. However, Iceland was very active in the question of

---

[6] http://www.nordcaps.org/start.htm

[7] See more in Martin Lundmark, "Nordic defence materiel cooperation," in Bo Huldt, Tomas Ries, Jan Mörtberg and Elisabeth Davidson (eds.), *The New Northern Security Agenda*. Strategic Yearbook 2004. (Stockholm and Helsinki: Swedish National Defence Collegeand Finnish National Defence College, 2004.) Pp. 207-230.

[8] The funds can be used for development and investment projects by different authorities, organizations and businesses. See the web site of the Norwegian Ministry for Foreign Affairs, http://odin.dep.no/europaportalen/norsk/eos_fin/p30005883/032141-130278/dok-bu.html

independence for the Baltic states and the first to recognize their independence from the Soviet Union in 1991.[9]

Norwegian regional interests have been centered on the North, the Barents region, and Russia, and less on the Baltic states. Nordic cooperation has for Norway represented an important indirect link to the EU, but a clearly limited one as the EU's political weight increases. Norway has organized a referendum on EU membership twice, in 1972 and 1994, and twice voters said "no." Pro-EU political parties hope for a third referendum after the next general elections in September 2005. Public opinion has for the past couple of years been quite positive towards eventually joining the Union, reaching 51% support in May 2004. EU enlargement has been seen as one factor increasing this support; also a sense of intensifying marginalization in European politics and European security might tip the balance in favor of the EU.[10]

### The Nordic EU members' attitudes towards EU enlargement

While the three Nordic EU countries have been supporting EU enlargement in general,[11] they have showed particular support for the membership of the Baltic States, mainly for reasons of security and stability. For Denmark, the Baltic states became the new focus of foreign policy after the end of the Cold War, with the aim of normalizing relations with them. Danish activism in recognizing their independence has even been seen as something revolutionary in that it meant an open confrontation with great power interests. Subsequently, Denmark has become an important key ally and bridgehead for the Baltics towards both the EU and NATO.

---

[9] See, e.g., Baldur Thorhallsson, "The Distinctive Domestic Characteristics of Iceland and the Rejection of Membership to the European Union," *Journal of European Integration* 23:3 (2001), pp. 257-280.

[10] *Aftenposten* 18.5.2004, http://www.aftenposten.no/nyheter/iriks/politikk/article793064.ece; see also *EUobserver* 10.8.2004 at http://www.euobserver.com/?sid=9&aid=17065 and Nina Græger, "Norway and the EU security and defence dimension: A 'troops-for-influence' strategy," in Nina Græger, Henrik Larsen and Hanna Ojanen, *The ESDP and the Nordic countries: Four variations on a theme.* (Helsinki and Bonn: Programme on the Northern Dimension of the CFSP, Finnish Institute of International Affairs and Institut für Europäische Politik, 2002).

[11] See chart.

## Chart.   Public Attitudes

| | Membership good thing | Support for enlargement | Support for a common Foreign Policy | Support for a common Defense/ Security Policy |
|---|---|---|---|---|
| **EU25** | **47 (–2)** | **46 (–4)** | **66 (+2)** | **74 (+3)** |
| Denmark | 54 (–3) | 59 (–4) | 50 (–6) | 61 (+1) |
| Finland | 46 (+7) | 48 (–5) | 55 (+3) | 57 (+6) |
| Sweden | 37 (–3) | 54 ( = ) | 49 (+1) | 55 (+6) |
| **EU15** | **48 ( = )** | **42 (–5)** | **65 (+1)** | **72 (+2)** |
| Estonia | 31 (–7) | 58 (+2) | 62 (+1) | 77 (+1) |
| Latvia | 33 (–13) | 67 (–2) | 67 (–1) | 77 (–3) |
| Lithuania | 52 (–3) | 67 (+5) | 61 (–1) | 70 (–5) |
| **NMS10** | **43 (–9)** | **71 ( = )** | **68 (+3)** | **79 (+3)** |

**Eurobarometer Spring 2004 (EB 61), European Commission**
http://europa.eu.int/comm/public_opinion/archives/eb/eb61/eb61_en.pdf
**(Parenthetical: Change since autumn 2003)**

One can perceive several Danish motives for supporting enlargement. Among them, security has been prominent: the most important Danish interest has been stabilization and democratization of North-Eastern Europe. Economic and environmental motivations have played a role, particularly questions related to pollution of the Baltic Sea and the safety of old-fashioned nuclear installations such as in Ignalina in Lithuania.[12] Moreover, motivations related to identity can be perceived: support for enlargement has been seen as a moral obligation but also a way to cash-in on substantial goodwill and prestige from the applicant countries.[13] Public support for enlargement has, in fact, been exceptionally high in Denmark.

Regional security motivations also contributed to Denmark's support for the so-called "regatta model" in enlargement, that is, starting negotiations with all the applicant countries at the same time. As Heurlin and Zepernick put it, allowing for all the three Baltic states to proceed together towards membership served to stabilize and enlarge

---

[12] Bertel Heurlin and David M. Zepernick, "Denmark and the EU's Eastern Enlargement," in Helmut Hubel (ed.) *EU Enlargement and Beyond: The Baltic States and Russia.* (Berlin: Berlin Verlag, Arno Spitz GmbH, 2002), pp. 180-182, 189, 191.

[13] Lykke Friis, *An Ever Larger Union? EU Enlargement and European Integration.* (Copenhagen: Danish Institute of International Affairs, 2000), p. 60.

a specific but not exclusively Danish sub-regional sphere of interests, while guaranteeing a common European response to any serious security threat emanating from the region in the future. The "regatta model" was initially heavily opposed by the Commission and other member states that favored a small enlargement, but supported by Sweden, and it was indeed a Danish-Swedish non-paper that brought the official enlargement agenda in line with their view at the Helsinki Summit in 1999.

The massive enlargement has, however, led Denmark into a complicated position with its partners. For many EU members, enlargement had to be accompanied by deepening integration, and this led to domestic difficulties in Denmark that already has its opt-outs from the more federal elements of the Union. Heurlin and Zepernick put forward the idea that furthering enlargement might be a Trojan Horse for a country like Denmark which could use it to halt further integration: by helping the Baltic states catch up with the front runners in the negotiations and letting more members in, the number of member states skeptical towards deeper integration might increase.[14]

Sweden, for its part, has for a long time played a central role in the Baltic Sea region. It also strongly supported Baltic independence and contributed to the negotiations in 1994 that led to the withdrawal of Russian troops. Sweden's regional initiatives started in 1991 with Prime Minister Carl Bildt and continued when Göran Persson became prime minister in 1996. Sweden worked through, for instance, the "Baltic Billion Fund"[15] and the Council of the Baltic Sea States, the secretariat of which was established in Stockholm in 1998.

Sweden has supported enlargement basically because the Baltic countries are its close neighbors: enlargement is a question of security and stability, while also transboundary problems are easier to meet within the EU. Also popular support for enlargement has been strong in Sweden. Indeed, EU enlargement and Sweden's central role in the

---

[14] Bertel Heurlin and David M. Zepernick, "Denmark and the EU's Eastern Enlargement," pp. 6, 182-188. Similar arguments have been presented about the United Kingdom.

[15] SEK 1 billion approved by the Parliament in 1996 for projects in areas such as energy, infrastructure and environment and to stimulate trade, investments and cooperation in the Baltic region. The Fund was closed at the end of 2002. http://www.sweden.gov.se/sb/d/3095/a/18411/m/wai;_kBbz4ej0F8.

Baltic Sea region are less controversial for the general public than Sweden's own EU membership. Support for the EU in Sweden has actually been in sharp decline since its membership application in 1991. Two major political parties, the Green party and the Left Party, are very critical towards the Union.

During the Swedish EU presidency in 2001, enlargement was one of the three priorities, the "three e's," together with employment and environment. The Gothenburg Summit decided on the conclusion of the membership negotiations in 2002 and accession before EP elections in 2004, which meant that Latvia and Lithuania were to catch up with Estonia.[16]

Finland's national strategy towards the neighboring areas has consisted of support for the political and economic transition process and a balanced social development. Enlargement has been a policy priority for Finland, essentially geared to avoiding the emergence of new dividing lines in Europe, and at increasing stability and prosperity. The consequences of enlargement have been perceived perhaps somewhat more critically than in Sweden and Denmark. On the positive side, there are the gains in stability and trade; on the negative side, however, one perceives a relative loss of influence in the Union in, e.g., as far as votes and the number of members of the European Parliament are concerned. The domestic opinion on enlargement has been rather negative. Enlargement has not been perceived as an important issue to be furthered, and it should not imply extra costs. There have also been fears linked to adverse effects on trade and unwanted immigration of labor force. A possible "watering down" of supranational features as a consequence of enlargement might not play as well in Finland as in Denmark, either, at least if it is to continue on its early pro-integrationist line.

Although Finland has supported the Baltic countries EU membership, it was, contrary to Sweden and Denmark, for a long time much

---

[16] See notably Gunilla Herolf, "Attitudes and Policies of Sweden in the Baltic Sea Region," in Helmut Hubel (ed.) *EU Enlargement and Beyond: The Baltic States and Russia.* (Berlin: Berlin Verlag, Arno Spitz GmbH, 2002). See also Hanna Ojanen, "Sweden and Finland: What difference does it make to be non-aligned?," in Nina Græger, Henrik Larsen and Hanna Ojanen, *The ESDP and the Nordic countries: Four variations on a theme.* (Helsinki and Bonn: Programme on the Northern Dimension of the CFSP, Finnish Institute of International Affairs and Institut für Europäische Politik, 2002).

more cautious towards their membership in NATO. This difference can be explained by security policy considerations: Russia is a more central security factor for Finland than for the Scandinavian countries, and its opposition to NATO enlargement affected the Finnish position as well. As to the procedures of EU enlargement, Finland was first in line with its Scandinavian neighbors: in early 1997, it favored the regatta model. Even the White Book on Defense (March 1997) mentioned the importance of starting negotiations with all applicants simultaneously, in order not to endanger the stability-enhancing effect of enlargement. In the summer, however, as the Commission recommended the 5+1 approach—starting negotiations only with Estonia, Poland, Czech Republic, Hungary, Slovenia and Cyprus—Finland changed its position: Estonia could in the first round pave the way for all the Baltic states towards membership. Enlargement was a central issue also during the Finnish EU presidency in 1999. There, however, the Swedish-Danish sponsored regatta model gained ground, and thus in the Helsinki Summit, six more countries were included in the negotiations, while Turkey was given the status of an applicant country.

*The Baltic states' road to EU membership*

EU accession of the Baltic states has to be viewed in the context of their overall "return to the West"—a process that started in the late 1980s and culminated with achieving the two main goals, membership in the EU and NATO. From a Baltic perspective, the transition was at the same time miraculous and self-evident. Miraculous because of the unexpected, rapid, radical and all-encompassing nature of changes that took place on both domestic and international scale within less than two decades. In 1988, at the height of the "Singing revolution," even full independence was considered by most Balts to be an unrealistic goal; hardly anyone gave a serious consideration to membership in the EU and even less in NATO.[17] Yet as the changes unfolded, each step was perceived as a natural part of rectifying the wrongs of the Soviet era and restoring the historic European identity of the Baltic nations. Europe— and more broadly "the West"—symbolized freedom and prosperity and was seen as a natural context for national identity and development.

---

[17] On the struggle for independence of the Baltic countries, see David J. Smith, Artis Pabriks, Aldis Purs and Thomas Lane, *The Baltic States: Estonia, Latvia and Lithuania.* (London and New York: Routledge, 2002).

The EU was hesitant in its support for the independence of the Baltic States up to the attempted coup in Moscow that took place August 1991, in order not to endanger the position and reforms of Michail Gorbachev in the Soviet Union.[18] Thus, the Baltic countries lagged somewhat behind the Central European transition countries when they regained independence in 1991. They were still treated as "former Soviet republics" by the EU, as distinct from the Visegrad countries, which had started to develop bilateral relations with the Union in the late 1980s. Contractual relations between the EU and the three Baltic states were not established until in May 1992 when the Trade and Co-operation Agreements were signed. By that time, the Visegrad countries had entered much further-reaching Association Agreements that incorporated the prospect of EU membership. The objective of full membership of the Baltic countries was eventually officially confirmed by both sides in the Free Trade Agreements that were signed in the summer of 1994.

Meanwhile, during the first half of the 1990s, the foreign policy agendas of the Baltic countries were largely dominated by relations with Russia. Although Russia initially supported the Baltic independence, the positive tide in relations was soon replaced with mutual hostility. Reluctant to accept complete "divorce" of former Soviet republics, Russia adopted the policy of "near abroad" from 1993 on, aimed at maintaining control over the Soviet area. For the Baltic countries, the Russian threat to their independence and to the Western orientation remained tangible until the withdrawal of the Russian/ex-Soviet troops, which was completed by August 1993 in the case of Lithuania and by August 1994 in the cases of Estonia and Latvia.

It was only after the dispute over the Russian troops had been resolved that the Baltic countries could properly focus on closer integration with Western structures of cooperation. All three submitted applications for membership in the EU in late 1995. Estonia gained a temporary lead when it was included in the first group of accession negotiations that were opened in March 1998. This decision was hotly

---

[18] Sven Arnswald, "The Politics of Integrating the Baltic States into the EU—Phases and Instruments," in *The European Union and the Baltic States: Visions, Interests and Strategies in the Baltic Sea Region*, Programme on the Northern Dimension of the CFSP, Vol. 2., ed. Mathias Jopp and Sven Arnswald (Helsinki and Bonn: The Finnish Institute of International Affairs and Institut für Europäische Politik, 1998), pp. 35–44.

disputed in the EU and came as a disappointment to Denmark and Sweden, and even more to Latvia and Lithuania. On the other hand, several EU countries were at that time reluctant to open negotiations with any of the Baltic States, one of the main reasons being their wish not to irritate Russia. Hence, the inclusion of Estonia was a major accomplishment for the Baltic region, as it gave a clear sign of the readiness of the EU involve the Balts in the accession process on an equal basis with the Visegrad countries. The label of "former Soviet republics" was losing relevance.

To the surprise and astonishment of many observers, the closer the goal of EU membership came, the more it actually became questioned by the Baltic people. Two important distinctions should be noted here, however. First, among the Baltic countries, the Lithuanians on average are considerably more positive towards the EU than the Latvians and Estonians; and second, between the political leadership and the broader public. The political elites of all three countries were indeed unequivocally committed to the twin-track accession to the two major Western organizations, the EU and NATO. Eurosceptic opposition groups of any notable size only emerged on the eve of referenda on EU membership, held in 2003. Until then, EU integration was consistently pursued by all three countries, in spite of frequent changes of government and instabilities in domestic politics. The broader public, by contrast, never questioned the Western orientation and the rhetoric of European identity and history, but it did take a skeptical stance towards the EU, especially in the cases of Estonia and Latvia. While membership in NATO has been constantly supported by a clear majority in all the Baltic countries, public support of the Estonians and Latvians to the EU was so low at some point prior to the referenda that there was a real possibility of a "no" outcome. Nevertheless, a strong majority voted for EU membership in the referenda (67% in Estonia, 69% in Latvia and 91% in Lithuania). Now Estonia and Latvia belong to the most eurosceptic member states, being close to the United Kingdom and Sweden in terms of public opinion on the EU (see chart above).

The main reason for both support and opposition is, perhaps paradoxically, the same: security and independence, and even the existence of the nations. This paradox is a key to understanding the position of the Baltic countries in the EU and in particular in EU foreign policy.

According to official policies, the main purpose of both EU and NATO membership is to safeguard the future independence, security and well-being of the nations. The main perceived threat to both independent state and national existence is obviously Russia—a threat not labeled as such in the official rhetoric, not necessarily named in public discussion, but considered so obvious that it needs not be mentioned. In official circles, the EU and NATO have been assigned different, but complementary and mutually supportive roles in guaranteeing the Baltic independence: the former is needed for economic development and non-military aspects of security, whereas the latter provides "hard" security guarantees. To use the words of Vaira Vike-Freiberga, the President of Latvia, the inevitability of both, and reluctance to prioritize either one, has been as obvious as the fact that a person needs two arms and does not wish to choose which one could be cut off.[19]

Yet public opinion has not easily agreed with this position. EU membership has been considered necessary for state security, but at the same time a threat to national identity and sovereignty. Many Balts have been reluctant to give away part of their sovereignty to Brussels, after having been independent for just over a decade. Even comparisons between the Soviet Union and the EU have not been unusual in public debate: both symbolize foreign power and a large, complex set of bureaucracy and rules being imposed on small nations. Still, it has been impossible to separate identity and sovereignty from security, and to promote or protect one of them without incurring implications for the others. This has created a dilemma that provides one of the main explanations to the euroscepticism of the Balts: in order to gain the security and stability provided by EU membership, one has had to pay the price of weakening national self-determination.[20] The particular significance of this dilemma in the cases of Estonia and Latvia is explained by the fact that both countries have inherited a large

---

[19] Address by Vaira Vike-Freiberga, President of Latvia, Marshall foundation lunch, Istanbul, 28 June 2004. Available at http://www.mfa.gov.lv/en/nato/news/4457/?pg=5037

[20] For an elaboration of this point, see Kristi Raik, *Democratic Politics or the Implementation of Inevitabilities?—Estonia's Democracy and Integration into the European Union* (Tartu: Tartu University Press, 2003), pp. 166-176. On the security/identity –dilemma, see also Pami Aalto, *Constructing Post-Soviet Geopolitics in Estonia: A Study in Security, Identity and Subjectivity*. Doctoral Dissertation, Department of Political Science, University of Helsinki (2001), pp. 43–45, 164–166; and Merje Kuus, "European Integration in Identity Narratives in Estonia: A Quest for Security," *Journal of Peace Research* 39:1 (2002), pp. 91-108.

Russian-speaking minority from the Soviet era, which has made nation-building more complicated than in most other post-communist countries in East Central Europe.[21]

The political leaders of the Baltic States have stressed, however, that it is membership in Western organizations, including the EU, that strengthens national self-determination by giving to their countries a seat and a voice at the tables where crucial decisions concerning their future and well-being are taken. Nevertheless, the Baltic leaders tend to share the concern of their citizens over sovereignty. They tend to be reluctant to give more power to Brussels and to strengthen the supranational elements of the Union. On the other hand, it is very important for them that the EU functions effectively and that they are included in integration in all fields, in order to be able to take part in decision-making that affects their countries in any case. They also tend to agree with the position that the interests of small states in the EU are best protected by strong common institutions. This brings again a dilemma into the Baltic views on the EU: the wish to protect sovereignty seems to speak for intergovernmental decision-making and for less rather than more integration, but then again, the influence of small states in intergovernmental cooperation is usually weak, and possible exclusion from certain EU activities would leave them with no influence whatsoever. The Baltic States might adopt a compromise solution of neither promoting the deepening of integration nor acting as a brake—in other words, going along with what is happening. This would obviously leave them in a rather passive position in the Union.

While more precise positions of the Baltic countries on the EU's development are still taking shape, it is worth to emphasize that full membership in the EU and NATO has given to the Baltic countries the sense of being anchored in the West for which they have quested since the regaining of independence. The year 2004 marks the end of the post-independence transition period and the insecure position on the border between two regional centers of power, the EU and Russia.

---

[21] The Russian minority constitutes approximately 29% of the population in Latvia and 26% in Estonia. Up to now, nearly half of the Russian population of Estonia and Latvia have been granted citizenship of their country of residence, almost the same number are stateless, and the rest are Russian citizens. In Lithuania the Russian speakers account for only 7% of the population, and the great majority of these are Lithuanian citizens.

## The impact of enlargement on the role of the EU in international affairs

*Nordic views on the role of the EU in security policy*

The strategic and security political implications of EU enlargement for the Nordic countries depend on what role they give for the EU in their security policies. For all of them, this role has become more central in recent years. For Sweden, the EU has been a central forum in that it is not a NATO member, but "federal" elements such as common defense are not a Swedish goal. Rather, Sweden has been working in the EU for civilian crisis management and conflict prevention.[22] Sweden's foreign policy role conceptions have been delineated as follows: a pragmatic minimalist in the EU, a bridge-builder in the Baltic Sea region, and a non-aligned collaborator in NATO.[23] To this, one could add emphasis on the importance of the United Nations. Sweden still sees its non-alignment as a stabilizing factor in the region. Alongside its contribution to soft security in the region, it has also contributed materially to the Baltic countries' defense. It sees NATO as a valuable partner in the region through the Partnership for Peace (PfP) and the Euro-Atlantic Partnership Council (EAPC).[24]

Danish foreign policy has traditionally been described as based on a structure where different organizations each have their specific roles. Some count four such cornerstones, NATO, the UN, Nordic cooperation and the EU, others would add the Organization for Security and Cooperation in Europe (OSCE) as a fifth one. Traditionally, thus, the EU's role has been limited and shaped by the other important fora; for instance, defense questions have belonged to NATO only. The EU has, however, gained importance as a consequence of enlargement and the strengthening of its security and defense dimension.[25] Still, Danish

---

[22] The Swedish EU presidency contributions were notably a programme for crisis prevention, establishment of the Committee for Civilian Aspects of Crisis Management, and emphasis on EU-UN relations.

[23] Lisbeth Aggestam, "An End to Neutrality? Continuity and Change in Swedish Foreign Policy," in Robin Niblett and William Wallace (eds.), *Rethinking European Order. West European Responses, 1989-97.* (Basingstoke: Palgrave, 2001.)

[24] See Gunilla Herolf, "Attitudes and Policies of Sweden in the Baltic Sea Region," pp. 225-228.

[25] See Henrik Larsen, "Denmark and the EU's defence dimension: Opt-out across the board?," in Nina Græger, Henrik Larsen and Hanna Ojanen, *The ESDP and the Nordic countries: Four variations on a theme.* (Helsinki and Bonn: Programme on the Northern Dimension of the CFSP, Finnish Institute of International Affairs and Institut für Europäische Politik, 2002), p. 91. Cf. also Bertel Heurlin and David M. Zepernick, "Denmark and the EU's Eastern Enlargement," pp. 179-180.

policies within the EU are dramatically limited by the Danish opt-
outs, which have in practice made Denmark into a passive observer.
Moreover, a gap has emerged between what Denmark supports in the
EU and what it can take part in. Traditionally, Denmark has placed
great importance to peacekeeping, mine clearance and humanitarian
aid. Yet, even such activities, if taking place within the framework of
the ESDP, are excluded because of the opt-out. As a consequence,
Danish influence in this field is even less than that of other small
states. Thus, it is understandable that for Denmark, transatlantic relations and a continued role for NATO are preferred alternatives in
security and defense. Denmark has underlined this through, e.g., participation in the Iraq war.[26]

Among the three, Finland has counted most on the EU as a strong
international actor. Finland's position on the external border of the
Union is a factor that has clearly influenced its security and defense
political thinking. Cross-border cooperation and involvement of non-
EU partner countries have been central in the Finnish view on the
EU's neighborhood ever since its "Northern Dimension" initiative in
1997. Through the initiative, Finland has aimed at increasing the efficiency of the EU's presence in the North, including the Baltic countries, Poland and Russia as "partner countries" of the EU, while also
multilateralizing its relations with Russia by making them an issue of
the EU as a whole.[27]

In the EU, Finland has been very flexible in its interpretation of
what the policy of military non-alignment allows. Yet, it did react in
December 2003 when the mutual defense clause was, against Finnish
expectations, on its way to the Constitutional Treaty. Finland gathered
the other non-aligned countries to propose a watered-down version of
the clause, leading in the end to a weaker compromise formulation. To
a great extent, Finland and Sweden have become each other's reference points in security policy. They have also jointly taken initiatives
such as including the Petersberg tasks in the Amsterdam Treaty. They
share a similar pragmatic view on crisis management. The public

---

[26] See Henrik Larsen, "Denmark and the EU's defence dimension: Opt-out across the
board?," pp. 106-111, 141.

[27] See more in Christer Pursiainen, "Finland's Policy Towards Russia: How to Deal with the
Security Dilemma?," in *Northern Dimensions. Yearbook of the Finnish Institute of International
Affairs.* (Helsinki: The Finnish Institute of International Affairs, 2000) pp. 63-84.

opinion is not against crisis management in the EU in either of the countries, and not even against defense-related cooperation, even though it is against NATO. Finland has, like its Nordic neighbors, also supported the build-up of the Estonian armed forces, and together with the other Nordics, the Baltic Defense College and the formation of a Baltic peacekeeping force.

Even though Finland differs from Denmark and Sweden in that it sees that a strong union and deeper integration is good for small states, all three have similar views on EU foreign policy, favoring pragmatism, and a civilian EU as opposed to a military one. Interestingly, Norway also shares many of the other Nordic countries' security political views. In general, Norway's foreign political profile is one emphasizing human rights, the non-military crisis management capacity of the EU, humanitarian aid and disaster relief—also because it is seen that the humanitarian arena is where small states have a "comparative advantage." NATO and American military engagement in Europe are important for Norway. In the ESDP, it shares the non-EU NATO members' position with, for instance, Turkey. Norway is interested in participating in ESDP, even though it might paradoxically reduce the need for American presence and thus cause problems for Norway. It has used a "troops-for-influence" strategy in the EU to gain political influence through contributing forces to the EU Headline Goal.[28]

Similarities and differences between the four Nordic countries, thus, do not follow the simple logic of their formal status as allied and non-allied. They are similar in that they do not subscribe to the aim of territorial EU defense, but focus on non-military crisis management, and favor comprehensive involvement of third countries.[29] One could argue that for all the Nordic countries, the EU is becoming an increasingly important security political actor in the region, compared with other regional organizations[30] and also with NATO. They are also ready to

---

[28] See Nina Græger, "Norway and the EU security and defence dimension: A 'troops-for-influence' strategy," pp. 41, 49, 61.

[29] Nina Græger, Henrik Larsen and Hanna Ojanen, *The ESDP and the Nordic countries: Four variations on a theme.* (Helsinki and Bonn: Programme on the Northern Dimension of the CFSP, Finnish Institute of International Affairs and Institut für Europäische Politik, 2002), p. 231.

[30] From the early 1990s, the Baltic and Barents Sea regions have seen the birth of a variety of different regional and sub-regional organizations, notably the Council of the Baltic Sea States (CBSS), the Arctic Council and the Barents Euro-Arctic Council.

upgrade their own participation: the latest form of cooperation between Sweden, Finland and Norway is the formation of an EU Battle Group among the three. Sweden has already shown readiness for more demanding crisis management operations through its contribution of special troops to the operation Artemis in Congo in summer 2003.

### The growing importance of the EU in the Baltic countries' security policies

During the time of their accession negotiations with the EU, the Baltic countries did not pay much attention to the rapidly evolving integration in the field of foreign, security and defense policies. According to the twin-track strategy mentioned above, the EU was mainly relevant for the economy and trade, whereas security and defense was the realm of NATO.[31] Reluctance of the Baltic countries to recognize the security role of the EU may thus also be explained by their unwillingness to accept the EU as a substitute for NATO.[32] In recent years, however, the progress of CFSP/ESDP, as well as the cracks in transatlantic relations that emerged during the Iraqi crisis, have forced the Baltic leaders to give more consideration to the EU as a foreign and security political actor. The clear role division between NATO and the EU, and between the Americans and Europeans, which constituted the backbone of Baltic foreign policies in the post-Cold war period, has eroded. Among other things, this means that the Baltic and Nordic countries are coming closer to each other in their views on the EU as a security political actor.

The views of the Baltic countries on EU foreign and security policy have been primarily defined by their relations with two major partners of the EU, Russia and the USA. As regards the former, the division of Europe into "east" and "west" has not lost significance for the Baltics. Membership in the EU and NATO gives them confidence that they are now on the western side of the east-west border, but they do remain concerned about threats coming from the East. They have fol-

---

[31] For an analysis of Estonia's position, see Kristi Raik, "Does the European Union still matter for Estonia's security?—Positioning Estonia in CFSP and ESDP," in *Estonian Foreign Policy Yearbook 2003*, ed. Andres Kasekamp (Tallinn: Estonian Foreign Policy Institute, 2003), pp. 163-180. Available at http://www.evi.ee/lib/valispol2003.pdf

[32] Sven Arnswald and Mathias Jopp, *The Implications of Baltic States' EU Membership.* Programme on the Northern Dimension of the CFSP, Vol. 14. (Helsinki and Bonn: The Finnish Institute of International Affairs and Institut für Europäische Politik, 2001), p. 43.

lowed with particular concern the revitalized efforts of Russia under the leadership of president Vladimir Putin to strengthen its regional power status and control over the CIS. The revived regional ambitions have also been reflected in Russia's policies towards the Baltic States: for example, in 2004, Estonia and Latvia were subject to a renewed wave of Russian accusations directed at alleged violations of the rights of the Russian-speaking minorities, although the EU and other Western organizations have repeatedly assured that there is no evidence of such violations. The simultaneous weakening of democracy in Russia accentuates the Baltic perception of their Eastern neighbor as a threat. Even though there is no likelihood of a military assault in the foreseeable future, the regional power ambitions and the uncertainty of the future path of Russia are of great concern for the Baltic states.

Continued US commitment to European security is therefore one of the main foreign policy priorities of the Baltic states. From the viewpoint of security, good bilateral relations with the US are considered perhaps even more important than membership in NATO, since only the US has the resources to provide credible territorial defense. The Baltics share with other Central and East Europeans a suspicion towards European great powers—primarily Russia, but also Germany, France and to a less degree other big countries—that has long historical roots, which makes the Atlantic link even more important. They have also been willing to support the US in order to pay back the "debt of gratitude" for the support of Americans during the Cold War. However, like elsewhere in Europe, the Baltic attitudes towards the international role of the US have become much more critical during the past years. Although labeled as "new Europe" during the Iraq crisis, the views of the Baltic countries on questions that divide Europe and the US, such as multilateralism and the use of force, are European. Furthermore, it is currently not an unusual view in the Baltic countries that, by participating in the Iraq war, they have now paid the debt of gratitude to the US, and that it would not be in their interest to support "another Iraq."

The increased criticism of US foreign policy together with uncertainty over continued US commitment to European security has pushed the Baltic States to give more relevance to the EU. Public opinion in all three countries gives a strong support to full participation in EU foreign and security policy, the support figures being considerably higher than in the Nordic EU members (see chart). The high level of public support for a common foreign and security policy is in sharp contrast with the lukewarm attitudes towards EU membership in general, which reflects the fact that for these countries, security was one of the main reasons for joining the EU. Nonetheless, the Baltic countries continue to support good transatlantic relations and a strong Europe, not wishing to prioritize either one. The regional dimension is an additional element in the Baltic countries' security policies, having both practical and symbolic significance. So, for example, the Estonian foreign minister Kristiina Ojuland has identified the following four pillars of Estonian security policy: membership in NATO and EU, bilateral relations with "allies, especially the US," and cooperation in the Baltic Sea region.[33]

The prioritization of US presence in Europe has conditioned the attitudes of the Baltic countries towards a common European defense. The Balts stress their willingness to make an active contribution to EU defense policy, but on the condition that this would not duplicate or undermine the position of NATO. They have participated in several EU operations undertaken so far—although with very small resources, this has been an important message of commitment, motivated by a wish to prove that they are not just consumers, but also producers of security.[34] Nordic support and cooperation has been of great importance for developing their crisis management capabilities.

While the US is seen to provide the indispensable "hard" security guarantees, the EU seems to be actually more relevant, and increasingly so, for the daily relations and current problems of the Baltic countries' relations with Russia. Prior to enlargement, there was concern in the EU that the Baltic membership would have a negative impact on EU relations with Russia. Indeed, the issues that cause tensions in Baltic-Russian relations, primarily the Russian-speaking minorities and the border treaties that Russia has so far refused to

---

[33] Address by the Minister of Foreign Affairs of the Republic of Estonia Kristiina Ojuland to the Riigikogu on behalf of the Government of Estonia, 8 June 2004. Available at http://www.vm.ee/eng/euro/kat_314/4567.html

[34] For data on the participation of the Baltic countries in EU operations, see Kristi Raik and Teemu Palosaari, "It's the Taking Part that Counts: The new Member States adapt to EU foreign and security policy," *FIIA Report* 10/2004, The Finnish Institute of International Affairs, Helsinki, November 2004. Available at http://www.upi-fiia.fi/english/publications/upi_report/reports/FIIA%20report%2010.pdf

sign, are now part of the agenda of EU-Russia relations. However, the Baltic countries do not wish to be portrayed in the EU as countries that continue to have "problems with Russia," and expect that EU membership helps them to improve and normalize their relations with Russia. They strongly support the attempts of the EU to develop a more coherent and effective policy towards Russia.

The Balts regard themselves as good experts on Russia and the CIS, and are willing to offer their expertise to be used in developing EU-Russian relations and the Eastern dimension of the European Neighbourhood Policy (ENP). At the same time, they are concerned about their ability to defend their interests in the EU's Eastern policies. The aim of the big member states to preserve their good bilateral relations with Russia is particularly dangerous from the Baltic states' perspective. Such concerns were expressed, for example, by Artūras Paulauskas, acting president of Lithuania, in May 2004: "We should be at the forefront... in order to defend our national interests and to avoid a situation where we are made an item of trade or other states pursue their interests at our expense."[35] When it comes to the ENP, the Baltic countries are eager to transmit their own experience of transition, successful reforms, and adoption of EU norms to the new Eastern neighbors of the Union.[36] Estonia has shown interest in particular towards Ukraine and Georgia, while Lithuania prioritizes support to Belarus and the Russian enclave of Kaliningrad. As a sign of its activeness in the Eastern neighborhood, Lithuania was also actively involved in solving the presidential crisis of Ukraine that burst out in late 2004.

Apart from Europe, Russia and the US, the scope of Baltic countries' foreign policy has so far been very limited. One of the implications of the accomplishment of "return to the West" is that it is now time to broaden the foreign policy horizon. The wish to be full-fledged members of the EU and the Western community requires the Baltic countries to develop their capabilities in the fields of crisis management, development cooperation, etc. Membership in the EU and

---

[35] Speech by H. E. Mr. Artūras Paulauskas, Acting President of the Republic of Lithuania, at Vilnius University, on Lithuania's New Foreign Policy, 24 May 2004. Available at http://www.urm.lt/data/2/EF51153536_Paulauskasspeech.htm

[36] For an Estonian view, see T.H. Ilves, "The Grand Enlargement and the Great Wall of Europe," in *Estonian Foreign Policy Yearbook 2003*, ed. Andres Kasekamp (Tallinn: Estonian Foreign Policy Institute, 2003, pp. 181-200. [http://www.evi.ee/lib/valispol2003.pdf]

NATO has brought both more leverage and more responsibility. Compared with the Nordic countries, the Balts do not have a similar devotion to non-military aspects of security. Yet they might end up contributing more to the EU's civilian capacities than they intend, because it is important for them to be active in EU foreign and security policy, and to cooperate closely with the Nordic countries. Furthermore, they emphasize the civilian capacities of the EU in order to avoid duplication with NATO. Participation in EU activities alongside with the Nordic countries might over time shape the security identities of the Balts, bringing them closer to their Nordic partners.

## Conclusion: potential for Nordic-Baltic cooperation in the EU?

*Enlarging Nordic cooperation to the Baltic states*

Despite the different affiliations with the EU and NATO, or perhaps partly because of these differences, the Nordic countries have developed among themselves a very far-reaching system of integration. It has been institutionalized into, but not limited to, the Nordic Council, established in 1952, and in the Nordic Council of Ministers, established in 1971. The most far-reaching goals of common Nordic labor market and a passport union were achieved in the 1950s, completed by a social security convention and the special rights of the Northerners. Regular ministerial meetings have taken place since late 1920s and 1930s, the foreign ministers meeting since 1932 at least twice a year. Since 1993, the ministers of defense have broadened their joint meeting agendas from UN issues to other international questions, while the prime ministers have been assigned a particular responsibility for Nordic cooperation.[37]

From the 1980s, Nordic cooperation has suffered from increasing competition from the wider European framework. To some extent, it gave impetus to Nordic endeavors, as Nordic cooperation helped the Nordic countries—also those outside of the EU—to keep on track

---

[37] For more background, see Hanna Ojanen, *The Plurality of Truth: A Critique of Research on the State and European Integration.* (Aldershot: Ashgate 1998, pp. 233, 246-7.)

with European integration.[38] In the 1990s, new impetus for Nordic cooperation came from the increasingly central role of the Baltic Sea region. The Nordic Council of Ministers (NCM) has had a special policy for its neighboring areas—first the Baltic states and then also Northwest Russia—since 1991. The official objectives of neighborhood cooperation have included, e.g., strengthening democracy and widening of the community of shared values with the northern parts of Europe.[39] In total, some 150 MDKK is allocated to the adjacent areas per year by the NCM.[40]

At the same time, the Nordic countries have helped the Baltic countries to set up institutions similar to their own, and invited them increasingly to participate in Nordic meetings that from an early "5+3" came to be called simply "the 8." Their possible membership in Nordic institutions has also been discussed. The first institution to open for their full membership has been the Nordic Investment Bank.

The continued relevance of Nordic cooperation has, however, regularly been questioned. In particular, Finland was reluctant to emphasize Nordic links during its first years of EU membership, which seemed to bloc the possibilities for closer regional cooperation within the Union. Instead, it was taking initiatives on its own (notably the Northern Dimension initiative) and underlined that there was no bloc building taking place, as it was perceived to be unwelcome in the Union. Moreover, Finland may not have been keen in being associated with the two "reluctant" Nordic EU members, Denmark and Sweden, as they were less supranational in their emphases.

Still, it was at least partly due to Finnish initiatives that Nordic coordination within the EU gained ground again with regular pre-

---

[38] The EEA agreement stressed the compatibility of Nordic cooperation with European integration, and while signing their membership treaties with the EU in 1994, Finland, Sweden and Norway gave a joint declaration on their intention to continue Nordic cooperation among themselves as well as with other countries and territories (the self-governing territories of Greenland, Faeroe Islands and Åland).

[39] Framework programme 2003-2005 for the Nordic Council of Ministers' activities in the adjacent areas. Adopted by the Nordic Ministers of Cooperation 30.10.2002. NSK/MR-SAM 59/2002 REV.1

[40] Hanna Ojanen, "Assessment of the Nordic Council of Ministers' Policies for the Adjacent Areas: Small but Smart?" Report for the Nordic Council of Ministers, 8 May 2004. [http://www.norden.org/naromraaden/uk/naer-m-app.pdf]

summit meetings been held since 2001 among the three. Soon, they were joined by the three Baltics, while Norway and Iceland are being kept informed. Now, the formula that is used is "3+3+2."

*Baltic cooperation*

The Baltic countries developed close ties and strong mutual solidarity in early stages of their transition. The common struggle for independence culminated in August 1989 in the "Baltic chain": a human chain formed by over two million people standing hand-in-hand on the way from Tallinn to Vilnius in order to commemorate the 50th anniversary of the Molotov-Ribbentrop pact. In the latter half of 1990s, cooperation gave way to competition in the pre-accession process of the EU. The Baltic relations were cooled by the EU's decision to include only Estonia in the first group of enlargement—Latvia and Lithuania were, in their view, unjustly excluded and reacted to the proposal made by the European Commission in July 1997 to start accession negotiations with 5+1 countries with bitter criticism.[41] Estonia, by contrast, emphasized its superiority in terms of membership criteria, and supported the Commission strategy of assessing each candidate country according to its own merits.

During the 1990s, the Baltic cooperation was to some extent "imposed" by the West. The grouping together of the three countries by Western actors caused some annoyance, especially in Estonia. In their desire to become a "normal" western country, the Estonians were orientating more to the north than south and attempted to construct a Nordic identity.[42] The Baltic identity was perhaps most important for Latvia, while Lithuania was looking towards Central Europe and had a special relation to Poland, based on historical ties and common religion.[43] Lithuania and Poland are not, however, likely to become important partners in the EU, since Poland, being one of the six large member states, has its own specific interests and strives for a position not comparable to that of the small Baltic states.

---

[41] See Sven Arnswald, "The Politics of Integrating the Baltic States," pp. 74-77.

[42] See Mikko Lagerspetz, "How Many Nordic Countries? Possibilities and Limits of Geopolitical Identity Construction," *Cooperation and Conflict* 38:1 (2003), pp. 49-61.

[43] Lithuania, like Poland, is a strongly Catholic country, whereas Estonia and Latvia are predominantly Protestant and more secular.

Now that the three countries are members in the EU, there are new prospects for cooperation in advancing their common interests in the Union. Yet, the usefulness of maintaining trilateral Baltic institutions has been questioned, again, in particular by the Estonians. The future of the Baltic Council of Ministers and the Baltic Parliamentary Assembly, designed according to the model of Nordic cooperation, have been actively debated and the institutions are undergoing reforms.[44] Another example of pressures to cut down trilateral cooperation is the Baltic Battalion BALTBAT which was established in 1994, aimed at improving the abilities of the Baltic countries to take part in international crisis management and advancing their aspirations to join NATO. BALTBAT was ceremoniously ended in September 2003 because it had "successfully fulfilled its goals."[45] Instead of developing BALTBAT further in the framework of EU crisis management, the Baltic countries decided to look for other partners in the EU, which shows their reluctance to be profiled as a distinct Baltic group. As an alternative to trilateral cooperation, the Baltic countries would be willing to merge their trilateral institutions into the broader framework of Nordic-Baltic cooperation. However, the Nordic countries, although promoting enhanced cooperation, have so far seemed reluctant to welcome the Balts as full and equal members in the Nordic institutions.

*Nordic-Baltic cooperation within the EU*

The new form of regional cooperation would now seem to be cooperation within the EU on issues of common interest among the Nordic and Baltic members. Some politicians have argued that such regionalism will be increasingly important in the Union. The Speaker of the Finnish Parliament and former Prime Minister Paavo Lipponen[46] among them has argued that as the EU enlarges, it is important that the "3+3" take care of Northern interests in the EU, speaking with one voice, and notably develop cooperation with Russia,

---

[44] See Hanna Ojanen, "Assessment of the Nordic Council of Ministers' Policies for the Adjacent Areas: Small but Smart?" Report for the Nordic Council of Ministers, 8 May 2004. http://www.norden.org/naromraaden/uk/naer-m-app.pdf

[45] Lauri Lepik, "Nordic-Baltic Defence Cooperation and International Relations Theory," in *Estonian Foreign Policy Yearbook 2004*, ed. Andres Kasekamp (Tallinn: Estonian Foreign Policy Institute, 2004), p. 156. http://www.evi.ee/lib/valispol2004.pdf

[46] See Paavo Lipponen, "Norden och EU." *Internasjonal politikk*, vol. 62 (2), pp. 259-266.

Ukraine and Moldova. Cooperation should in practice take the form of pragmatic consultations before the Council meetings rather than "bloc building." Even Poland and Germany could be included in some of that cooperation. The Swedish ambassador to the EU, Sven-Olof Petersson,[47] has similarly argued that in the enlarged union, there will be new forms of meetings; more and more work will be carried out in small working groups and regional groupings.

But what are the realms in which the Nordic and Baltic countries have shared interests and where such instrumental coalition-building might be expected? For some observers, the potential for regional cooperation on EU issues does not seem bright at all. Stålvant[48] has found that the eight countries (Sweden, Finland, Denmark, Estonia, Lithuania, Latvia, Poland and Germany) do not agree on any single item.[49] In his view, thus, the asserted subgroup cohesion does not exist. Partially, this view might result from his different conception of which countries constitute the subgroup: in fact, Germany is perhaps the most divergent country. Stålvant also puts emphasis on the division in "old" and "new" Europe: Fennoscandian countries abstained from lending political and physical support to the Americans, the Baltics were more outspoken about their political participation in the antiterrorist coalition, and Poland and Denmark committed themselves at an early stage to the coalition forces.[50] However, as argued above, the Baltic countries do not regard the transatlantic link as an alternative to the strengthening of EU foreign and security policy. As they are to some extent readjusting their views on the US and EU as contributors to their security, membership in the EU is likely to further increase their emphasis on the EU.

---

[47] Sven-Olof Petersson in a seminar by UD and UI, May 2004, see http://www.regeringen. se/sb/d/2810/a/23027.

[48] Stålvant produces a table about the stands of the "Baltic Sea players" on 10 different issues at the European Convention. See Carl-Einar Stålvant, "Interests, loyalties, and the lures of power: the Baltic Sea States in future European governance," in Bo Huldt, Tomas Ries, Jan Mörtberg and Elisabeth Davidson (eds.), *The New Northern Security Agenda*. Strategic Yearbook 2004. Stockholm and Helsinki: Swedish National Defence College and Finnish National Defence College.

[49] Finland and Sweden agree most. 60% joint positions appear in the pairs Germany/Denmark, Estonia/Sweden, Estonia/Finland, and Lithuania/Poland.

[50] See Carl-Einar Stålvant, "Interests, loyalties, and the lures of power: the Baltic Sea States in future European governance," p. 95.

There are clear indications of the Baltic countries' interest in the Nordic countries as a reference group within the Union, more so than in the Southern members or indeed in their neighboring Poland— partly because of similar mentalities, and partly because they are all small countries. This need not lead to having common positions, however. Increasing coordination may simply mean consultation to get acquainted with each other's points of view and possible areas of disagreement. There are also areas of clearly joint concern, and thus possible realms of cooperation within the EU in the 3+3 formation, such as research and development, education and technological innovation. In the area of foreign and security policy, the wider neighborhood, issues concerning the EU's eastern border, and security political cooperation in the form of crisis management are possible examples of cooperation fields.

At the same time, the differences in views on Russia, and on NATO, are considerable. There might be some competition over the "expertise on Russia" for which Finland was praised when joining the EU. However, in spite of their good expertise on Russia, the Baltic countries are not up to taking an active role in the EU's policy towards Russia at least in their first years of membership. This is due to their lack of experience as regards the functioning of EU system, very limited human and financial resources, and last but not least, their bilateral problems in relations with Russia. Finland has some major advantages, such as experience in the EU and good relations with Russia. While Finland is closest to the Baltic states as to threat perceptions, its official policy has been different, as it has avoided taking critical stands on Russia.

Enlargement has been seen to contribute notably to stability and security in the region. Without doubt, however, the Baltic countries' membership in the EU also profoundly changes the regional setting, inserting a new kind of stability into it. From a broader international relations perspective, the Nordic-Baltic area has become less important and interesting than what it was in the 1990s. After "dual enlargement" of the EU and NATO, it has been argued, the Nordic-Baltic area has become "just one European sub-region among others."[51] At

---

[51] Helmut Hubel, "The Baltic Sea Subregion after Dual Enlargement," *Cooperation and Conflict* 39:3 (2004), pp. 283-298. (Here p. 294.)

the same time, promoting the regional interests within the EU becomes a new joint challenge for the "3+3." The new setting in which the Nordic and Baltic countries work as equals through the EU increases the need to get to know the neighbors better. There would also seem to be increasing similarity between the eight countries—in particular if Norway and Iceland join the EU and Denmark gives up its opt-outs—notably as regards the EU's international role. When looked at from the inside, the differences between the eight may outweigh the similarities. When seen from further away, however, the region does look increasingly homogeneous.

## Chapter 3

# Consequences and Strategic Impact of Enlargement on the (Old) EU

Ulrike Guérot

## A 'Tour d'Horizon' of enlargement and its complexity

There is no doubt that the biggest enlargement of the European Union will change its nature and chemistry. None of the previous enlargements has with this intensity opened the debate on the scope of the European Union, its future, the degree of integration as well as regarding its geographical limits. Never in history has the debate about European identity and its 'finalité' been so ardent. This is also due to the coincidence that the discussion about potential next enlargement rounds had started, even before the enlargement of the ten new members states had been completed in May 2004, let alone digested: Only a few months after the "big bang," Turkey got green lights for the opening of accession talks in October 2005 at the EU Summit meeting in Brussels in late 2004; the European Parliament adopted a resolution requesting a membership perspective for Ukraine in January 2005[1]; and other countries like Georgia do not miss one single opportunity to express their perspective for membership. This enlargement had, thus, a tremendous watershed effect. It ultimately opens 'Pandora's box' and puts into question the undertaking of European integration as a whole, especially the notion of further political integration along the lines of 'an ever closer union.' Many in the 'old' member states who had never had warm feelings about European integration can now easily hide behind the new difficulties and challenges to claim the project's end. Although exaggerated, there are already voices that put monetary union into question.[2]

---

[1] http://www2.europarl.eu.int/omk/sipade?PUBREF=-//EP/TEXT+PRESS*DN-20050113-1+0+DOC*XML+VO//EN&L=EN&LEVEL=2&NAV=X&LSTDOC=#SECTION4

[2] Sebastian Dullien,"Der Euro steht auf der Kippe,"*Financial Times Deutschland*, March 8, 2005.

Also, communication on the benefits of enlargement has been a disaster so far, to the extent that old and new states (and publics) believe they are both on the 'loser' side. Large publics in the old member states believe that their countries are becoming less influential in the enlarged EU. The people in the fifteen old EU countries worried primarily about the costs of enlargement and the influx of cheap labor from the East, and whether the Union's institutions can cope with twenty-five and more members. The newcomers are concerned about a 'second class' membership position. Therefore, the big psychological risk is the one of a self-fulfilling prophecy: enlargement is not going to work, because everybody thinks it is not going to work. The irony is that the EU is a best-selling model, but only for states and people outside of the EU!

And as if the challenge of digesting ten new countries institutionally and financially would not be a huge task in itself, enlargement comes at a time and in a political environment that is particularly difficult. On the one hand, integration and deepening is under strain, since the new European Constitution needs still to be ratified, mostly through national referenda. At least ten countries[3] will therefore be forced to engage in a difficult campaigning on institutional issues that are difficult to explain and to sell to the European citizens.[4] More broadly, citizens feel uneasy accepting heavier financial burdens and continuous pooling of sovereignty without knowing what the 'finalité politique' of the EU could look like. This is especially true in France where the debate about the constitution is overshadowed by the question of Turkish accession to the EU.[5]

Europe is becoming a scapegoat, with nationalist tendencies and right-wing movements rising.[6] It is not a young, dynamic, innovative and rich European Union that is confronted with—cost-generating—

---

[3] Belgium, Denmark, France, Ireland, Luxemburg, Netherlands, Portugal, Spain, UK, Czech Republic, Poland, Slovenia. Spain voted 'yes' on February 20, 2005, with 76% favourable votes, but only 42% participation.

[4] Communication about the issue has failed, see: "One third of EU citizens unaware of European Constitution," in: euobserver.com, January 28, 2005; for an analysis see: Daniel Keohane: 'A guide to the referenda on the EU constitutional treaty, Centre for European Reform, Briefing note, October 2004.

[5] Sylvie Goulard, *Le Grand Turc et la République de Vénise* (Paris, Fayard, 2004), p. 127.

[6] The German right-wing party NPD got some 10% in the last regional elections in Saxony.

enlargement, but an 'old' Europe that is over-aging and economically rather poorly performing. All of this fuels the discussion about 'financial overstretch' of the EU. There are many voices in the old member states that believe that the end of political integration has come, and that it is not worth believing in a bright future for the EU.[7] If anything, the political project could only survive in a 'core-Europe' structure, with some countries moving ahead in integration.

There are at least four factors, why enlargement matters both in terms of institutional structure as well as geo-strategy of the EU.

1. First, the ten new member states come with very distinct national and historical features into the European Union. Most of them struggled for freedom and independence in the 1990s. They have a more powerful feeling about national sovereignty and are, in average, more reluctant to renounce to it. In the EU terminology, these countries belong more to the 'intergovernmental' camp than to the 'supranational,' meaning that they are not—at least for the time being—inclined to push for more integration or deepening of the Union.[8] This clearly poses the question of a 'two-speed Europe.'

2. Second, with nine of the countries that recently joined the EU being rather small (if not: very small[9]) countries, this wave of enlargement tilted the balance between larger and smaller member states at the advantage of the latter. This is not only as such a burden for the institutional equilibrium; it will also, above all, make the question of internal leadership in the EU a salient and disputed one, as the chasm between 'small' and 'large' member states will inevitably grow bigger.

3. Third, the newcomers have, in average, strong transatlantic feelings and ties, which poses problems for the shaping of a common approach in defence policy. Not that 'West-European' countries dismiss a transatlantic component; the United Kingdom or Italy under the Berlusconi government or the former Aznar-government of Spain were also proud to be counted among the best 'allies' of Washington

---

[7] Michael Stürmer in his presentation at the conference of the Herbert Quandt Foundation: "Realism in international policy," October 28-29, 2004.

[8] Vladimir Bilcik, "Shaping the EU as an external actor: Slovakia's shifting role conceptions," in: *Slovak Foreign Policy Affairs*, Fall 2004, pp. 40-51.

[9] Malta does account for only some 300 000 citizens; Cyprus is equally very small. All three Baltic States have less than 6 million citizens.

in the war against Iraq. But the transatlantic orientation in the West does no longer have the 'existentialistic' odor that it has in the East.[10]

4. And finally, most of the ten new members being, in the East, at the geographic periphery of the EU have a solid interest of not remaining 'border' country, but bringing its various neighbors also into the European Union. This poses the ardent question how to deal with the European neighbourhood and how to develop a European geo-strategy towards the countries beyond its borders.

The first two of these factors will impact on the EU's institutional system; the two latter will impact on its geo-strategy and on the EU's ambitions to become a global player. All the four factors together will definitely put the UE under strain for the years to come.

The 'adieu-bells' of the *'Europe de Charlemagne'*[11] are ringing, and this compiles dozens of questions about its near and mid-term future: How can the EU, especially the 'old' member states, cope with these developments? Does enlargement mean the renouncement of a 'political union'? What if the EU-Constitution is rejected? Is a 'core-Europe' conceivable and which countries would be part of it? What kind of flexibility mechanisms do we really need? How will leadership of the EU function in the future? And last but not least: Where does Europe end?

## Some misperceptions about the EU Constitution

The biggest misperception about the European Constitution is to think that this text reinvents the European Union or that it starts European integration from scratch. In fact, the European constitutional treaty is more a comprehensive and transparent re-writing of the existing treaties, and shows more the current state of achievement in European integration than it does reinvent something radically new. Of course, there are new things in the constitutional treaty[12]:

---

[10] Jan Winkler, State Secretary for Defence Policy, Czech Republic, at a conference of the German Council on Foreign Relations: "A Common Security Strategy for 'Old' and 'New' Europe," January 27, 2004.

[11] Expression for the former Europe with initially six member states in 1957.

[12] The CER guide to the EU's constitutional treaty, Centre for European Reform, policy brief, July 2004 and Ulrike Guérot: "Europe could become the first 'post-modern' superpower," *European Affairs*, Fall 2004, pp. 36-42.

most importantly the position of a permanent president of the European Council, together with the abandonment of the rotating presidencies; the position of a common European foreign minister; a new voting system stipulating that a qualified majority vote needs 55% of the states representing 65% of the Union's citizens; further the EU gets a legal personality, a human rights charter, and its legal system is unified which also means that large parts of policies in the field of home and justice affairs (i.e. asylum and visa policies) are now becoming supranational[13] instead of intergovernmental; the competences of the EU and its member states are clarified, the 'subsidiarity principle' is improved—meaning that the control of national parliaments on EU legislation is enhanced. Moreover, the means for flexible approaches within the EU are being set up, especially in the field of European defence policy through the creation of a tool called 'structured co-operation.'[14] But there is nothing in the constitution that would radically overcome the traditional pattern of institutional reform through small and tiny steps. The constitution is quite an intelligent compromise and mixture of 'accelerators' of integration and 'emergency brakes' for member states. It does not tilt the balance for a European federal 'super-state,' but it may make the EU more efficient and transparent in its decision making.

The other illusion is that stopping the constitution would mean to stop European integration or roll it back. Many of the adversaries of the constitution cannot clearly specify what it is precisely in this constitution that they disagree with; their uneasiness is more a general feeling that the Maastricht treaty already has gone to far in integrating European nations. The European Constitution stands, indeed, for continuity, for the wish to further deepen European integration; but this might be incompatible with enlargement that stands for rather a fresh start of the EU. Therefore, it might precisely be the ratification process of the European Constitution which will eventually create a momentum for a 'core-Europe,' supposing one or more countries fail to ratify the constitutional treaty.

---

[13] Supranational in the EU-jargon means four things: 1. right of initiative for the Commission, co-decision by the European Parliament, qualified majority voting by the Council and competence of the ECJ (European Court of Justice)

[14] Draft Constitutional Treaty, Article I 40-6, in combination with article III-213.

## From a 'magnetic core' to exclusion?

In order to analyse the possible consequences, one needs to retrace shortly the long lasting discussion about 'core-Europe.' Already during negotiations on the Treaty of Maastricht in 1992 and in the context of monetary union, the question of a core was on the table. A famous German policy paper[15] argued that those countries 'able and willing' to join monetary union (on the basis of the convergence criteria) should also be the 'hard core' of a political union and go for further political integration—as monetary union would spill over on many other policy areas. However, the paper described a temporary, open 'core' as it assumed that eventually all EU countries would meet the criteria for EMU and then join in, meaning also that all would be at some point in the 'political union.' Today's discussion is different in the sense, that the bottle-neck of ratification[16] and the problem that the constitution may be rejected in just one single country (or only in very few countries) stops the entire European Union from pursuing its deepening process. Therefore, the discussion centers more on what to do with the countries that do not want to sign up for more integration—and that are neither willing nor likely to catch up, at some point in history, with the 'core' states.[17] In the history of European integration there have always been the 'big hesitators,' namely the United Kingdom and Denmark. But interestingly, up to present, the common ground of integration has never been put into question. Today's discussion, nevertheless, seems to cement a 'two-speed' Europe with two different paths of integration rather than focus on a magnetic 'core.'

## The legal vs. the political dimension of the referenda: some scenarios

There is a twofold answer to this problem: a legal and a political one. Legally there is no option for a 'core' to be born. If the constitu-

---

[15] Wolfgang Schäuble and Karl Lamers: "Reflections on European Policy," CDU/ CSU-Fraktion des Deutschen Bundestages, September 2004.

[16] Gian Luigi Tosato and Ettore Greco: "The EU Constitutional Treaty: How to deal with the ratification bottleneck," Document, IAI 0417E, Paper presented at the Seminar on: "Riflessioni in terma di ratifica e anticipazione del Trattato Constituzionale per l'Europa," Rome, November 15, 2004.

[17] Andres Maurer et al.,"Ratifikationsverfahren zum EU-Verfassungsvertrag,"Stiftung Wissenschaft und Politik, January 2005.

tional treaty fails, the EU's legal basis is the Nice Treaty signed in 2000. The constitutional treaty only comes into force if adopted by all member states.[18] But the political answer is not that simple, as many member states are determined not to accept a blocking of the constitutional treaty by just one or a small number of countries.[19]

Although all EU countries are formally equal, in fact, the French and the British votes on the Constitution matter most. Both are highly important for the 'core-Europe' discussion, but both are different in essence. The British referendum will determine the UK's role in Europe—in a steering group or as part of the periphery; the French referendum will decide about the future of Europe. A French *Non* means the deadlock for the constitution and a sudden end to the idea of a core. France has been, together with Germany, in the driving seat of European integration for decades. Therefore, one can hardly imagine a group of countries moving ahead with integration leaving France aside. With Spain being already part of the 'yes'-camp, a Dutch, a Czech or even a Polish 'no' to the treaty would be harmful, but probably not fatal to the constitutional project. For various reasons, their rejection would have less impact. The Netherlands and the Czech Republic are small countries, and Poland is a newcomer. A "nay" from these would not be as dramatic as a British, let alone a French one. What then is the likely outcome?

Among the unlikely scenarios are the ones that either nothing happens or that the constitutional treaty is renegotiated, independently of which country(ies) vote no. The EU has spent far too much political energy with the set-up of a constitutional convention. The acceptance of sticking to the present Nice Treaty is contested by most member states. They will not agree to shelve the work of the Convention. But renegotiating the treaty is equally unlikely. Assuming the likely event of a UK rejection the others that have worked hard to push the project through their own parliaments or via referenda would not be keen to renegotiate; the more so as the treaty is a subtle equilibrium of intertwined compromises. This scenario would leave the question open whether the concerned country would go for a second referen-

---

[18] Gian Luigi Tosato and Ettore Greco, op. Cit, p. 2-4.

[19] Charles Grant: "What happens if Britain votes no?" Centre for European Reform, Policy Paper, February 2005, p. 2 and following.

dum[20] or whether this country could be excluded.[21] The problem about the constitutional treaty, in contrast to earlier treaties, is that it does very little to extend the EU's remit into new policy areas. So it is hard to see what a country could opt out of. Most of the treaty is about institutions and decision making procedures. One country could not opt out say of the double majority voting or the creation of a foreign minister—such rules either apply to everyone or they cannot work.[22]

The more likely but unspectacular scenarios are that either some small (and superficial) changes are being made to the treaty without touching the substance and therefore putting into menace the chances of success for a repeated referendum or that member states would start the informal implementation of parts of the treaty. Indeed, many of the Constitution's stipulations could be implemented through inter-institutional agreements of the EU and the (willing) member states,[23] or the willing member states could choose the possibility of 'enhanced co-operation' to achieve a higher degree of integration in some policy fields. Yet, these two solutions do not suffice in themselves to resolve the institutional crisis, as the most important innovations, i.e. the 55%/ 65% rule for qualified majority voting, could not be adopted through these procedures. The Nice Treaty made it slightly easier to set up an enhanced co-operation, by removing the right of one member state to wield a veto, except in foreign policy, and by reducing the minimum number of states required to eight.[24] So far no group of countries has made a serious effort to use this procedure. In 2004, however we saw the first attempt of enhanced co-operation on tax.[25] Opinions differ as to why the procedure has never been used. For

---

[20] As Denmark did with the Maastricht Treaty in 1992 and Ireland with the Nice-Treaty in 2000.

[21] There are various different analyses on whether this would be legally feasible, most of them agreeing on the fact that it would, if both parties, the EU and the concerned country, agreed upon, see Gian Luigi Tosato and Ettore Greco, op. cit, p. 11 and Andreas Maurer: "Austritt, Ausschluss oder institutionelle Anpassung: Optionen nach dem Scheitern des EU-Verfassungsvertrags," Stiftung Wissenschaft und Politik, (unpublished paper), p. 5.

[22] Charles Grant, op. cit, p. 7.

[23] Andreas Maurer, ibid.

[24] See Brendan Donnelly and Anthony Dawes: The beginning of the end or the end of the beginning? Enhanced co-operation in the constitutional treaty, Federal Trust European Policy Brief, November 2004.

[25] Commissioner Frits Bolkestein suggested that a sub-group of member states might wish to harmonise rules on corporate tax.

some, the problem is that the rules establishing enhanced co-operation are too onerous and bothersome. Others did not detect the need
to go this path.[26] The technique was designed to overcome the veto of
just one member state, in a policy area subject to unanimity, but neither the UK nor anyone else has yet created the kind of blockages that
would provoke the use of the procedure.[27] A British "no" would bring
up the question of a 'core' with new acuity.

## A 'Union' within the Union?

Beyond 'core' developments *within* the treaty—like enhanced cooperation—there is also the option of a 'core' or avant-garde *outside*
the treaty. Since Joschka Fischer's famous speech at Humboldt-
University in Berlin,[28] recalled by Jacques Chirac's suggestion of a
'pioneer group,' much thought has been given to how a 'centre of
gravity,' a sort of 'Union within the Union' could be created. And
there is little doubt that many French and German high-ranking officials argue that the best response to a British no would be to proceed
without the UK.[29] France and Germany have been pushing this idea
far in November 2003, when they announced the possibility of a
'Franco-German Union.' This idea became an immanent threat, when
the European Council failed to adopt the constitutional treaty in
December 2003.[30]

However, the Franco-German Union is still pretty much abstract.
The first question would be which and how many member states
would follow such an initiative. Would France and Germany be able
to create a critical mass? It is highly likely that countries like the
Czech Republic or Estonia for example would oppose isolating the
UK. These countries feel squeezed between their wish to be first class

---

[26] Charles Grant, op. cit. p. 12.

[27] See Franklin Dehousse, Wouter Cousens, Giovanni Grevi: "Integrating Europe: multiple
speeds—one direction?'" European Policy Centre, April 2004.

[28] Joschka Fischer: "From confederacy to federation: thoughts on the finality of European
integration," Speech to Humboldt University, Berlin, May 12, 2000.

[29] i.e. Valéry Giscard d'Estaing: "Vite, la constitution de l'Europe," *Le Monde*, July 10, 2004;
Francois Lamoureux: "Draft Constitution: why a 'rear-guard' should be established,"
*Notre Europe*, April 2004.

[30] See i.e. Dominique Strauss-Kahn: "Building a political Europe: 50 proposals for tomorrow's
Europe," Report presented to the President of the European Commission, April 2004.

members without harming UK's position in the EU. Even if counting Luxembourg, Belgium, Italy, Spain, Hungary, Slovenia and Finland among the likely countries to push for more integration, this does not add up to more than half of the member states that would go for a 'hard core.' In addition, complex questions how the core would relate to the EU would need to be solved. Would the Commission be in charge for core activities? Would this require a new 'foundations act'? Would it require a special budget? What about the EP? Would still all MEP's vote or would this necessarily lead to a doubling of institutions and structures? If created outside of the treaties, the 'core' would probably dismiss the use of the European key institutions. There are plenty of arguments to assume that such a structure would not be sustainable. And again: in case of a French no, this option is a futile one.

However the most likely option remains what could be called a 'messy core,'[31] in case that some of the referenda fail. Let us assume that Britain votes decisively against the constitutional treaty, but that the other twenty-four members ratify the document. In the ensuing crisis, one group of countries tries to persuade all the others that have ratified the treaty to adopt it—and force the British to accept a special status. But that effort fails when friends of Britain refuse to go along with the scheme. France and Germany then work on plans for a core Europe that would have its own constitution, but it gathers little support and the legal and political obstacles prove insurmountable. The integrationist countries would try to do the best they could in difficult circumstances. They would seek to maintain the momentum towards a political union in every way they could, without contravening the existing treaties. They would try to implement as much of the constitutional treaty as was legally possible, especially the provisions on foreign policy. They would try to establish enhanced co-operation, under Nice Treaty rules, in certain policy areas, such as tax, R & D and educational exchange. They could also set up vanguard groups outside the treaties in other areas, such as border guards, police co-operation, a European Public Prosecutor and the harmonisation of criminal law. They could formalise the institutions of the Euro Group. And they would probably cajole the British into agreeing to a mini-IGC that would adopt one or two of the central provisions of the constitutional treaty, such as double

---

[31] Charles Grant, op. cit, p. 31.

majority voting rules. The consequence of all this would be further European integration, some of it involving the whole EU, but some of it based on perhaps half a dozen over-lapping yet distinct smaller groups of member states. And it would remain to be seen, if over time, one of these groups would acquire de-facto leadership functions within the EU and could further institutionalize as a 'core.'

Two conclusions are to be drawn from the impact of enlargement and the constitutional debate on the EU's institutional future. The first is that the constellations and coalitions will vary, according to the issue in question. There will be few permanent alliances or power-blocs in the enlarged EU. In particular, the new members will not form an 'Eastern bloc' that usually votes together, for their views and interests are far from identical. Even though most of the new members are small, they could tip the balance in favour of one or other coalition of members on any given issue.

The second conclusion is that the EU will institutionally change much more than either the old or new members expect, or have prepared for. The new constitutional treaty, far from being satisfying, is a good compromise and an important step into the right direction—the enlarged EU would be in a deadlock if it were to stick to the Nice Treaty.

However, even if the EU countries eventually agree on and ratify the new constitutional treaty, its provisions are, over time, unlikely to enable the enlarged Union to work smoothly. Further and forthcoming waves of enlargement will put further pressure on the EU's institutional machinery, which is increasingly rattling and wheezing. More radical reform is needed. The EU has thus entered a period of perpetual revolution that may well continue for the next decade.

## What about leadership?

It might be one of the most important impacts of EU-enlargement on the EU-15 system that the traditional leadership pattern is undoubtedly loosing ground in a 'messy core' scenario. It is conventional knowledge that France and Germany have been the driving force of European integration throughout the decades. The European Community for Coal and Steel was mostly designed to overcome war between France and Germany. Both are founding members of the Rome Treaties in 1957 and both have been at the origin of any initiative towards deeper integration ever since. The Elysée-Treaty of 1963 laid the ground for this intense cooperation through two annual bilateral summits. There is nothing comparable to this relationship within the European Union. From the shaping of the European Monetary System by Helmut Schmidt and Valéry Giscard d'Estaing in 1978 to the Maastricht Treaty in 1992, from the Euro-Corps in 1992 to the European headquarter cell for military operations in 2003, there is no single major initiative in European integration in which France and Germany have not taken the lead. Also the deadlocking capacity of the two countries is enormous. The two constitute critical mass within the EU institution; together France and Germany combine more than 50% of population and of the votes in the Council, let alone their economic weight within the Union. And, thus, it had become conventional wisdom that, where and when the two agree, the Union can move forward. This 'symmetry of the asymmetry' meant that most of the time, France and Germany where coming from two very different positions; i.e. on monetary union, France has always been in favour of more economic coordination while Germany was concentrated on price stability; in European Security and Defence Policy (ESDP), France wanted always a more independent security policy for Europe, and Germany wanted to keep it within the NATO-frame. But when both could bridge their differences that would give solid ground for the rest of European countries to jump on board of a common initiative. Everybody could find its own position somehow reflected in a Franco-German compromise. This dynamic has lost its exclusivity. As regards the Lisbon agenda, the UK and Portugal have been shaping the economic outlook of the EU in 2000. The EU policy towards Russia is mainly driven by the new member states, above all Poland and Lithuania. Aznar and Blair issued together important proposals for the European Convention, and the small countries—nick-named the seven dwarfs[32]—had their own positions in the Conventions. All this shows shifting coalitions within the EU with no longer one clear pattern, but rather ad-hoc collations on given topics. Another example are the ongoing talks about the next EU budget: France and Germany have been both signatures of a memorandum of the net-contributors in July 2004 together with four other net-contributors[33]; but on the

---

[32] The Benelux countries together with Slovenia, Slovakia and Austria.

[33] Sweden, UK, Austria, Netherlands.

other hand Germany is not inclined to support unconditionally France's interests as regards the agricultural policy of the EU, where France could align rather with Poland—or with Spain that will probably defend its position as regards the cohesion funds. It is merely in the field of foreign policy where, at some point, France and Germany can still pretend to have some leading position, if one looks at Iran. However, it shows clearly that France and Germany need the UK backing to be credible and influential, as shows their attempt to lift the arms embargo against China which failed, precisely because of missing British backing.

## The dysfunctional Franco-German tandem

Enlargement, thus, has radically changed realities for EU-leadership. The Franco-German engine is still a necessary, but no longer a sufficient condition for the Union to move ahead. Quite the opposite, in recent years, the Franco-German leadership has been perceived has an unhealthy 'condominium'—or dictate—by other EU countries, especially by the newcomers. Even more worrisome, it had become dysfunctional to a large extent. Dysfunctional meaning that the former Franco-German engine became a 'train without carriers'[34] as it lost its triggering power on other states. A Franco-German initiative would no longer be automatically be followed by other states. On the contrary, some countries would refuse the initiative only because it came from France and Germany. Many reasons added up for this to happen. Primarily the Franco-German deals of the past years have been—rightly—perceived by other member states as serving Franco-German interests more than the common good of the European Union. In particular the EU Summit in Göteborg, Sweden, in June 2001 showed that France backed Germany in getting special phasing-in regulations concerning the free movement of people after EU enlargement (Germany feared a massive influx of workers from Eastern countries). Germany, in return, helped France to defend a special regime for Eléctricité de France (EDF) within the EU Commission's effort to promote the liberalisation of the European electricity and gas market. Another example is the 'deal of Copenhagen'

---

[34] Ulrike Guérot: "Frankreich und Deutschland—Lokomotive ohne Anhänger?" Johannes Varwick and Wilhelm Knelangen (ed.), *Neues Europa—alte EU? Fragen an den europäischen Integrationsprozess*, p. 285-299.

at the EU Summit of October 2002, where France and Germany shaped a compromise on agricultural spending without any consultation process with the other member states.

Furthermore, Germany has lost its special attention to the smaller member states. With Gerhard Schröder in power, Germany shifted towards a European policy based on national interests, rather than keeping the 'neutral European broker' position, that it had during the Kohl era and became more 'intergovernmental,' whereas it had traditionally defended a strong European Commission. This resulted in loosing the bond of affection with the small member states. Finally, leadership requires moral authority, and France and Germany lost a lot of their credibility because of their behaviour regarding the stability and growth pact. The two countries broke the 3 percent deficit rule for several years in a row, and both succeeded in circumventing the EU Commission's authority on the sanction mechanism, whereas small countries (Ireland and Portugal) received the famous 'blue letter.' All this added up to a huge amount of suspicion of joint Franco-German initiatives within the Union and especially among the smaller members. There is no doubt that France and Germany lost their relative power within the EU's decision making process. In other words: France and Germany are no longer steering the EU's agenda, but they are more perceived as actually blocking it. As regards the neighbourhood policy of the EU, i.e. the case of Ukraine, Poland and the Baltic countries are actively in the driving seat, whereas France and Germany seem more reluctant to embrace the new European geostrategy. In simple terms, France and Germany are—rightly or wrongly—but at least perceived as being 'anti-liberal,' 'anti-American' and 'anti-enlargement,' and differ in that strongly from most of the other member states. Their request for leadership in the enlarged EU cannot work as long as France and Germany move back to the center of Europe and catch up with mainstream thinking in the rest of the EU.

## No credible ESDP without Britain. . . .

This sentiment culminated, when France and Germany declared themselves against a military intervention in Iraq in 2003 at the occasion of the 40th anniversary of the Elysée-Treaty, and pretended to speak on behalf of the European Union. A large number of European countries did not follow the couple.[35] Yet supported by the over-whelming majority of the European public, the tandem fueled the European split failing to unite the Europeans around a common stance. What implications does this have for leadership in the enlarged EU?

Special attention must be given to the United Kingdom, because only the UK can bridge between 'the old' and the 'new' member states. Many feel and think like the UK, when it comes to European integration. There is often reluctance, distance and skepticism, more than enthusiasm about further pooling of sovereignty. Many of the newcomers to the Union modeled their economic and social systems after the liberal UK system and therefore feel closer to the UK in societal terms.[36]

Evidently, the leadership question of the EU is intertwined with the constitutional question. In case of a British No to the Constitution, the UK could not play the role of broker between old and new member states. But supposing a British yes: Could the 'Big Three' drive the EU? The answer is two-folded. On Iran, a recent example for an initiative of the 'Big Three,' France, Germany and Britain have been influential, and could trigger a move of the whole Union. However, the concept of the "Triumvirate" is not likely to become the uncontested winning leadership team. First, because the other 'sort-of-big' countries (Italy, Spain, Poland) are not inclined to give leadership powers exclusively to the 'Big Three.' 'Big Three' would instantly mean 'Big Four,' as either Italy or Poland would like to be included. And second, because some sort of institutionalized leadership of the 'Big Three' would increase the chasm between the 'small' and the 'large' member states. One winning principle of the EU has always been the relatively bigger power of small states in the institutional system. To institutionalize a permanent leadership position of the 'Big Three' would mean to give up a fundamental principle in European policy. In sum, leadership within the EU will require more than two shoulders, but which ones will vary according to the issues. And any leadership group of the EU

---

[35] For a comprehensive analysis of the genesis of the transatlantic rift and the Franco-German role see Philip H. Gordon and Jeremy Shapiro, *Allies at War*, A Brookings Institution Book (McGraw-Hill, 2004).

[36] Thomas Ilves (Estonia) at the conference of the Centre for European Reform: "Britain and the Constitutional Treaty," London, December 8, 2004 .

in the future will need to have small and Eastern countries on board. Considering a likely rejection of the Constitution by the British electorate, Britain will lose its opportunity to play a central role in the integration process. Leadership in the enlarged EU will be diffuse and vary along the issues. Nevertheless, these ad-hoc alliances will have to take into account that their acceptance depends on guarding the interests of the smaller member states. The 'messy core' will give birth to a European Union which will be far less predictable, less coherent, but also less monolithic and more flexible.

## . . . and the transatlantic dimension of 'core-Europe'

It is then essential to look at the question of what impact the leadership problem in the EU will have on the development within ESDP. The Iraq crisis has made evident that France and Germany cannot claim leadership in foreign policy, or, in other words, they cannot determine the relationship of the EU towards the US for the whole EU. The moment they tried, at the famous Tervuren meeting (nicknamed the 'Chocolat Summit') in April 2003, in the middle of the Iraq war, to spell out an initiative for a European Defence Union, including a European Headquarters for EU-lead military missions, they met high resistance of most of the other member states.[37] Only Luxembourg and Belgium sided with them. There is neither European readiness nor majority to construct the EU as a 'counterweight' to the US. This basically means that there is no credible foreign policy of the EU without the UK on board, which points again to the difficult situation the EU would be in if ever the UK drops out through a failure of its referendum. In foreign policy, Britain is again the most important glue between 'old' and 'new' member states. Whereas Franco-German actions in this field raise immediately suspicion, British participation is the guarantee for a friendly transatlantic environment. In this sense, there are at least two conditions to get a decent leadership in the enlarged EU and to hold the whole, enlarged union together: the first is that the UK votes 'yes'; the second that Britain and France work harder together,[38] as France is a defender of

---

[37] Charles Grant and Ulrike Guérot: "A military plan to cut Europe into pieces," *Financial Times*, April 8, 2003.

[38] Timothy Garton Ash, *Free World. America, Europe and the surprising Future of the West* (New York: Random House,, 2004), p. 83.

'multi-polar' ambitions, whereas the UK bridges the Atlantic and Germany must again regain a mediator role. Two conditions must be met to enable Germany again to be the European broker for compromise and mediation: Germany must be economically performing, and Germany needs the American backing for its European compromises. None of the two are met today.

The transatlantic dimension of 'core-Europe' is that a European 'core' is likely to be less atlanticist. But nearly more important would be the fact that a 'core' Europe would necessarily be weak and unable to shoulder the huge challenges that are waiting in the European neighborhood. A 'core-Europe' could neither develop global actor ambitions, nor shape a regional power-projection for the European near-abroad. This is why German Foreign Minister stated in an interview in 2004 that 'plans for small-size Europe do not work any longer.'[39] The crux is that France does not buy into this German conception. With Germany being squeezed between its deepening and widening ambitions, between its strategic partner France and the rest of the enlarged Union, the whole Union could fall apart.

## Europe in search of its geo-strategy: between a political project and a universal mission

Whereas many citizens within EU member countries feel uncomfortable about further integration and popular resistance is rising, other countries are literally lining up in order to join the prestigious club called European Union and they make the future of their countries depending from future EU-membership. Not only Turkey, but also Ukraine, and increasingly countries like Georgia or Moldova belong to this category, let alone the Balkans. The 'Europe-boom' is also mirrored in literature. Jeremy Rifkin's book: *The European Dream. How Europe's Vision of the Future is Quietly Eclipsing the American Dream*[40] has set the tone in this discussion, echoed recently by Mark Leonard's

---

[39] Interview with Joschka Fischer, *Berliner Zeitung*, February 28, 2004.

[40] Jeremy Rifkin, *The European Dream: Why Europe's vision of the future will quietly eclipse the American dream* (New York, Penguin, 2004).

'Why Europe will run the 21st Century.'[41] EU-Commissioner Günter Verheugen says that the EU should become a world power.[42] All the three argue mainly that Europe, the EU, acts like a magnet to border countries precisely because it exerts no threat and has no power or 'empire' ambition of its own. The EU does not seek to impose a 'model,' it just *is* or constitutes a model that other countries find so attractive that they want to join and other regions of the world (Mercosur, Asean, African Union) so attractive that they want to imitate it. And this would be the EU's way to achieve 'world-power' status. This is, of course, good news for Europe, but has inherently a complex dimension, to say the least. The point is the EU that formerly meant to be a political project of unification, has become a kind of 'civilisatory project' or a synonym for a universal mission, which is bringing peace, democracy and prosperity into neighboring regions. Yet, the 'political project EU' is threatened to get lost in the 'civilisatory project' of Europe. It is the enlargement of the ten in 2004 that tilted the balance from the EU as a 'political project' towards the EU as a 'civilisatory project,' and this is the perhaps most massive impact of Eastern enlargement on the 'old' EU. The reason for this is that no new member state wants to be the 'external border' of the EU; every state wants to bring its new neighbors in. Poland openly favours Ukraine; Turkey would promote Georgia and others and so on and so forth.[43] This pattern is evidently true in the European East, but increasingly so southwards of the EU. As the famous membership 'criteria of Copenhagen' are quite vague, many countries surrounding the European Union could feel invited to apply for membership, as they turn democratic and shift to market economies. The problem is, however, that EU-membership is and cannot be the prize for democracy! On the other hand, the EU's influence on the democratization process in neighboring countries depends to a large extent on the fact, that the EU has the 'golden carrot' of membership to offer. The EU has real 'transformative power' only if it offers full membership. How

---

[41] Mark Leonard: "Why Europe will run the 21st Century?" Fourth Estate, UK, 2005.

[42] Günter Verheugen: „Europa muss Weltmacht werden,"Interview in *Internationale Politik*, January 2005.(1/2005), p. 34-45.

[43] In a meeting with a person of the EU department in the Turkish Ministry for Foreign Affairs in September 2004, I have been told that Turkey, once in, would immediately promote membership of Ukraine, Georgia and Israel.

then to disentangle the democratization process from membership perspectives?

There is no easy answer to the question where does the EU will draw the borderline between its political and its 'civilisatory' project in the future. 'An ever closer Union' as imagined under the Treaty of Maastricht in 1992 cannot function with 35 or more states. The EU has already reached its institutional capacities. The consequence is that the more the EU focuses on its 'civilisatory' project, the political project suffers; and the more countries are lining up for membership, the less citizens in the EU member states are willing to support the project.

There is no ultimate answer to this deepening-widening matrix of the EU. On the other hand, it is evident that the EU can only become a global actor, if it actively takes part in the shaping of the European neighborhood and builds up a geo-strategic dimension by giving the border countries a perspective for membership. In short: with Turkey joining, the EU could have a geo-strategic role to play in the broader Middle East; the EU's future relation to Ukraine will impact on the EU's relationship to Russia. Both will help the EU to become a 'player.' There are not only inter-state relations at stake. Ukraine, harboring many pipelines, is essential for the energy supply of the EU. The same applies to the Black Sea and Caucasian Countries like Georgia, Moldova or Kazakhstan. The EU has no interest leaving these countries in a grey zone. As a geo-strategic actor in the region, the EU has all interest to tie these countries closely to its own power center, to help improve political and economic stability and, finally, to tie them up to the single market. This means basically, that the EU will have to face a trade-off between domestic redistribution and a global actor role. The narrow concept of a political union had also a huge component of financial redistribution among the EU member state through the structural funds. This redistribution cannot be extended too many more member states. Membership perspectives for the 'ring of friends' of the European Union[44] will therefore depend on a new design of the domestic structures of the EU, that are less based on homogenous living standards, but more on free and liberal markets, especially labor and agricultural markets. But this potential perspective again brings the EU far away from its initial *Charlemagne*-concept of a

---

[44] Die EU schafft eine ‚Ring von Freunden,' in: *Financial Times*, March 7.

political union, and it is not sure that European citizen will buy into a concept of power-projection for the EU.

Enlargement has basically faced the old member states of the EU with the necessity to become an 'empire against will.' Weak core, messy entity or grand design: the future of the EU is an open question again!

## Chapter 4

# The Strategic Implications of EU Enlargement on Central and Eastern Europe[1]

László J. Kiss

## Impact of Enlargement in the EU

The entry of eight Central and Eastern European countries together with Cyprus and Malta into the European Union on May 1, 2004 was a historically unprecedented achievement both in scope and in diversity, ending centuries of division. Europe reunited means a stronger, more democratic and more stable continent, with a single market providing economic benefits for all its 450 million citizens. The enlargement is the biggest and perceived as the cheapest one in Central and Eastern European (CEE) countries, due to the different budgetary arrangements from the earlier ones.[2] Furthermore it is a part of a double "big bang" enlargement, a "geopolitical revolution," a form of globalization and a response to globalization, raising the issue of how the "West" and "East" should be defined again.

In fact, the debate about Eastern enlargement of the EU has been accompanied by widely diverging estimates of the actual costs involved. Skeptics prefer to cite maximum figures, while proponents adopt minimum estimates. According to some experts, on the whole, the impact of enlargement on the current EU will be negligible, simply because the economies of the acceding countries are small: taken together, they amount to no more than 5 percent of the EU-15. In economic terms, the eastward enlargement is the equivalent of adding an economy the size of the Netherlands to an economic area with

---

[1] "The costs of Eastern enlargement of the EU are exaggerated," Frion Research Institute, Division Foreign Policy Research Working Paper, No.2, 1999.

[2] See F.E.Marek Grela, "Accession and After: What Do the Candidate Countries Expect from Membership?" Available at www.cicerofoundation.org/lectures/speech_grela.html

380 million people and a GDP of €9 trillion euro.[3] Nevertheless, perception is one thing; reality is another thing; both are explored in the old and new member states.

The addition of the Central and the Eastern European countries to the EU means a more fluid, differentiated, and possibly divided EU. According to some observers, the future of enlarged EU is a "neo-medieval empire" rather than a "post-Westphalian Super-state."[4] The "Westphalian Super-state" is about "concentration of power, hierarchy, sovereignty, and clear-cut identity," whereas the neo-medieval empire is about "overlapping authorities, divided sovereignty, diversified institutional arrangements and multiple identities."[5] This is evident from the fact that the integration process is progressing via alternative routes, involving the use of opt outs and formulas for variable geometry as seen in European Monetary Union (EMU), Common Foreign Security Policy (CFSP) and the area of freedom, democracy and justice. As the EU has expanded to new policy areas, the homogeneity of membership was compromised.

It may be assumed that the new members will further complicate the integration process. Differences of opinion and differences in implementation of the *acquis communautaire* will make a single-speed Europe less likely.[6] In contrast to this, another approach tends to state that the emergence of a multi-speed EU of the future will be a "post-Westphalian regional state" displaying a distinct form of supranational governance as well.[7] The gradual alignment of economic, monetary, foreign and security, as well as border and internal security policies may lead to the strengthening of the EU as not only an economic but also a political and strategic actor in medium term. In this sense the method of integration will be more flexible, multi-

---

[3] See Barysch, Katinka: Does enlargement matter for the European Union economy? Centre for European Reform. <http://www.cer.org.uk/pdf/policybrief_enlarged_economy.pdf>www.cer.org.uk/pdf/policybrief_enlarged_economy.pdf

[4] Jan Zielonka, "How New Enlarged Borders will Reshape the EU." *Journal of Common Market Studies*, vol. 39, no.3, September 2001, p.30.

[5] Ibid. p.509

[6] See Cigdem Nas, "The Current Enlargement Process of the EU and Turkey's Position," Fornet, Available at www.fornet.info CFSP Forum vol.1, no.3, p13.

[7] See Charles C. Pentland, "Westphalian Europe and the EU's Last Enlargement" *European Integration*, vol.22, no.3, 2000

faceted, diffuse and patchy, but the core of the EU will become more integrated.

In all likelihood, the Union will move from being a predominantly rich country club to a continental Union comprising the poor new-comers. Accordingly, the former external gap of development between West and East has become an internal one. Following the enlarge-ment, the increased diversity will change the EU's political and cultural nature, and it will reinforce current EU trends toward slower legislative and reform output, greater conflict over structural funding, more pressure to reform the CAP, a stronger Council vis-à-vis the Commission, more recourse to coalitions-of-the-willing and flexibility.

The enlargement has made the EU not only more complex and het-erogeneous than ever has existed before, but it provides an increased pool for forming coalitions in different issue areas reinforcing and inter-secting cleavages between "rich" and "poor," net payer and net receiver, "Atlanticists" and "Continentalists," and new and old peripheries. The new diversity of Union will put its compromise culture to the test, as well. Moreover, the newcomers challenge the balance between the old fifteen members. The dominant mode of behavior is likely to be an assertive policy based on defense of national interests. Among the old member states' publics, as seen in the French case, the enlarged EU is perceived as a new status quo emerging at the expense of France. "In the past, for the French, Europe was a way of pursuing national ambi-tion through other means, of prolonging past glory, whereas for the Germans it represented a way to break from their past."[8] Consequently, in the postwar history Europe was a way of both prolonging the nation state and substituting it, a project of historic continuity and discontinu-ity at the same time. Against the backdrop of German political class the more Europeanized Germany was, the more "German" Germany seemed to be emerging. In the enlarged EU an increasing incongruity has developed between the EU and the national interests of old mem-ber states. From this point of view, people are inclined to regard the new status quo in *statu nascendi* as not so advantageous, aimed at dimin-ishing the institutional power of old member states and undermining,

[8] See Dominique Moisi, "Handing the 21st Century to Asia," *International Herald Tribune,* May 26, 2005. Available at http://www.iht.com/articles/2005/05/25/opinion/edmoisi.php

for example, the social peace and the leading role of the Franco-German alliance.

The EU seems to be becoming introspective during the initial period after enlargement. The new members bring in their own views, positions and priorities, and it will take some time for all the member state governments to establish alliances on different issues. Accordingly, during the first years after enlargement, there will be little spirit of solidarity as countries argue about power and money. In the years 2006-2007, the member states are preoccupied with settling the EU's next budget, for 2007-2013. The net contributors such as Germany and The Netherlands are pitted against the net recipients such as Spain and Poland and all countries will take tough stands to defend their positions. The old members try to hang on to their acquired rights—Spain and Portugal to their regional aid and Britain to its budget rebate. The gulf between Britain and France over European spending widened when the French President rebuffed a suggestion from Britain's Tony Blair that subsidies for farmers be reviewed.

Germany, the traditional "paymaster" of the Union has displayed increasingly self-interested behavior owing to its costs of integrating the eastern Länder and its decreasing soft power capabilities. It is remarkable that the German taxpayer is the only one in the "old" EU who knows from very tangible experience what is meant by bridging the double European and national division by sharing its own resources and what adjustment costs should be paid for transformation in European and German frameworks. It is not surprising that the German public's willingness to pay for solidarity with poorer parts of the Union has consequently diminished and more and more Germans are questioning their country's traditional role as net payer in the Union. Therefore, an additional difficulty is emerging since no member state is capable of replacing Germany's structural role as "economic locomotive" and the biggest net payer.

The new CEE members find themselves under unprecedented fiscal pressure after accession closely related to the diminished direct payments to their agrarian sectors to the detriment of competitiveness and due to being committed to meet the Maastricht criteria. Even before they actually joined the Union, opposition politicians and the domestic presses in several CEE countries were demanding that their governments get a better financial deal out of the EU. Any government which tries to claim to be acting in the "spirit" of solidarity these days is likely to be asked by an angry domestic press why it is not defending the national interest. Disillusionment with politics is growing across Europe, and in many countries the EU is becoming unpopular as the layer of government that is furthest away from the people. In Central and Eastern Europe, this disillusionment with politics in general and the EU in particular is compounded by "enlargement fatigue." People are tired of hearing of the need for more reform and greater austerity, especially in countries with high unemployment and public debts, such as Poland and Slovakia, last but not least Hungary. Voters in the new member states might blame the EU for their countries' economic problems—criticizing in particular fiscal tightening—over the next few years.

## Need for "Effective Membership" and New Conflict of Interests in EU

Following de facto membership during the pre-accession process (which really meant a high level of asymmetric interdependence between the Union and candidate states in economic terms) and the subsequent de jure membership on May 1, 2004, an "effective membership" is supposed to be acquired by the CEE member states. Against the backdrop of domestic pressures, the concept of "effective membership" is taken to refer to the capabilities of new members necessary to reshape the EU from within in accordance with national interests and objectives. The membership in EU means that the new members in Central and Eastern Europe want to have a say on the future shape of a united Europe and to participate in the efforts to accomplish the reforms of EU. Nevertheless, the integration of the new CEE member states into the EU's political system takes several years before they are settled into the EU's institutions in Brussels. During that period, the EU could find that its decision-making structures work more slowly, and consensus may be harder to establish.

In addition to that, "effective membership" involves the capability of new member states to form ad hoc coalitions in order to assert their policies and joint sub-regional objectives in different issue areas. The ten new members and the next two candidates, Romania and Bulgaria, will have votes and limited veto power, not sufficient to develop a blocking minority, but their institutional power cannot be left out of consideration if they align themselves with a big member state. They want to exercise these rights to the full to ensure that they get better deals in the future. At the same time, the old members will be trying to hang on to their long-standing privileges. This combination of defensiveness among the old members and resentment among the new ones will make for longer and more bitter arguments than before—and reduce any sense of solidarity between countries.

The new members are, however, unlikely to form an enduring "Eastern bloc," by voting together too often in Visegrád framework, even if they have a common interest in focusing the EU's budget for economic catch-up policies, because most are much poorer than the old fifteen. At the same time, there has been some fear in the Czech Republic, Slovakia and Hungary that their northern neighbor, Poland, is drifting away towards other big European states. Poland competed to be "America's best friend in Europe" vying for that role with Spain on the voting rights in the Council of Ministers, and with UK on transatlantic relations. With Germany and France it has had the so-called Weimar Triangle agreement. On the other hand, there is a fear in Poland that the rest of Visegrád group might lean closer towards each other and Austria, and eventually recreate some sort of a privileged Austro-Hungarian cooperation. Nevertheless, none of these fears is justified. Poland's close relations with Spain changed easily with a change of government in both Warsaw and Madrid. Special ties with the UK are more a dream than based on reality, as Warsaw does not look for disintegration, as do many British political forces. The Polish fears about a Franz-Josef monarchy are also unfounded, because even if Hungary, Czech Republic and Slovakia preferred close relations with Austria to Poland, one should bear in mind that a part of Poland was part of that monarchy; not to mention that bilateral relations are burdened with serious problems between Austria and the Czech Republic and between Austria and Slovakia ranging from the Benes decrees to nuclear power stations, respectively.

With regard to the Visegrád Four (V 4), it should be underlined that cooperation by no means stands for uniformity in behavior, and the geography in itself cannot make a long-term policy. The Visegrád countries do not have to agree on every single issue. As other European close cooperation mechanisms—like Nordic states—show, states sometimes disagree fundamentally, but this does not put an end to their special status. In Central and Eastern Europe a sometimes manifest, sometimes latent, rivalry can be observed among the newcomers. From time to time the regional pioneer role has undergone major changes. In the 1990s during the first period of transformation, Hungary and Czech Republic could play pioneering roles, while from the beginning of the new century the Baltic States and Slovakia have seemed to take the lead. The Baltic States and Slovakia seem to be on a high growth path, with lowest labor cost in the region, driven by inflows of foreign direct investment and capable of promoting the substantial domestic reforms, even meeting the Maastricht criteria earlier than other new member states. It is of great significance to what extent the major political parties are able to make consensus in the individual new member states beyond the traditional divisions necessary for creating comparative instititutional advantages and what is more, asserting and protecting their own countries' rights in EU.

The differences existing and emerging do not preclude the possibility of maintaining the Visegrád Four or "Visegrád plus" (Visegrád plus Slovenia and Austria) in the EU because it provides a framework for coordinating some crucial policies well in advance, like finding a budget settlement between 2007-2013 and the new neighborhood policy. In other words, the EU works in terms of functional, not geographical logic. It would be, however, a mistake to rule out in advance the possibility of synergic coincidence of the functional and geographical logic in Central and Eastern Europe, especially in the case of Visegrád frameworks. The countries concerned are not only rivals in a single European market but they are linked to each other by a lot of structural problems arising from both history and geography. Furthermore, it would be a mistake to overlook that the Union getting bigger and more heterogeneous inevitably gives rise to the regionalization and regrouping processes. It is sufficient to mention the conflicts of distribution that are expected to emerge between "new" and "old" peripheries demonstrating the conflicting priorities between the Barcelona-process and the new Eastern dimension.

The increased economic diversity constitutes an additional impetus for the differentiation and conflict of interest in the enlarged Union. Despite the economic growth in the new member states, there is a large wealth gap with the old EU-15. EU GDP per capita now averages more than €20,500, but the Czech average is only €11,380, while Hungary's is €10,384 and Poland's €8,001.[9] However the richest Central Europeans have converged with the poorest EU-15 countries. Slovenian GDP per capita has now overtaken that in Greece. The range of economic performance and income across Central Europe is wide. The Czech Republic, Hungary, Poland, Slovakia and Slovenia enjoy GDP per capita between one-third and two-thirds of the EU average, whereas the rest are below one-third of the EU-average. GDP per capita in Slovenia, the richest newcomer in EU, is over €15,000 while it stands at just a third of this level in Bulgaria and Romania. Regional inequalities, the rates of unemployment and growth, even the compliance with fiscal policy based on Maastricht criteria vary enormously not only between, but within the new member states along the West-East economic divide. The income levels in region around capital cities usually greatly exceed the national average. Budapest, Prague and Warsaw seem to be ineligible for some of the EU's regional aid funds while several regions along the internal East-West economic divide seem to be left out of catch up process.

Furthermore, the wage differences based on the former external and the present post-accession internal disparity gap between West and East have challenged the social model in the old member states, as well. From the point of view of old member states, the services liberalization in the single European market involves the risk of losing their usual advantages in terms of competition. Some politicians in the old member states have started to exploit anti-enlargement sentiment and the new members are accused of "social dumping"—a politically charged word for low-wage competition. In the old member states the trade unions fight against the services liberalization while others argue that this is a way to protect their members rather than help all the 19 million unemployed Europeans. As there are still lower salaries and social protection in some Central- and East-European EU states, the fears are that the new rules on services—which represent

---

[9] See Solidarity in Europe. A Think-Tank Forum Warsaw, June 6-8, 2002. Centre for European Reform—British Council Warsaw—Konrad-Adenauer-Stiftung. Available at <http://www.britishcouncil.pl/governance/concept%20paper-solidarity.doc>www.britishcouncil.pl/governance/concept%20paper-solidarity.doc

up to 70 percent of the European internal market—would lead to "social dumping."

In other words, the newcomers can enjoy considerable advantages over their competitors in the old member states due to their low wages. Nevertheless, the newcomers should face the same challenge, if the process of "enlargement of enlargement" takes place in the future. Some old member states like Germany and France feared that low tax rates in the new member states would lure companies eastward, taking jobs and investment with them. Politicians gave expression to the opinion that it was unacceptable for Germany as the EU's biggest net payer to finance unfair tax competition against itself. Germany has openly threatened to cut EU regional aid unless the new members rethink their tax policies. Germany and France have dusted off old plans to introduce a minimum rate of corporation tax in the EU. The tax debate has been an opening shot in the EU's budget battle. What is more, in their attempt to cap EU spending, Germany and France could use allegations of "unfair" tax competition to limit transfers to Eastern Europe.

The vanguard of new economic Europe is made up of countries like Luxembourg, Estonia and Ireland. The economic divide does not always follow national borders, however, in three of Europe's biggest economies—France, Germany and Italy—internal battles are under way over policies that would reshape labor markets, making it easier to hire and fire workers. The roots of these differences lie primarily in Europe's experiment with socialism, and people's impressions of the results. There are those who consider socialism a failure and wish to replace it with its opposite and those who believe the state should protect workers from the uncaring actions of capitalists. It is somewhat strange that Britain and other more traditionally reform-minded countries in old Europe have found new allies in the East, even though these countries in many ways have very large, even overblown, welfare states themselves. Germany and France have used the specter of tax harmonization to show that they are still the motor for European integration. The British government, supported by the new members in Central and Eastern Europe, insisted on keeping the national veto for all tax matters in EU's new constitutional treaty. In turn, Paris and Berlin added procedures that will make it easier for a small group of EU countries to go ahead with a policy initiative on their own. They are now talking about using these "enhanced co-operation" procedures to harmonize their corporate tax systems.

## The Eastern Periphery and a New Geopolitical and Foreign and Security Policy Agenda

The enlarged EU will have to cope with neighborhood policies that receive support from different member states. Scandinavians focus on the "Northern Dimension," Central Europeans on the former communist countries of East and South East Europe, and the Mediterranean member states on the Barcelona process. The EU tradition of package deals takes care of the balance (e.g. Germany supported the Barcelona process in the mid-1990s partly because it needed the support of the Mediterranean member states for eastern enlargement).

With the first wave of EU eastward enlargement in 2004, the eastern and southeastern borders of the new member states have become the new external borders of the EU (only the Czech Republic will be entirely surrounded by EU member states). It is here that the key functions of customs and immigration control and security are to be carried out on behalf of the whole EU. This requires implementation of an array of measures, including strict control of the external frontier according to common rules (contained in Schengen Manual for the External Frontier), accession to the Schengen Information System, the computerized database, etc. Due to the new Eastern enlargement, which is nothing like the previous ones, the EU faces the task of reinventing itself as foreign policy actor towards the new neighborhood.[10] A policy towards the immediate geographical neighborhood is an essential feature and requirement of any regional power, and if EU intends to become a full-fledged one, it is not only normal but also consistent with the Union's nature that it aims at building "a ring of friends" around its borders.

The geographical extent has brought new geopolitical perspectives and diverging geopolitical priorities and national interests into the

---

[10] See: Dov Lynch, "The New Eastern Dimension of Enlarged EU" in Judy Batt, Dov Lynch, Antonio Missiroli, Martin Ortega and Dimitros Triantaphyllou, *Partners and Neighbors: a CFSP for a wider Europe*. Chaillot Paper No. 64 (Paris: European Union Institute for Security Studies) p.59.

enlarged EU. The same goes for wider disparities in threat perception.[11] Added to this are the different security cultures and the lack of strategic culture in the new member states due to the historical heritages of the Great Powers' "divide et impera" policy, as well as the different prisms through which each sees its security situation and defines its strategies. It may thus become more challenging to harmonize truly "common foreign and security policies" in the enlarged Union although the new member states attach particular importance to the Union's Ostpolitik to ensure security and stability in neighborhood.

The most important contribution of the new member states to the Union's external policies is the "Eastern Dimension." The interesting test cases in this respect were the controversies over the transit to and from the Kaliningrad enclave, Poland's joint crisis management with the EU in "Orange Revolution" in Ukraine, and Hungary's democracy- and region-building activity in the Western Balkans in the framework of Stability Pact.

The so-called Szeged Process initiated by Hungary in 1999 has significantly contributed to the local capacity-building for effective cross-border co-operation. Since 1999 the Process has provided support to Serbia-Montenegro, Albania, Macedonia and Bosnia-Herzegovina in the fields of democratization: strengthening the rule of law, assisting local governments and strengthening the civil society. The renewed and broadened Szeged Process intends to engage all political forces, local governments, NGO's, think-thanks, scholars and students, as well as the media and other opinion leaders of the beneficiary countries that share the same perspective and align themselves with the goals of Euro-Atlantic integration. The instruments of the Szeged Process are seminars, trainings, information, brochures, teaching and educational materials, twinning projects, exchange of experts etc.

The region-building process in Southeastern Europe implies that there are a large number of core problems to be coped with, ranging from unresolved statehood and national determination issues, to matters of military security and border demarcation, to multilayered regional cooperation and to mundane low-politics issues. Until the present, the containment and treatment of such conflicts has been the

---

[11] Jiri Sedivy, "The Impact of the New (Post-Communist) EU Member States on the CSFP." Fornet. www.fornet.info CFSP Forum, vol. 1, .no.3, p.8.

paramount concern of the international community. The varying priorities and the ensuing differentiation within the region, which is even more serious if one takes into account that states such as Greece and Turkey are to be included, may cause some questioning of the potential for intergovernmental co-operation to foster common political identities—a necessary prerequisite for a sustainable and deepening integration—is significant.

The European Commission unveiled a strategy to prevent new "dividing lines" in Europe by embracing countries on the margins of the newly expanded EU. The European Neighborhood Policy (ENP) is distinct from the issue of further accessions, and addresses to countries that do not currently have the prospect of accession. The aim is to draw countries on the EU's eastern and southern fringes into a reinforced partnership centred on trade and political goals including human rights and the fight against terrorism. In the economic field, the partner countries would be invited to align themselves with the EU's internal market by adopting approximate laws and open up their markets in accordance with the WTO rules. A ring of well-governed countries around the EU, offering perspectives for democracy and economic growth is in the interests of Europe as whole. In addition to that, the European neighborhood policy is closely related to an existential dilemma the Union is facing, namely the apparent choice to be made between over-extending the enlargement process to the point of destroying its own governability, versus denying one of its founding values to be open to all European democracies and possibly generating negative effects from the exclusion of countries in its neighborhood. The newly emerging ENP could provide a way out of this dilemma.

From the point of view of the member states, the new geopolitical situation of being situated on the EU periphery calls for a new foreign and security policy agenda for shaping the new external environment. Due to their new geopolitical situation and considering the fact that Poland, Slovakia and Hungary have a special responsibility promoting the European orientation of the countries in the region, they represent the Union's newest resource, which could greatly contribute to a successful ENP. Slovakia and Hungary expect a visible differentiation of the neighborhood policy in relation to each region and proclaim themselves in favor of the development of the "Eastern Dimension" as a mechanism coordinating for the eastern policy activities and a platform for regional cooperation.

The EU has rediscovered that its new members on the EU's periphery can be strategic partners on the "stronger" and more active side of the new borders. These new members are expected to adopt the role of "patron" or "supporter." Therefore it is important to stress that the new strategic borders should be as friendly and safe as possible, while complying with the Schengen regimes. The borders should be opened for complex cooperation projects ranging from cross border activities to region-building, and in some cases, crises prevention and post-conflict rehabilitation. Difficulties exist in implementing Europe's Schengen rules on border controls relating to immigration, asylum policy, political cooperation and judicial assistance. Central and Eastern European states are becoming the "buffer zone" of refugees displaced by conflicts in the Balkans, Africa and Asia as migrants seek access to the West.

From the point of view of some new member states like Poland and Hungary, on the one hand, the old historic mission seems to be revisited; in the name of "Europe" providing a protective shield against the "invaders." On the other hand, the new member states want more integration and more enlargement transcending their peripheral status. This means more competition, flexibility but also a stronger Europe to deal with the new challenges. The new countries want to embrace an EU that tackles more issues on the community level instead of having more powers reside with the member states, particularly the bigger ones. Their allegiance to Europe is all the more heartfelt because they are not convinced about Russia's road to democracy.

What is less well appreciated is the potential impact of the EU's external border regime on those regions, which fall just on each side of the EU's new external border. The EU's external border regime seems likely to have a damaging impact on the economic stability of the borderland regions themselves, on each side of the new eastern border between Poland and Hungary and their eastern neighbors. In the last decade of relatively free movement across the border, there has been a significant cross-border trade and the possibility for labor to commute jobs, which has become a vital means of surviving for many inhabitants in these peripheral areas. Moreover, many borderland regions are multi-ethnic in composition. Open borders have provided opportunities not only for discovering suppressed national minority identities, but contributing to the diminution of mutual animosities over the past decade.[12]

Intensified cooperation with non-EU countries in Central and Eastern Europe ought to prepare for closer ties with and eventual admission to the Union. Since most of the newcomers are small and medium-sized states, their geographical focus lies on the European continent and its direct vicinity. Poland and Slovakia border on Belarus and Ukraine. Hungary borders on the Western Balkans and Ukraine, and last, but not least, on "itself" meaning the existence of Hungarian minorities in all neighboring countries. For Hungary, the main concern about Schengen is the impact of EU visa policies on the access of the ethnic Hungarians living in surrounding countries. These "external minorities" total up to 3 million people, a significant number in relation to the 10 million living in Hungary. Ensuring the welfare of these communities is a main tenet of Hungarian foreign policy and is a central issue in its bilateral relations with its neighbors. Moreover, much cross-border trade and investment depends on family and cultural ties with diaspora communities, and pendulum migration into Hungary provides jobs that support many families in poorer neighboring countries.[13] A number of proposals have been put forward to deal with the problem of admitting ethnic Hungarians without visas, ranging from a national visa via permitting a stay of over 90 days for citizens of neighboring countries, but in Hungary alone, to the proposal to offer dual citizenship offering to millions of ethnic Hungarian which failed in a Hungarian national referendum in 2004.

At the same time, the existence of external minorities is an additional impetus making Hungary interested in extending the Euro-Atlantic regimes to all its neighboring countries as soon as possible. From this it follows that the EU opens up new avenues for Budapest to be able to unite the "Hungarian nation" as whole in the integration structures based on sharing and pooling sovereignty even if all of Hungary's neighbors are

[12] Judy Batt, "The Impact of EU Enlargement on Regions on the EU's New Eastern Border," Available at www.crees.bham.ac.uk/research/wgb.pdf [13]    See:    George Schöpflin, "Hungary and its Neighbours," in George Schöpflin, *Nations Identity Power* (London: Hurst Company) pp.378-410.

[13] See: George Schöpflin, "Hungary and its Neighbours," in George Schöpflin, *Nations Identity Power* (London: Hurst Company) pp.378-410.

hardly to be expected to become EU member states simultaneously. Moreover, this serves as an example showing how the minority questions can be defused, how the incongruence of state and nation—a very sensitive problem in Central and Eastern Europe—can be managed by enlargement in positive terms. Accordingly, the Union is considered to be not only a complex multi-level system of governance but the community of communities or "community of minorities" to cite then Commission President Romano Prodi,[14] in which each individual has to have the right to be the member of several freely chosen communities simultaneously, and every community has the right to promote the different cultures and languages of each individual. Furthermore, the history of the Union also shows that integration does not mean the end of nation state at all. Rather, it offers a suitable institutional framework for transforming the traditional nation into a post-traditional, Europeanized, integrated one, which never has existed in the history before.

## New Member States: "Atlanticists" or "Balancers" Between NATO and CFSP/ESDP?

Unlike the new small-sized member states in Central and Eastern Europe, Poland seems not to be confined exclusively to a subregional role of agenda-setting in its direct vicinity. Poland, like Hungary, observes the process of stabilization on the Western Balkans and desires to participate in the Barcelona Process and Mediterranean Partnership, which aim to develop close relations between EU and its neighbors on the south coasts of the Mediterranean Sea. Moreover, Poland seems to have a global vision of its role in the second pillar and to be keen on joining a "directoire" which the great powers may find all the more attractive in an enlarged EU. Poland is vitally interested in preventing the reintegration of the post-Soviet area back under Russian domination, maintaining close cooperation between the U.S. and the EU to build a common security structure. The reestablishment of Russian control over Ukraine and the stabilization of control over Belarus would re-create a material base for neo-imperial ambitions that are still present in Russia. This is why the independence and Europeanization of Ukraine and, if the internal conditions of the

---

[14] János Martonyi, "Europe at a crossroads ("Európa válaszúton")," *Magyar Szemle*, XII, No. 11-12, December 2003, p.231.

country allow, of Belarus are crucially important for Polish security. From the Polish point of view, the strategic relationship with US could be used to counterbalance its low profile economic position in the EU. Also, the anti-Iraq axis between Germany, Russia and France recalled bad memories of the interwar period. The replacement of US domination in the Euro-Atlantic security architecture with a Franco-German tandem supported by Russia is contrary to Polish interests.

From this point of view, the ESDP must not be based on anti-American sentiments. Poland questioned the proposals for enhanced, "structural" cooperation in the ESDP, as well. The "structural cooperation" is open to all EU members, but it still duplicates NATO's function without having NATO's resources. According to Polish perception, the entire project seemed to be based on the idea of a "European directorate," which aimed to exclude Atlanticists—among others Poland—from the core of European security structure.[15] At the same time Warsaw, like other countries in Central and Eastern Europe, promotes the Eastern Dimension of the EU, based on the Northern one, and cooperation with Visegrád countries, Baltic States and possibly, when it enters the EU, with Romania regarding Moldova. The contradiction with the Mediterranean priorities of France, Italy and Spain is obvious, while cooperation with Germany will be complex, given Germany's Russia first policy versus Poland's Ukrainian priority.

The question may be raised whether the new enlargement of EU is likely to generate a shift of balance toward a more Atlanticist Union. Though this point should not be exaggerated since the new invitees—maybe Poland is an exception to the rule—can hardly be considered to be political heavy weights neither within EU nor outside the EU. With most of the new NATO members either in or about to be EU members and thereby, fully included in the EU's Common Foreign and Security Policy (CFSP), the latest round of NATO expansion to Central and Eastern Europe seemed also to reduce the strength of the eurocentric tendencies within the EU's European Security and Defense Policy (ESDP).

The new members of EU, getting closer to the fragile zones of instability, to its "near abroad" are interested to tie the ESDP as closely as possible to NATO, since the only alternative would be an EU duplica-

---

[15] See Przemyslaw Zurawski vel Grahewski, "ESDP: A view from Poland," Fornet, www.fornet.info, CFSP Forum, vol 1, no.3, p.9.

tion of some of the structures and functions that the Alliance already possesses. That would be a costly and time-consuming process, and even more importantly, would seriously undermine the transatlantic link. Moreover, it is hard to find any European country—in particular a new member state—that would be willing to multiply its national defense budget to cover the costs of duplication. In order for the ESDP to be successful, it must not interfere with the role of NATO. Given that the ESDP is not designed as a substitute to NATO, ESDP is oriented toward stabilization and peacekeeping, these should not be a conflict. Moreover, most European countries hope that the ESDP is limited to the periphery of the EU; whereas NATO operates further afield, in places like Afghanistan, and is considering operations in the Middle East.

At first sight the enlargement process has brought pro-Atlanticist countries into the EU. There has been a strong resistance by the new members to attempts to communitarize CFSP/ESDP or to detach it from NATO. Many CEE countries feel that the United States was instrumental in their quests for independence, as well as bringing them into NATO, especially so in Poland's case. As a result, the new members seem to be close to the Atlanticists and those favoring incremental reforms in CFSP rather than "revolutionary approaches." Nevertheless, a gradual re-balancing of the pro-Atlantic bias can be expected in due course as they are fully integrated and socialized into the EU, particularly in that case, when they feel that they have an equal say in shaping the future of the CFSP/ESDP.[16] Therefore, their first priority is to preserve the balance between NATO and EU/ESDP and not to harm NATO. It is clear that if Europe would remain divided into pro- and anti-US camps, the ESDP will achieve little. It is in the interests of the new members to make sure that ESDP develops in a way that does not deepen the "new-old" divide in Europe. At the same time, Hungary, Czech Republic and Slovakia have expressed their interest in the development of ESDP as an indispensable element and instrument of CFSP. The countries believe that a flexible, inclusive approach and effective links to NATO are essential to the success of ESDP.

Moreover, the Czech Republic's views and positions on CFSP/ESDP matters come closest to the UK's intergovernmental approach. For

---

[16] See Juri Sedivy, "The Impact of New (Post-Communist) EU Member-States on the CFSP," Fornet, www.foirnet.info CFSP Forum, vol.1, no.3, p.8-9.

the British, NATO plays as important a role as it does for the Czech Republic, as confirmed by the following statement: "We believe that a flexible, inclusive approach and effective links to NATO are essential to the success of ESDP. We will not agree to anything which is contradictory to, or would replace, the security guarantee established through NATO."[17] According to the Security Strategy of Czech Republic, the creation of the EU's Common European Security and Defense Policy is a natural part of the European integration process. It is, however, important for this process to be in line with developments in the European Security and Defense Identity within NATO and for it to lead to a strengthening of transatlantic ties.[18] One expert identified the status of Hungary as one of the free riders in NATO. In this view Hungary upheld a "soft" Atlanticist position in the ongoing debate on the relationship between the US and Europe.[19]

The enlarged EU of 25 will face an intensified need for flexible ad hoc coalitions. Along these lines, European security culture as well as strategic thinking will be formulated. A promising example is Javier Solana's European Security Strategy. Most important for the new member states is perhaps Solana's assertion that "the transatlantic relationship is irreplaceable" and that "NATO is and will remain key to safeguarding or security: not as a competitor but as a strategic partner."[20] According to Hungary's ambassador to the United States: "I wouldn't say Old Europe/New Europe. We Hungarians want to make sure that everybody understands we are not about to choose between Europe and the United States...we spell it out clearly: "'more Europe, not less America.'"[21]

The ESDP and the EU were not invited to play an operative role in the war on terrorism, though a case can certainly be made for the EU's increased relevance in peace support operations for example in the

---

[17] A Constitutional Treaty for the EU—The British Approach to the European Union Intergovernmental Conference 2003, White Paper, p.38.[18]    See: Hana Motková, "CFSP and Czech Republic," Available at fesportal.fes.de/pls/portal130/ does/ Folder/ Worldwide/Westsuedue 2005.o4.14, pp.6-7.

[19] See: "Report on the 7th Export Conference: Converging and Diverging. NATO and CFSP on the eve of enlargement," November 17, 2003, Available at fesportal.fes.de/pls/portal30/docs /FOLDER/WORLDWIDE/WESTSUEDEUR, p.4.

[20] For reference see: Draft European Security Strategy presented by the EU High Representative for the Common Foreign and Security Policy, Javier Solana, to the European Council, June 20, 2003 in Thessaloniki, Greece

[21] Interview with András Simonyi, *The San Diego Union-Tribune*, June 29, 2003.

Balkans. Both sides of the Atlantic share the desire to rid the world of terrorism. The scenario of weapons of mass destruction (WMD) in the hands of terrorists driven by anti-Western ideologies poses a serious threat. Consequently, Europe has a vital interest in assuring that it becomes the counterpart, rather than the "counterbalance," to the United States in the campaign against international terrorism, even if threat perceptions could differ from each other regarding the methods and timetable.

## Eastern Enlargement and the EU External Relations

After eastern enlargement, the EU will be not be the same to the outside world, but the changes affect foreign policy much more than external economic relations and they are focused on the EU's post-communist immediate geographical neighborhood. Because of their modest economic weight, the new members will hardly affect the external trade and investment relations of the Union with third countries. Accordingly, the new members will little add to the EU aid effort. On the one hand the new member states' economic relations to third countries might decline with the adoption of EU regulation in middle term, on other hand the relations might increase due to the improving infrastructure and the attractiveness of the newcomers as location of investment in long term.

The EU's external policy follows the principles based on concentric circles. The most intense relations are established with the candidate states like Croatia and Turkey, although the Commission is going to involve all democratic states in the Balkans, holding out the prospect of membership, as well. This is approach aimed at integration proper i.e. at bringing neighboring countries directly into the EU through bilateral process based on strict "conditionality." The next circle relates to the target countries of new neighborhood policy—embracing North Africa, Middle East and Eastern Europe and Caucasus. This is an approach aimed, first and foremost, at stabilization, mainly based on fostering regional cooperation and broad partnerships (regionalism) and more modest means. In addition to that the EU has a global development and aid policy aimed at supporting the developing world in accordance with the millenarian objectives of the UN.

From the point of view of CEE countries, it is surprising that on average—despite priorities based on principles of concentric circles—about 49 per cent of the expenditure envisaged by the Commission goes to development policy in the chapter of the EU's budget plan entitled "EU as global partner." Meanwhile, only 15-17 per cent goes to the pre-accession funds and new neighborhood policy in the next financial period of seven years. That is the reason why politicians in CEE member states have expressed an opinion that the percentage rates in the controversial budget plan reflects a policy detrimental to newcomers. What is more, these disadvantages cannot be compensated by the structural and cohesion policy. Consequently, the EU's external policy should be regarded as a traditional means of maintaining and strengthening privileged relations of the former colonial powers to their earlier colonies. Nevertheless, it hardly need be discussed that the CEE member states also have vested interests, like other countries in the developing world catching up with the core states; even they can benefit by this.

Nonetheless, the new threats and transnational risks, emanating from the immediate geographical neighborhood make the new CEE members more interested in placing more emphasis on pre-accession processes and on a new "Eastern Dimension" based on a division of labor between new members and the Union. Additional funds are also required to address the new strategic environment ranging from Ukraine, Moldova, the Balkans to the Caucasus region and the Middle East.[22] From this it follows that the discussion about and a conflict of interest over the new financial period might open a window of opportunity for the CEE states to restructure the budget plan in favor of their geographical preferences. No matter which final decision will be taken, but it is certain that the "enlargement of enlargement" continues to put the issue on the agenda in the years to come. The institutional "size" of EU in terms of politique finalité is defined by the constitutional treaty which waits to be ratified, while the "territorial finalité" is a question still to be defined and negotiated.

From the point of view of CEE member states, the foreign policy of the former superpower, Russia is of utmost importance. In this case, the positions of the individual member states in Central and Eastern Europe, like those of Poland and Baltic states, may differ from the other ones regarding the threat perception of Russia.

Unlike the NATO enlargement, the EU's historic eastern enlargement caused no difficulties between EU and Russia. On the contrary, in the

---

[22] István Szent-Iványi, "Hogyan legyünk önzőCEek? ("How to be egoistic?")," Népszabadság March 17, 2005.

context of work to create the common economic space, the Commission underlines the benefit of enlargement for Russia and for EU/Russia economic relations, of taking forward bilateral negotiations for Russia's World Trade Organization accession. It will also recall the importance of cooperation on energy and transport issues, including the Energy Dialogue and satellite navigation (Galileo). The Commission calls also for increased cooperation on environmental matters, including an assessment of the prospects for ratification of Kyoto protocol by Russia.

Russia's foreign policy on Europe is to a greater extent reactive and not supported by coherent strategy. This policy depends on the situation . An illustrative example of this could be the antiwar axis between Paris-Berlin-Moscow. Russia's relationship with Germany and France will remain a priority issue for Russia. And it is particularly Germany, and its leadership that never shown signs of losing interest in developing relations with Russia. This, however, may change if Berlin needs to coordinate its policies towards Russia with the new member states, such as Poland.

Moreover, for the last four years the results of the Russia—EU Partnership and Cooperation Agreement—have been quite modest. Kaliningrad has remained a region in focus following the enlargement of EU in May 2004. The new Ukraine, Belarus and Moldova form a top-priority group of countries where Russia may use the whole arsenal of political and economic policies. In this region Russia maintains the possibility to conduct policy aimed either at destabilizing or stabilizing countries' internal situation. The EU, in this case, may read Russian policies towards "near abroad" as messages of Russia's intentions on a wider European scale.

The eastern enlargement brings the European Union close to the vital spheres of Russia's interest—its "near abroad." Ukraine is the largest country in the post-Soviet space where rear-guard actions over geopolitical influence have taken place between the USA and Russia. That is one of the reasons why the American strategy considers both Poland and Ukraine as important geopolitical partners to contain and to prevent Russia from becoming a world power again. Following the "Orange Revolution," the EU cannot evade either moral or political commitment to fight for a country like Ukraine belonging to Europe both in geographic and historic terms. The US' strategy does not rule out either the partnership with Russia against terrorism, or the competition with Europe, or the containment of Russia. Regardless of the future policy of the EU towards Ukraine, Belarus and Moldova, Russia is likely to regard it as a penetration of her orbit of influence, thus leaving no choice for Moscow but to adopt assertive and active policy towards its near abroad. The present intensification of Russian policies towards her near abroad is apparent. The goal is to remain a dominant political and economic player in the region. The key tool of Russia's policies towards Ukraine, Belarus and, to a lesser extent, Moldova even towards the CEE member states of EU has been economic. It is, however, an open question whether Russia will be able to build up its "raw material-colonialism"—as a substitute for its lost super power status—in the post-Soviet and European space. It is very likely that Russia as a primary energy supplier to and through Eastern Europe will continue to be a major player in Europe for the foreseeable future and will use its economic interests to exert political influence or will endeavor to gain influence over the foreign and security policies of nearby countries.

An additional question is how will the energy supply policy of the EU be shaped and to what extent will an integrationist or dependent structure be established between EU and Russia? On the one hand, President Vladimir Putin's effort to recreate a Russian sphere of influence in the Commonwealth of Independent States (CIS) are partly economic (to secure oil and other revenues), partly geopolitical (to enhance political control over neighbors and secure a buffer security zone against Islamic extremism in the South) but also domestic: to increase respect for the state among the Russians themselves. On the other hand, Russia is likely to make a distinction between the new member states from Central and Eastern Europe and the old EU members. The Kremlin's attitudes towards the new member states will be to a great extent determined by the latter's relationship with Brussels and key European countries. And if something resembling a two-speed Europe emerges, one of the Kremlin's responses could be a differentiated European Policy. Another one of Russia's instruments, which is essentially European is the concept of human rights, which the Kremlin applies to some of the new EU members such as Latvia and Estonia. But the durability and potential of this approach is already questioned following Putin's domestic policy development. The benchmark for protection of human rights established by the Council of Europe and the OSCE stand in marked contrast to the current situation in Russia, where the vertical power of government increasingly leaves less room for the individual in favor of a more powerful centralized state.

## Conclusions

Eastward enlargement of the EU will have a range of effects on the CEE countries and the EU as a whole. The increased diversity will change the EU's political and the cultural nature, and will reinforce the current trends in the EU, as well, ranging from greater conflict over structural funding to more recourse to flexibility.

Following the eastern enlargement there are two kinds of solidarity, solidarity in Europe, and solidarity between Europe and America. Solidarity in the enlarged EU can be discussed in its economic and socio-political dimension. From economic point of view, during the first years after enlargement, there will be little spirit of solidarity, as countries argue about power and money under pressures of domestic policy. Due to its low-wage competition and services liberalization, the newcomers can enjoy advantages over their competitors in old member states giving rise to anti-enlargement sentiments. Nevertheless, the new CEE member states will face the same problems in the process of "enlargement of enlargement," too. In terms of "effective member-ship," the EEC newcomers find themselves under unprecedented fiscal and "success" pressures closely related to financial transfers and requirements of Maastricht criteria and an accelerated catching-up process. An important political dimension that will make solidarity dif-ficult in the enlarged EU is the lack of permanent strategic alliance. The new members need time to get accustomed to the new political mechanisms already operating in the Union, such as flexible coopera-tion or multi-speed integration, which may not be conducive to politi-cal solidarity in the future and involve the risk of remaining second class members. Unanimity is not to be expected in the future EU, but mastering the art of dialogue and winning back people's trust in European institutions is one of the most important tasks.

The existing and emerging differences do not rule out the possibil-ity of maintaining regional frameworks like the Visegrád Four (or "Visegrád plus") coincident with the functional and geographical logic in the EU. The Union is getting bigger and more heterogeneous, inevitably favorable to rationalization and re-grouping processes. The geographical extent, however, has brought new geopolitical perspectives and diverging geopolitical priorities and national interests, even different threat perceptions into the enlarged EU. The new geopolitical situation of the CEE member states, meaning the emergence of new external strategic borders of EU, calls for new foreign and security policy agenda-setting. The European neighborhood policy is meant to manage the existential dilemmas, among others the choice between over-extending the enlargement and the possibly negative effects from the exclusion of countries in its neighborhood. The new CEE member states have a special responsibility promoting the European orientation of countries in the region and they represent the EU's newest resource, which could greatly contribute to a successful neighborhood policy. The most important contribution of the CEE member states to the Union's external policy is the "Eastern Dimension" consisting of different sets of problems and tasks. From the point of view of Baltic States and Poland, the major problems are the transit from and to Kaliningrad, the westernization of Ukraine and, not to a lesser degree, to prevent Russia from becoming "re-emergent" imperial power.

Unlike the new small states, however, Poland seems not to be confined exclusively to subregional role of agenda-setting. Poland seems to have a global vision of its role and to be keen on joining a "directorate" in certain situations. For geopolitical reasons, Hungary, like other new member states, faces a large number of problems coming from its immediate geographical environment, interest in protecting Hungarian minorities, as well as the unresolved statehood, region- and state-building, and regional cooperation.

The history of EU points to the fact that integration is very conducive to managing the problems of nation states given the incongruence of state and nation in Central and Eastern Europe. Integration does not mean the end of the nation state at all; rather, it offers a suitable framework for transforming the traditional nation state into an post-traditional integrated, Europeanized one and a "community of communities," making the minority issues more manageable in an enlarged European space.

Although the enlargement process has brought "soft" and "hard" pro-Atlanticist countries into the EU, it would be a mistake to conclude that the East-West conflict will be replaced by a "West-West conflict." Nevertheless, the double big bang enlargement has justly raised the issue of how the "West" and "East" should be defined again.

The new CEE member states have as a priority to preserve the balance between NATO and EU/ESDP and not to harm NATO, and last but not least, to avoid choosing between Europe and United States. It is clear that if Europe would remain divided into pro- and anti-US camps, the ESDP will achieve little. Therefore the new member states have vested interest in making the European and Atlanticist assets as balanced as possible. Both the US and the EU have had their share in the process and both paid their price. America was left alone to bear the financial burden and moral costs of an intervention lacking international support and credibility. It also turned out that building European identity by means of opposing America could cost Europe its unity.

Following the eastern enlargement, the EU is not the same to the outside world, but the changes affect foreign and security policy much more than external economic relations. From the point of view of the CEE member states, the major problem is related to the disproportionate percentages allocated for international development in the budget plan for the next financial period 2007-2013. The controversial plan reflects namely the geopolitical priorities of the former colonial powers' privileged relations with their former colonies rather than the financial needs of the CEE countries in framework of their new neighborhood policy in an enlarged Union. Therefore, the CEE states are interested in restructuring the budget in favor of the foreign and security policy preferences, taking the short- and long-term processes of "enlargement of enlargement" into consideration.

# The Larger EU and its Near Abroad

## Chapter 5

# The EU's Neighborhood Policy

Michael Leigh

## EU Enlargement and "Europeanization"

This chapter explores the European Union's new Neighborhood Policy which was introduced to accompany the current phase of EU enlargement. Its goal is to avoid the creation of new barriers between the EU and neighboring states in eastern Europe and the Mediterranean region. It offers closer links with the EU, stopping short of membership, in exchange for commitments to political and economic reform and key foreign policy goals. The chapter examines the scope and limits of this policy, especially given the European aspirations of some of the states concerned.

Enlargement is widely regarded as the European Union's most successful foreign policy. In the 1980s the accession of Greece, Spain and Portugal served to consolidate democracy after the overthrow of authoritarian regimes. It ruled out any return to dictatorship in these three countries, bringing gains to the West as a whole in terms of stability and security. The short-term economic costs, in extending the Common Agricultural Policy to cover certain Mediterranean products or making transfer payments under the EU's funds for economic restructuring, were considered well worth the price. The accession of Austria, Finland and Sweden in the 1990s, after the end of the Cold War, firmly anchored these three neutral countries to western institutions, while providing a bridge to transition countries in central and eastern Europe.

These transition countries found a focus in the European Union for their aspirations to build new systems based on political and economic freedom. At a time when NATO membership was still unthinkable, association agreements with the EU, eventually embodying the goal of EU membership, enabled them to rejoin the mainstream of international life. Later, the political and economic criteria for EU membership and the accession negotiations themselves guided the reform process. The EU's regulatory environment provided a ready-made set of rules for economic reforms and the prospect of free trade with the EU attracted foreign direct investment, bringing new capital, technology and management skills. Governments could mobilize support for unpopular reforms as a necessary stage on the way to EU membership. Facilitating the peaceful transformation of half a continent, with scarcely a shot fired or loss of life is perhaps the EU's most far-reaching achievement. It, too, came at a certain economic cost, but one which was negligible when compared with the gains in European security and, indeed, the EU's overall weight in world politics.

## The Balkans and Albania

The former Yugoslavia and Albania had been less successful than the countries of central and eastern Europe in transforming themselves into modern societies. The wars of the 1990s, persistent conflicts over minorities and borders, and weak governance precluded a dash for modernity through "Europeanization" (that is the adoption of European values, standards, laws and administrative practices as part of the process of transition and *rapprochement* with the EU). Yet the EU could not envisage with equanimity continued instability in this neighboring region, bringing with it threats ranging from warfare itself to state failure, organized crime, illegal migration and trafficking. The Dayton-Paris agreements, after the war in Bosnia, and later, the establishment of a UN administration in Kosovo, the Belgrade Agreement creating the state union of Serbia and Montenegro, and the Ohrid Agreement setting up a framework for reconciliation in Macedonia, all required strong international backing. Could the process of "Europeanization," which had proved so successful in central and eastern Europe, be adapted to the requirements of the "Western Balkans"?

The response was not long in coming. The international community devised the Stability Pact as a means to persuade recently warring parties and their neighbors to cooperate in the interest of economic development and eventual political reconciliation.[1] A greater inducement was needed, however, given the depth of resentments and the

---

[1] Stability Pact for South Eastern Europe. Available at http://www.stabilitypact.org

complex multi-level systems of governance in the region resulting from post-war arrangements. The EU provided that inducement in the form of the "perspective" of membership, which, alone, gave credibility to the Stability Pact. Membership would result from fulfillment of a set of criteria, modeled on those applied to the countries of central and eastern Europe, adapted to the circumstances of the western Balkans. "Stabilization and Association" Agreements mirroring, *mutatis mutandis*, the earlier "Europe Agreements" would set out the path towards membership.[2] EU financial assistance would address urgent reconstruction needs, shifting gradually to institution-building and support for political and economic reform.

The EU's strategy was founded on a simple calculation. There could be no "final settlement" in the Balkans which would be satisfactory to all the region's ethnic groups. Ethnicity and borders did not coincide and could not be made to do so by further fractioning and sub-division. But if all the groups concerned were convinced that they shared a common future inside the EU, with its goal of political and economic union, remaining incongruities between ethnicity and borders would lose their significance and, hence, their potential for renewed conflict.

The key to success lay in the credibility of the process in the eyes of the population. To peoples weary of war, grappling with day-to-day necessities in reduced economic circumstances and skeptical of politicians' promises, talk of EU membership must often have seemed like pie in the sky. Realizing this, the EU took steps to make the process more credible. At the Thessaloniki summit in 2003 the EU brought into the "stabilization and association process" many of the techniques which had proved their worth with the candidate countries which were to join the EU the following year.[3] But it would take a long time for any number of action plans, twinning arrangements and technical assistance to bring tangible perceived benefits to the public at large.

---

[2] The Stabilisation and Association process, Available at http://europa.eu.int/comm/external_relations/see/actions/sap.htm

[3] Progress of Western Balkan countries towards the EU within an enriched Stabilisation and Association Process. Available at http://europa.eu.int/comm/external_ relations/ see/ gac-thess.htm] European parliament 4th parliamentary conference "Stability pact countries recommendations to the Thessaloniki EU-South East Europe submit," Brussels May 22, 2003 [http://www.europarl.eu.int/comparl/afet/stability_pact/4th_conference/conclusions_en.pdf

More visible and hence more capable of seizing the public's imagination were palpable achievements by western Balkan countries in
moving towards EU membership. Slovenia's success in joining the
first wave of new EU Member States had some impact elsewhere in
the Balkans, although this was limited as Slovenia assumed the identity of a central European rather than a Balkan country. Later Slovenia
sought to share its experience with neighboring countries through
training programs and regional cooperation. The conclusion by the
Former Yugoslav Republic of Macedonia and by Croatia of
"Stabilization and Association" (S.A.) Agreements with the EU,
accompanied by various forms of pre-accession support, made the goal
of EU membership more credible.[4] Croatia's application for EU membership, endorsed by the Commission and the Member States in 2004,
was further proof that the EU meant what it said about the perspective of membership.[5] Understanding what was at stake, Croatia
renewed its commitment to Balkan regional cooperation, progress on
refugee return and cooperation with the International Criminal
Tribunal on the Former Yugoslavia. Nonetheless its failure to arrest
and send to the Hague tribunal the indicted war criminal Ante
Gotovina held up the start of accession negotiations. FYROM's application for membership in 2004, though seen by some as premature,
gave further credibility to the S.A. process.[6]

These important steps forward are not yet conclusive in demonstrating that, in the western Balkans, Europeanization can repeat its
earlier success. Reform is painfully slow and the region is beset by
organized crime and corruption. Albania has scarcely succeeded in
moving beyond the initial stages of reform, despite entering into

---

[4] Council of the European Union Interinstitutional file 2001/0049 (ACV) "Stabilisation and
Association Agreement between the European Communities and their Member States, of
the one part, and the former Yugoslav Republic of Macedonia, of the other part" Brussels
March 26, 2001. Available at http://europa.eu.int/comm/external_ relations/see/ fyrom/
saa/saa03_01.pdf Commission of the European communities file 2001/0149(AVC)
"Proposal for a COUNCIL DECISION Concerning the signature of the Stabilisation
and Association Agreement between the European Communities and its Member States
and the Republic of Croatia on behalf of the European Community" Brussels July 9 2001.
Available at http://europa.eu.int/comm/external_relations/see/croatia/com01_371en.pdf

[5] Commission of the European communities file COM (2004) 257 Final "COMMUNICA-
TION FROM THE COMMISSION Opinion on Croatia's Application for Membership
of the European Union" Brussels April 20, 2004. Available at http://europa.eu.int/
comm/external_relations/see/sap/rep3/cr_croat.htm

[6] Negotiations began on March 22, 2004.

negotiations for an S.A. agreement with the EU and receiving related assistance.[7] The question of Kosovo's final status still needs to be addressed, in conjunction with its ability to meet standards set by the United Nations. Meanwhile it remains a UN administration and there is a constant risk of renewed violence. In addition to the Kosovo question, Serbia and Montenegro face problems of governance and constitutional order which are among the factors holding back progress towards eventual EU membership.

Despite impressive reforms in FYROM and significant efforts to implement the Ohrid Agreement,[8] an EU police mission, the presence of an EU Special Representative, and an unsuccessful referendum challenging the process of decentralization showed the need to consolidate what had been achieved. The decision that an EU Force should replace that of NATO in Bosnia-Herzegovina in 2004 underlined the degree of the EU's commitment to the country's stability.[9] But this important step should not lead to the country's situation being viewed in the EU mainly through the prism of security, if the process of "Europeanization" is to remain the key to growth and development in the region. Above all, reconciliation throughout the western Balkans is held back by the continued impunity of indicted war criminals. When the key outstanding cases are at last addressed, the credibility of the vision of parallel progress towards EU membership will receive a major, and perhaps decisive, boost.

## Turkey

The EU's impact on Turkey's reform process is incontrovertible. Since the EU recognized Turkey as a candidate for membership at Helsinki in December 1999, successive governments have introduced reforms more far-reaching than any since the time of Ataturk.[10] The

---

[7] Negotiations began on January 31, 2003.

[8] The Ohrid Agreement. Available at http://www.coe.int/T/E/Legal_affairs/Legal_co-operation/Police_and_internal_security/Police_cooperation/OHRID%20Agreement%2013august2001.asp

[9] EUROPEAN SECURITY AND DEFENCE POLICY—EU military operation in Bosnia and Herzegovina—Council conclusions. Available at http://europa.eu.int/comm/external_relations/cfsp/intro/gac.htm#cfsp120704

[10] Conclusions of the European Council on Turkey since Luxembourg (December 1997). Available at http://europa.eu.int/comm/enlargement/turkey/pdf/european_councils_.pdf

rhythm of reform grew markedly when a single party, the Justice and Development Party (AKP), formed a government with control of the parliament in November 2002. A series of constitutional and legal changes have enabled Turkish citizens to enjoy a wider range of fundamental rights and freedoms. Freedom of expression, freedom of association, freedom of religion, freedom from abuse by the security forces, greater civilian control of the military, the reform of the judiciary, the use of languages other than Turkish in broadcasting and education are among the areas where striking progress has been made.

As in central and eastern Europe, the EU insisted throughout on practical results that would bring real benefits. This meant going beyond paper reforms to ensure proper implementation and enforcement. To be sure, retraining and, possibly, a new generation would be needed to bring about profound attitude and behavioral changes among judges, prosecutors and the security forces throughout the country.

The EU's customs union with Turkey, dating from 1995, requires the country to align itself with the EU's common commercial policy.[11] Turkey advanced more fitfully in meeting the economic criteria for EU membership—mainly requiring the state to pursue sound fiscal and monetary policies, to reduce its role in economic life, by dismantling monopolies and promoting privatization, and to create the foundations for a competitive market economy. The severe financial crisis and recession of 2000 contributed to the electorate's rejection of the traditional parties then ruling the country and to the subsequent victory of the AK party, with its commitment to EU-oriented political and economic reforms.

The pull of the EU has also led to better relations between Turkey and neighboring countries. The reduction in tensions with Greece, following mutual assistance after earthquakes in the two countries in 1999, the apparent strategic decision in Ankara to support UN efforts to solve the Cyprus problem, crowned by the favorable referendum vote in the northern part of the island in 2004, and even tentative steps to begin a dialogue with Armenia, all owe something to Ankara's wish to project an image of a country dedicated to good neighborly relations, in the context of its EU membership bid.

---

[11] Conclusions of the European Council on Turkey since Luxembourg (December 1997). Available at http://europa.eu.int/comm/enlargement/turkey/pdf/european_councils_.pdf

Turkey's candidacy has been a powerful catalyst for change. There is a growing consensus in favor of liberal democracy and there has been a considerable convergence with European standards. There is now better protection of human rights in Turkey and the role of the military in public life has been reduced. The Turkish authorities have been willing to enter into dialogue and cooperation with the EU on a range of subjects which would, hitherto, have been considered taboo. Turkey has collaborated in monitoring progress and, on the whole, has accepted EU advice on areas where further efforts are needed. After one fairly critical regular report from the EU Commission, a Turkish minister asked: "How can we reject this report when it is a mirror held up to ourselves?" The challenge now is to maintain the momentum of this process with the added impulse of the accession negotiations beginning in October 2005 and to support reformers in Turkey whose vision is of a modern, western-oriented, secular nation, taking its place in the mainstream of European political and economic life.

## The European Neighborhood Policy

The EU's enlargement process has, thus, achieved a large measure of success in creating a zone of stability, security and increasing prosperity in Europe. As the EU's fifth enlargement loomed on the horizon the question arose as to whether this success could be replicated, in whole or in part, among the neighbors of the new EU of twenty-five without an offer of membership. As a result of enlargement, the EU acquired borders with Belarus and Ukraine, and extended its frontier with Russia. The EU's land border with these three countries now covers 5,100 kilometers. With the accession of Romania, scheduled for 2007, the EU will share a border with Moldova. The accession of two island states, Cyprus and Malta, has brought a number of Mediterranean countries closer to EU territory.

These impending geopolitical changes led to the design of a policy, initially known as "wider Europe" now the European Neighborhood Policy, with a number of objectives.[12] The EU's fundamental objective

---

[12] Official journal of the European Communities n° L 35/1"Council decision n° 1/95 of the EC-Turkey association council of 22 December 1995 on implementing the final phase of the Custom Union" February 13 1996 [http://europa.eu.int/comm/enlargement/turkey/pdf/ec_tk_ass_council_1_95_en.pdf]

is to "export" stability to neighboring countries so that its own peaceful development is not hampered by instability in its new hinterland. A related objective is to improve security at the border of the enlarged EU, without alienating neighboring countries. A third objective is to improve living standards in these countries, as a means to enhance political stability and to reduce migratory pressures. The ENP seeks to strengthen commitments to the rule of law, democracy, and the respect of fundamental rights and freedoms. Such an approach, if pursued judiciously, taking into account the nature of the regimes in question and the threats they face, will contribute to general security in the EU's immediate environment.

To achieve these objectives, the EU offered partner countries a kind of bargain. If they accept precise commitments, which can be monitored, in the area of "common values" and core foreign policy objectives, the EU is willing to open up certain of its own policies and programs to their participation. The "common values" imply specific steps such as the holding of free and fair elections, improving conditions for detainees, facilitating the activities of non-governmental organizations, and allowing greater media freedom. The core foreign policy objectives include counter-terrorism and the non-proliferation of weapons of mass destruction, as well as dialogue and cooperation to resolve existing conflicts.

For its part the EU will invite partner countries to participate in several important aspects of its own activities: the internal market, police and judicial cooperation, border management, efforts to stem organized crime, corruption, money laundering and trafficking, as well as the development of energy and transport networks, exchange programs and other initiatives in education, science and research.

Thus, essentially, there are two baskets, one containing commitments mainly by partner countries and one containing commitments mainly by the EU. At first various formulas were considered for establishing mechanical links between these two baskets. The EU, might, for example, open up certain agencies or programs in exchange for confirmation that a particular election had been held in free and fair conditions. This approach was, however, found to be unrealistic. Instead a broad balance was to be struck between the extent of a partner's real progress in acting on the basis of "common values" and the ambitiousness of the EU's offer.[13]

The contents of the two baskets differ from country to country, according to its particular needs and capacities and its existing relations with the EU. The particular mix is the result of consultations with each partner to establish agreed "action plans." These then serve as the point of reference for programming EU assistance and for working together in the joint bodies set up under the EU's cooperation or association agreement with each country. The EU will monitor implementation and if, after an initial three year period, sufficient progress has been made, it will be ready to consider a new and more ambitious bilateral agreement as the framework for future relations.

For the policy to be credible and effective, it needs to be backed up by additional financial resources. For this the European Commission proposed a new "European Neighborhood and Partnership Instrument," which will replace existing funds (TACIS and MEDA) and include a special cross-border facility. The Commission has proposed that funding, under the EU's next financial planning period, 2007-2013, should be significantly increased to match the political priority given to ENP. The cross-border facility will support projects implemented both in the territory of the enlarged European Union and of adjoining partner countries, a useful innovation.[14]

This approach was largely inspired by the EU's enlargement experience. The commitments to shared values contained an echo of the 1993 Copenhagen accession criteria.[15] The "action plans"—a blue print for *rapprochement* with the EU—draw on the "accession partnerships" with the candidate countries, and the "European partnerships"

---

[13] Commission of the European communities COM(2004) 373 final "COMMUNICATION FROM THE COMMISSION European Neighborhood Policy STRATEGY PAPER" Brussels, May 12, 2004. Available at http://europa.eu.int/comm/world/enp/pdf/strategy/Strategy_Paper_EN.pdf

[14] Commission of the European communities COM(2003) 393 final "COMMUNICATION FROM THE COMMISSION Paving the way for a New Neighborhood Instrument "Brussels, July 1, 2003. Available at http://europa.eu.int/comm/world/enp/pdf/com03_393_en.pdf

[15] European Parliament activities SN 180/93 "European Council in Copenhagen 21-22 June 1993 Conclusions of the presidency" Copenhagen June 22, 2003. Available at http://www.europarl.eu.int/summits/copenhagen/ default_en.htm] [http://www.europarl.eu.int/summits/copenhagen/co_en.pdf

with the western Balkan countries.[16] The degree of approximation with EU standards proposed differs from country to country, according to its needs, capacities, internal priorities and its readiness to adopt the EU model for economic and regulatory reforms. The main difference with the enlargement process is in the second basket, the "EU's offer," as it does not include the perspective of accession. From the outset, the EU made clear that the European Neighborhood Policy would bring its own inherent benefits which are distinct from the possibility of accession.

And there, of course, is the rub. Can the ENP provide sufficient incentives, in the absence of the prospect of accession, to induce partners to embark on the process of "Europeanization"? The final answer to this question will only be given on the basis of several years' experience with implementation. At this stage, however, it can be said that most countries, to which the offer was made, have responded positively. Admittedly, there is some skepticism about the ENP's benefits. The initial action plans fall short of expectations that partners would be admitted to all EU activities except participation in its own institutions and that the "four freedoms" of the EU's internal market would soon be extended to them. Nonetheless nearly all the countries concerned are now fully engaged with the EU in the neighborhood policy. There has also been a certain amount of healthy competition among neighboring countries seeking to advance their relations with the EU.

The ENP has created a process, a methodology, and a set of priorities for joint action as well as medium-term objectives. This lays the basis for a much more structured and systematic relationship in the future. Despite feelings that the carrot could be juicier, few partner countries have chosen to absent themselves from the process. This chapter's tentative conclusion is, therefore, that "Europeanization," albeit in a more flexible form, has a future beyond the confines of enlargement as such.

---

[16] Commission of the European communities COM(2003) 285 final "COMMUNICATION FROM THE COMMISSION to the council and the European Parliament European "The Western Balkans and European Integration "Brussels, May 25, 2003. Available at http://europa.eu.int/comm/external_relations/see/docs/index.htm#eip] [http://europa.eu.int/comm/external_relations/see/2003.pdf

## Eastern Europe

The scope and limitations of the ENP are best examined in terms of its significance for particular countries or groups of countries. To clarify this, let us first consider the ENP's geographic reach. The policy's initial focus was in eastern Europe, that is the countries beyond the enlarged EU's eastern border. The main challenge for the new member states in the region, especially Poland, Lithuania, Slovakia and Hungary, is to preserve and develop cross-border links with these neighboring countries, which are beneficial to their citizens, while strengthening their external border controls sufficiently to permit their eventual full participation in the Schengen system. In 2003 the Polish government circulated a "non-paper" calling for an eastern dimension to the enlarged EU's external relations. It proposed an array of initiatives to strengthen links between local and regional authorities, civil society groups, and economic actors across the eastern border of the enlarged EU.

These proposals dove-tailed with the EU's own desire to send a message to Russia, Ukraine, Belarus and Moldova that enlargement was in no sense directed against their interests and that, on the contrary, they too could expect to benefit from it. These potential benefits include access to a larger market, governed by a single set of trade and regulatory rules, a significant measure of economic integration with the enlarged EU, technical assistance and financial support and enhanced cooperation over a wide range of issues.

## Russia

Russia made clear from the outset that it preferred to develop a strategic partnership with the EU, separate from that proposed to smaller countries.[17] There is little place in Russia's world view for economic integration with the EU, as implied by the ENP, especially if part of a scheme which extended from Moldova to Morocco. Russian representatives pointed out that the country was not, in any event, a new neighbor, already sharing a border of well over a thousand kilometers with the EU. Russia's vision was of a "twenty-five plus one" approach, in which Russia was recognized implicitly as a political equal.

---

[17] EU-Russia Summit St Petersburg, May 31, 2003, Joint Statement. Available at http://europa.eu.int/comm/external_relations/russia/sum05_03/js.htm

In fact Russia, while willing in principle to engage with the EU in developing its own strategic partnership (in much the same fields proposed by the ENP), was seeking a largely political relationship of the type it had established with NATO. Indeed some observers consider that Russia favors an ad hoc approach which lets it pick and choose parts of the EU *acquis* judged favorable to its interests, play member states off against each other, and against the Commission, and which enables it to give priority to efforts to bring back together parts of the former Soviet economic space.[18] Russia may consider that the ENP could conflict with its own efforts to establish a "Single Economic Space" with Ukraine, Belarus and Kazakhstan, announced in September 2003.[19]

In fact the EU and Russia form part of each other's immediate neighborhood and need to develop practical policies for dealing with this reality. The EU has offered to extend its proposed new European Neighborhood and Partnership financial instrument to Russia, not least to permit the further development of cross-border projects with Finland and several new Member States. Russia and the EU should work closely together, in a structured rather than an ad hoc manner, to achieve results in such areas as energy policy, trade, nuclear safety and the prevention of terrorism and organized crime. No doubt Moscow will be following closely its own neighbors' rapprochement with the EU under the ENP and may adjust its position in this light. It would be better for Russia to cooperate with the EU through the proposed "strategic partnership" on issues arising in our common neighborhood rather than to view it as the setting for a new struggle over spheres of influence.

To make a success of this partnership the EU needs to engage with Russia, to formulate clear-cut objectives, and to speak with one voice in developing and implementing policies to meet these objectives. The EU must be forthright in defending its values and its interests in order to leave Moscow in no doubt that the EU as such is a partner to be reckoned with.

---

[18] Commission of the European communities COM(2004) 106 final "COMMUNICATION FROM THE COMMISSION to the Council and the European Parliament on relations with Russia "Brussels, February 9, 2004. Available at http://europa.eu.int/comm/external_relations/russia/ russia_docs/com04_106_en.pdf

[19] EU/Ukraine Summit, Yalta, 7 October. Available at http://europa.eu.int/comm/external_relations/ ukraine/intro/ip03_1343.htm

## Belarus

As for Belarus, there are scant hopes of developing a relationship based on common values under the Lukashenka regime. But Poland and Lithuania, in particular, attach great importance to the message that the ENP also applies potentially to Belarus. The EU has indicated that as soon as Belarus has a government based on the will of the people expressed through free and fair elections it will be ready to develop normal relations with the country and to bring it fully into the scope of the ENP.[20] Meanwhile contacts are being developed with civil society. Modest funding is available for NGOs in Belarus, although the government in Minsk continues to create legal and administrative obstacles to their receiving EU support. The Commission and the government of Lithuania organized a workshop in Vilnius in March 2005 to coordinate assistance for civil society from different donors.

## Ukraine

For now, the ENP's initial coverage in eastern Europe is limited to Ukraine and Moldova. Consultations on Action Plans took place in the first half of 2004. These talks revealed clearly the two countries' main desiderata. Even before the "Orange Revolution" of November 2004, Ukraine's principal objective was to obtain from the EU a commitment to negotiating a new bilateral agreement, to replace the 1998 Partnership and Cooperation Agreement (PCA).[21] The new agreement, in Ukraine's view, would resemble the Europe Agreements which paved the way for accession by countries in central and eastern Europe. Kiev sought an EU commitment to such an agreement, with the perspective of accession, as the main benefit it would derive from the ENP. This was clearly not on the EU's agenda in 2004, although it has indicated that no door has been closed for the future.

---

[20] Commission of the European communities COM(2004) 373 final "COMMUNICATION FROM THE COMMISSION "European Neighborhood Policy STRATEGY PAPER "Brussels, May 12, 2004 [http://europa.eu.int/comm/world/enp/pdf/strategy/Strategy_Paper_EN.pdf]

[21] Official journal of the European Communities n° L 49/3 " PARTNERSHIP AND COOPERATION AGREEMENT between the European Communities and their Member States, and Ukraine" February 19, 1998 [http://europa.eu.int/eur-lex/pri/en/oj/dat/1998/l_049/l_04919980219en00030039.pdf]

Ukraine's second major objective was to conclude a Free Trade Agreement (FTA) with the EU, as foreshadowed by the PCA. The EU insisted on a step-by-step approach, beginning with a review of the feasibility of such an agreement, Ukraine's accession to the WTO, and then negotiations for an FTA. The EU also insisted on the resolution of a number of outstanding trade disputes. Ukraine also sought "market economy status" under the EU's anti-dumping rules, a status that had already been granted to Russia.

A third major objective was progress towards the lifting of visa requirements for Ukrainian citizens visiting the EU. This went well beyond prevailing opinion in the EU. Agreement was reached, however, on an approach which would combine measures to facilitate the issuing of visas, back-to-back with the conclusion of a Readmission Agreement between the EU and Ukraine.

While these were the chief top priorities for Ukraine, the Action Plan covers virtually all aspects of bilateral relations.[22] The EU obtained assurances from Ukraine on common values (notably free and fair elections and media freedom) and foreign policy objectives (especially greater efforts to solve the Transnistria conflict by better control of the break-away region's border with Ukraine). For reformers in Ukraine, the ENP opened up new possibilities and provided a counter-balance to pressures from Moscow for faster realization of the Single Economic Space, embracing also Russia, Belarus and Kazakhstan. The ENP added weight to the position of reformers and westernisers in Kiev against those representing the vested interests of non-competitive economic sectors, which could still find markets in Russia and other former Soviet states, and more generally those who still looked towards Moscow for support.

The Presidential election in November 2004 put to the test one of Ukraine's key undertakings in the Action Plan: free and fair elections. The popular uprising in protest against the manipulation of the results in the second round of the Presidential election led to a re-run

---

[22] Europen Commission, "Proposed EU/Ukraine Action Plan, September 9, 2004. Available at http://www.europa.eu.int/comm/world/enp/pdf/action_plans/ Proposed_Action_Plan_EU-Ukraine.pdf

The EU-Ukraine Cooperation Council approved the Action Plan on February 21,2005. See "Ferraro-Waldner welcomes adoption of Ukraine Action Plan." Available at http://europa.eu.int/comm/external_relations/ukraine/intro/bfw_210205.htm

of this round, in conditions broadly considered free and fair, and the election of Viktor Yushchenko, on a strongly "pro-European" platform. This orientation was reinforced by the role of European leaders in the resolution of the political crisis leading up to the re-run of the election.

The new President sought to obtain further commitments from the EU, in particular to a membership perspective, going beyond the scope of the ENP Action Plan, agreed by the government of Viktor Yanukovich, his defeated adversary in the Presidential election.

During the political crisis, the EU withheld approval of the ENP Action Plan with Ukraine.[23] Now that one of the Plan's key requirements had been met, it was ready to approve it and to speed up implementation. A ten point programme was added, going beyond what had been agreed with the outgoing regime, but stopping short of offering a membership perspective.[24] Clearly, in early 2005, there was no consensus among the twenty-five Member States in offering such a perspective although some favored it.

The challenge for the EU in early 2005 was to convince the new Ukrainian authorities of the usefulness of the ENP Action Plan in guiding their own reform priorities and in working out a path to close links with the EU. In Kiev there was recognition of the need for hard work on the necessary reforms but also a desire to see the "Orange Revolution" recompensed with a promise of eventual EU membership and a refusal to accept "neighborhood" status.

## Moldova

Moldova's principal objective in embarking on ENP talks was to obtain a fast-track with the destination of EU membership. As a member of the Stability Pact, Moldova aspired to the negotiation of a Stabilization and Association Agreement, like FYROM, Croatia and other western Balkan countries, which would include the goal of EU

---

[23] December Council Conclusions [http://ue.eu.int/ueDocs/cms_Data/docs/pressData/en/ec/83201.pdf]

[24] Reform to letter of Mr Javier SOLANA, High Representative for the Common Foreign and Security Policy and Mrs Benita FERRERO-WALDNER, Member of the European Commission [http://register.consilium.eu.int/pdf/en/05/st05/st05799.en05.pdf]

membership. EU negotiators explained that such agreements had been devised mainly to meet the particular needs of the countries which had emerged from the break-up of the former Yugoslavia and the resulting wars. As such they were not adapted to the historical experience and present needs of Moldova, which was linked to the EU by a Partnership and Cooperation Agreement.[25] At the same time, the EU was clearly not ready to extend the membership perspective given to these countries to Moldova.

A second Moldovan objective was to obtain greater EU support for Chisinau's position in the conflict over Transdniestria. This took the form, mainly, of seeking EU pressure on Ukraine to impose controls on its border with the break-away province, with a view to preventing contraband trade and reducing its economic viability. By reinforcing its links with the EU and obtaining the prospect of better market access and increased assistance, Chisinau hoped to increase Moldova's attractiveness to the population of Transdniestria. In its ENP Action Plan, Moldova obtained some satisfaction on these issues. The ENP should in time help to create a more favorable environment for existing efforts to resolve the conflict.

A third objective was to obtain trade preferences from the EU, modeled on the autonomous measures offered to the western Balkans. Here the EU proved to be responsive, provided that Moldova takes measures to control the origin of goods exported to the EU under such preferences. This will require upgrading of the Moldovan customs service and staff training. Finally, Moldova sought improvements in the visa regime applied to its citizens when visiting the EU, a sensitive issue for EU Member States.

As to common values, Moldova proved largely ready to provide the EU with the assurances it had been seeking. The EU attached particular importance to the implementation of these commitments in practice, given shortcomings in Moldova, with respect to human rights and fundamental freedoms, which had been the subject of EU diplo-

---

[25] Official journal of the European Communities n° L 28 3/36" COUNCIL AND COMMISSION DECISION of 12 October 2000 on the conclusion of the Protocol to the Partnership and Cooperation Agreement establishing a partnership between the European Communities and their Member States, of the one part, and the Republic of Moldova, of the other part" November 9 2000. Available at http://europa.eu.int/eurlex/pri/en/oj/dat/2000/l_283/l_28320001109en00360036.pdf

matic demarches. The March 2005 parliamentary elections were a first test of these commitments.

Overall, the EU Action Plan with Moldova, the first to be concluded with a partner country demonstrated the extent of common interests in closer links.[26] The prospect of Romania's accession in 2007 and the fact that up to forty percent of Moldova's citizens might then obtain "EU passports," through dual citizenship, gave a sense of urgency to the need to improve living standards and to accelerate political and economic reform in the country.

## The Southern Caucasus

Georgia, Armenia and Azerbaijan were not included within the scope of the ENP when it was announced in 2003. These three countries in the southern Caucasus would not be neighbors of the EU of twenty-five, although, like Romania and Bulgaria, scheduled for EU accession in 2007, Georgia has a Black Sea coast. While belonging to the Organization for Security and Cooperation in Europe and to the Council of Europe, all three fell below the standards set by these bodies in terms of free and fair elections and respect of human rights.

All three were beset by "frozen conflicts" and Georgia suffered a degree of spill-over from the Chechen conflict, leading at one point to Russian bombardment of the Pankisi Gorge, a part of Georgia considered to be a place of refuge for Chechens involved in armed conflict with Moscow.

All three expressed dissatisfaction at their exclusion from the ENP and the EU's Council of Ministers subsequently promised to return to

---

[26] Consultations between Moldova and the European Commission were effectively concluded in July 2004

[27] "COUNCIL CONCLUSIONS ON WIDER EUROPE—NEW NEIGHBORHOOD" June 16 2003. Available at http://europa.eu.int/comm/external_relations/we/doc/cc06_03.pdf

[28] Commission of the European communities COM(2004) 373 final "COMMUNICATION FROM THE COMMISSION "European Neighborhood Policy STRATEGY PAPER "Brussels, May 12, 2004. Available at http://europa.eu.int/comm/ world/enp/pdf/strategy/Strategy_Paper_EN.pdf

[29] Council of the European union file 10679/04 "BRUSSELS EUROPEAN COUNCIL 17 AND 18 JUNE 2004 PRESIDENCY CONCLUSIONS" Brussels June 18, 2004. Available at http://ue.eu.int/ueDocs/cms_Data/docs/pressData/en/ec/81035.pdf

the question, on the basis of a recommendation by the Commission.[27] In May 2004, the Commission recommended their inclusion within the scope of the ENP.[28] The Council endorsed this recommendation in June 2004.[29]

What happened to reverse the EU's position in the intervening period? EU enlargement contributed to a growing awareness of the region's strategic significance for the EU in terms of energy supply, transport links with central Asia and the prevention of trafficking in drugs and human beings. Several new EU Member States, especially the Baltic countries, attached particular importance to energy and transport links between the EU and the southern Caucasus. These would become more significant with the planned entry into service of the Baku-Tblisi-Ceylan oil pipeline in 2005, to be followed, subsequently by a parallel gas pipeline.

The EU decided to raise its profile in the region by the appointment of a Special Representative, in particular to support efforts to resolve the frozen conflicts in South Ossetia, Abkhazia, and Nagorno-Karabakh.[30] If prolonged indefinitely, these conflicts could bring renewed instability to this strategically important region and complicate EU relations with Russia. The EU's Security Strategy, approved by the European Council in December 2003, gave a new priority to the southern Caucasus.

The "Rose Revolution" in Georgia in November 2003 brought to power a President, Mikhail Saakashvili, and, following elections in January 2004, a government bent on reform, which recognized the need to fight corruption and to maintain good relations with all the countries of the region, including Russia. Mikhail Saakashvili's success in bringing to an end by peaceful means the Ajara secession in June 2004 at first seemed to augur well for progress in South Ossetia. But the situation there deteriorated sharply in August 2004. The EU had become the main source of civilian assistance to Georgia and, together with the World Bank, convened a donors' conference in Brussels in

---

[30] Official journal of the European Communities n° L 157/72" COUNCIL JOINT ACTION 2003/473/CFSP of June 25, 2003 regarding a contribution of the European Union to the conflict settlement process in Georgia/ South Ossetia " June 26, 2003. Available at http://europa.eu.int/eurlex/pri/en/oj/dat/2003/l_157/l_15720030626en 00720073.pdf

[31] OSCE "INTERNATIONAL ELECTION OBSERVATION MISSION Presidential Election, Republic of Azerbaijan"—October 15, 2003. Available at http://www.osce.org/documents/odihr/ 2003/10/806_en.pdf The final ODIHR report. Available at http://www.osce.org/documents/odihr/2003/11/1151_en.pdf

July 2004. Besides raising more funds than expected, this Conference provided a showcase for the government's new policies.

Elections in Azerbaijan in 2003, while still below international standards, showed some limited improvement on past practice.[31] They were further marred, however, by police violence after the election. It was felt desirable to engage more directly with Baku to push for greater efforts on political and economic reform.

Turkey's progress in 2003-2004 towards meeting the conditions for accession negotiations meant that the southern Caucasus had become, potentially, a region neighboring the EU. Overall, the ENP provided the best available tool to enable the EU to engage more fully with the region. In doing so it could mobilize its existing Partnership and Cooperation Agreements with all three countries and TACIS assistance program, in support of ENP objectives.

For the three countries concerned the ENP represented an opportunity to diversify their foreign policy, to provide a certain counterweight to Russia, and to obtain new forms of support. This seemed more pressing in light of continuing violence and terrorism in Chechnya and northern Ossetia. Besides these pressing concerns, Georgia and Armenia, in particular, insisted on their European identity and proclaimed EU membership as their long term goal. Azerbaijan sought to remain in step with its neighbors. All three countries wished, through the ENP, to move closer to the mainstream of political and economic life in Europe, just after the accession of three former Soviet republics to the EU and the previous extension of the ENP to Ukraine, with which they had close links, and Moldova. Armenia hoped that through closer links with the EU it could increase pressure on Turkey to re-open the border, closed in 1993 following the war with Azerbaijan over Nagorno-Karabakh.

Overall, both the EU and its partners in the southern Caucasus viewed the ENP as a means to increase the salience of the region. This was reflected in a series of high level visits to the three capitals in the summer of 2004. In March 2005 the Commission issued detailed reports on all three countries and recommended that Action Plans be developed.[32]

---

[32] Communication from the Commission to the Council COM(2005)72 of 2 March 2005.

## Mediterranean countries

While the initial impetus for the ENP came from the situation along the enlarged EU's eastern border, the Commission proposed from the outset that the policy also cover the entire Mediterranean region. The objective is "to promote a ring of well governed countries to the east of the European Union and on the borders of the Mediterranean with whom we can enjoy close and cooperative relations."[33] The ENP provides a means to focus more attention on issues which concern the EU as a whole and in particular its southern Member States. These include terrorism, a top priority in the EU's security strategy approved by the European Council in December 2003 and which became even more pressing after the murderous attacks in Madrid in March 2004 and subsequent threats to other Member States.[34]

The ENP requires commitments on preventing terrorism and the proliferation of weapons of mass destruction. Illegal migration to the EU, transiting through or originating in North Africa is of growing public concern, highlighted by the loss of life at sea by migrants who were victims of unscrupulous traffickers. Member States hope the ENP will provide additional incentives for partners to tackle regional conflict and that it will contribute indirectly to the Middle East Peace Process. The ENP is a means to promote better governance and the respect of human rights. This means encouraging governments to live up to commitments made through the Barcelona Process and in various international conventions.

In exchange for commitments in these areas, the EU is ready to promote economic and social development, through the different instruments at its disposal, and to enable the Mediterranean countries to participate in certain of the EU's own activities and programs. These countries already benefit from free access to European markets for industrial goods (which remains a major goal for Ukraine and

---

[33] Commission of the European communities COM(2004) 373 final "COMMUNICATION FROM THE COMMISSION "European Neighborhood Policy STRATEGY PAPER "Brussels, May 12 2004. Available at http://europa.eu.int/comm/world/enp/pdf/Strategy_Paper_EN.pdf

[34] Council of the European union "BRUSSELS EUROPEAN COUNCIL 12 And 13 December 2003 PRESIDENCY CONCLUSIONS," Brussels December 13, 2003. Available at http://www.statewatch.org/news/2003/dec/SecSecurity+ESDP.pdf

Moldova, as noted above). The accumulation of rules of origin, already agreed in principle, and measures to modernize and diversify their economies, will enable the Mediterranean countries to take fuller advantage of the access to European markets already accorded. The added value of the ENP in the economic area comes mainly in other areas, such as trade in agricultural goods and services, as well as technical assistance in adapting to EU standards.

A similar methodology was proposed to countries to the south and east of the EU. Action Plans will be implemented through existing instruments, the Barcelona Process, when multilateral action is called for, and the Association Agreements, when the issues are essentially bilateral. Implementation will be monitored closely by both sides and the Commission will issue periodic progress reports. On the basis of these reports, a decision will be taken on whether progress is sufficient to warrant moving towards a new and more intense relationship between the EU and the individual countries concerned. The Commission's suggestion that this kind of enhanced relationship could take the form of "European Neighborhood Agreements" received a more enthusiastic response from partners in the Mediterranean region, who do not aspire to EU membership, than from those in eastern Europe.

The Commission proposed and the Member States accepted that the ENP should be extended to all Mediterranean countries participating in the Barcelona process. Action Plans were concluded, in the first instance, with partners having EU Association Agreements, or interim agreements, in force. This meant that in 2004 a first round of Action Plans were negotiated with Israel, Jordan, Morocco, the Palestinian Authority and Tunisia, to be followed in 2005 by Egypt and Lebanon. The offer is also open to Syria, when its Association Agreement is signed and ratified. In early 2005 Algeria still had not ratified its Association Agreement with the EU and initially showed little interest in the ENP. Despite hopes raised by Libya's decision to renounce weapons of mass destruction and by Colonel Gaddafi's visit to Brussels in June 2004, Libya still has not formally accepted the principles underlying the Euro-Mediterranean partnership and in early 2005 had not resolved the problem of Bulgarian and Palestinian medical workers condemned to death following legal proceedings whose fairness has been widely contested outside the country.

The EU sought to ensure consistency between positions taken in its Common Foreign and Security Policy and the terms for political dialogue and cooperation in the Action Plans with Mediterranean countries. This meant finding mutually acceptable language on issues such as terrorism, WMD, the Middle East Peace Process and human rights. The Action Plans with most partners in the region reflect a delicate balance between the EU's desire to promote human rights and fundamental freedoms and the concern of governments to maintain stability. Commitments in the political field reflect each government's own intentions with respect to political reform.

Israeli officials were attracted by the ENP as an opportunity to develop bilateral relations with the EU at a pace which reflects Israel's own capacities and aspirations. They were particularly interested in participation in EU programs and agencies building, for example, on Israel's existing involvement in the European Union's Research Framework Program and in the Galileo satellite communication program, agreed in June 2004. Some Israeli representatives look to an arrangement similar to the European Economic Area, as an ultimate goal, falling short of membership. The Action Plan calls for a closer political and economic partnership with Israel and includes explicit commitments on political dialogue and cooperation on human rights, the prevention of terrorism and the proliferation of weapons of mass destruction and the Middle East Peace Process. The Israeli side gained a greater degree of openness to Israeli participation in EU activities through the Action Plan, while the EU obtained far-reaching commitments by Israel in the foreign policy and security field.

Palestinian leaders proved ready to engage with the EU in developing an Action Plan as part of the ENP. Its main features are further efforts to reform the Palestinian Authority, to prevent corruption, to ensure the proper control of public funds and to protect human rights, backed up by continuing EU financial support. It includes commitments on the prevention of terrorism and of the proliferation of WMD and the Middle East Peace Process. Clearly this Action Plan will need to be further developed when progress is made in the peace process towards a two state solution.

The development of Action Plans both with the Palestinian Authority and with Israel is a clear sign of the EU's willingness to engage further in the region and to create additional incentives for progress in the peace process. This is of particular value in the new climate created by the election of Mahmoud Abbas as President of the Palestinian Authority in January 2005 and the formation of a new Israeli government under Ariel Sharon committed to withdrawal from Gaza and certain parts of the West Bank.

The ENP was one of a number of initiatives seeking to improve governance and to expand political and economic freedom in the Mediterranean region and the Middle East in 2004. These included the EU's own European Security Strategy for the Mediterranean and the Middle East and the "Forum for the Future" approved by the G-8 and the EU-US Summits in June 2004.[35] These initiatives all seek to narrow gaps in knowledge, freedom and individual rights and should, therefore, be complementary. Indeed, there was a marked convergence between EU and US goals in the region in 2004. The EU's approach, however, is strongly influenced by its position as a neighbor of the countries concerned and by traditional ties. This is reflected by the scale of the resources it provides through the MEDA program and the European Investment Bank.

The ENP is seen as a means to reinvigorate certain aspects of the Euro-Mediterranean partnership, to give a new priority to subregional cooperation, for example in North Africa, or between Israel, Jordan and the Palestinian Authority, and to give countries a chance to strengthen their links with the EU bilaterally, without waiting for the entire Barcelona Process to move into higher gear. This particular aspect is particularly appreciated by Jordan and Morocco, which seek a form of advanced status through the ENP, and by Israel, whose level of economic and technological development creates the basis for closer links in many fields.

## The ENP—a first step

The ENP is still at the initial stages of its development. Any conclusions must, therefore, be provisional and subject to confirmation by

---

[35] Press release from EU-US summit 25-26 of June "EU-U.S. DECLARATION SUPPORTING PEACE, PROGRESS AND REFORM IN THE BROADER MIDDLE EAST AND IN THE MEDITERRANEAN" Dromoland Castle, 26 JUNE 2004 [http://europa.eu.int/comm/external_relations/med_mideast/intro/index.htm][http://europa.eu.int/comm/external_relations/us/sum06_04/]  [http://europa.eu.int/comm/press_room/presspacks/us20040625/dec_mideast.pdf]

subsequent experience. The main question posed in this chapter is whether the process of "Europeanization," which has proved an effective spur to political and economic reform in central and eastern Europe and, to a certain extent, in the western Balkans, can also be effective in countries neighboring the EU, in the absence of a perspective of EU membership for them.

In responding to this question, it is important to consider the ENP's scope and limits. The ENP seeks to *promote* "common values," recognizing that these values are not necessarily already well grounded in the political systems of all partner countries. The issue in most cases is improving governance, respect for human rights, protecting minorities and broadening political and economic freedom rather than strengthening an existing democratic political system. These objectives gained in credibility following the "Orange Revolution" in Ukraine, free and fair Presidential elections in the West Bank and Gaza, as well as demands for greater freedom in Lebanon and Egypt.

The ENP creates incentives for political and economic reform. The closer neighboring countries come to standards prevailing in the EU, the more scope there will be to involve them in EU policies and programs. Techniques for supporting reform developed with candidate countries, involving legislative approximation, support for administrative and judicial reform, technical assistance, twinning, and monitoring, regular reports and the fixing of deadlines are being adapted to the needs of neighboring countries. This will be backed up in the future by a new financial instrument and increased levels of support.

Undoubtedly the leverage given by the ENP is limited, compared with that provided by an offer of membership. The enlargement process has led to the most extensive "interference" in internal affairs ever willingly accepted by sovereign states. Candidate countries have opened their books to the EU and welcomed the spotlight shone on dark nooks and crannies. They have accepted the EU model, as a whole, as the basis for their modernization and development. Neighboring countries, which are not on a path to membership, do not have the same incentive to conform to the requirements of "Europeanization." They have many priorities in their internal and external policies of which closer links with the EU, through the ENP, are just one. Governments need to maintain a delicate and shifting balance among internal and external pressures in their region.

Nonetheless "Europeanization" as defined in this chapter has proved relevant to the concerns of many of the countries in the EU's immediate vicinity. This is confirmed by their positive response. The incentives which are on offer, as well as competitive pressures among participating countries, have been sufficient to bring them to the starting line.

The Action Plans agreed in 2004 are a first step. In themselves they represent a significant step forward, with far-reaching commitments made in the two "baskets" described at the beginning of this chapter. The credibility of the ENP as a lasting framework for relations between the EU and its neighbors will depend very much on the extent to which both sides deliver on these commitments. This will require political will, good organization, and the allocation of sufficient human and financial resources.

In the light of real progress with the implementation of commitments in the Action Plans, the EU and its partners will consider further steps, including new and more comprehensive bilateral agreements and a more systematic approach to the opening of EU programs and agencies to the participation of neighboring countries. This will take place in a differentiated manner, reflecting the needs, capacities and desire of each country to engage with the EU.

The ENP creates the basis for a more effective presence of the enlarged EU in its own neighborhood, with states in the region viewed increasingly as "partners" rather than "third countries." It structures relations between the EU and its neighbors in a manner largely inspired by the enlargement process. Henceforth relations with these countries, while being influenced by foreign policy considerations, will also incorporate significant aspects of the EU's internal *acquis*. The ENP has set a new process in motion, established priorities for action and defined medium-term goals. This should produce gains in stability, security and economic development which will benefit the participants, the EU and the international community as a whole.

## Chapter 6

# The Strategic Implications of Turkey's Integration in the European Union

Henri J. Barkey and Anne-Marie Le Gloannec

When the European Union in its December 2004 Summit invited Turkey to begin accession negotiations in October 2005, it set into motion what potentially can represent one of the most profound set of changes in EU politics, transatlantic relations, and Europe's interactions with its near-abroad. Turkey's accession process has already engendered an important debate within the EU about its own future, the structure of its institutions and its ultimate status in global politics. The beginning of negotiations with Ankara has been a singularly important American strategic goal that has had broad bipartisan support in the US. The Europeans who in the past had always emphasized the economic, social and budgetary implications of Turkey's membership, in deciding to extend an invitation this time around paid attention to strategic arguments.

Washington, initially concerned by the fact that Turkey, because of its size and cultural heritage, was getting a cold shoulder from the EU pushed the Europeans hard to level the playing field for Ankara. The real push started after the EU's 1997 Luxembourg summit when the Europeans refused to even consider Turkey's application while making room for many others, especially formerly Communist bloc countries. The US strategic perception has evolved over the years. Its early worries were more Turkey specific. In the EU accession process, Washington saw an opportunity to achieve what Ankara had been unable to do in recent decades: democratize its polity, improve its human rights record and liberalize and modernize its economy. US pressure and admonishments not having succeeded in turning Turkey around, Washington was clearly worried of possible implications for its own security and the region of a potential Turkish descent into radical politics.[1] The EU membership accession process was viewed in the US as a means of achieving all of these with EU support. Here Turkey's own desire to become an EU member would help what best can be described as burden sharing between Washington and Brussels. This said, the US has always maintained that it saw its role as one of vigilance, that is, making sure Turkey got a fair hearing in Brussels and that beyond that Ankara had to live up to the demands put forth by the EU club.

Following the September 11 events, the US view of Turkey became somewhat less clear. On the one hand, there was for a brief moment the possibility that Ankara would step into the breach created by "old Europe's" unwillingness to back the Iraq war effort. However, these hopes were dashed when the Turkish parliament, contrary to expectations, refused to allow the Pentagon to open a northern front against Saddam Hussein. Instead what became more important was that Turkey make progress towards EU accession negotiations while ruled by a moderate Islamic party, the Justice and Development Party, AKP. As such, it could become a powerful example for democratic governance in the Middle East. To be sure, US officials have always played up Turkey's secular democratic tradition as a model for the Arab world, although such entreaties had fallen mainly on deaf ears. Hence US support for the beginning of EU accession negotiations after September 11 gained another raison d'être often discussed under the rubric of avoiding a potential "clash of civilizations."

Europeans have chafed at US intervention and "heavy handed" lobbying techniques in support of opening negotiations with Ankara. They have been disturbed by what they perceive to be Washington's lack of concern for the difficulties that any enlargement of the European Community/European Union[2] involves and the fact that it also ignores the extreme complexities of these arrangements for the European Union, which is not only a Common Market but also a community of solidarity and common destiny. Turkey, because of its size, of its location and of its culture, is the biggest challenge that the

---

[1] Turkey has had a history of domestic instability and violence which has often resulted in military interventions. Even when there was no violence as in the ascent of the Islamic Welfare Party to power in the late 1990s, the military intervened to sideline them.

[2] The twin name refers to the fact that the European Communities, founded in 1957, were subsumed by the European Union in 1993.

European Community/Union has ever faced. Perhaps not surprisingly, this difference in perceptions led Jacques Chirac to tell George W. Bush at a NATO summit in Istanbul to mind his own business when the American President advocated Turkey's integration into the EU.

What is new now, however, is the fact that the European Union has come to perceive the strategic benefits of Turkey's inclusion or, on the contrary, the strategic problems linked with it. Certainly, it does not only look upon Turkey in strategic terms. The very workings of the EU and the necessity for Turkey, as for any candidate country, to adopt the lengthy and complex list of *acquis communautaires*, the regulations and legislation that the EC/EU has produced over the years, do not allow to frame the Turkish question in strategic terms only. Yet, never have the strategic implications of a country's accession to the EC/EU attracted as much attention as in Turkey's case. Certainly each past enlargement involved some strategic considerations which were however limited and subdued. When Finland joined the EU in 1995, attention was drawn to the fact that from then on the EU shared a common border with Russia. When former Soviet satellites entered the Union in 2004, not only the EU's borders with Russia lengthened, it also acquired the Russian Kaliningrad enclave. It seems that the further the EU reaches eastwards, the more vivid the strategic implications of enlargements will be because with new countries the EU's reach increases as it penetrates into unstable areas, encountering undemocratic or transitional neighbors such as Belarus and the Ukraine. The case of Ukraine bolsters this argument. Considerations such as how to deal with Russia will become increasingly more important in the overall judgments passed by EU members about yet another enlargement.

Turkey is strategically all the more important as it draws the EU into territories hitherto unknown. EU's borders will be extended to the likes of Iraq, Iran, Syria and the nations of the Caucasus. Even for those who advocate Turkey's entry into the EU, Asia Minor is not Europe. On old maps which show Europe as well as the Ottoman Empire, there were two Turkeys: one in Europe, starting in Istanbul and one in Asia. Turkey also is a big country, larger than any other European country and, according to projections, the most populated by 2020. It is a country which is experiencing a tremendous transformation under the leadership of a moderate Islamic party, a country still underdeveloped in many ways but also developed in others, with its political, intellectual and business elites, a country where indeed the West meets the East. Its relations with minorities inside the country and with neighbors outside are far from settled. In short, it is the biggest challenge that the EU has ever met, were it to integrate this country once referendums are held in a number of member states.

To that extent, it is not surprising that strategic considerations loom large in various analyses, reports and recommendations such as The Report of the Independent Commission on Turkey[3] or the reports produced by CEPS,[4] among others, and that in the arguments formulated for or against Turkey's entry they play an important role. In this chapter, we will look at these implications in two ways. We will first turn to the geopolitical constellation of enlargement which—apart from the possible opposition of public opinion in those countries where Turkish accession is submitted to a referendum or were the European Constitution to fail—may hinder or on the contrary foster Turkey's accession: far from being a done deal, negotiations may still derail and accession fail if some questions such as Cyprus' political status are not solved, or again if Iraq fails to stabilize and democratize, if Iran reaches for nuclear weapons or if Russia further seeds trouble in the Caucasus. Were Turkey to become a member of the European Union in a number of years, its membership will entail a number of strategic implications which we will analyze in a second part with their whole complexity, leaving aside the somewhat mechanistic, if not simplistic arguments sometimes resorted to. Here, though we both favor Turkey's membership in the European Union, we want to touch the complexity of this process, with all its nuances.

## The geo-political constellations of enlargement: possible roadblocks and their consequences.

Turkish accession to the EU will be unlike any other in the past. Turkey poses a challenge to Europe in just about every single dimension imaginable. With a current population of more than 70 million, it

---

[3] Independent Commission on Turkey (under the chairmanship of Martti Ahtisaari), "Turkey in Europe: More than a Promise?," September 2004, p. 51.

[4] Kemal Dervis, Michael Emerson, Daniel Gros and Sinan Ülgen, *The European Transformation of Modern Turkey* , Brussels and Istanbul,: Centre for European Policy Studies and Economics and Foreign Policy Forum, 2004, p. 116.

is populous. It also has the lowest per capita income level of any joiner. It is culturally distinct in a way in which Greece, with its Orthodox past and institutions, was not. The strategic challenge it poses by expanding the borders to the volatile Middle East and to a lesser extent the Caucasus is unprecedented. If expansion to Finland, the Baltic states and Poland brought the EU to Russia's borders, there is little doubt in the minds of most Europeans that Russia with all its faults is part of Europe. The same cannot be said of the Middle East; it is not Europe. Turkey has been involved in a number of conflicts with some now EU members, such as Greece and Cyprus where from a legal point one can argue that it is occupying EU territory. The kind of internal political problems, especially regarding the disposition of minority rights, is nothing like the ones experienced by other Europeans. Turkey's Kurdish problem dwarfs even Spain's, which has had to contend with the violent ethnic-based opposition of ETA.

The negotiations for accession into the EU will be far more difficult for Turkey than anything it has experienced in getting to a yes vote at the EU's Brussels Summit in December 2004. What makes Turkey different in many respects from other candidates is that many factors, some not directly related to Turkey, including the symbolic issue of the headscarf in France or a hypothetical new wave of terrorism in Europe, will bear upon its successful candidacy. This is institutionally complicated by the fact that, again unlike other candidate countries, Ankara will have to face the added bar of public opinion now that the French have promised their electorate a referendum on Turkey's accession while other governments might follow suit.[5] Already, as the French government and pro-EU forces in France are trying to win a referendum on the EU constitution they are put on the defensive by opponents to ratification who have made use of Turkey's candidacy to defeat the document. Were the constitution to be rejected, the enlargement process to both the Western Balkans and Turkey might be put to a halt or at least become more difficult.

---

[5] In certain countries like Austria, France and Germany a clear majority of public opinion opposes Turkish membership in the European Union and so do prominent intellectuals left and right in those countries. Last but not least the new Pope Benedit XVI denied that Turkey belonged to Europe, saying that it could not join the EU when he was, as Cardinal Ratzinger, heading the Congregation of the Faith.

This section will focus on the problems that are likely to arise during the accession negotiations. We can look at the challenges facing Turkey in the following three categories:

1. Political and Procedural problems;

2. Strategic concerns, and

3. Domestic European consensus and the future of the EU. These are not distinctly separable from each other.

## Political and Procedural Problems

In view of the controversy generated so far by the prospect of Turkey's accession, EU countries are likely to delve into every detail and minutiae of Ankara's progress. Unlike in the case of a small country of the size of Latvia or even Croatia, EU countries will be negotiating with Turkey conscious of the size of the stakes involved. Pressure from public opinion and their own needs will propel them into thinking they have to get it right. Complicating matters is the dynamic nature of the enlargement process. Hence, the Union is likely to be doubly careful not to repeat past mistakes. As Heather Grabbe argues, "the Union has learned that it is not enough for a country to change its legislation, because EU policies do not function properly without implementation and enforcement."[6] In other words, Grabbe argues "Turkey will have to prove it is enforcing the relevant EU laws before it can 'close' each chapter."[7]

While making sure that implementation and enforcement procedures are in place before closing a chapter will be one of the many details the Union will be insistent on, this will undoubtedly create resentment on the Turkish side for two reasons. First, Ankara, which to date, has succeeded in changing legislation without implementing the changes in many instances is likely to cry foul. Second, given the size of the country and the moribund state of the Turkish bureaucracy and judicial system, implementation is likely to take much longer than envisaged. It is easy to see how some countries, for domestic reasons,

---

[6] Heather Grabbe, "When negotiations begin: the next phase in EU-Turkey relations," Center for European Reform, London, p. 2.

[7] *Ibid.* There are 31 chapters in all.

may insist on demanding full compliance by Ankara before signing on to Turkish membership.

Before Turkey completes its own accession talks, Europe is scheduled to admit at least three other countries, Romania, Bulgaria and Croatia. The Romanian experience and especially the difficulties entailed in that process is likely to further inform the Turkish process. Any difficulty on Romania's path to accession will necessarily be amplified in the public's mind when it comes to Turkey. Of all the former Soviet-bloc countries Romania's transition has been the most difficult. In any case, "the European Commission in Brussels has already made it clear that **all** the Balkan countries are potentially eligible for membership, in the hope of encouraging them to make peace and introduce democratic reforms."[8] Yet their accession process might hamper Turkey's own accession process. If the inclusion of the Western Balkans is to proceed with greater determination—as the International Commission on the Balkans recommends[9]—this might deflect attention from Turkey for three reasons: because they are obviously European countries while Turkey's European identity is contested, because the amount and depth of problems to solve will absorb energies and might even preclude further enlargements and finally because including Kosovar and Albanian Muslims might deprive Turkey of one of its "trump cards," i.e. helping reconcile Islam and democracy, Muslim and Western worlds to avert the post-9/11 "clash of civilizations" argument.

In the absence of a Cyprus settlement, the Greek government of the Republic of Cyprus (ROC) as the recognized representative of Cyprus and an EU member has very few incentives to make Turkey's road to accession an easy one. Although under enormous pressure not to veto the December 2004 Summit resolution, the Greek Cypriot leader Tassos Papadopoulos was reported to have said he may have given up "one "big veto" against Turkey's starting membership talks, he retained 62 'small vetoes.'"[10] The stalemate on Cyprus is already

---

[8] "Outgrowing the Union: A Survey of the European Union," *The Economist*, September 25, 2004, p. 5, emphasis added.

[9] International Commission on the Balkans, "The Balkans in Europe's Future," Robert Bosch Stiftung, King Baudouin Foundation, German Marshall Fund of the United States, Charles Stewart Mott Foundation, 2005.

[10] *Financial Times*, December 20, 2004.

having an impact on Turkey's relations with the Union; at the December 2004 Summit Ankara had promised that it would amend the customs union agreement with the EU in advance of the October 3, 2005 starting date of negotiations to include the ROC it does not officially recognize. While Turkish diplomats do not anticipate any problems with the signing of the amended customs union agreement, it is the Greek Cypriots who see the EU accession process as the only means through which they can get the Turks to make concessions on the UN Secretary General Kofi Annan's plan. Even though the Turkish government and Turkish Cypriots under their new leader Mehmet Ali Talat have effectively executed a 180-degree turn in their traditional uncompromising policy positions, they have few cards to play. The EU has been singularly incapable or unwilling to overcome Greek Cypriot objections to the opening of minimal trade relations in order to reward Turkish Cypriots for voting in favor of a resolution of the problem in April 2004 and to strengthen the moderate camp among them. As long as the stalemate continues, the likely probability is that there will be more European court decisions against the Turkish position on Cyprus further damaging the atmosphere between Ankara and Brussels. Having engineered a reversal of Cyprus policy, the government in Turkey is in need to demonstrate to its public that it has received benefits. Cypriot attempts at making life difficult in EU conclaves are likely to sour the mood in Ankara. Already, Turkey is retaliating by blocking NATO-EU military cooperation because of Cyprus's membership in the EU.[11]

Looming on the horizon is the domestic impact of the Iraq war on Turkey. Many Europeans may have decided that Turkey is closer to their position on the transatlantic divide than originally thought given the Turkish parliament's rejection of US demands on the eve of the war. The context for the Iraq war in Turkey is very different than in Europe. The war has opened the way for robust Kurdish autonomy and perhaps even independence in northern Iraq were Iraq to succumb to the orgy of violence or simply a civil war and not to recover as a unified state. For many years, Ankara has tried to prevent the

---

[11] Mehmet Ali Birand, "Simdi de NATO'da Kibris Krizi Yasaniyor," *Posta*, February 23, 2005. Turkey, NATO and the EU had agreed in 2002 that any EU-NATO joint operation that included NATO wherewithal would not include Cyprus in its operation area. With Cyprus now a member of the EU, it is impossible for the EU to ignore a member country, whereas the Turks are sticking by the letter of the 2002 agreement.

Kurds in Iraq from achieving such goals precisely because it fears a contagion effect that could lead Turkish Kurds to perhaps emulate their Iraqi brethren. In the process, they have created the Iraqi Turkmen Front, which under Ankara's tutelage, is designed to mobilize Iraqi Turkmens against Kurdish ambitions. Increasingly, this issue has come to dominate all Turkish discussions of the future of Iraq. Having established "red lines" in the matter, Turks have occasionally threatened to use force to roll back Kurdish ambitions to not only declare independence but also incorporate the contested city of Kirkuk within the Kurdish autonomous region in a future Iraqi federation. An added complication is the remnants of the PKK, the Kurdistan Workers' Party, holed up in the northeastern corner of northern Iraq and the fear that a Kurdish managed northern Iraqi region would be incapable of controlling the border much less deal effectively with the PKK.

In view of the sensitivities associated with the Kurdish question, which range from ideological opposition to existential fears, there is a distinct possibility that the future of northern Iraq may prove to be a breaking point in the Turkish political system. This is in part due to the fact that opponents of the ruling party have few if any political opportunities with which they can weaken the AKP. The politics of the Kurdish issue cuts across all political persuasion, including in the dominant AKP which makes it particularly vulnerable to a sudden change in the fortunes of the Turkmens and/or the Kurds in northern Iraq. Any Turkish incursion into Iraq to intervene with the developments there, assuming this was possible, may serve to reignite the Kurdish question in Turkey itself. The very act of intervening into Iraq and the resulting resumption of inter-ethnic violence in Turkey is likely to draw the ire and opposition of Europe. The reemergence of the Kurdish question would bring back to the forefront discussions of Turkish human rights policies, democracy and its treatment of minorities. This would represent an important setback in Turkish goals towards European accession.

## Strategic Concerns

In the period leading to accession, will Turkey's strategic predicament help it on the road to EU membership? Complicating matters for the EU is the transatlantic dimension of the relationship with Turkey. With the second-largest military force in NATO and a proclivity to take questions of security seriously, Ankara is poised to play an important role in any future European security architecture. At the same time, Turkey has had a profound, though recently strained, relationship with the US. Originally, some European countries saw in Turkey a stalking horse for the US—or perhaps a second one depending on one's view of Great Britain. However, far more important than the relations with the US, it is Turkey's proximity to the Middle East and to a lesser extent the Caucasus that will help determine European perceptions of Turkey in the years up to accession. Five important issues dominate the Middle East, the Arab-Israeli peace process, the future of Iraq, Iran's nuclear ambitions, the Caucasus and terrorism.

Turkey, which hitherto had tried to remain aloof from Middle East developments, has found itself far more engaged because of developments in Iraq. Moreover, the new Turkish government has made a conscious effort to repair its relationship with the Arab and Muslim world, both by trying to open a dialogue with it and by cooling its relations with Israel. Ankara worked hard to assume the mantle of the General Secretary of the Islamic Conference Organization and the AKP leadership has made no secret that it wants Turkey to play a much more robust international role commensurate with its size and importance. However, the problem Turkey faces in the Middle East is the real possibility that none of the issues listed above will improve in the medium term. On the contrary, all the countries that border it (apart from Europe) are susceptible to internal domestic instability. The most obvious is Iraq where that is already in evidence on a daily basis with the violence perpetrated by insurgents on the American forces as well as on Iraqi civilians and government authorities. The chances that Iraq will succumb to an even worse fate are not inconsiderable and, therefore, future Iraqi developments may undermine Turkish political stability and its foreign and domestic political goals.

Similarly, Syria and Iran are marked by transitional regimes of sorts; Bashar al-Assad has not proven to be on par with his father and his ability to guide Syria into a reformist future is very much in doubt. Recent events in Lebanon, specifically, the accusations by the Lebanese opposition of Syria's role in former Prime Minister Rafiq Hariri's assassination and the pressure brought upon Damascus by both France and the US, have shaken the al-Assad regime. Although recent events in Lebanon unleashed by Hariri's assassination are more representative of a nationalist reaction than of a democratic movement—though as Ghassan Salame pointed out, one may be the precondition of the other—the fact remains that they are likely to have an important and immediate impact on Syria.[12] In addition to the "contagion" effect of the demonstrations, Damascus has to contend with the possible loss of control of its stranglehold over Lebanon's economy and financial centers and the possibility that with it its access to foreign exchange resources will be severely compromised. Whether this will hasten changes in Syria, including a transformation of the regime, remains to be seen. Nonetheless, Bashar's choices will not be many: he will have to choose between autarky and reliance on Iran to an opening towards the West and Israel which, in turn, may require much greater efforts to resolve the Golan Heights problem. He also has to contend with the consequences of the Iraqi war and conflict. He not only feels the pressure of the United States unhappy with his inability or unwillingness to stop the incursion of jihadists into Iraq, but also has to worry of the demonstration effect of a successful transformation in Iraq would have on his largely disenfranchised population.

By contrast, in Iran, the strengthening of the conservative forces at the expense of the reformists does not bode well for its future dialogue with the West, especially on nuclear arms proliferation. Unlike Syria, the regime in Iran has the ability to buy itself some time because of the continuing high oil prices. It faces none of the foreign exchange pressures Syria does. Having more time translates into a better bargaining position. Should European-Iranian relations turn sour, how will Turkey respond, especially if it is clear that Iran acquires a nuclear device? Will this propel Turkey, a NATO member presumably protected by the NATO umbrella, opt for a weapon acquisition program of its own? Such concerns are likely to influence European perceptions of Turkey's role.

The Caucasus is also pregnant with severe internal pressures. The territories in the Northern Caucasus are increasingly slipping out of Moscow's control as the populations succumb to the violence perpetrated by a few. Any instability that travels south from that region is likely to involve Turkey as Ankara has tried to play a constructive role in the Caucasus while maintaining its opposition to the Armenian

---

[12] Ghassan Salamé: "Un Liban déconfessionnalisé, nouveau, est à inventer," interview, Dossier: "Le réveil des Libanais," *Le Monde*, Thursday, March 31, 2005

government's occupation of Azeri territory. Ankara has had to be careful in the Caucasus not just because of the ethnic linkages between its own population of Chechen and Abhkhaz origin, but also because of the general danger of instability to oil-export routes.

Greater instability in the Middle East, especially the possible dismemberment of Iraq because of its own internal intra-ethnic and intra-sectarian divisions, might lead to increased violence, greater movements of people across boundaries, and possibly involve Turkey in direct conflict with Iraqi Kurds. In addition, the Iraqi imbroglio will force the Europeans to question the wisdom of extending the continent's borders to the Middle East. As such it will reinforce those who argue that Turkey remain a buffer state of sorts between the Middle East and Europe while enjoying a privileged relationship with Europe. If Turkey wants to avoid being painted with the broad brush of Middle Eastern instability, it will have to redouble its efforts to secure its boundaries, reduce the trafficking of all kinds of peoples and goods, and most importantly do not become an easy transit route for refugees, economic or political. This may require decisions such as imposing visa restrictions on neighbors such as the Iranians as well as a more stringent control regime for its Central Asian and other Turkic speaking nationalities (which we discuss in the second part of this chapter).

## The Domestic European Consensus and the Future of the EU

All these problems have to be analyzed against the backdrop of domestic politics which makes Turkey's European vocation different, if not more difficult. The current progress that made the positive December 2004 EU decision possible was the result of Herculean efforts by a new ruling party which, in many ways, represents the most "dissimilar" of Turkey's constituencies when compared to EU's core. The ruling Justice and Development Party, AKP, is a conservative party for which religion is an integral part of its identity and many of whose members and leaders were once virulent opponents of the EU. There is no question that this turnabout by the AKP is good news in that the segment the furthest away from Europe culturally is able to make its peace with what it hitherto saw as a "Christian club." It is, however, worrisome that the secular elites in control of the Turkish state were incapable of introducing the necessary reforms leading to negotiations with the EU earlier. In their nationalist or leftwing variants, these elites have come to represent the new center of the opposition to the EU in Turkey. Complicating matters is the fact that what divides the ruling AKP from its secular opposition are fundamental questions pertaining to the nature of the regime in Turkey. Many of the reforms demanded by the EU are viewed as "regime-threatening" by these elites and hence for them, the EU is a poisoned chalice precisely because it prescribes changes that will force the democratization of the Turkish political space. Hence as Turkey encounters increasing requirement from the EU, the opposition to the EU will undoubtedly assume a more intransigent form and lead to domestic instability.

Unlike many of the recent adherents to the EU, Turkey is likely to have the greatest difficulty adapting to what Robert Cooper has called the "new post-modern order" in Europe where the order of the day is about the breaking down of the distinction between foreign and domestic policy, "mutual interference and mutual surveillance" of each other's domestic affairs, and "security based on transparency, mutual openness and mutual vulnerability."[13]

Domestic European concerns, ranging from unemployment to the integration of Muslim minorities, are far more likely to determine perceptions of Turkey. In a number of countries specific events or issues have helped sour perceptions vis-à-vis the Muslim minority. These include the controversy over wearing the "veil" in public schools in France, the murder of the Dutch cinematographer Theo van Gogh by a fanatic, the honor killings of young Turkish women in Germany, and the debate on the Armenian demands for Turkey to recognize the 1915-16 Ottoman state's killings of large numbers of Armenian civilians, acrimoniously culminating in 2005 with the 90th anniversary of the beginning of the massacres.

Here too, the government's behavior in the next few years will go a long way to shaping perceptions of Turkey. When on the eve of the EU Summit, Prime Minister Tayyip Erdogan's government tabled a law proposal to criminalize adultery, it took the EU by surprise. It was not so much the surprise element as it was the fact that the EU, per-

---

[13] Robert Cooper, *The Post Modern State and the World Order* (U.K.: Demos, 1996), 25-26.

haps mistakenly, interpreted the move as a concession to the hard line and religious elements of the party thus giving rise to the fear regarding the hitherto unmentioned suspicions of AKP's agenda. Europe's misgivings about Turkey have increased recently as it perceives the AKP government clamping down on demonstrations and pursuing laws deemed unfriendly of journalists' rights. Whether these are a temporary sign of weakness or indication of things to come, remains to be seen. In any case, it has served to nurture further unease in the European Union.

In any case, Turkey's possible accession is going to trigger a discussion over the future of Europe or again conflagrate with such a discussion were the project of European constitution to unravel. For those who wish to see a deeper integration of European institutions, Turkey is a serious impediment. Ankara will not only have enormous needs but for the most recent joiner to have possibly the largest population and, therefore, the greatest influence in EU bodies will deter any efforts at deepening. The prospect that Turkey will have some 15 percent of the voting power in EU councils is enough to engender stiff opposition to its accession. On the other hand, for those not interested in deepening but rather in a diversified and loose European arrangement, a Europe with "multiple speeds," then Turkey is a welcome addition.

## Will the EU Need Turkey for Strategic Purposes?

What will Turkey's strategic benefits for the EU be when the country joins? Of course by that time Turkey itself may be a different country—just as the EU, with even more members, from the Balkans mainly, will be a different beast. Yet it is safe to contend that the most immediate impact will be the extension of Europe's boundaries as discussed earlier. Overnight the enlarged EU with Turkey as a member will acquire 2949 km of land borders, mostly mountainous and 8330 km of sea borders. Assuming no major developments, the newly acquired neighbors of the EU will be situated in a region made up of fledgling states, of mostly repressed civil societies and of ongoing violence. Countries such as Syria, Iraq, Iran, and the Caucasus states will all be struggling with various forms of pressures ranging from economic and political reform to instability generated by domestic and external forces.

In the long run the success of these countries is fundamentally important to the future of the EU. Europe, whether it likes it or not, will increase its involvement in the Middle East partly because of the greater number of immigrants, legal or illegal, in its midst and partly because of the remnants of the civilizational issues that will be separating the West from the East. The quest for stability in the Middle East, in an age of missile and WMD proliferation, will demand that Europe's defense start far away from its own borders. Similarly, without any serious prospect of a reduced dependence on hydrocarbons, the Caspian Basin and the Middle East as a whole will require increased attention.

This is where Turkey's contribution will be most significant. Both opponents and advocates of Turkey's membership in the EU make their case by pointing out to this new strategic reality. Detractors recoil at the possibility that instead of exporting, the EU will be importing instability from Turkey and through Turkey from its neighbors as well. By contrast, proponents of Turkey's membership look upon it as an opportunity for the EU to stabilize Turkey and beyond and help this body become a major player in the regions adjacent to it. Both arguments may very well be true: Turkey's inclusion is a gamble where stability will be exported against a calculated measure of instability.

The EU's enlargement to Turkey is in keeping with the past tradition of the EU. First by including Turkey the European Union may well play the same stabilizing role it has in the past by accepting new democracies as members, i.e. countries which had hardly come out of their fascist or communist pasts. In the 1980s and 1990s, the leaders of the EC/EU bet on democracy and each time they proved to be right: both the Southern rim of Europe and the Central European countries prospered and developed, economically and politically, while anchored in the EU—or while still in the process of anchoring themselves in the EU. Certainly in Turkey's case, the bet may be somewhat more audacious: the Europeanization of Turkey will entail not just the transformation of Turkish politics, including the ruling AKP, should it still remain in power at the time, but also some of its most notable institutions like the military. Whereas the AKP is suspected by some in Turkey of harboring a hidden agenda, one of trying to Islamicize the country—albeit through surreptitious means—the military has been the institution at the forefront of defending secularism and yet blocking attempts at genuine democratization. To that extent, the support of the European Union for democratization entails a certain irony as it means pushing the military back to where it belongs and stop being the guardian of Kemalist principles, including secularism— as well as extending the rights of minorities, including religious ones. The democratic principles the EU is advocating may well be used against the consolidation of democracy. The aim is to begin a process of change that is principled and yet not controllable by any single dominant force, whether this is the military or the AKP, in other words to foster a vibrant, autonomous, civil society. To that extent, even if Erdogan and his party were to entertain a "hidden agenda" — they might be overtaken by the dynamics of events: after all Gorbachev lost his own bet, that of reforming communism without giving up all communist perspectives, and he could not control all evolutions and revolutions. In any case a prosperous and democratic Turkey with its European future will be one which will shed many of its insecurities and almost xenophobic approach to its friends and foes alike.

## Turkey as an Example for the Muslim World?

Certainly some evolutions will be very slow because they cannot be imposed from above or from the West—meaning here both European elites and Turkish western-oriented ones: the rights of women may be decreed yet difficult to enforce in the Anatolian East or in the sprawling shantytowns of the large cities.[14] If Europe's bet however is won and if Turkey's democracy deepens, not only will Atatürk's—and even the Ottomans'—original dream of westernizing Turkey be fulfilled but also the twinning of Islam and democracy will have proven possible. Turkey certainly has shown that state and religion may be separated on the soil of Islam but the "Christian-democratization" of Islam has still to happen, i.e. Muslim parties should evolve along the path that European Christian-democratic parties followed in the past, allowing political parties to entertain religious values, yet within the context of a separation of state and church. That in of itself would be a

---

[14] As the writer Orhan Pamuk fears in his novel *Snow*, (London, Faber and Faber), 2004, first published in Turkey in 2002. Yet the government is starting a wide campaign to change public attitudes vis-à-vis so-called "crimes of honor."

dramatic achievement. It would put in evidence the reconciliation of Islam and democracy both in Turkey and within the wider European framework: Turkey and its overwhelmingly Muslim population would be a fully-fledged democratic country while the democrats of Europe would embrace a democratic Turkey with a Muslim party, assuming the AKP remains a dominant political force in the foreseeable future.

Yet it remains to be seen whether other Muslim states and societies would follow suit. A democratic Turkey may serve as an example to be emulated by others: this argument is more to be heard in the United States than it is in Europe, for a number of reasons. Those in Europe who want to embrace Turkey emphasize the latter's internal developments. Just as the southern brim of Europe and its central core strengthened their democratic credentials through their adhesion to the EU, the main aim of EU's enlargement to Turkey is for many to consolidate first and foremost the democratic process in that country. Although Bush's vision of a greater Middle East is only reluctantly shared, if at all, by Europeans, the fact remains that if Europe is to become what it was envisaged to be in the imagination of its founders and most ardent supporters, a liberal space devoid of conflict, then Turkey may have a demonstration role to play beyond its borders. Certainly the Turkish example cannot simply be translated to other neighboring countries. The Ahtisaari report underlined for instance that "Turkey's experience is unique, based on diverse cultural roots, two centuries of western orientation and Atatürk's revolutionary transformation to secular democracy; it cannot simply be transferred to other Islamic countries. Each country has its own dynamics and the Arab world has shown little inclination for Turkey." Still, just as Turkey was influenced by Europe and developed the desire to join it, "it would show the Islamic world that it is indeed possible to find answers to the dilemma of combining religious beliefs and traditions with the universally accepted principles of modern societies."[15]

## The Export of Stability

Even if it were not to serve as an export-model of democracy, Turkey would however be expected to contribute to the export of sta-

---

[15] Ahtisaari, op. cit., p. 17.

bility. First it might help to protect Europe from possible energy disruptions and even from potential political blackmail linked to the suspension of energy deliveries. Currently 26 percent of European oil imports originate in the Middle East, whereas the comparable figures for the former Soviet area and North Africa are 41 and 15 percent respectively.[16] By contrast, Europe depends exclusively on Russia for its imports of gas (there is significant production in Norway and the UK which gets exported to other European countries and liquefied natural gas, LNG, imports from Algeria). Clearly some countries such as Germany, Poland or the Baltic states are even more dependent on Russia than others and this dependence is likely to increase over the next fifteen to twenty-five years. Certainly, as some analysts point out, Russia—or its predecessor—has never resorted to crude pressures and turned off the faucet of gas and oil. Yet the danger exists that some leaders might be willing to accommodate Russia lest deliveries be stopped. In any case, Turkey has already emerged as an energy hub with the Bosporus, the Kirkuk-Ceyhan and the Baku-Tbilisi-Ceyhan oil pipelines while connections with Europe exist, through Greece, or are being planned, through Bulgaria, Romania, Hungary and Austria, adding prospective additional oil transport routes from the Caspian Sea Basin.[17] In addition, gas is been transported from Iran to Turkey via the Tabriz-Erzurum line while a pipeline from Baku to Erzurum is to be built and other projects are under consideration.

There is no question that Turkey's attempts at becoming a transport node for oil and gas will enhance the perception of its importance to Europe. As pent up oil demand from China and India weigh on traditional Middle East suppliers, Europe is keen to develop a network of pipelines from the NIS. So far the industrialized world has weathered the storm of skyrocketing oil prices in 2004-5 well. Still, the prospect of future price increases is potentially destabilizing and, in turn, it will encourage Europeans to create an infrastructural network that not only provides some redundancy in the event of disruptions but also reinforces the distribution networks in accordance with their needs. It is here that Turkey will play a critical role in anchoring its oil-producing former Soviet-bloc neighbors and act as a conduit.

---

[16] British Petroleum Statistical Review of World Energy. June 2004.

[17] On energy issues cf. John Roberts, "The Turkish Gate: Energy Transit and Security Issues," (Brussels: CEPS), September 2004.

Second, Turkey may not only ensure the stability of energy supplies to the EU; it may also help to stabilize the environment. Both Turkey and the EU have a vested interest in securing stability in the Middle East, the Caucasus and Central Asia. This is a major aim of the security strategy, "A Secure Europe in a Better World," which was adopted in December 2003 and of the neighborhood strategy, "Wider Europe— Neighbourhood: A New Framework for Relations with our Eastern and Southern Neighbours." Certainly Europe should not need to wait for impulses from Turkey to care for its near abroad, for the Caucasus for instance. Here one can only deplore the lack of interest and engagement of the European Union for such countries as Georgia up to the revolution of 2003-2004 and the subsequent publication of the "Neighbourhood Policy." Turkey too has an interest in promoting good relations with its neighbors, as it has with Syria or Armenia in recent years, or in helping settle disputes, between Armenia and Azerbaijan, in helping Central Asian countries move towards a democratic future or in controlling fluxes of all sorts. In this respect, it is not deprived of instruments and policies.

Turkey's borders North, East and South should become secure, both open and controlled. The EU "Neighbourhood Policy" states very clearly that border management is likely to be a priority item in the action plans adopted for each of the participant countries.[18] In the past few years, Turkey has joined a number of (European) institutions to intensify the surveillance of borders, participated in twinning projects with EU members, signed readmission agreements with other countries to curb illegal migration and started to impose visas on neighboring countries, following the necessity to adopt the acquis.[19]

One of the arguments for opponents of Turkey in Europe is the extension of the EU's borders to areas of the world that are unstable and prone to civil conflict. As a result, with Turkey's accession, the EU will be directly bordering regions that are already exporting illegal migrants and, therefore, amplifying the existing problem. In effect, these opponents worry about both Turkish migrants as well as those

---

[18] http://europa.eu.int/comm/world/enp/pdf/strategy/Strategy_Paper_, p. 16.

[19] For a detailed analysis, see Joanna Apap, Sergio Carrera and Kemal Kirisci, "Turkey in the EU area of Freedom, Security and Justice," (Brussels: CEPS), EU-Turkey Working Paper n°3, August 2004.

from the Levant. The EU's migrant problem has three geographical dimensions. The first is Eastern Europe and is considered the least important. The second originates from the southern shores of the Mediterranean and is focused primarily on Italy and Spain. The third originates in the Levant and Turkey and at the moment the primary conduit is Greece (and its Aegean islands). With the accession of Bulgaria and to a lesser extent Romania, the EU's exposure will increase. What opponents of Turkey's entry hope is to outsource the border management problem to Ankara as part of the neighbourhood policy. Turkey, which already is cooperating with the EU on a number of issues,[20] may find the outsourcing notion unacceptable and, therefore, be inclined to reduce its cooperation. On the other hand, having Turkey in the European Union may offer a considerable advantage: it will allow the latter to better control its external borders thanks to a synergy of Turkish and European techniques and know-how of border control and management.

## Assets and Liabilities

As far as projecting stability is concerned, Turkey is endowed with some instruments and means, in both military and civilian areas. It has substantial military capacities, military and police forces and a gendarmerie. It is the largest NATO army in Europe, with considerable combat experience in difficult terrains, yet limited strategic lift capacity, as the report on The European Transformation of Modern Turkey underlines.[21] The Turkish military infrastructure has been in much need of modernization and while progress was made along this front, the economic crisis of 2001 severely diminished the country's ability to purchase arms abroad. It has had an extensive experience fighting a non-conventional enemy, the Kurdistan Workers' Party, the PKK, throughout the 1980s and 1990s. The combination of domestic and external threats has enabled the Turkish military to have an inordinate degree of influence in politics even at times of diminished resources. The Turkish military makes up for its deficiencies in modernization and agility with sheer numbers and willingness to deploy itself when necessary. In 1998, for instance, the military took upon itself to

---

[20] Joanna Apap et al. Turkey in the EU area of Freedom, Security and Justice, op. cit.

[21] Kemal Dervis et al., *The European Transformation of Modern Turkey*, op. cit. pp. 50.

threaten Syria with war in the event Damascus did not rid itself of Abdullah Öcalan, the leader of the PKK. Damascus complied rather quickly even though it was not clear whether the Turks would have engaged in large-scale military action. What was important was the perception that they would have. Among other things it has participated in the stabilization operations undertaken by SFORII and KFOR as well as by ISAF, even leading ISAF II operation in 2002-2003.

Last but not least, Turkey has some interesting know-how and experience in promoting relations with the Turkic world. A common linguistic background allowed Turkey to develop relations with the newly independent republics of Central Asia after the demise of the Soviet Empire: students' exchanges, the establishment of elite high schools, cooperation in drug and crime-fighting etc. were among the tools that the country resorted to.[22]

## Turkey as a Regional Power?

Yet does this suffice to turn Turkey into an active promoter of a European CFSP and will Turkey's admission foster *per se* an active CFSP, making a global player, or at least, an important regional player out of the European Union? The advocates of Turkey's entry into the EU seem to believe so: the Ahtisaari report emphasizes the beneficial effects of a Turkish membership on Europe's Foreign and Security Policy, underlining that "… Turkish accession would considerably strengthen the Union's capabilities as Foreign Policy actor,[23]" as it would add a new geo-strategic dimension to the Union's Foreign Policy efforts. This is a view which both overlooks the difficulties which Turkey encounters with some of its neighbors and entails some mechanistic reasoning as to the workings of the EU.

One should remember that Turkey itself is embroiled in difficult relations with some of its neighbors such as Iraq or Armenia. To that extent, it may not be the perfect intermediary, supposedly neutral, that it wishes to be, for instance in the relations between Armenia and

---

[22] For details cr. Michael Emerson and Nathalie Tocci, "Turkey as Bridgehead and Spearhead—Integrating EU and Turkish Foreign Policy," (Brussels: CEPS), EU-Turkey Working Paper n° 1.

[23] Op. cit. p. 17.

Azerbaijan over the Karabakh. Its ability to serve as a bridgehead or as a spearhead to the EU, to use Michael Emerson's and Nathalie Tocci's formula, is also limited for the same reasons. Certainly relations between Turkey and Armenia have improved recently on all accounts: Turkish historians have for instance started looking at the genocide issue, sometimes together with Armenian authors.[24] Yet the question of the massacre perpetrated against the Armenians is not being officially addressed and the demands of French or German politicians even lead to a stiffening of public attitudes. Finally, the Turkish-Armenian border remains closed. Here membership in the EU could help—just as being part of the same union eventually helped Turkey and its arch-enemy, Greece. More actively, the EU could ask from Turkey to engage into a process similar to that in which the Hungarian government and its neighbors defused and settled the question of Hungarian minorities: treaties were signed in the framework of a so-called Stability Pact.[25] Such a step might be welcome on the part of Turkey all the more so than Suleyman Demirel himself called for such a pact in 1999, albeit in a very general way. On the whole, a democratic Turkey inside the EU might be favorably perceived by a number of actors in the region, softening the image that Ankara may have projected over decades—though an undemocratic Russian government might not welcome the accession of Turkey to the EU.

Some structural problems will however remain. Turkey in the Middle East still suffers, although at a diminishing rate, from its Ottoman past. Here the most important stumbling bloc will be the Kurds, especially if they were to gain independence or autonomy. Beyond this, its relations with the Iraq and Syria will be affected by the disbursement of the waters from the Euphrates and Tigris rivers. Although its relations with Israel once driven by Turkey's dislike of Syria have suffered under the AKP government, it remains rather solid especially on the economic front. The greatest contribution to European Union goals in the region that Turkey can bring is on the economic front. As a member of the EU, Turkey is likely to become a regional economic workhorse, not only sup-

---

[24] Even the Turkish government is taking steps to deal with the issue as the two Turkish political leaders , Erdogan and leader of the opposition Deniz Baykal, met recently to advance a strategy to combat and yet also engage critics of Turkey on the Armenian issue, see *Hürriyet*, March 9, 2005.

[25] cf. Anne-Marie Le Gloannec: « Le 'soft power' plutôt que l'union politique », in *Le Figaro*, December 18-19, 2004.

plying Europe with its wares, but also it may become an entrepot of sorts for European companies wanting to operate closer to Middle East and Central Asian markets. The Turkish private sector, especially its construction companies, has extensive experience in these regions and to the extent that Turkish business can serve as a conduit for Europe as well as better economic management techniques, the Middle East will be better off. As to Central Asia, initial Turkish efforts in the 1990s certainly appeared to those in the region as an attempt at dominating them. Yet, there is no question that Turkey remains in a privileged position in Central Asia as it has natural affinities. As an EU member, Turkey's influence in the region will increase significantly. For one, the region's states will not have to balance their interests between Ankara and Brussels and Brussels will help soften the contours of Turkish foreign policy. A more confident Turkey will also be able to do what it has shied away from doing until now, that is, push for the democratization of Central Asian regimes.

## Conclusion

In any case, a positive synergy might then emerge between Turkey and its European partners, allowing them to subtly turn some of Turkey's means and instruments into advantages. Yet there is nothing inevitable about this. Nor is there any inevitability about the EU becoming stronger as it adds Turkey to the mix. Here too the argument, often resorted to by proponents of Turkey's membership, is too mechanistic. It overlooks the fact that Turkey might be a difficult partner for years to come, as it has proven to be when the agreement between the EU and NATO was negotiated. Certainly, as many have come to understand, Turkey probably will not be the American Trojan horse feared by the 'Europeanists'. The refusal by the Turkish Parliament, on March 1, 2003, to allow US troops to transit the country to launch a second front against Iraq, and the subsequent difficulties the two countries have had, especially over the future of Iraq, have shown that Turkey and the US are not always on the same wavelength. Also membership in the European Union brings with it a socialization process that all other countries have undergone during their accession process. On the other hand, Turkey's special relationship—the current problems over Iraq notwithstanding—with the U.S. *may* actually help bridge the Atlantic divide. In many ways, Turkey is more likely to emulate Britain rather than any of the continental European powers. It will be on the edge of Europe; although far from the U.S., Ankara will be close to the Middle East, an area where the Washington will continue to have strong interests. With Britain, therefore, Turkey may come to represent one of the two bookends of a strong transatlantic relationship.

Yet there is the possibility that Turkey will be a difficult partner; this combined with the difficulties of negotiating with twenty-nine plus countries,[26] will render the EU even more cumbersome at hammering out positions in foreign and security policy. The greatest problem facing the EU with Turkey as its member is the possibility that Ankara will not have made the transition to the post-modern world order as practiced by the EU. A Turkey that remains wedded to older conceptions of the nation-state and intent on pushing its own security agenda onto Europe is likely to create havoc. Whether this comes to pass depends on the effectiveness of the accession negotiations.

Last but not least, it is not because the EU, penetrating deep into Asia Minor and the Middle East, will have to deal with such issues as turmoil in the Caucasus or the Israeli-Palestine peace process that it will do so and that it will do so efficiently. On the one hand, as we have underlined earlier, Turkey may only add a limited comparative advantage to European capabilities in terms of diplomacy because of its own entanglements which will have to be undone first. On the other hand, the EU has turned out to be a pretty heavy body to move. In the past, the addition of countries neighboring Russia, such as Finland, Poland or the Baltic ones certainly have helped, to some extent, to draw European attention to certain issues: a Northern dimension was added which helps resolve such problems as pollution in the Baltic sea. Yet the so-called strategy vis-à-vis Russia is not convincing either by its coherence or by the determination of EU members to adopt a common attitude. Yugoslavia too is a case in point: though the Europeans had to intervene in their backyard and though they thought that 'Europe's hour' had come, they helplessly witnessed the descent of the various communities into violence. It is in that respect astonishing that political leaders in the EU expect a more muscular European foreign policy from the sheer fact of adding one more member to the Union, albeit a powerful country such as Turkey.

---

[26] Since Romania, Bulgaria and Croatia at least will be members of the EU by the time Turkey joins.

# Chapter 7

# Russia and EU Enlargement: Starting the Endgame

Timofei Bordachev

"The Eurocrats are coming. Lord make us so strong." For many years, by and large Russia dealt with the European Union (EU) by ignoring it. Now Europe is here and has already started to exercise its own proactive policy towards Russia. After the EU's biggest enlargement become a reality, a newly emerged 500million monster appeared on the western Russia's borders and seems to be quite confident in setting the common agenda. And Russia looks like it is not ready for this change.

However, the choice Russia faces now is extremely simple: it can either become a satellite of a renewed and vibrant Europe or an equal partner. The answer to this question depends on many factors of internal and international nature. Europe can move either towards deeper integration and supranational character or become a less consolidated common market. Russia can also continue the way it goes presently or turn back to become a normal market democracy. It would not be an exaggeration to say that in the next few years Russia will face an internal policy choice, which might be no less crucial than the one it made in August 1991. Both Europe and Russia will be affected by major international events and tendencies. Yet an effort must be made if that challenging choice (*partner* or *satellite*) is to be understood and effectively answered.

## On the Eve

Although preparations for the eastward enlargement of the European Union (EU) officially began as early as 1993, those who then held power in Russia did not attach much importance to it. In effect, no response was forthcoming from Moscow until the end of summer 1999, by which time the matter had already been settled in the EU and the technical parameters, including the adherence of the candidate countries to the community *acquis* and Schengen legislation, had been agreed. It is, therefore, unsurprising that, of all of the issues related to enlargement, the most important to Russian politicians and diplomats has been the issue of land access for Russian citizens to the Kaliningrad *oblast*, following changes made by Lithuania to the visa regime while adopting Schengen legislation. Other issues, such as changes to Russia's foreign trade arrangements with the EU accession countries or the prospects of cross-border cooperation, remain on the periphery of the Russian foreign-policy agenda.

The reason for this lies both in the way that the Russian ruling class has traditionally perceived the EU and in the idiosyncrasies of the entire process of European integration—of which enlargement has become a part—that prevent third countries from organizing a timely and adequate response to it. In the EU itself, fundamental questions concerning enlargement were under discussion for a long time, despite the fact that Copenhagen membership criteria were approved in 1993. Moreover, the slow pace of the enlargement debate and open discussion among EU nations of the major enlargement-related problems left Russia with the impression that it would still be a long time before any practical steps were taken.

However in reality, and despite their calm appearance, throughout the 1990s, Russia—EU relations were characterized by a series of fundamental disagreements that affected Russia's perception of EU enlargement. The most significant was the opposing views of the parties regarding who constituted Russia's main partner in Europe. Moscow and the European capitals had different answers to this question, which impacted on day-to-day relations and was a major contributing factor to their noticeable breakdown in 1999. At that time, nearly all of the EU countries backed the North Atlantic Treaty Organisation (NATO)'s operation in former Yugoslavia (which Russia opposed) and later strongly condemned the Kremlin's assault on Chechnya.

A number of European authors believe that Russia failed to develop a coherent single policy on the EU in the 1990s.[1] Russia has always maintained relations with France, Germany, Italy, the UK and other European countries, and these have dominated its relationship with

---

[1] Kempe, I., *Direct Neighbourhood Relations between the enlarged EU and the Russian Federation, Ukraine, Belarus and Moldova*, (Gütersloh: Bertelsmann Foundation Publishers, 1998).

the EU. From the beginning of the 1990s, European integration also assumed a foreign-policy dimension, intended to address the imbalance between the EU's considerable economic weight and its humble contribution to international affairs. Nonetheless, as some Russian observers even admit today, Moscow has always viewed the EU as being on a par with other international organisations—the Council of Europe, NATO and the United Nations (UN)—in which national governments play a deciding role in all issues.[2]

Russian foreign policy inherited this particular attitude to the EU from the Union of Soviet Socialist Republics (USSR), which essentially refused to do business with the European Community as a supranational organisation until the late 1980s and regarded it on a superficial level as an economic appendage to NATO. In 1988, a declaration of mutual recognition was signed between the Council for Mutual Economic Assistance (the Soviet-dominated trade bloc of socialist economies) and the European Community, but until then the USSR had only maintained bilateral relations with EU member states. The first agreement on trade and cooperation between the EU and the USSR was signed in 1989 and a Partnership and Cooperation Agreement (PCA) in 1994 but it was not until six years after the Soviet Union's collapse that the PCA came into force between the EU and Russia in 1997. Moscow's reserved attitude towards cooperation with the EU is also reflected in the very limited written record of bilateral relations, which, until 1999, consisted of only three documents adopted in the EU and one PCA signed by Russia.[3]

The Europeans believe that Russia's flawed view of the EU is linked to one of the most significant characteristics of Moscow's European policy practice of the 1990s: the prevailing bilateral approach. For the duration of the 1990s, Russia strove to establish constructive ties with the leading European powers. A great deal of its diplomatic activity on the European front failed to bring about a rapprochement with the

---

[2] Leshukov, I., "Rossiya i evropeiskii soyus: strategiya vzaimootnoshenii" in Trenin, D., *Rossiya i osnovnye instituty bezopasnosti v Evrope: vstupaya v XXI vek*, (Russia and the Basic Security Institutions in Russia: the Path to the 21st Century (Moscow: Carnegie Moscow Center, 2000), pp. 23–38.

[3] European Commission communication: "The Future of Relations between the European Union and Russia" (1995); European Council general report: "Strategy for EU-Russian Relations" (1995) and "European Union Action Plan for Russia" (1996). Available at www.europa.eu.int/comm/external_relations/russia/russia_docs/index.htm

EU. This was primarily due to the fact that all of the EU countries' foreign economic activity had already (by the late 1970s) come under the jurisdiction of supranational bodies in Brussels, which Russia overlooked as before.

It is possible to identify at least three reasons for this situation. First, intense contacts were fostered with the leaders of the European states in the spirit of the personal diplomacy of the 1990s, which corresponded with the individual leanings of the head of state and was partly intended to compensate for the lack of competitiveness of the Russian economy.[4] Such a policy could not be applied to relations with the EU. It is hard to imagine an informal meeting between the Russian president and the representatives of the EU "Troika," let alone the twenty members of the European Commission. Second, focusing attention on the European "superpowers" coincided with the doctrine of establishing triangular geopolitical combinations, which was the chief obsession of Russian foreign policy in the 1990s. Finally, from the point of view of the workings of the bureaucratic machine, the Russian Ministry of Foreign Affairs was far more accustomed to dealing with European countries on a bilateral basis, as reflected by its internal structure, which to this day does not have a department devoted exclusively to the EU.

However, the main reason for the predominance of the bilateral approach in Russia's European policy was the fact that the phenomenon of European integration does not fit with the traditional points of reference of Russian foreign policy. As many Russian and foreign authors note, for Russia, the 1990s became a time of harking back to the principles of nineteenth-century diplomacy rather than searching for new solutions.[5] Although there are numerous reasons for this, the most significant was the prevalence of the principles of political realism in Russian foreign policy.[6] The notion of international relations as a state of chaos in which each country simply pursues its own interests contradicted the liberal institutionalist views that not only dominated

---

[4] On the idiosyncrasies of personalised Russian foreign policy, see Bogaturov, A., 'Pyat' sindromov Yeltsina i pyat' obrazov Putina, *Pro et Contra*,' Vol. 6, No. 1–2., 2001, pp. 122–137.

[5] See, for example, Fedorov, Y., 'Krizis vneshnei politiki Rossii: kontseptualny aspekt,' *Pro et Contra, 2001.*, pp. 31–49.

[6] Primakov, E., 'Mezhdunarodnye otnosheniya nakanune XXI veka: problemy i perspektivy,' *Mezhdunarodnaya Zhizn,*' No. 10, 1996, pp. 3–14.

Western foreign-policy thinking in the 1990s, but that had also long since become the ideological basis for the process of European integration. Whereas in the case of the US, the idiosyncrasies of the world views held by representatives of US President Bill Clinton's administration most likely played a significant part in foreign policymaking and it was foreseeable that the paradigm of American foreign policy would change once the Democrats left the White House, in the "Old World," Russia encountered a model of relations between the countries of the region that was fundamentally at odds with Realpolitik. Russia's attempts to formulate European policy with an emphasis on the self-centred interests of the EU's leading powers were predestined to failure.

Consequently, throughout the 1990s, Russia regarded the EU as an intergovernmental regional association in which the supranational element played little part and the European 'superpowers' took all of the key decisions independently—in accordance with the current demands of intrinsically chaotic international relations. Needless to say, Moscow's stance was a source of active displeasure to Brussels and the European capitals and was countered by their efforts to act in apparent defiance of it by taking all of the most important decisions on Russian matters collectively. Here one can see a fundamental contradiction that not only prevented progress in bilateral relations, but also hindered fulfilment of the terms of agreements already in place.

## First Strategy Documents

A clear example of the difference of opinion can be found in the tone and substance of the following conceptual documents adopted by Russia and the EU in 1999: the EU's Common Strategy on Russia; and the Medium-Term Strategy for the Development of Relations between the Russian Federation and the European Union (2000–2010).

It would be no exaggeration to say that Moscow misconstrued the EU's Common Strategy. In the first place, it was perceived as a sign of the EU's aspiration to develop some kind of special relationship with Russia. Even experienced Russian commentators and diplomats emphasised the significance that Russia was the first country with which the EU signed one of these new strategy documents for individual countries.[7] Meanwhile, other assessments of the document vary from the restrained to the openly sceptical. As a rule, these are the opinions of European experts and, at best, they underline the strategy's incompatibility with Russia's priorities and expectations.[8]

The Medium-Term Strategy for the Development of Relations between the Russian Federation and the European Union, presented in late 1999, is a largely declarative document intended to express Moscow's interest in a strategic partnership with the EU. Some observers attribute the very fact that it was adopted to the need to enhance the role played by Russian President Vladimir Putin at a meeting of EU leaders in Helsinki, Finland, on October, 22 1999.[9]

The basic provisions of the document included an initiative to build a strategic partnership between Russia and the EU and an appeal to the European Union to facilitate Russia's accession to the World Trade Organization (WTO), to increase assistance programmes and to revoke anti-dumping measures against Russian goods. The ritual passage about the need for cooperation in the security sphere had the greatest negative impact. The mention of a need to 'counterbalance NATO-centrism in Europe' immediately prompted an angry response from the majority of European observers and, as a relatively meaningless remnant of 1990s foreign-policy thinking, even overshadowed the constructive element of the Russian proposals. Whatever the case, the content of all the official documents and the consequences of their adoption demonstrated that Russia lacked a clear idea of whom it was dealing with in Europe.

Moreover, the aims set out in the two documents are completely different. The EU describes its strategic goal as the construction in Russia of "a stable, open and pluralistic democracy ... governed by the rule of law and underpinning a prosperous market economy benefiting alike all the people of Russia and of the European Union."[10] In Moscow's opinion, a strategic partnership with the EU "can manifest itself in joint efforts to establish an effective system of collective secu-

---

[7] Danilov, D., 'Potentsialny soyuznik Moskvy,' *Nezavisimaya Gazeta*, 3 December 1999; 'Rossiya na putyakh mirostroitelstva,' *Nezavisimaya Gazeta*, 12 September 1999.

[8] Gowan, D., *How the EU can Help Russia*, (London: Centre for European Reform, 2001).

[9] Leshukov, I., *Rossiya i evropeiskii soyus: strategiya vzaimootnoshenii, op. cit.*, p. 24.

[10] In regard to the Common Strategy of the European Union on Russia, Available at www.eur.ru/eng/neweur/user_eng.php?func=rae_common_strategy

rity in Europe on the basis of equality without dividing lines, including through the development and implementation of the Charter for European Security. . . ."[11]

Whereas the EU made it its main objective to change the internal situation in Russia with an emphasis on the need for progress in the human-rights field and the creation of civil institutions, Moscow called on the EU for cooperation on 'equal terms' in a broader international context. The aims of the parties again proved completely at odds, thereby effectively bringing the potentially positive effect of the two new documents to naught.

Hence, the main problem in Russian-European relations in the period 1993-2003 was that Russia was unable properly to identify a partner in Europe and to draw up its foreign-policy measures accordingly. This failure to understand the role and potential of the EU as a single international player, at least as far as the fundamental issues of enlargement were concerned, inevitably resulted in a heedless and even dismissive attitude towards the matter of the EU's physical advance towards Russia's borders.

The process of NATO enlargement, which began to be discussed in 1994, following a summit in Brussels, played an important part in shaping the dismissive attitude taken towards EU enlargement by the Russian elite and authorities. If one looks at the main foreign-policy declarations and documents adopted by Russia in the 1990s with respect to European security issues, one is struck by the pronounced difference in Moscow's views of the role, essence and potential of the two largest institutions in the Western world, namely the NATO bloc (with the US as its backbone) and the European Union.

The former is depicted as a Cold War relic, a completely meaningless and potentially aggressive military instrument, the very existence of which is supported by the 'hawks' in Washington and the bureaucrats in its Brussels headquarters who are afraid of losing their jobs. Conversely, the EU is perpetually viewed as a constructive element that facilitates the region's economic development and represents an

---

[11] In regard to the Medium-Term Strategy for the Development of Relations between the Russian Federation and the European Union (2000–2010), see: www.eur.ru/eng/neweur/ user_eng.php?func=apage&id=53

important partner for Russia.[12] Moreover, on the level of public opinion, by its own long-term anti-American propaganda, the Russian government and elite have made too good job of turning most of the ordinary Russians into pro-Europeans to be able to turn them all overnight into Europhobes.

No attention was paid to the fact that, of the EU's fifteen member states in 1995, eleven (the largest and most significant of which included France, Germany, Italy, Spain and the UK) were members of NATO and acted in full accord with the US. Despite the fact that disagreements periodically flared up between Moscow and Washington and that the leading EU countries invariably stressed their adherence to the principles of transatlantic solidarity, Russian foreign policy never identified the US with its Western European allies.

Moscow's attitude towards the two parallel processes of eastward enlargement of these Western institutions likewise differed. NATO enlargement was always treated as a factor that would undermine European security, whereas the possibility of the countries of Central and Eastern Europe acceding to the EU was seen as more of a positive phenomenon by Russia, even though all of the candidate countries also aspired to become members of NATO. Furthermore, during the 1990s, the EU did not disguise its intention to increase its military potential in part with the help of American resources and in no way in opposition to the US.[13]

## New EU Policy Towards Russia

Things changed very noticeably after the EU stated the intention to enlarge and practical consequences of this process affected Russia directly in 2001—2002. However, what was most important was that some of the consequences, such as Kaliningrad transit issues or new

---

[12] Pichugin, B.M., 'Rasshirenie ES na Vostok i ekonomicheskie interesy Rossii,' *Doklady Instituta Evropy RAN*, No. 29, 1996; Maximychev, I.F., 'Ugrozy bezopasnosti Rossii, svyazannye s nachalom rasshireniya NATO (Vneshnepoliticheskie aspekty)' *Doklady Instituta Evropy RAN*, No. 42, 1998; Zhurkin, V.V., 'Evropeiskii soyuz: vneshnyaya politika, bezopasnost,' oborona' *Doklady Instituta Evropy RAN*, No. 47, 1998; Danilov, D.A., 'Rossiya v Bolshoi Evrope: strategiya bezopasnosti,' *Sovremennaya Evropa*, No. 2, 2000.

[13] Schmidt, P., 'ESDI: "Separable but not separate"?,' *NATO Review*, Vol. 48, No. 1., 2000, pp. 12–15; Heisbourg, F., "European defence takes a leap forward," *NATO Review*.

EU policy towards CIS, raised questions about the ability of a new Russian leader to seem effective in resolving foreign policy issues. Surprisingly, very soon relations between Moscow and Brussels reached the point of major disagreement. It is fair to say that in the beginning of 2004 both Russia and the European Union demonstrated some dissatisfaction with the general state of their relationship, as well as with each other's actions in specific situations.

As it has been mentioned above, the first signs of this discontent became apparent during discussions over Russia's Kaliningrad Region following the EU's enlargement. The controversy centered around the ability of Russian citizens to travel freely between the region and the Russian mainland. Russia and Europe realized for the first time that, despite the ambitious integration agenda, they not only spoke different languages but also failed to accept the intrinsic logic of each other's actions. Later, President Vladimir Putin sharply criticized the European Commission for its unyielding position at the talks on Russia's accession to the World Trade Organization. He accused the Brussels bureaucracy of "attempting to arm-twist Russia." Following this disagreement, there arose the diplomatic conflict over the settlement of the Transdniestria problem. That was the first time the Europeans clearly demonstrated to Moscow that it could no longer consider itself absolutely free in taking independent actions within the post-Soviet space.

Later on, this new trend was confirmed in Ukraine. Based on some very personal attitudes towards the leaders of Ukrainian opposition, the Russian government offered a substantial backing to the candidate supported by President Kuchma, Viktor Yanukovich. For its part, the EU clearly sympathized with the leader of opposition, Viktor Yushenko. After the second round of the presidential elections, when the opposition took the streets of Kiev, the EU gave assistance and soon became a major interlocutor between the authorities and opposition. As a result, the Ukrainian question overshadowed the Russia—EU summit on November 25, 2004, and did not make it the most friendly one.

Against this background, attempts are being made in the European Union to revise the basic parameters of its relations with Russia. In December 2003, the European Council instructed the Commission of the European Communities to assess the state of the EU's Russia pol-

icy and offer recommendations on how to improve it. The EU
Council of Ministers was asked to consider the Commission's proposals and make its conclusions. The European Parliament decided to
formulate its own position as well.

These efforts resulted in three documents approved by the EU offi-
cial bodies: a report of the European Parliament Committee on
Foreign Affairs, Human Rights, Common Security and Defense
Policy; Communication from the Commission to the Council and the
European Parliament on Relations with Russia; and Conclusions of
the European Council on Relations with Russia.[14]

These documents clearly differ from each other in tone. The
European parliamentarians gave an unambiguously negative assessment on the run up to and the results of Russia's State Duma elections, the settlement process in the Chechen Republic and the
question of human rights there, the status of mass media and law
enforcement practices in Russia, and Moscow's role in Transcaucasia
and Moldova. The report pointed out that "Chechnya is not only an
'internal affair' to Russia because violations of human rights are self-
evidently threats to international security." The report drew special
attention to Russia's reluctance to extend the 1994 Agreement with
the EU to the countries in Central and Eastern Europe that were to
join the European Union, and to Russia's delay in ratifying border
treaties with Latvia and Estonia. Finally, the parliamentarians called
for a better coordination of actions by individual states and pan-
European institutions with respect to Russia.

---

[14] The three documents are:

1) European Parliament 1999-2004 Session Document (FINAL A5-0053/2004), Report
with a proposal for a European Parliament recommendation to the Council on EU-Russia
relations (2003/2230(INI)), Committee on Foreign Affairs, Human Rights, Common
Security and Defence Policy - Rapporteur: Bastiaan Belder, February 2, 2004. Available at
http://www2.europarl. eu.int/omk/sipade2?PUBREF=-//EP//NONSGML+REPORT+A5-
2004-0053+0

2) Communication from the Commission to the Council and the European Parliament
on Relatons with Russia (COM (2004) 106), February 9, 2004. Available at
http://europa.eu.int/comm/external_relations/russia/russia_docs/com04_106_en.pdf

3) Council of the European Union, Brussels European Council 25 and 26 March 2004 -
Presidency Conclusions (POLGEN20 CONCL1), Brussels, May 19, 2004. Available at
http://ue.eu.int/ueDocs/cms_Data/docs/pressData/en/ec/79696.pdf

The Communication document contained much less emotional assessments of Russia's internal developments and relations with the EU. In particular, the Commission stressed the need to continue with the dialogue on the creation of four common spaces. At the same time, the document drew attention to the latest elections to the State Duma and an assessment by the OSCE and the Council of Europe. It restated concern over the human rights situation in the Chechen Republic.

The Commission proposed a more efficient policy for protecting the basic interests of the European Union. These were the ratification of the Kyoto Protocol, maritime and nuclear safety, and readmission negotiations fostering the Russian side to agree on reciprocal cooperation over the return of illegal residents to their country of origin. These agreements form part of the European Union's broader aim of developing a balanced, coherent and common approach towards immigration and asylum, the facilitation of humanitarian aid delivery, the ratification of border agreements with Latvia and Estonia, the extension of the PCA to the countries that are to join the EU, Siberian over flight payments, cooperation in the exploration of outer space, energy sector reform, and Russian safeguard measures. The Commission intends to improve the coordination of the EU members' policy vis-à-vis Russia.

The Commission recommended the EU Council "move away from grand political declarations and establish an issues-based strategy and agenda." The Euro-bureaucrats pointed out that "Russian practices run counter to universal and European values," as well as to the basic goals of cooperation. The Communication proposed "drawing up an objectives paper for Summits, which should clearly draw 'red lines' for the EU, positions, beyond which the EU will not go," and presenting a "draft joint Action Plan to Russia covering all four [common] spaces."

However, the final word belonged to the EU Council, which met in Brussels on February 23, 2004, in the foreign ministers format. The Council's conclusions expressed the EU's resolve to build "a genuine strategic partnership with Russia based on equal rights and obligations, mutual trust and an open and frank dialog." It also stated that the EU "has a strong and genuine interest in an open, stable and democratic Russia."

The Council said the European Union is "open to discuss any of Russia's legitimate concerns over the impact of (EU) enlargement," but added that "this shall remain entirely separate from PCA extension." The Council pointed to the need to identify and formulate EU interests, objectives and priorities in its dialog with Russia.

All the three official documents expressed dissatisfaction with the state of EU-Russia relations, criticized the EU's ability to conduct a single and well-coordinated policy vis-à-vis Russia, and recognized the need to continue the course toward Russia's integration through joint long-term projects, such as the creation of four common spaces.

In contrast with the EU's previous official statements, the documents call on the European Union to build relations with Russia on the basis of an increased rationalism, proceeding primarily from its own interests. Until recently, the EU official bodies did not mention EU interests as the basis for their negotiating positions. On the contrary, the EU always emphasized a community of interests between the European Union and Russia.

In other words, this new approach of the EU is of a dual nature. On the one hand, the dissatisfaction is accompanied by the desire to improve and develop, rather than freeze, its relations with Russia. On the other hand, the EU has already shown signs of a readiness to decrease the significance of this mutual relationship; a diplomatic conflict is not out of the question should events not develop in accordance with the EU's scenario.

## Russia and "The Ring of Friends"

This new policy is a part of a wider EU agenda of developing relations with its neighbors. In March 2003, the European Commission presented a communication entitled "Wider Europe—Neighbourhood: A New Framework for Relations with our Eastern and Southern Neighbours" for consideration by EU heads of state. The document in question is the result of a joint initiative by the EU Commissioner for External Relations, Chris Patten, and the EU High Representative for Common Foreign and Security Policy, Javier Solana, and is supposed to stipulate the basic outline and strategic parameters for expanding EU policy in relation to those neighbouring countries that are not regarded as candidates for accession.

An examination of the European Commission's proposals shows that, even before completing the process of its own enlargement, the EU set about establishing a circle of friends closest to its borders that, although formally independent, will nonetheless have to assimilate the lion's share of European rules and legal standards. It is no secret that the more detailed development of the "ring-of-friends" idea (first proposed by the President of the European Commission, Romano Prodi and possibly inspired by "Lord of the Rings" movie appeared just shortly before)[15] also presupposes tangible conditions for such relations. These include the fulfilment of a series of EU requirements and the reformation of the national economies and political systems of the partner countries on the basis of these demands. By way of reward, the especially worthy would be granted access to the EU common market and the opportunity to enjoy fundamental European freedoms of movement (of goods, services, persons and capital).

For its part, Moscow has advanced the idea of building up a strategic partnership between Russia and the EU in the climate of a multipolar world. In Russia's opinion, such a partnership could entail working together in the international security arena, increasing the export of Russian energy resources to Europe and stimulating the investment process. However, the EU has not yet reached the state of internal unity necessary for a responsible foreign policy. As a result, most attempts to establish a military and political dialogue with Moscow are limited to tactical cooperation between Russia and certain influential EU countries. Furthermore, the poor compatibility of the political and economic systems of Russia and Europe make it difficult to lay the economic foundations for such a strategic partnership.

Striving to put forward a model of "special partnership," which was not included in the concept of Wider Europe, led Moscow to propose the concept of "common spaces" at the EU—Russia Summit in St. Petersburg in May 2003. Moscow responded after French President J. Chirac suggested establishing four "common spaces" between Russia and Europe: a common economic space, a common justice and home affairs space, a common security space, and a common education space. This way of constructing bilateral relations should potentially

---

[15] Romano Prodi, "Building our future together," European Parliament, Strasburg, 10 February 2004.

make a distinction between Russia and other "new neighbours" of the enlarged EU.

## Endgame: A Strategic Choice to be Made

Indeed, the strategic choice Russia faces is extremely simple: it can either become a satellite of a renewed and vibrant Europe or an equal partner. Unlike the United States, Russia cannot limit its relations with the European Union to trade alone, however successful that may be, without going deeper to integrational relations. The vast extent of their common border, Europeans' interest in Russia's resources, their concerns over non-military threats emanating from the East and the democratic expansionism of the European Union—all these will inevitably lead both parties toward closer relations. Moreover, Russia is tied to Europe by a common cultural heritage, and neither the United States, with its global interests, nor a dynamic China can offer Russia more beneficial economic and political alternatives than Europe.

In the 1990s relations between Russia and the European Union were not clearly defined. This can be explained by the fact that the partners themselves were undergoing internal transformations: The European Union was preparing to enlarge and was therefore revising its legislation, while Russia was witnessing a change in socioeconomic relations, forming a new political regime and developing new ways of acting on the international scene. Although the Partnership and Cooperation Agreement between the Russian Federation and the European Union was signed back in 1994 and entered into force in 1997, the quality of bilateral relations has not yet given grounds for optimism. Furthermore, the lack of progress in mutual economic relations, the huge asymmetry in the balance of trade and occasional diplomatic wrangles show that Russia and the European Union have yet to agree on a common agenda. As of 2004, Russia had developed a regime that some analysts characterize as authoritarian state capitalism reliant on bureaucracy. However, the possibility that this might change, turning in one direction or another in the coming decade, should not be ruled out. What Russia will become in ten years is still an open question.

The European Union, for its part, is gradually changing in appearance and substance. The united Europe has been working steadily toward a common Constitution. In May 2004 eight states of Central and Eastern Europe, as well as Cyprus and Malta, became full-fledged members of the EU, and in 2007 Bulgaria and Romania will join them. The EU has established a virtual protectorate in the Balkans.

It is clear that the European Union is now at a critical juncture with the sharp increase in membership and the attempt to advance toward a federal model of organization. Several outward manifestations of these processes have led some critics to warn of a crisis and even an end to the integration process. But such alarmist observations are hardly worth taking seriously.

It is possible to point out several internal and external characteristics of a united Europe that are not likely to change in the coming decade. First, the Europeans will remain committed to the principle of bringing their legislation closer in line as a more advanced instrument for cooperation than just trade. The Europeans believe that drawing partners' legislation and regulations closer to EU laws is a natural and integral part of constructive relations.

Second, despite growing military and political integration, an enlarged Europe will continue to resolve disputes by peaceful means and exert pressure through economic influence. The success of European foreign policy will largely depend on the extent of economic ties and interdependence.

Third, by expanding the common market to 25-27 countries, Brussels's role as coordinator will slowly but steadily increase. Despite resistance from national bureaucracies and the conservative mood of average citizens, the course toward removing internal barriers will result in Brussels's increasing responsibility for the administration of Europe, and its significance in the foreign policy of a united Europe will grow. Fourth and finally, Brussels will retain the trademark inflexibility that has at times elicited the unconcealed irritation of the Russians and the Americans. This unwieldiness, however, is an objective result of the complex internal organization of the EU and the need to find agreement among many varying interests as common policies are developed.

In the coming years, the European Union will strive for a dominant position in the western part of the post-Soviet space, proposing closer forms of cooperation with Belarus (after Lukashenko leaves the political scene), Moldova and Ukraine, which would enable these countries to raise the issue of formally entering the EU within ten to fifteen years.

The democratic expansionism of the European Union in the East is rife with the potential for serious conflicts with Russia. Under the current regime, Moscow considers the CIS directly in its sphere of interests and will view the interference of Europeans as an openly hostile act. In the near term, there could very well be serious clashes surrounding the settlement of the conflict in the Transdniestria region. For the EU, the self-proclaimed republic has become a convenient testing ground for new instruments of military and political integration. If the Europeans begin putting on the pressure for a solution of the Transdniestria problem, their discussions with Moscow could quickly become even more heated than the well-known dispute over transit through Kaliningrad. However, even an acute diplomatic conflict is unlikely to impede the growth of the EU's influence in the western part of the CIS and the movement of the three above-named post-Soviet states toward some form of integration with Europe.

Russia will remain an onlooker in this process. The model of preparations for full-fledged membership in the EU, which has worked so well with the countries of Eastern and Central Europe, does not apply in Russia's case. Furthermore, Russia is not separated from Europe by natural barriers as are the United States or states of the Middle East or North Africa. Russia will hardly be able to limit its relations with the EU to trade, but the patronizing model of cooperation that Europe has adopted with respect to the Maghreb and is expected to adopt in the Middle East will not suit Moscow either. Russia has never been a colony of any European country; on the contrary, it once controlled part of the present territory of the European Union.

The prospects for bilateral relations will largely depend on an extremely important component—energy. In the medium-term, Russia will remain the largest supplier of energy resources, foremost among them natural gas, which is becoming increasingly important in the 21st century. However hard the Europeans try to find alternative energy resources and to diversify their sources of supply in terms of geography, the Russian share of energy supplies on the European market is unlikely to decrease. And for Russia as well, the countries of the EU will remain virtually irreplaceable customers, given, first of all, that the infrastructure for supply has already been established; second, neither the Russian government nor domestic private business has sufficient means to develop production of liquefied gas; and, third, there are no players on the international market with the same purchasing power as the Europeans.

Given the immediate geographic proximity and scale of potential non-military threats from the East, the Europeans would hardly risk excluding Russia from its immediate sphere of influence or, as European Commission president Romano Prodi put it, from the "circle of friends" of a united Europe. By its very nature, the EU objectively strives to develop a special international environment where integration partners receive compensation for the partial renunciation of their state sovereignty in the form of advantages resulting from access to the common market.

With respect to Russia, a distinctive model of integrational relations is likely to emerge, and those relations will be formed in the coming decade. The essence of this model will depend above all on the domestic evolution of Russia itself.

## Basic Prerequisites

Democratic countries delegate aspects of their sovereignty; authoritarian ones sell theirs in exchange for various kinds of material and moral support to the state as a whole or to some of its representatives. The main question Russia will face in ten years with respect to its relations with the European Union concerns the terms on which Moscow will agree to renounce part of its sovereign rights in exchange for some measure of integration. Theoretically, two scenarios for closer ties are now possible. The first of them resembles the current model of relations between the European Union and Norway.

For a variety of reasons, Norway is not ready to enter the EU, although it meets all the criteria for membership. The compromise solution: in 1992, the European Union signed an agreement with the

European Free Trade Association (EFTA), comprising Norway, Iceland and Liechtenstein, on the creation of a European free trade area. Under the terms of the agreement, the partner states were obliged to adopt a lion's share of European law domestically, and in exchange the EU would grant them free movement of goods, persons, capital and services. The European Union benefits more from this, but compared with other EU partners—such as Switzerland, Turkey, the countries of North Africa and the CIS—it is the Norwegians who have retained the most rights and opportunities to defend their interests in Brussels. For them, many formal and informal channels through which to influence the drafting and adoption of decisions have remained open. It should be emphasized that both within the EU and in its relations with nearby countries, the decisive role in protecting the players' sovereign rights is played by the opportunities afforded to their own civil society and business communities.

If Russia, in the coming years, develops according to the optimistic scenario, Europe will have a chance to use the Norwegian model in its relations with Moscow, albeit with some adjustments. If, however, the country adopts an authoritarian regime, ties with the EU would take on an alternative less attractive form. On one hand, authoritarianism would be accompanied by a decrease in the role of the legislative branch, and consequently the weakening of democratic oversight over national foreign policy. But on the other hand, an authoritarian government would be forced to cooperate with the European Union—not just for the sake of Russia's modernization but for its very preservation. The only place that can provide Russia with the necessary resources and technology is Europe, so it is only a question of the price to be paid.

An undemocratic government that restricts the opportunities for private enterprise and carries out populist social policies will hardly be able to mobilize sufficient internal resources for the development of resource-production sectors. Meanwhile, maintaining the necessary volume of energy supplies and the development of new fields and deposits require considerable funding. Given such conditions, the reinforcement of bureaucratic control over foreign trade will reduce its transparency and most likely lead to a veiled "sale of the homeland." Furthermore, the EU would be sure to criticize Russia's domestic policy, which would compel the Russian authorities occasionally to "buy off" the Europeans, granting them new assets and rights on the cheap without the knowledge of the general public. Therefore, the state of Russian-European relations ten years from now will depend on whether Russia turns into a democratic country with a market economy during that period or not. If it does, relations with a united Europe would be on an equal footing and based on Russia's delegation of some of its sovereign rights to Brussels. If, on the contrary, authoritarian trends prevail, Russia could effectively find itself becoming a satellite of the EU, with virtually no rights. Some form of integration between Russia and Europe is inevitable; its terms, however, are for Russians themselves to choose.

## Chapter 8

# The Larger EU and the New In-Between Lands: Ukraine and Belarus

Nicolae Idu

## Introduction

Belarus and Ukraine were the Slavic heart of the former Soviet Union, but Russia was and still is, economically and politically, the most influential neighbor. Alexander Lukashenko, the current Belarus president, was re-elected in 2004 and succeeded in getting a referendum passed to change the Constitution to let him rule on until 2015. In Ukraine, the former President Leonid Kuchma tried to find a safe successor to win the elections for the presidency in November 2004. While some of Leonid Kuchma's opponents faced all sorts of bureaucratic and legal "obstacles," Lukashenko's rivals just simply disappeared.

In the old member states of the European Union (EU) there is a deep-rooted perception that these countries are geographically in Europe, but mentally and culturally not, except, somehow, the western part of Ukraine. They are typical transition countries.[1] The public institutions are weak, creating in the people a deeply ingrained distrust of the state and political parties. The education system has preserved the collectivist mentality, which is consistently reflected at the level of the decision makers. One can add to this the lack of independence of the judiciary and a deficit of transparency in the government and political structures. The media is controlled or influenced by the state by different means. Entry into the media market is restricted. The emerging civil society structures are not able to exercise control over government activities or to influence them. In economic terms,

---

[1] Romanchuk, Jaroslav—*Integration challenges for Belarus, Ukraine, Moldova . . .* , September 2003, http://liberty-belarus.org/english

these countries are still facing big structural problems, low competitiveness of the real sector combined with backward financial institutions. On top of this, corporate management is weak, while marketing, intellectual property rights and customer protection are minimal. Powerful lobbyists who were in the former communist party are active in the front lines of the new politics.

For the time being, however, the squalor on Europe's Eastern frontier poses a dismal prospect for the West. Both Ukraine and Belarus are weapons markets for the worst sort of customer and provide transit for just about everything the West wants to keep at bay. While the United States (US) succeeded in substantially improving its relations with Russia, Western policy towards Ukraine and Belarus in the past ten years has been much less successful, though Ukraine has managed at least to maintain its independence from Russia.[2] In spite of these common features, Ukraine and Belarus have, each of them, their own peculiarities and objectives. Therefore, they do relate differently to the EU and perceive the impact of EU enlargement accordingly.

## Who Are They, Ukraine and Belarus?

Ukraine is the largest country in Eastern Europe outside Russia, and its success or failure affects the whole region. Despite the western media's gloomy reports, scores of foreign investors already have been successful in Ukraine, raising interest in the prospects for growth in the medium term. Considered to be the next "tsunami to hit Europe,"[3] Ukraine is a big, undeveloped market, but with a promising investment perspective. In addition, companies have opened production facilities here and are exporting to Russia or Eastern Europe. However, after 1990, only $5 billion was invested in Ukraine, a tenth of the amount that has flooded neighbor Poland in the same period. Most of this sum is not even genuine foreign direct investment (FDI), but is repatriated capital routed through offshore tax havens. That is why Cyprus ranks as Ukraine's second largest source of foreign cash (see Table 1).

---

[2] *Sour Slavs in the slow lane, Kiev and Minsk*, from *The Economist* Print Edition, May 30, 2002.

[3] Rathbone, Sharon—*The next best thing*, EUROINVEST, Autumn, 2003.

**Table 1. Sources of Ukraine FDI (1992—2002, percent)**

| | |
|---|---:|
| USA | 16.6 |
| Cyprus | 10.4 |
| UK | 9.5 |
| Netherlands | 8.4 |
| Russia | 7.2 |
| Germany | 5.7 |
| Virgin Islands | 5.6 |
| Other | 36.6 |

Source: Dragon Capital, State Office for Statistics

According to World Bank, which took into consideration both the political and the business climate, the protecting investors index in Ukraine for 2004 is scored at 3.0, compared with the regional score of 3.6 and the Organisation for Economic Co-operation and Development (OECD) score of 5.6 (the index varies between zero and seven).[4]

Ukraine produced a third of the Soviet Union's steel, nearly half its iron ore, over half its sugar and was considered to be the breadbasket of Europe. Following independence, a World Bank report even said that it had the potential to become "one of the richest countries in the world."[5] With its rich soil and vast open spaces, agriculture still represents about 65 percent of Ukraine's gross domestic product (GDP). The emerging banking sector has around 150 active banks, of which two are state owned (savings bank Oschadny and UkrExImbank) and seven are wholly-owned Western banks (including Credit Lyonnais Bank Ukraine, ING, Citibank, Raiffeisen Bank and HVB).

Ukraine's true oil and gas potential is not really assessed, current production being marginal. In the wake of the Chernobyl disaster, Ukraine still relies heavily on nuclear energy. The European Bank for Reconstruction and Development (EBRD) is to make finance available for two further nuclear power plant units. Ukraine's current power capacity is twice as high as peak demand, according to Central and Eastern European (CEE) Bankwatch network, 2000. Therefore,

---

[4] Snapshot of Business Environment—*Ukraine*, World Bank, 2004. Doing Business Environment—*Ukraine* and *Belarus*, September 2004, http://www.worldbank.org/DoingBusiness/ExploreEconomies/BusinessClimatesSnapshot.aspx?economy=19

[5] Beichman, Arnold—Who Lost Ukraine?, The Washington Times, October 2, 1998, pag.121, at http://www.ukr.org/beichm01.html.

increasing nuclear energy production could be a key strategy for its future development. The new century has brought economic growth for the first time, with rising industrial output, improving exports, and falling inflation, and spells a promising future. According to the Ukrainian authorities, during the years 2000-2003, Ukraine has registered the average GDP annual increase at 7.2 percent, and that of industry at 15.1 percent. Labor productivity in the industries increased by 85.9 percent, and export of goods by 80 percent during the same period. 114 countries have invested in Ukraine. The most important investments were made by non-residents from the US—$1.019 billion (16.6 percent) and Cyprus—$647.6 million (10.4 percent).

In Ukraine, September 11 determined a pro-Western reorientation of the foreign policy. Until that moment, Ukraine had tried to balance between Russian interests and Western orientation. After Vladimir Putin had taken a more pro-Western attitude, the opportunities for Ukraine to orient its security policy toward the West also increased. Ukraine also declared its support for the US in combating terrorism. This attitude is a continuation of the relations with the Western security organizations, primarily North-Atlantic Treaty Organisation (NATO), which have, to date, already been quite constructive. In contrast to Russia, Ukraine welcomes NATO's Eastern enlargement, being, also, an active participant in co-operation within the framework of the Partnership for Peace (PfP) program. Even officially Ukraine is very much orientated toward strengthening Western co-operation and integration, internal weakness makes its foreign policy contradictory. American-Ukrainian relations have been in the most serious crisis since Ukrainian independence because of a secret tape-recording of president Kuchma from July 2000, apparently authorizing the sale of the Kolchuga early-warning radar system to Iraq. The downing in October 2001 of a passenger aircraft coming from Israel over the Black Sea during Ukrainian army manoeuvres was a sign of weak command and control.

Belarus or "White Russia" has a fairly high standard of living in comparison to other states in the region. Private business, however, is virtually non-existent. Foreign investors avoid this market and even Moscow was disappointed with Belarus' evolution in recent years. President Lukashenko embarked on a move towards authoritarian rule in 1996 by a reform of the 1994 Constitution, which led to concentrating powers heavily around the president. Democratic conditions were undermined in particular by the replacement of the democratically elected parliament with a national assembly nominated by the president, but also by a brutal approach to the opposition and the media, and interference with the judiciary. A key element to understanding Lukashenko's success and the failure of democracy is the lack of history and tradition of Belarussian statehood and national identity.[6] Belarus is now the only European successor state of the former USSR without a ratified Partnership and Co-operation Agreement (PCA) with the EU. The EU tightened sanctions against Belarus after Western observers reported that the parliamentary election and referendum organized on October 17, 2004, fell "significantly short" of international standards. They underlined that the authorities largely disregarded democratic principles. Official results showed 77.3 percent of registered voters supported the referendum, though an independent exit poll by Gallup suggested that just under half had voted for the extension of President Lukashenko's mandate.[7] In response, the US Congress passed in October 2004, the Belarus Democracy Act 2004, which calls for funding of the Belarussian opposition and economic sanctions against the state.

In 2003 Belarus' economy posted 6.1 percent growth and continued expanding through 2004, albeit at a slower growth rate. High inflation, persistent trade deficits, and ongoing rocky relations with Russia, Belarus' largest trading partner and energy supplier, hampered it. Belarus has seen little structural reform since 1995, when President Lukashenko launched the country on the path of "market socialism." Lukashenko re-imposed administrative controls over prices and currency exchange rates and expanded the state's right to intervene in the management of private enterprises. Belarus retained its self-imposed isolation from the West and its open-market economies. Its policy towards the West is isolationist and confrontational.[8] 1997 boundary treaty with Ukraine remains unratified over unresolved financial claims, preventing demarcation and diminishing border security;

---

[6] Davidomis, Ramunas, *The challenge of Belarus and European responses*, EU-ISS Occasional Paper, July 29, 2001, at http://aci.pitt.edu/archive/00000696

[7] Wheeler, Carolynne, *Belarus faces EU wrath for disputed poll result*, in Guardian Unlimited, October 19, 2004, at: http://www.guardian.co.uk/russia/article

[8] Shushkevich, Stanislav, *Belarus: Statehood and Security*, presentation at Harvard University, Davis Center for Russian Studies, April 17, 2000, at: www.daviscenter.fas.hardvard.edu/seminars-conferences

boundaries with Latvia and Lithuania remain undemarcated despite European Union financial support. In economically weak Belarus, for which the transition is torturous, trafficking in the material of the Soviet army has become a profitable business. Belarus hit the headlines in the autumn of 2001, when it was discovered that when it had sold weapons to rogue states, such as Iraq.

## Strategic Relevance of Ukraine and Belarus

Including Romania, the new EU Eastern border from Narva on the Baltic Sea to the Danube Delta on the Black Sea will add 3700 km of frontier with Russia, Belarus, Ukraine and Moldova to the current 1470 km of Finnish-Russian border. Diseases, drugs and the smuggling of migrants and prostitutes from the western side of the former Soviet Union are a running sore. A "green corridor" for smugglers leads from Ukraine's notoriously corrupt port of Odessa to Riga in Latvia. By using the estimates of Belarussian experts, at the present time there are from 100,000 to 200,000 illegal immigrants on the territory of Belarus who aim to reach the West.

With respect to the strategic interest in the energy supply to West, one could underline the Ukrainian oil pipeline transit system consisting of two main pipelines (Druzhba 1450 km and Prydniprovski 1540 km) with an export capacity of more than 100 million tons per year in 2002. Despite this capacity, the amount of crude oil shipped through Ukraine to Central Europe is decreasing. As a component of this system, the construction of the Odessa-Brody-Plock Oil Pipeline started in 1995 with technical assistance from the EU and the official opening tooking place in 2001. The pipeline is expected to handle oil supplies from the Caucasus and the Middle East (projected capacity 14.5 million tons per year). The Polish and the Ukrainian governments plan a further extension of the pipeline to Plock, in Poland. This connection pipeline is approximately 500 km in length, with 100 km in Ukraine. It would create a link to refineries in Poland and permit oil to be exported from the petroleum terminals in Poland and Germany as well as supplying refineries in Germany, Slovak Republic and Czech Republic, via the northern and southern branches of the Druzhba pipeline. The project would have several advantages:[9]

---

[9] http://www.ukraine-eu.mfa.gov.ua

- It could strengthen the security of supply of Ukraine and Central Europe, in particular the new EU member states Poland, Slovak Republic and Czech Republic;

- It could contribute to safe and secure transportation of oil from the Caspian Basin and the Russian Federation while avoiding the increase of oil maritime traffic in the Bosphorus and the Black Sea as well as related risks of accidents;

- It would support the European Commission's policy to increase environmental standards.

President Viktor Yushchenko underline that Odessa-Brody pipeline extension is important for the whole Europe, having an "enormous significance" in diversifying Europe's energy supply sources and transport options by using Caspian oil and Ukrainian transit route.[10]

The EU and Belarus are direct neighbors with a common border of more than 1000 kilometers. Belarus is the main land transit route from the EU to Moscow and to Russia in general. Any transit through Belarus is 1.5 times shorter than the transit route through neighboring countries. Belarus, Poland and Ukraine are obviously the most important countries for the western EU members from the point of view of energy transit. Belarus has the strategic Yamal-Europe gas pipeline on its territory. The largest system of the Druzhba oil pipeline is also situated on its territory. It is supposed to build a new gas pipeline, Kobrin-Velke-Kapushany through Belarus and Poland to the Western Europe.

On top of the economic aspects, the most important strategic element related to Belarus is its foreign and security policy designed in close relationship with Russian Federation's interests, as was clearly illustrated during the Kosovo crisis. There are, also, two Russian military bases on its territory.[11] Belarus provides to the connection between the borders of East European states and Russia, and the land link between the Russian enclave of Kaliningrad and the rest of the Russian Federation. Belarus' position means that there is not a

---

[10] Socor, Vladimir—*Surge of Interest in Odessa-Brody Oil Pipeline*, Eurasia Daily Monitor, March 17, 2005.

[11] Marple, David R., *Belarus a Denationalized Nation*, Harwood Academic Publishers, 1999.

Baltic—Black Sea belt of western oriented countries around Russia. There are two explanations for this situation. One is related to ethno-nationalism, because Russians and Belarussians share the same values and mentality, and practice the same religion, Orthodox Christianity.[12] The other one is the economic factor. The economy of Belarus was one of the most integrated in the Soviet system. After gaining inde-pendence, the country was not able to gain access to the markets of other countries and was extremely dependent on energy resources from Russia. Through these factors, Belarus enforces the geopolitical position of Russia.

The risks concentrated in the post-Soviet territories generated by illegal migration, cross-border crime, drug trafficking, smuggling and corruption can have direct impact on the West as long as Ukraine and Belarus are permeable buffers between the two regions.[13] Non-demar-cated and mostly uncontrolled borders such as the one between Russia and Ukraine are a fertile breeding ground for these problems. In addi-tion, as the former Soviet empire had expanded up to the borders of Afghanistan, the resulting borders provide direct contact with a source of Islamic fundamentalism. Arms or drug trafficking and the risk of conflicts spilling over neighboring regions are latent threats, which are difficult to measure.

## Strategies and Attitudes Related to EU

Ukraine and Belarus have significantly different visions regarding their present and future relationships with the EU. Although Belarus is not looking for a close and integrative link with Western Europe due to the incompatibility of its political and economic system with the EU values and model, Ukraine has even expressed, rather incon-sistently, its wish to join, at a certain moment, the Union, but lacking achievements in Europeanizing its legal and institutional system.

Ukraine's three strategic priorities are forging closer ties with NATO (with which it already has a special deal), with the EU, and

---

[12] Davidomis, Ramunas, *ibid.*

[13] Zagorski, Andrei, *EU Policies Towards Russia, Ukraine, Moldova and Belarus*, Geneva Center for Security Policy, Occasional Paper Series, No.35, http://www.gcsp.ch/e/publications/occ-papers/35-zagorski.pdf

getting into the World Trade Organization (WTO). Kiev has further specified these goals in a roadmap included in the conception of the socioeconomic development of the country for the period 2002-2011.[14] The latter envisaged that, by 2004, Ukraine was supposed to finalize the negotiations of an association agreement with the EU to replace the PCA of 1994, and complete negotiations on the introduction of free trade area, which din not happen. By the year 2007, the domestic legislation of Ukraine shall be harmonized with the EU requirements in key areas and a customs union shall be established. In the years 2007-2011, the association agreement should be fully implemented, and Ukraine should meet the Copenhagen criteria thus becoming ripe for full EU membership. Since 2002, former foreign minister Anatoly Zlenko pledged, as many others did, that a clear commitment of Ukraine to prospective membership would be an important motivation to boost domestic reforms: "we speak about a clear landmark to which Ukraine could direct its efforts now."[15] For the time being, Kiev looks for a sort of an association agreement that has been concluded by Turkey in 1961. But, Brussels avoids taking a clear stand, providing a sort of 'positive ambiguity.'

Both the government and the main opposition of Ukraine advocate joining the EU and developing ties with Europe rather than with Russia.[16] But, as with Russia, many are wary of Ukraine's sheer size. A Ukraine-EU Troika meeting in April 2004, dealt a blow to Ukraine's European aspiration when the EU ministers failed to grant market economy status to Ukraine. For the time being, Ukraine will most likely develop some sort of intermediate relation with the EU,[17] even it is strongly backed by all major political forces in Poland, a member state with strong historical ties with Ukraine (through the Polish-Lithuanian Commonwealth).

---

[14]The Address of the President of Ukraine to the Supreme Rada of *Ukraine*. The European Vocation. The conceptual basis of the strategy of the social-economic development of Ukraine in 2002–2011, http://www.kuchma.gov.ua/main/?sp/index

[15]Statement of Anatoly Zlenko, Minister for Foreign Affairs of *Ukraine*, at the conference of East-West Institute "European Home is a Home for *Ukraine*," Kiev, April 27, 2002.

[16]Emerson, Michael—*Vade Mecum for the Next Enlargements of the European Union*, CEPS Policy Brief, No.61, December 2004, http://www.ceps.be

[17]Ferrero-Walder, Benito—*Article on Ukraine*, 19 February 2005, at: http://www.delukr.cec.eu.int/site

Anyhow, public attitudes are changing. According to a survey conducted by the Ukrainian Center for Economic and Political Studies in September 2001, 32 percent of Ukrainians believed that European integration was a priority for Ukraine, while 41 percent chose ever-closer co-operation with Russia. By 2004, according to some Ukranian parliamentarians, 50 percent of the population was supporting the EU membership for Ukraine.

Analysts seem to share the view that Ukraine's weak position in promoting its European integration aspirations results from inconsistent and slow domestic reform; domination of political declarations over practical implementation of Ukraine-EU documents; weakness of administrative and institutional support for Ukraine's European integration ambitions; lack of expertise on European integration processes in the government. Key challenges are seen as a lack of coordination and coherence in the actions of state institutions with regard to European integration efforts and lack of institutional capacity, as well as lack of public interest, awareness, support and demand for European integration.[18]

By July 2004, Ukraine has apparently abandoned its goal of joining NATO in a sign of its growing tilt towards Russia. The former Ukrainian President, Leonid Kuchma, signed a decree ordering changes in the country's defense doctrine to remove reference to membership in the EU and NATO as the ultimate goal of Ukraine's foreign policy. But, the new President Viktor Yushchenko reintroduced these objectives into the national strategy. Previously, after repeated refusals, Ukraine finally signed up to a Single Economic Zone pact with Russia, Kazakhstan and Belarus. The accord provides for a customs union, free movement of goods, capital and labor, and common tax, monetary and foreign trade policy. For Belarus, signing this document meant keeping its already known foreign policy direction, while for Ukraine this was a new demonstration of lack of coherence and systematic approach in defining its foreign policy priorities. Under these conditions, for example, it will be difficult to imagine the creation of a free trade zone between Ukraine and EU. The 'unification' of legislation, which is a final aim of this ongoing agreement, renders impossible the harmonization with the European legislation.

---

[18] Pidluska, Irina, *EU Relations: Enlargement and Integration*, http://www.policy.hu/pidluska/EU-*Ukraine*.html

Belarus, which is increasingly dependent on bilateral co-operation with Russia, its main partner, does not have a wider policy choice either. Its agenda is currently to keeping good relations with Ukraine, Poland and Lithuania as well as with Russia and to seeking normalization of relations with the EU, Council of Europe and the Organisation for Security and Co-operation in Europe (OSCE) Parliamentary Assembly. Taking into consideration the extension of the EU, the authorities of Minsk started to emphasize the need of a 'rapprochement' with the European Union.[19]

For the Belarusian regime the stakes were too high. The linkage between the progress in domestic reforms and progress in co-operation with the EU (including the provision of technical assistance), has failed to reach the objectives.[20] Belarus went on the way of an authoritarian regime, despite the crucial importance of its trade with the European Union. The EU (and Germany within the EU) is not only the second biggest trade partner for the country, but the main source of hard currency income and of the modernization of Belarusian industrial enterprises. In 2001, the country's trade turnover with the EU came to only 37 percent of its total trade turnover with non Commonwealth of Independent States (CIS) countries.[21]

## The EU Policy Towards Ukraine and Belarus

The European Commission has approved on December 9, 2004, special agreements with Israel, Ukraine, Moldova, Morocco, Tunisia, Jordan and the Palestinian Authority with the goal to spread stability on the EU borders. Talks to expand the policy to cover Egypt, Lebanon, Armenia, Azerbaijan and Georgia started in February 2005. This is concrete expression of the European Neighborhood Policy (ENP) developed by EU in order to promote close and constructive relations with its neighbors for whom accession is not a clear target, at least from the EU point of view. Thus, the EU is strongly interested in implementing

---

[19] Alekseyeva, Tatyana; Gordeychik, Alexandr; Dostanko, Elena—*The Interaction of the Republic of Belarus with the Leading European Organizations in the late 1990s*, Belarusian Journal of International Law and International Relations, Minsk, 2000, N 2.

[20] Svirko, Yuri, *Belarus presidential elections may not be recognized*, in Central Europe Review, Vol. 3, No. 5, 5 February, 2001.

[21] Source: COMEXT, Eurostat.

suitable strategic partnership[22] with *Ukraine*, Russia and Mediterranean Basin. These agreements have an important financial follow up.

In the past, the EU's technical and financial support for Ukraine and Belarus was marginal. Belarus was not a real target for this assistance for reasons related to its authoritarian regime. The Technical Assistance to Community of Independent States (TACIS) Indicative Program for the period 2000-2003, worth €5 million, was focusing on the development of civil society, the training of managers and educational exchanges. Still under the same program a further €5 million was allocated for 2003, targeting civil society and activities related to the effects of Chernobyl accident. Belarus made repeated requests in 2002 for additional assistance to its efforts in keeping illegal immigrants on its side of the border. EU support reached €16 million in 2001—2003 after these appeals.

For Ukraine, the EU was the largest donor over the last ten years, its total assistance amounted to €1.072 billion, while the member states disbursed, for example, only €157 million in the period 1996–1999. This consists of technical assistance through TACIS programme, macro-financial assistance, and humanitarian assistance. In the field of technical assistance, the Commission established a Country Strategy Paper for the purpose of setting out the overall policy objectives for TACIS planning for the period 2004—2006. If the EU assistance allocated to Belarus was negligeable, those allocated to Ukraine was at the modest level of €21 per inhabitant over the period mentioned above, few times less than the neighboring former or present candidate countries. An important part of this assistance has been devoted to environmental protection, particularly to minimize and eliminate the consequences of the Chernobyl accident. Therefore, the effectiveness and the impact of this assistance in reforming the country is definitely questionable. The other EU instruments the EU largely concentrate on the task of "bringing Ukraine in line with the legal frameworks of the single European market and the WTO system" with a prospective option of establishing a free trade regime.[23]

---

[22] Beatty, Andrew, *Brussels approves 'neighborhood' deals*, at http://www.euobserver.com/?aid=17950&print=1

[23] European Council Common Strategy of 11 December 1999 on *Ukraine* (1999/877/CFSP), L331/1

Meanwhile, the consensus of EU and member states with regard to the "soft security" threats envisioned after the enlargement of the EU were reflected in developing co-operation in the field of justice and home affairs as long as Ukraine is part of a large ex-Soviet zone where illegal migration and transnational organize crime, including trafficking in drugs and human beings are prevalent.

Though, the EU—Ukraine "strategic partnership" is an example of a misfortune relationship between the two entities, which seem to pursue different agendas. In 2002 EU enlargement Commissioner Gunter Verheugen said that "a European perspective" for Ukraine does not necessarily mean membership in ten or twenty years; however, that does not mean it is not a possibility. This gave a clear indication as regards the limits of EU policy on Ukraine. As reasons for the EU's lack of interest in Ukraine's accession, experts referred to the slow pace of democratization and economic, legal, institutional and administrative reform in Ukraine, the low quality and, hence, low competitiveness of the bulk of Ukraine-made goods and, finally, the fact that Ukraine's share in EU's foreign trade is very low. Conversely, the EU has replaced Russia as Ukraine's foremost commercial partner, with 35 percent of its external trade in 2003.

On February 21, 2005, a three-year action plan was signed between the EU and Ukraine to govern bilateral relations. It sets out the main areas of reform Ukraine needs to implement in order to meet EU standards. The areas covered range from safeguards to steel import quotas and a relaxed visa regime.[24] The agreement aims to facilitate the granting of market economy status to Ukraine. In this context, the action plan offers EU backing to Ukraine's bid to join the WTO. Under the pressure of the "Orange Revolution" that brought Viktor Yushchenko to power in Kiev, Ukraine reiterated that its long-term aim is to apply for full membership. However, the EU responded that Ukraine's accession to the EU was not a question for discussion, the ENP remaining the framework for the EU's relations with Kiev.

On the other hand, the EU has no common strategy on Belarus because it represents a political black spot for Europe. It would be possible to freeze all forms of contact and co-operation and cut aid

---

[24] *EU, Ukraine Sign Three-Year Action Plan*, Euractiv.com, February 22, 2005.

and assistance programs. By doing so, however, the West would completely lose the marginal influence and credibility on Belarus it still has. There would be no channels of communication left, and the relationship would deteriorate even further. In terms of positive-sum diplomacy, there are limits on what the EU can offer Belarus if the country keeps its current domestic and foreign policy orientation.[25] Belarus's trade with the West is rather insignificant, and Minsk is not seeking either EU or NATO membership. What type of attitude, therefore, should the different European institutions adopt towards Belarus? In November 2004, EU foreign ministers offered Belarus the prospect of a "gradual development of bilateral relations" if concrete moves are taken towards democratization. EU foreign ministers called President Lukaschenko's government to "reverse the present policies and to embark on fundamental democratic and economic reforms."[26] In return, the EU is offering increased trade and political ties as part of its ENP. The peculiarity of the situation in the EU-Belarusian relations implies, however, that the distortion of this relationship since the 1996 political crackdown has liberated both sides from the need to take any decision concerning the long-term policy options of Belarus in Europe. The authoritarian regime of Lukashenko is a good excuse for the EU not to be exposed to the question whether or not an eventual European vocation of Belarus, which would be logical in the context of its geographic location, should be given serious consideration.[27] The case of Belarus most explicitly reveals the weakness of the instruments so far available to the Common Foreign and Security Policy (CFSP).[28] Developing one single common strategy covering the EU's policy towards the non-candidate European Newly Independent States (NIS) situated to the west of Russia may miss the distinct problems that should be addressed in each specific case. EU policy towards the two countries was, and remains a work in progress, for the European Union itself, and the CFSP in particular. The underlying assumption of the EU policy towards the two countries in the early

---

[25] Davidomis, Ramunas, *ibid.*

[26] Beatty, Andrew, *EU to offer Belarus olive branch after rigged elections* at http://www.observer.com/?aid=17800&sid=9

[27] Alekseyeva, Tatyana; Gordeychik, Alexandr; Dostanko, Elena—*ibid* http://www.cenunst.unibel.by/journal/2002

[28] *The Forgotten Neighbor—Belarus in the Context of EU Enlargement to the East*, on the Future of Europe, Policy Paper 4, Stefan Bathory Foundation, Warsaw, 2001.

1990s was determined by the expectation that the Soviet successor states would form a relatively coherent group of countries around Russia within the framework of the CIS, never considering offering any of the NIS either membership, or any sort of association.[29] Instead of this, EU should treat Ukraine and Russia differently by decupling their strategic agendas for reasons related to their attitude on international policy. Russia wishes to be recognized as a great power, Ukraine does not. More than this, EU and Russia have different agendas in Ukraine.[30] The gap in mutual expectations of the developing co-operation between the EU and those NIS countries, which clearly articulate their reasons for membership, becomes the source of mutual frustration and controversy. This is especially true with regard to Ukraine. PCAs offered neither a prospective membership, nor any sort of association with the EU.[31] Pending substantial progress in transition, the most appropriate objective was to develop free trade with the EU. These provisions clearly distinguished the PCAs from the Europe Agreements with the former and current aspirant countries. And they differ in that respect from the Stabilization and Association Agreements currently considered for the Western Balkan. The EU is the second largest trade partner of these countries and this should place the EU in a special position.[32] The attempt of the EU to find a way out of this debate and to further diversify its relations with Belarus and Ukraine and offer a status of special neighbours, as proposed by the UK at EU summit meeting in Luxemburg on 15 April 2002, has only emphasized the concentration of Brussels on its 'soft security' concerns, and is unlikely to put an end to the continuing debate over EU membership. Ukraine wanted EU to adopt a new strategy, but definitely not the one that would put Kiev into the same position with Minsk and Chisinau.[33] The neighbor status, as proposed in Luxembourg, is rather an attempt to clarify the nature of relations with the new neighbors by reducing common interests only to prob-

---

[29] See: "The EU's relationship with the countries of Eastern Europe & Central Asia," available at: http://www.europa.eu.int/comm/external_relations/ceeca/index.htm

[30] Kuzio, Taras—*EU and Ukraine: a turning point in 2004?*, Occasional Papers, European Union Institute for Security Studies, Paris, 2003.

[31] Zagorski, Andrei—*ibid.*

[32] Dempsey, Judy—*Enlarged EU agrees new ties with neighbors—Moldova, Ukraine, Belarus,"* at http://www.europa.yam.ro/articles/2002/aprili

[33] European Council—*Common Strategy of 11 December 1999 on Ukraine*, L 331/2.

lems of migration, trade, and international crime.[34] From over the EU's Eastern border the perception is that the Wider Europe concept is the result of a member states multiple interests, and proposes to embrace the EU neighborhood policy and the competition occurring inside the EU regarding its priorities in geographical direction. At present, the EU's external relations are targeted on accession guidelines that are unilaterally fixed by Brussels, while the relations with countries that do not have clear prospects for membership must be based on mutual agreements. Cooperating in managing crises and security policy partnership with these countries should become an important priority for the EU given the new framework provided by the Constitutional Treaty.

## Russia's Influence

On the one hand, Russia, based on its common communist past with the two countries, is competing with the EU on exercising influence on Belarus and, mainly Ukraine. Russia continues to increase its control on Ukrainian economy. Ukraine currently imports 75 percent—80 percent of its oil, almost all of which comes from Russia. President Vladimir Putin has named a Russian former prime minister, and gas magnate, Viktor Chernomyrdin, as his ambassador to Ukraine, with the task of "strengthening economic ties." Kremlin-backed industrialists have been buying up Ukrainian industry on the cheap, with political influence part of the bargain.

On the other hand, Russia has broadly viewed Belarus as a loyal Slav ally and a political buffer against the West.[35] Nevertheless, when Russia joins the WTO, Belarus will be in no position to join the organization, but would suffer gravely without its customs union with Russia. Belarus, like most former Soviet states, has an active manufacturing export-oriented economy with an accent on high technologies. Belarus exports more than 55 percent of its GDP and 80 percent of industrial production. Approximately 180 enterprises of the Republic of Belarus and more than 250 Russian ones take part in joint programs.[36]

---

[34] *Ukraine*–European Union Summit, Yalta, 11 September 2001, Joint Statement, p.1.

[35] Lewis, A (edit), *The EU and Belarus: Between Moscow and Brussels*, Federal Trust, London, 2003.

[36] Antczak, R, Bogdankiewich, S, *Impact of the Russian Crisis on the Belorussian Economy*, Studies and Analyses no 206, CASE Foundation, Warsaw, 2002.

Notwithstanding, Russia seems to be sincerely interested in stabilizing its western neighboring areas for rather obvious reasons. On his attempt to build a strong Russia, Vladimir Putin is aware that not only the military component is important, but the economic one too. According to his vision, the unified economic area with the former soviet countries (Russia, Ukraine, Belarus and Kazakhstan) would be complementary with the common economic area agreed with the EU. Therefore, a closer Ukraine to the EU—even with a membership perspective—is supported by Russia. As a consequence the NATO-Russia Council meeting on December 9, 2004, addressed the situation in Ukraine in a joint statement, reiterating "our support for the independence, the sovereignty, the territorial integrity of and democracy in Ukraine."[37] Because the EU-Russia relationship improved, they could play a positive role in reaching the objectives established by the ENP for this zone. The common economic space between EU and Russia, a concept that was agreed upon in November 2003, has a relatively higher degree of relevance for the whole ENP zone of action, although it is still very much on paper.[38] The Russian attitude can provide both cooperative and competitive incentives for ENP in this area. Russian officials publicly confirmed Russia's commitment to common values shared with the EU and its interest to harmonizing processes related to post-Soviet space with the European integration one.[39] Nevertheless, the eastern enlargement of the EU is much more challenging to Russia than the NATO enlargement, creating a will for a pro-active response in Russian policy.[40] Russia cannot accept that ENP would somehow dilute the integration process within the CIS or affect Russian interests in Central and Eastern Europe, even after EU enlargement. But, Russia and the EU member states act as allies in the anti-terrorist fight and EU-Russia opposition could be very active in addressing cases of regional or sub-regional conflicts.

---

[37] http://www.nato.int/issues/nrc/index.html

[38] Nikolov, Krassimir, *European Neighbourhood Policy and Bulgaria-challenges and opportunities*, in Hayoz, Nicolas, Leszek Jesien and Wim Van Mems (eds.) *The New Neighbors of the European Union: Prospects and Risks*, Peter Lang publishers, 2004.

[39] Chizhov, V.A., Russia-EU: *A Strategy of Partnership*, in International Affairs, No. 9, Moscow, September 2004.

[40] Barko Yury, *Will Wilder Europe come into being?* A comment to Michael Emerson, *in Contemporary Europe*, Institute of Europe, Russia Academy of Sciences, No. 4, Moscow, September 2004.

## The Impact of the Enlargement and the ENP

The last EU enlargement granted to both Belarus and Ukraine the EU's neighbor status. During the same month, May 2004, the European Union launched the ENP, the aim of which is to promote prosperity and stability amongst its neighbors. However, not all of these neighbors have responded to the policy as the EU might have hoped or expected. While the southern neighbors of the EU have welcomed the ENP, which carries a promise of the extension of "four freedoms" to the EU's neighbors, in Eastern Europe its perception was opposite. Ukraine, for example, refused to sign the Action Plan in July 2004. The ENP is not seen as an acceptable substitute for EU membership, even the new government led by Yulia Tymoshenko accepted in February 2005 a new three-year action plan. Belarus seems to be definitely less reactive to ENP. Therefore, in the absence of an action plan, the enlargement impact for this country is rather questionable. While the proximity of the EU creates a certain pressure on the Lukashenko's regime, stimulating the political opposition and the civil society.

On top of these perceptions in the two countries, the enlargement and the ENP favor the strengthening of the political dialogue in the areas of security and crisis management, border management, migration, visa policies, and organized crime. The after-election crisis in Ukraine showed the important role the EU can play in determining the course of democracy along its impressively border. The EU will exert a stately attractive pull on Ukraine, creating efficiency and welfare gains via liberalized access to the single market, trade promotion, business creation, better market access, enhanced dialogue and cooperation on social and employment policies, encouraging reforms directed at reducing poverty and increasing the effectiveness of the social assistance.

In the new circumstances, Ukraine could expect to get finally an EU association agreement and EU support for full membership at WTO. At the same time, for both countries, but particularly for Ukraine, the ENP's focus on energy safety and security is an important opportunity to improve and extend their energy transport systems.

"It is our strong belief" stated Françoise Le Bail, Director for Ukraine in the EU Commission's Directorate—General Trade, "that

Ukraine—contrary to common belief—will do well out of enlargement."[41] She argued that EU enlargement will give Ukrainian operators direct access to one, larger, harmonized EU market of some 450 million people. Ukraine, perhaps more than all other countries because the majority of acceding countries are traditional partners for Ukraine, will benefit from single set trade rules, a single tariff, and a single set of administrative procedures which will apply across the enlarged Union. Furthermore, she expected that EU enlargement will be positive for the Ukrainian economy, in terms of an increase in welfare and in trade flows. The overall level of tariff protection in the new member states will decrease after enlargement, as long as the current average tariff in the EU is around four percent while the average tariff in the ten new member states is around nine percent.

But, for Ukrainian officials, the EU enlargement led to negative consequences for their country. They mention the problems encountered in the area of border co-operation between Ukraine and its neighbors who became member states. Also, the bilateral trade relations are affected. According to some estimations, Ukraine's losses will amount to $ 500—600 million per year.[42] The agrarian sector will suffer due to the new non-tariff restrictions, as will the metallurgical and chemical industries as a consequence of the EU's anti-dumping measures. A non-preferential access to markets in Central European countries, particularly Poland, will generate losses for Ukrainin producers estimated at about one percent of exports for 2004—2005.[43] The human dimension is also important. The number of Ukrainians able to cross the common borders with the neighboring EU member states diminished considerably with the introduction of a stricter visa regime. This created difficulties in promoting contacts for business, tourism, education and cultural relations.

Different from the Central European countries, which have directed much of their effort over the last decade in order to meet the

---

[41] *Ukraine Will Benefit from Enlargement*, Press Release, EC Delegation, Kiev, June 19, 2003 at http://www.ukraine-eu.mfa.gov.ua

[42] *Ukraine and its Neighbors*, Speech of the Minister for Foreign Affairs of Ukraine, K.Gryshchenko at the Conference *"Ukraine in Europe and in the World,"* Kiev, February 21, 2004 at http://www.ukraine-eu.mfa.gov.ua

[43] Milcher, Susanne; Slay, Ben—*The economics of the ENP: An initial assessment*, CASE, March, 2005, Warsaw.

Copenhagen criteria and to prepare for adapting the *acquis communau-taire*, the transformation policies in Ukraine and Belarus were initiated based on the consensus of relevant domestic interest groups.[44] Though some projects have been implemented successfully, the TACIS program has failed to help to produce any serious systemic effect on the reforms in these countries. The instruments of conditionality developed and applied by EU were supposed to be a way to get the desired impact. Unfortunately, the existing agreements between EU and its neighboring countries are seen sometimes more as simple statements of intent than as a real framework for co-operation. The EU should try to avoid unfulfilled membership prospects, which will not contribute to a safer and more stable Europe; indeed, exclusion and unfulfilled promises might bring about the opposite result.[45]

The EU's technical support should be more related to neighborhood requirements and keys components of this aid should focus on regional development and foreign investment orientation. The neighboring countries are important allies for strengthening the European Security and Defense Policy (ESDP).[46] Although the process is first and foremost oriented around the current enlargement, European integration must also meet larger requirements, related to the entire continent. It is not only Russia that challenges the EU to strengthen its CSDP. Furthermore, the EU should identify other areas for integration co-operation with non- candidate states. Differentiated integration can offer solutions for strengthening co-operation without full membership. In any case, future capacities and capabilities for European integration promote the conditions for a multi-speed Europe. At the same time, EU cannot ignore this problem, because expectations beyond the

---

[44] Ulakhovich, Vladimir, Center for International Studies (Belarus State University); Grimaldi, Marcello (University of Messina, Italy), Minsk–Messina, 2003, *Belarus and the European Union: Experience and Prospects for Co-operation*, Report in the Framework of the Project "Learning from the EU: Support for a More Democratic Constitutional and Legislative Reform Through Educational and Public Awareness Activities, Contract ?CSDP/1/45-B7/5200B00 (Civil Society Development Program for Belarus).

[45] Kempe, Iris; van Meurs, Wim—*Towards a Multi-Layered Europe*, Bertelsman Group for Policy Research, Center for Applied Policy Research, (Munich: Ludwig Maximilian University) November 2002.

[46] Grabbe, Heather, *The Sharp edges of Europe: Security Implications of Extending EU Border Policies Eastwards*, Occasional Papers, March 13, 2000, Institute for Security Studies, WEU.

Union's borders would either be constantly increasing or would be disappointed. In such a situation, the EU might lose its influence in promoting peace, democracy and welfare in Europe.

To integrate countries without current accession prospects into a "Europe+" integration model a new neighborhood policy is needed.[47] Only the EU cannot shape the neighborhood policy; the neighboring countries must also agree. Being a EU neighboring country does not necessarily mean strictly harmonizing legally and institutionally to the *acquis communautaire*, but does mean strengthening co-operation.[48]

For the EU, developing a new strategy towards this region will take place in parallel with the enlargement process until 2007, the integration of the new 12 members at that point, the Intergovernmental Conference, and the discussions over the new EU budget for 2007-2013. In the "Wider Europe" Communication,[49] the European Commission proposed to work in the initial phase until 2006 within the existing legal framework. From 2007, new neighborhood instruments will be introduced following an assessment of the relevant legal and budgetary issues.[50]

The different components of the European integration process, like accession, neighborhood, and the wider Europe policies have to be flexible. The Union should be open for every European country, but that does not mean that every European country should receive a membership guarantee.[51] Membership depends on EU capacities, strategic decisions and internal developments of the eastern and southeastern European states.[52]

---

[47] *Europe+* could be what the former French President François Mitterand called "la Grande Maison Européenne," where the *europeanisation* process could be extended to areas like Caucasus, Middle East and North Africa.

[48] Kempe, Iris ; van Meurs, Wim, *ibid.*

[49] Communication from the Commission to the Council and the European Parliament, *Wider Europe—Neighborhood: A New Framework for Relations with our Eastern and Southern Neighbors*, Brussels, March 3, 2003, COM (2003)104 final.

[50] *Paving the Way for a New Neighborhood Instrument*—European Commission Communication, COM (2003), 393 final, Brussels, July 1st, 2003.

[51] Emerson. Michael, Noutcheva, Gergana—*From Barcelona Process to Neighborhood Policy*, Assessments and Open Issues, CEPS Working Document, No.220, March 2005, available at http://www.ceps.be

[52] Kempe, Iris ; van Meurs, Win—*ibid.*

## Is There a Role for the New Member States?

The EU external policies were not the best examples of coherence in the past years, relying essentially on the experience and capacity of one member state who performed leadership functions, according to its geographical position and the target of the policy.[53] Based on this assumption one could imagine that some of the new and future member states (Poland, Hungary and the Baltic states, but Romania and Bulgaria as well) could take up responsibilities as regards EU policy towards Belarus and Ukraine. Even the Commission mentioned the role that new member states can play in ENP,[54] there are opinions according to which allowing such a role it could jeopardize the community spirit and damage the coherence of ENP. Nevertheless, on behalf of the EU the Polish and the Lithuanian Presidents accompanied Javier Solana, the high representative of the EU for foreign and security policy, in an attempt to promote a democratic solution during the presidential election crisis from December 2004 in Ukraine. The Commission already has withstood pressures from new member states (such as Poland) and from a number of think tanks to launch a new "Eastern Dimension" of the external community policy, following the example of the "Northern Dimension" of the regional co-operation.[55] Although one should not over value the role of the new member states in this respect, even Poland is prepared to have an active attitude. On the one hand, noting fears that current policies are isolating Belarus further and having little effect in encouraging opposition movements, some officials pressed for greater engagement and more concrete measures. Poland has pressed for the Commission to look into the possibility of opening an EU representation office in Minsk, to build ties with national level, regional and local authorities. However, member states agreed instead to "make use" of the OSCE's offices in Minsk. They also agreed to limit contacts with the authorities, but left open the possibility of cross-border co-operation. On the other hand,

---

[53] Wehmhorner, Arnold, *The new neighbors of the EU and the challenges to Bulgaria*, available at: www.fes.bg

[54] See reference no.43; Commission of the European Communities, *European Neighborhood Policy—Strategy Paper*, Communication from the Commission, Brussels, 12.5.2004, COM (2004) 373 final.

[55] Bertelsmann Foundation & Center for Applied Policy Research (eds), *Thinking Enlarged. The Accession Countries and the Future of the European Union, A Strategy for Reform* by the Villa Faber group on the future of the EU, Munich, 2001.

the Ukrainian-Polish relations have a positive consolidating impact on the situation in the Central and Eastern Europe. The election events in Ukraine promoted Poland into a leading position as regards EU's involvement in the post-election crisis. Moreover, the realization of the joint Austrian-Hungarian initiative regarding Ukraine would promote improvement of trans-border co-operation and of the entire complex of relation between Ukraine and the EU. For Hungary and Romania to approach Ukraine under the umbrella of ENP would give a new dimension to the relationships with their national ethnic groups from this country.

The profile of the EU in Eastern Europe is not high. Stimulating reforms requires deep, extensive and constant engagement with target countries. The potential of the ENP to engage the whole societies is limited given the fact that so far the EU did not succeeded to establish a clear political role in Eastern Europe. If the EU is to make an impact, Europe needs to be approached mainly politically. The ENP should enhance the political and societal dimensions such as the liberalization of the visa regime between neighbors and the EU, as this issue has a direct bearing for many people. Moreover, it is in the interests of the EU to promote reforms by stimulating pro-European aspirations in the neighboring states.[56]

---

[56] Roman and Kataryna Wolczk, Challenge Europe, issue 12, European Policy Center, Brussels, October 2004. Available at http://www.theepc.net/en/default.asp? TYP=SEARCH&LV=279&see=y&PG=CE/EN/directa&AI=379

## Chapter 9

# The Mediterranean and the Greater Middle East

Lothar Rühl

## Who Is In The Region?

With the southern enlargement of the EU all of Southern Europe is within the Union. Only Turkey, North Africa and the Levant, in European geopolitical terminology usually set apart from the wider Middle East as the "Near East" (Naher Osten or Proche-Orient), remain outside in 2005. Most of the myriad of Aegean islands to within a few miles off the Anatolian coast, with Crete and Rhodes as the main pieces, are Greek, hence part of the EU. Thus, this region means Israel and the Arab countries from Morocco in the West across the Maghreb to Egypt and Syria.

Malta and Cyprus acceded to the EU in 2004. Cyprus was admitted as a whole, however practically without the Turkish occupied Northern part, the "Turkish Republic of Cyprus," a separate entity created after the Turkish military occupation in 1974 and only recognized by Turkey itself. The Cyprus issue therefore remains without conclusion, but since negotiations on Turkish EU membership have been agreed to, Ankara will have to yield eventually on the central point of one Cypriot state under majority rule, which means a Greek one—whatever the political conditions for Turkish-Cypriot participation and the rights of Turkey, Greece and Britain as "guarantor powers" of the independence and constitutional order of the Republic of Cyprus since 1959-1960. Cyprus is definitely part of the EU and a sovereign state with UN membership, even if a dual special relationship exists with Greece and Turkey, and Britain still possesses the two "exterritorial" military bases on the southern coast under UK sovereignty. This position, as well as the US/UK electronic listening station on Mount Trodos within the territory of the Republic of Cyprus, has a certain strategic value as a springboard into the Middle East.

Cyprus was used as such in 1956 by the Franco-British Expeditionary Force for the Suez Operation in conjunction with the Israeli war against Egypt in order to reoccupy the Suez Canal Zone, and again in 2003 by the US as a waiting position for its transport flotilla, held ready for several weeks around Cyprus in view of the planned landing of an expeditionary force of army corps strength in Southern Turkey for an offensive against Iraq.

The "Mediterranean" geopolitical context of European policy, therefore, includes other than Malta and Cyprus, Turkey, Israel and nine Arab countries: Morocco, Algeria, Tunisia, Libya, Egypt, Jordan, the Palestinian territory, Lebanon and Syria. Of these, Libya is the only country outside the "Euro-Mediterranean partnership" framework, pending a satisfactory settlement of outstanding differences on terrorist acts in the past and the acceptance by Libya of "the Barcelona acquis in full," which means all the agreements between the EU and the other Mediterranean partners. In spite of the change of Libya's relations with the West following the agreement of 2003 with the US and Britain to give up nuclear, chemical and other toxic weapons research and development, Libya has not yet been admitted by the EU to the political cooperation program of the "EU Strategic Partnership with The Mediterranean and The Middle East," adopted by the European Council (EC) in March 2004, and to the "Euro-Mediterranean Partnership" in the framework of the "Barcelona Process." The EC decided in June 2004, that Libya must make "a formal undertaking" to accept "the full acquis" of the Barcelona agreements prior to being admitted to the process. [1]

It is also noted in the same text that Mauritania is a member of "the Arab Maghreb Union, a significant regional organization within the geographical scope of the initiative." This statement of simple fact

---

[1] European Council, "Final Report on an EU Strategic Partnership with the Mediterranean and the Middle East," Approved by the European Council June 2004, para. 10. Available at http://ue.eu.int/uedocs/cmsUpload/Partnership%20Mediterranean%20and%20Middle%20East.pdf The "Final Report" and an annex are available in European Union Institute for Security Studies, *EU security and defence core documents 2004*, Vol. V, Chaillot Paper No. 75 (Paris: European Union Institute for Security Studies), February 2005, pp. 129-141. Available at http://www.iss-eu.org/chaillot/chai75e.pdf Language on Libya appears in the in "Final Report" and the "Annex to Annex" to the "Final Report," p. 139-140. See also European Commission, "EU's Relations with Libya," Available at http://www.europa.eu.int/comm/external_relations/lybia/intro/index.htm

without further political qualification translates into a possible future interest of the EU to include Mauritania in the "Euro-Mediterranean Partnership" as well, however on conditions to be agreed upon. Strategically Mauritania with its Atlantic coast is part of NATO's "Mediterranean Dialogue," created in 1995 for "promoting regional security and stability" between its participants in a co-operation framework around NATO. The other countries are Israel, Jordan, Egypt, Morocco, Tunisia and, since 2000, Algeria, which means that apart from Libya the entire southern and south-eastern coast of the Mediterranean has been drawn into the NATO network of co-operative relations, whatever the real political significance and reliability of these. Admission of Libya and Mauritania to the EU "Mediterranean Partnership" could complete the Western alignment of North Africa and the geopolitical configuration of the "Euro-Atlantic security system" encircling the Mediterranean Sea, apart from Syria and Lebanon on the Levant. NATO looks for a "strategic partnership" of its own with the EU, as NATO secretary general Jaap de Hoop Scheffer declared in Berlin in a public speech on May 12, 2005.[2]

Whether Mauritania would then constitute the outside border of the "Mediterranean" co-operation sphere for the EU in West Africa, remains to be seen, since there are other ethnically mixed, partly Muslim, Arab-African countries, all former French colonies, such as Chad and Mali, bordering via the Sahara desert on the Arab Maghreb. A further extension of the EU and NATO spheres of interest south of the Mediterranean as an annex to the Arab North Africa remains a possibility.

There is a potential for over-extension of European political capabilities and influence in the "Mediterranean" context of the "Barcelona Process" for association with "strategic partnership" policies in the Middle East, since the EU considers, in the same document, "regular consultations with the Arab League" and "outreach to other relevant organizations."[3] This ambition appears again in the EU's "European Security Strategy," adopted by the EC in December

---

[2] Jaap de Hoop Scheffer, "Perspektiven der Sicherheitspolitik im Zusammenspiel von EU und NATO, Speech at Humboldt University, May 12, 2005. Available at http://www.nato.int/docu/speech/2005/s050512a.htm

[3] "Final Report," p. 9, and EUISS, *EU security and defence core documents*, p. 134.

2003,[4] which formulates a European security and defense policy program with far-reaching strategic aims beyond the EU's extension in the Mediterranean and to the Black Sea via the planned inclusion of Bulgaria and Romania and the envisaged admission of Turkey. Even without Turkey (which was not mentioned in the 2003 document on the "European Security Strategy") the geopolitical scope of this strategic doctrine opens Europe's sphere of international security activities far beyond the Middle East and North Africa into the domain of global affairs by proclaiming the EU's interest in "strategic partnerships" with countries in Southern Asia, South America and the Far East: China, Japan, India, Brazil, South Africa are specifically mentioned as is Canada within the North Atlantic alliance (the special relationship with the US is mentioned apart as the foundation of the alliance). On the Mediterranean region the EU's European Security Strategy, as spelled out by the EU Council in June 2004, declares: "Our task is to promote a ring of well-governed countries ... on the borders of the Mediterranean with whom we can enjoy close and co-operative relations."[5]

## Strategic Priorities and the Greater Middle East

The first problem to be considered in this global context is that of priorities in a hierarchy of international security interests, which could be covered by European means with or without outside support. How does the "European Strategic Partnership with the Mediterranean and the Middle East" relate to this global concept and where are the priorities in European security and cooperation schemes within the wider region? This is a critical question in view of the fact that the "Greater Middle East" (in EU terminology also called "Broader Middle East") borders on the Indian sub-continent and in Central Asia on the continental approaches to China.

The "Greater" or "Broader Middle East" is an ambivalent geopolitical notion, since there is no conclusive agreement whether it includes North Africa, South West Asia with Afghanistan and even Pakistan or

---

[4] *European defence: A proposal for a White Paper*, Report of an Independent Task Force to the European Union Institute for Security Studies (Paris: European Union Institute for Security Studies, May 2004), p. 25 and 28.

[5] European Council, "Final Report," in EUISS, *EU security and defence*, p. 130.

Western Central Asia with the Caspian Sea Basin. If the largest Central Asian country, Kazakhstan (the core of the historical Turkistan), between Russia in the west and China in the east, were to be included, this enormous Oriental region would outsize the Europe of the EU several times and confront it with a variety of different regional and national interests, security problems, specific geostrategic situations, political structures and cultures. The EU with its envisaged "strategic partnerships" would have to move on the historical terrain of the French empire in North and West Africa, of the British and Russia empires in the East. There it would have to deal not only with Central Asia and South West Asia but also with neighboring China and India, let alone with Russia and America as external powers with economic and strategic interests in the geopolitical configuration of the Asian Eurasian continent. In practical terms of policy a delimitation has to be introduced: Where are the geographical borders of a "Greater Middle East"? The next question then is: What and where are the European means for action to fill out such a vast space between the Mediterranean, Central Asia and the Indian Ocean— even not considering the Far East and the whole of Africa with European economic interests and political involvement via France?

The main thrust of EU partnership with Oriental countries beyond the Mediterranean region seems to be directed towards the geographical Middle East, or more specifically, "east of Jordan," as the EU texts specify, towards the Gulf and possibly towards the Horn of Africa opposite Arabia with Somalia and Sudan as future objectives of "stabilization" and "reform" policies by the EU, once the situations in these countries would permit cooperation on a firmer basis than can be expected for the foreseeable future.[6] An extension to the North Eastern corner of Africa would later pose the problem of European political involvement in Ethiopia and East Africa as well—again, the European problem is limitation of the scope of EU activities for "partnership" and "security co-operation" to aims, that can be reached, and to realistic programs as well as to geopolitical configurations, which could be controlled in crisis by European means. These questions still remain open.

The EU strategic partnership with the Mediterranean and Middle Eastern countries was adopted by the European Council (EC) in June

---

[6] Ibid, p. 135.

2004 as the European contribution to the US "Greater Middle Eastern Initiative" for reform policies, security and stability of the wider Middle Eastern region, including the entire Gulf region. However, no mention was made or has so far been added of the region "east of Aden" or of Central Asia. The terms "wider," "broader" or "greater" have not yet been officially associated by the EC with the "Middle East." Beyond the "Mediterranean" region, which in EU terms includes Jordan, the EC has set the aim of working together in particular with the six states of the Gulf Cooperation Council (GGC): Saudi Arabia, Kuwait, Qatar, Oman, Bahrain and the United Arab Emirates, as well as with Iran and Yemen and "to work towards peaceful stabilization and reconstruction in Iraq," based on a "broad concept of security," which means a political/social-economic one beyond military security.[7] The political implication is a priority for civilian instruments of an indirect strategy.

"Partnership" is defined as a privileged relationship based on "geographical proximity" and "growing interdependence" as well as the existing "solid and substantial set of co-operation activities" in the "Barcelona process."[8] Partnership, therefore, must be characterized by "a co-operative spirit" and "dialogue." The "Strategic Partnership's objective" is given as "the development of a prosperous, secure and vibrant Mediterranean and Middle East." This strategy is meant by the EU to differentiate between the external partners, address specific situations, problems and interests and "to fully reflect the fact that there is no basis for a one-size-fits-all approach"; on the contrary "successful implementation requires a long term coherent engagement with a pragmatic approach."

As to the EU partnership agenda with the Arab countries of the region the EC document proclaims:

> The EU will seek to play its part in addressing (the) challenges . . . Among the security challenges which have already developed to worrying levels are regional conflicts, terrorism, proliferation of weapons of mass destruction, and organized crime.

---

[7] Ibid, p. 130

[8] Ibid.

Responses to these challenges comprise a wide range of measures, from promoting a WMD-free zone in the Middle East and preventing proliferation to ensuring economic growth and stability, managing and addressing migration issues, ensuring security of energy supply, promoting sustainable development, promoting the rule of law, respect for human rights, civil society and good governance.[9]

It is further said that "the primary political concerns" for the EU involve, inter alia, "respect for the rights of minorities, cooperation on non-proliferation, counter-terrorism, conflict prevention and resolution, and economic development as recognized by the declaration of the Arab League Summit on 23 May, 2004." "Mutual respect for their unique cultures" is set forth as one of the "principles of action" as well as the recognition that "there are shared security concerns" to be dealt with and that "a broad concept of security which addresses domestic concerns which foster insecurity, such as economic underdevelopment and unemployment, especially youth unemployment" should be followed by the partnership policies.[10]

## Palestine

The EU has also privileged a solution of the conflict over Palestine by international mediation, based on the UN resolutions adopted since 1967 —which means that Israel would have to withdraw from the occupied territories without a negotiation on the future international borders with an Arab Palestine and Syria. This strict interpretation of the historical UN position, never recognized by Israel, will, of course, not stand against Israeli resistance, supported by the US, and the facts on the ground, created by Jewish settlements on formerly Jordanian territory. The "road map" for a peaceful resolution of the conflict, proposed by the "Quartet" USA, EU, UN and Russia, envisages negotiations after the return to non-violence and a freeze in Jewish settlements on the West Bank of the Jordan and in the Gaza strip. The European policy is both in flux and its foundation in "international law" (the UN resolutions) undermined. The relevance of a European contribution to a

---

[9] Ibid, p. 130-131.

[10] Ibid, pp. 129-132.

resumed "peace process" within the "Oslo framework" cannot, therefore, be assessed before the results of future negotiations with Israel and
the Palestinian Autonomy Authority under American mediation would
be consolidated. An independent or European diplomacy in this conflict
is neither possible under the auspices of the "Quartet" nor realistic
without American agreement. Hence one of the corner stones of the
European-Mediterranean partnership, the resolution of the Israeli-Arab
conflict for peace in the Near East, remains out of reach of an
"autonomous" EU policy. The same is true for the suggestion of a
"WMD-free zone" in the Middle East, which poses the question of
Israel's nuclear armaments as the Arab countries and Iran have pointed
out in every discussion on Middle Eastern security. This was done by
Teheran as an argument for its own "peaceful" nuclear energy program
with a "full cycle" technology in a statement by foreign minister Kamal
Kharrazi at the UN in New York on May 3, 2005. He cited the nuclear
armaments of countries, which had not signed the NPT, i.e. Israel, as a
compelling reason not to confront non-nuclear weapons states like Iran
with "arbitrary...criteria" for definition of a "break-out" capability at a
given level of nuclear energy production.[11]

The combination of the demand that Israel withdraw from the territories occupied in the war of 1967—which is long-standing in
EC/EU resolutions—and of the proposal for an WMD-free zone,
implying Israel's nuclear disarmament as a counterpart to an effective
elimination of all WMD in the Middle East without resolving the
problems of military disparities between conventional forces and for
arms control in the region first, critically limit European influence on
Israel and the options of EU diplomacy in the Arab-Israeli conflict.

## Iraq

The same is not quite the case with the second corner stone in the
Middle East: the reconstruction of Iraq as an independent and unified
country in accordance with UN resolutions. But in Iraq the US is the
leading power and the UN is marginalized as long as insecurity prevails. The refusal by the European allies to participate with the EU or

---

[11] David E. Sanger and Warren Hoge, "Tehran to resume nuclear program," *International
Herald Tribune*, Paris, May 4, 2005. Available at http://www.iht.com/bin/print_ipub.php?
file=/articles/2005/05/04/news/iran.php

to let NATO take part in the military control of Iraq for a limited area (south of Baghdad) has prevented military cooperation and limited political cooperation with the US and any "multilateralist" approach to post-war crisis management in Iraq and in the Gulf region with Europe as a distinct political actor. The participation of Britain, Italy, Poland, the Netherlands, until the spring of 2004 Spain, and several other European allies in the US led "international coalition" with military contingents, while others, France and Germany in particular, refused to do so, has contributed to neutralize the "European Security and Defence Identity" in dealing with acute crisis in the Middle East. In consequence, the "European Security and Defence Policy" (ESDP) has been inoperable in this region ever since 2003.

Both the cases of the Israel-Palestine issue and Iraq, different as they are, but related to each other as to ESDP, show the limits of the international relevance of the European "strategic partnership" notion in terms of military or "hard" security contributions from European initiatives in crisis contingencies such as post-war Iraq under the US-led international military occupation and in the wider Gulf region for cooperative schemes of transformation and stability. Where high intensity insurgency and terrorism, arms and military forces, arms control, proliferation of nuclear armaments and missile technology or the illicit fabrication and possession of biological and chemical agents for "weapons of mass destruction," a major concern for both Europe and America, are the subject of international action, the EU as such is not yet prepared or able to join in counteraction other than by political, economical and technical means. So far, only Britain and France could act with military force or cooperate with the US in "counter-proliferation" to enforce the Non-Proliferation Treaty (NPT). However, the EU could not set the political conditions or exercise control. Insofar "strategic partnership" between Europe and countries in the Middle East is—and probably will remain in the foreseeable future—strictly limited to the civilian side of the coin, hence of conditional and limited significance in crisis and conflict.

## Libya and Iran

In this respect there are two cases in point: Libya and Iran. It has to be noted that Libya negotiated in secret to abandon its nuclear and other WMD armament programs in 2002-2003 not with the EU nor with France and Italy, the nearest European Mediterranean countries immediately concerned, but with the US and Britain. Libya's co-operative disarmament policy has been inaugurated and pursued, so far, outside the Mediterranean and the UN security context. A new relationship with America, covering regional security, nuclear non-proliferation and regional stability, was and has remained the central Libyan concern and Libyan President Mohammar Qaddafi's political priority. It is obvious that this American connection relates to American power over any other external influence in North Africa and the Middle East. Even on the major issue of Mediterranean security and of partnership options with the EU, where nuclear, chemical and biological arms were concerned, and even though their arms are nearer and more dangerous to Europe than to North America and Qaddafi did not turn to Europe or show any political concern for European interests in the "Euro-Mediterranean Barcelona process."

This Libyan orientation again points to the limits of European influence on major security and armaments issues of immediate concern to Europe, despite the extension of EU borders towards North Africa with the admission of Malta and Cyprus and the EU's Maghreb policies of cooperation.

The case of Iran is different but equally elucidating: Britain, France and Germany formed a common diplomatic approach to the problem of Iran's "full cycle" nuclear program (including uranium enrichment and reprocessing of used irradiated reactor rods) which in the view of the IAEA director general Mohamed El Baradei, as expressed in the spring of 2005, could reach the capability of nuclear weapons production within three years, if completely resumed. Since 2004 the three European countries, acting for the EU, not under control of the EC but as individual partners with their own authority and national interest, offered Teheran economic support and political co-operation if Iran gave up the "full cycle" program and conformed to the international demands, as set forth by the EU itself, the US and the IAEA.

This European approach follows the "soft security" line. However it is based on American power held in reserve while European partners are negotiating and on the US warning to Iran of possible adverse consequences in case of non-compliance with the demands of the international community.

Iran has also accepted the recent additional protocol to the treaty and the required safeguard agreements, including on "intrusive inspections," with the IAEA. The case of Iran is complicated by the wording of the NPT, that assures all signatories of the treaty the right to possess and use enrichment technology for peaceful purposes. As any other signatory of the NPT, Iran could reach the nuclear weapons "thresh-hold" within the treaty framework "legally" and later choose the time for a possible step over the thresh-hold and "break out" of the treaty, as North Korea has done.

The policy of the three EU partners therefore is at the same time risky by itself and reasonable, since it tries to entice Iran to forego the technical option of nuclear armament. It is an example of European thinking on international conflict and shows the conceptual core both of EU "strategic partnership" policy and of the ESDP itself: a clear preference for non-use of armed force and for caution in exercising political pressure. The initiative of the three EU partners may or may not have a satisfactory outcome, but it is not independent of the implicit American back up and implied threat with the use of armed force for military counter-proliferation in case of an Iranian step beyond the "nuclear thresh-hold." Hence, EU policy is not a self-supporting and therefore truly "autonomous" policy in crisis prevention and conflict resolution. Its "strategic" relevance is a function of Teheran's perception of the possible use of American power if the negotiation is in crisis or after talks break down, hence the importance of US strategy vis-à-vis Iran and ultimately of the deterrence value of American military power and political determination. The Iranian and the Libyan cases illuminate the ambiguous context of the European security strategy and policy in dealing with critical security problems outside Europe, in particular in the dangerous Middle East.

## Nonproliferation

The EU "strategic partnership" policy for the Mediterranean and Middle Eastern countries does not explicitly mention military security nor does it seem that it intends, presently, to include it in the program for the foreseeable future. But the June 2004 EC Final Report on the envisaged strategic partnership with the region lists "Non-Proliferation, Security Dialogue and Counter-Terrorism" as part of the cooperation program within the framework of the "Euro-

Mediterranean Partnership." "The EU's overarching objective should be to set up appropriate consultation and mechanisms for enhanced political dialogue on conflict prevention and crisis management, counter-terrorism and non-proliferation" by means of:

- The inclusion of the EU standard clause on non-proliferation of Weapons of Mass Destruction in all new Third Country Agreements;

- Establishment of expert sub-committees under the Association and other Third Party Agreements;

- Intensification of dialogue within the political chapter of the Barcelona Process on the implementation of relevant international agreements and export/ end use control policies[12]

This clearly is an arms control policy, that the EC has set forth for all its members and all Mediterranean partners with a view to strengthen the NPT and the international export/end use regime, agreed upon by the club of exporters of materials and technology. From 2004 onwards any agreement between a country in the Mediterranean region and the EU legally has to provide for such constraints. All EU members are bound by these political rules and future treaty obligations with "third countries." In the Mediterranean region itself these rules concern EU relations with Israel and all Arab countries on the Levant including Jordan and, of course, a future Palestinian state. The critical addressees of this clause are Libya, Syria, Lebanon and Palestine in the Near East.

Nuclear proliferation is not the only concern with respect to these countries, probably at present not even the most urgent one, but proliferation of other WMDs certainly is, especially as far as Syria and Lebanon are concerned, (because of the militant and armed Islamic "Hezbollah" party with its Iranian connection) but also Palestine with the various militant Palestinian organizations with terrorist cells and guerrilla tactics from "Islamic Jihad" and "Hamas" to the extremist nationalist wing of the PLO-core group "El Fatah," and the Damascus-based nationalist "liberation fronts." Teheran's still keen interest in destroying the Oslo peace process in Palestine and confronting Israel

---

[12] "Final Report," in EUISS, *EU security and defence*, p. 134-135.

indirectly in Lebanon via "Hezbollah" point to a persistent danger of WMD spread for terrorist use against Israel and to the escalation risks involved in this situation. Here clearly, the Mediterranean and Middle Eastern risk potentials touch upon each other and EU "strategic partnership" policies as the ESDP as a whole have to take these risks into account, which indeed means active crisis management, counter-terrorism and non-proliferation, the latter at least by diplomatic, economical and technical means, available to the EU.

As far as the non-Mediterranean countries in the "Middle East" ("east of Jordan" in the EU terminology) are concerned, all critical countries of the Gulf region are within the scope of strategic partnership. With them only "intensification of dialogue" on the "implementation of relevant international agreements and export/end use control policies" could be envisaged in 2004 "under the existing or future relevant instruments" (read diplomatic and technical agreements).

The countries addressed are the Gulf Cooperation Council member-states plus Yemen, Iraq and Iran. In this political context the essential profile of the non-military aspect of European security policy is the Franco-German-British negotiation approach to Teheran on constraints of the Iranian nuclear energy program to exclude uranium enrichment and reprocessing in return for EU cooperation. Technically the EU depends on the IAEA for verification of compliance with the NPT against the illicit spread of nuclear arms in the region as it is on the US for strategic reconnaissance, military security and enforcement of the NPT by "counter-proliferation." What, then, could "strategic partnership" with the Middle East mean in practical terms, where nuclear non-proliferation is the concern in an actual contingency, since non-proliferation is a stated objective of the EU Mediterranean and Middle Eastern political agenda? Nuclear proliferation had happened before 1991 in Iraq; it was successful in Pakistan in 1998; it may be current in Iran in 2005 or become a threat in the future. Nuclear material and technology were traded in the arms bazaar in the Gulf and given to Iran as to Libya from Pakistan since the 1970s (either on private initiative or with the knowledge of the government or the armed forces). Neither the IAEA nor the European Community had known it or suspected, that the USSR, later Russia, had exported nuclear technology to Iran, as France had to Iraq. EU "strategic partnership" policy, therefore, faces a huge problem in the Middle East, quite apart from terrorists, who may indeed acquire WMD.

As a consequence, the EC's policy for the Euro-Mediterranean partnership envisages a reinforcing the links between the ESDP and the Barcelona process by making the European security and defense policy "more visible," the cooperation "more substantial and concrete," using it with Mediterranean partners "case by case for exercises and training," which means including military and police forces, crisis management, civil defense and civil protection agencies. This was inaugurated in 2001 in Kuwait.

It finally does "consider, when the situation allows, re-launching the Euro-Mediterranean Partnership discussion on the draft Mediterranean Peace and Stability Charter and other similar types of frameworks." This rather convoluted formulation reflects the difficulties of making progress towards such an agreement on political principles and guidelines for European-Arab relations and on definitions of what is meant by "peace and stability," in particular in view of the Arab-Israeli conflict over Palestine, on which Europe has only little influence in spite of the EU participation in the "Quartet" and the negotiation on its "road map" approach to security and stabilization as prerequisites for progress towards a political compromise on borders, Jerusalem and an independent Palestinian state.

## Regional Security: CSCE Model?

As to the relations of the EU with "countries east of Jordan" the EC sets the aim of "launching internal reflections and consultations for a comprehensive approach to security in the area including encouragement to partners to consider confidence building measures such as notification of exercises, exchange of military observers etc." The EU is to develop "a framework for dialogue and confidence building at the regional level" with the countries east of Jordan.[13]

This is the adaptation of the 1975 Helsinki formula of the CSCE, the East-West Conference on Security and Cooperation in Europe, which lasted fifteen years until the end of the East-West conflict and

---

[13] European Council, op cit, p.10-11.

continues in the Organization for Security and Cooperation. The idea of applying the "Helsinki principles" of political security and military constraints of the CSCE process to the Middle East by "confidence building measures" certainly is a positive European contribution to the discussion of security in the Middle East. However it was already copied in the Madrid conference program of 1991 for Israel and Syria/Lebanon with some practical results such as the withdrawal of heavy arms from the border regions to enhance military stability against surprise and large-scale attack. The possibilities of the CSCE model in the Middle East are limited, since the CSCE process went parallel with the negotiations between the alliances on reductions of conventional land and air forces between 1973 and the Conventional Armed Forces in Europe (CFE) treaty in 1990. The CSCE could never be more than a diplomatic framework for "détente" in Europe, mostly of psychological reassurance and political promise via agreed principles, however without common definitions of substance, certainly not the foundation of security. Without such a foundation in multilateral arms control agreements on force structures, force levels and armaments, the application of the CSCE model in the Middle East could not create reliable and solid security, not even by verifiable military "constraints" and "confidence building measures," limiting troop movements and larger scale force concentrations or exercises in border regions, as it could not have done in Europe during the East-West confrontation.[14]

## Counter-terrorism

This leaves "counter-terrorism" as the last critical chapter of the Euro-Mediterranean and Middle East "strategic partnership." Under this heading the EC's June 2004 text notes as an objective within the Mediterranean context "implementation of reinforced operational co-operation in the fight against terrorism among judicial and police authorities; through the Justice and Security sub-committees existing or currently being established under Euro-Mediterranean Association Agreements and agreed Action Plans."[15]

---

[14] Lothar Rühl, "Can the CSCE be a Role-Model to frame the political process of the Greater Middle East with Europe and the United States?" in Andreas Marchetti (ed), *The CSCE as a Model to transform Western Relations with the Greater Middle East* (Bonn: ZEI/CEI), Discussion Paper C 134, 2004, p. 43-54.

[15] European Council, "Final Report," p. 11.

For "relations with countries east of Jordan" the ambition is more limited: "Build on existing engagement with the GCC (Gulf Cooperation Council) including on the question of tracking financing of terrorism and seek other opportunities for technical co-operation." Yemen, Iraq and Iran are not mentioned. Tracking terrorist international finance and logistics is one of the foremost European and American concerns. Co-operation between the Euro-Atlantic allies has been organized and is officially said to be functioning well. However, in the Middle East the European governments and the EU itself have only limited influence and less latitude for applying pressure for joint action. Again, there is no wide-open field for autonomous European policies.

## EU Enlargement to Turkey and the Broader Middle East

The major impact of enlargement on European strategic partnership with the Mediterranean Arab countries and the Middle East is obvious: The only important EU enlargement policy in this geographical area is the envisaged admission of Turkey, and later possibly of the three countries in the Southern Caucasus: Georgia, Armenia and Azerbaijan (the latter no more a "European" country than Turkey, but has been included in the all-European military security area of the 1990 Paris Conventional Armed Forces in Europe, CFE, arms reduction treaty "from the Atlantic to the Urals").

The inclusion of Turkey into the EU is also the only strategic move possible to close and cover the south-eastern flank of the EU as a defense community and dominate Europe's Southern periphery across the Levant and the Black Sea to the Middle East proper with the Gulf and to the Caucasus with access to the Caspian Basin of Western Central Asia. However, this move makes sense in geopolitical-strategic terms only if Turkey were to become a valuable, congenial and reliable European partner within both the EU and the NATO frameworks based on the American alliance, with a secular Turkish state and a majority Muslim population, and despite having most of the country in Asia Minor, which is mainly outside Europe and part of the Middle East. This is a tall political order.

The Eastern enlargement to Bulgaria und Romania as well as a future one in the Southern Balkans including Croatia, Bosnia,

Macedonia, possibly Serbia-Montenegro and Albania can be considered as irrelevant to security concerns, since the entire area has been part of the NATO sphere of strategic interests ever since the Kosovo war in 1999 under allied military control and politically in a partnership with the EU. As a result of that war, the ESDP—formulated in principle by the EC in June 1999 at the end of the Kosovo conflict—South-eastern Europe is more inward-looking for obvious reasons of political reform and stability. The international assistance pact, proposed by the German government at that time for "stability in Southeastern Europe" is supposed to serve this purpose as is the European participation in the post-war "peace consolidation" in Bosnia-Herzegovina.

While the Western Balkans has an Adriatic sea coast (mostly Croatian Dalmatia) and a Black Sea coast to the east in Bulgaria and Romania, and while it is also part of the Mediterranean co-operation policies of the EU as of the Black Sea co-operation scheme, launched by Turkey, South-eastern Europe is only marginal to the central Arab-European Mediterranean relationship both in historical and political as in economic and strategic terms. South-eastern Europe looks more to the Black Sea, to Turkey and to Eastern Europe as its second orientation after the West and Central European priority, represented by economic, cultural and political ties to Italy, Austria, Germany and France. For the EU and its ESDP the Eastern enlargement so far has little impact on the Mediterranean situation and European Middle Eastern policies. This could change somewhat in the future, if and when the independent countries of the European Caucasus, Georgia and Armenia, possibly neighboring Azerbaijan were to become members or close associates of the EU. In that case Europe would have to develop a new "Eastern" policy for the Caucasus-Caspian region and Western Central Asia, hence into the Northern part of the wider or "Greater Middle East."

An admission of Ukraine, still a semi-democratic country with massive internal problems even after the "Orange Revolution" which brought about a regime change with the presidential election, would again change the political equation. Ukraine, astride Central and Eastern Europe, draws the attention further to Russia, already associated with the EU for trade and co-operation in general. Russia under Putin seeks a close partnership with Europe and the Ukrainian policy of the EU will have to be harmonized with its Russian policy, in order not to create conflicts and contradictions. Several EU members, i.e. Germany which is Russia's most important trading partner and looks for investment in Russian energy resources and industry, Sweden, Finland and the three Baltic states (former Soviet republics for half a century 1940-1990) have developed considerable economic stakes in Russia or in energy and raw material imports from Russia. They are more occupied with Eastern Europe than with the Mediterranean. Germany does need a Middle Eastern policy, which is one of the reasons for the German government's support of Turkish membership in the EU.

The admission of Turkey to the EU cannot be considered exclusively or even predominantly as relevant to the relations of Europe with the Muslim Middle East, important as this is in political-strategic and cultural terms: The issue has an East European aspect, that would become even more commanding in case Ukraine joined the EU. Together Turkey and Ukraine would create a new political focus for Europe, a new strategic structure for the EU, as well as open the Eastern perspective wider than ever before, including relations with Russia and with the Caucasus. This means a North Eastern pole of attraction across the Black Sea, drawing political and economic force away from the Mediterranean and the Maghreb. The EU's problem in geopolitics of keeping a balance between its southern or Mediterranean/Oriental and its North and East European commitments in the allocation and use of its limited resources as between its Mediterranean and its Northern and Eastern member-states for an integrated European policy would weigh more heavily on the internal balance than at present. The "Greater Middle East" for Europe will develop a Northern tier across the Black Sea as across the Caspian with Turkey under the influence of EU enlargement to the east. The central strategic position has already shifted to Turkey, the key country in the "swing zone" of geopolitical dynamics away from Western Europe. This change of the structure of Europe's political geography began in 1991 with the end of the Soviet Russian empire and the "opening of the East." Since then, Turkey's central situation between the Balkans and the Caucasus, the Mediterranean and the Black Sea, which had been that of the Ottoman empire since the Turkish conquest in the 15th century until Russia's final victory under Catherine the Great in the Russo-Turkish wars during the last quarter of the 18th century, has been set free again.

It is in and around Turkey that EU enlargement and any European partnership, "strategic" or otherwise, with countries in the Middle East, whether in narrow or wider geographical boundaries, must be considered. Therefore, admission of Turkey to the EU is the central strategic choice of EU expansion policy prior to the still distant and hypothetical one over Ukraine.

The main reason does not lie in Europe, although the Ottoman empire was a European power for almost five centuries, with, at times, a large extension from the Aegean Sea and the Balkans across the Black Sea to Central and Eastern Europe. The main reason is in the Middle East proper and in the Caspian Basin of Western Central Asia, where strategic and economic interests meet historical and cultural-linguistic ties with the Turkic people, relatives to the Turks as the Turkomans in Northern Iraq. The Kurdish national problem, long denied as a fact and suppressed by authoritarian policies in Turkey as in Iraq, Iran and Syria, links all four neighbors in a negative common interest in preventing the emergence of an independent Kurdish state. This, however, is at stake in post-war Iraq since 2003. Therefore, Turkey has an immediate and a long-term strategic interest in the evolution of Iraq, as it always had from the Turkish domination of Mesopotamia until the end in 1918.

But Turkey has its own regional priorities beyond the Kurdish national question and the oil in the Kirkuk-Mosul region of Northern Iraq, which Turkey lost in World War I. As a Muslim country it cannot simply become the political, let alone the cultural elongation of Europe in the Middle East. As a large and economically viable country with the most important population of the region, important demographic growth and the only self-sufficient food supply from a developing agriculture, based on the single most vital natural resource even before oil and gas, the Anatolian water table, Turkey has a call to primacy in the Middle East as a rival of Iran and Iraq with Saudi Arabia being an insecure strategic partner of the USA.

It is in this strategic triangle, where the further development of the Gulf region and the wider or "Greater Middle East" around it, the ultimate issue of stability and security, of peace and war, may well be decided by the basic realities of economic geography and demography, which determine strategies and national policies in the long run. In this wider perspective, the politics of alliance and coalition, as does the politics of international organization and, hence, of the extension of associations or unions between countries, depend on those basic realities: water, oil/gas, demography and economic growth.

In this long-term perspective, can Europe be enlarged by Turkey and become a power or even a participant in the Middle East? And if not, how could it influence regional developments via Turkey as an EU member in its own interest? Two notions have been used to describe rather than define Turkey's strategic importance to Europe either as an external but "privileged" partner of the EU and ally in NATO or as a full member of the EU: "Bridge to the Middle East" and "Corner-stone" of Europe's security and defense in the Middle East. The notion of a bridge suggests a crossover from Europe into the Orient over a cultural and geographical divide. The question is, by what means and to what purpose? Could Turkey be such a bridge and would the Turkish people want to serve such a purpose, once it would have been jointly defined as a common vital interest? And why should Europe directly reach into the Middle East via Turkey? The more plausible notion of a corner stone or "Southeastern pillar" of Europe begs the question of the EU's strategic-geopolitical interests in the region. Is it to be an advanced forward-defense against possible threats or challenges from the Middle East under "the arc of crisis" between Pakistan and North Africa? A "glacis" in the Middle East from where to act in prevention or pre-emption to better shield "the Southern periphery of Europe" as the "New Strategic Concept for the Alliance" of 1991 suggested for NATO? Whatever the answers, Turkey is the key country in the central strategic position between the Mediterranean and the Black Sea, the Balkans and the Caucasus, between Europe and the Middle East. As the then US diplomat Richard Holbrooke put it in 1994: "a strategic partner on all three fronts of the confrontation: Balkans, Caucasus and Gulf" for the US.[16]

The EU has, so far, been extremely cautious, even shy, in dealing with Turkey as a "strategic partner." The reasons are obvious: The unresolved problems of Northern Cyprus, of the Kurdish question, of the internal situation in Turkey with the constitutional, legal and administrative reform and the human rights issues, which have to be settled according to the "Copenhagen principles" of the EU; but

---

[16] Richard Holbrooke, Cable News Network, 1994.

above all because of the political concern not to prejudice the later decision on Turkey's admission to the Union after the oncoming negotiation. Had the Solana document on the "European Security Strategy," adopted by the EC in December 2003, mentioned Turkey as a "strategic partner" as other countries outside the EU, Ankara would have protested, since the formula could be read as foreclosing the membership option and negate in advance future results of the negotiation between the EU and Turkey.

For the reason, of not to giving too much to Ankara in advance, the EU had refused in the past to let Turkey participate in the military crisis reaction force and contingency planning for crisis response. This denial has been maintained, and Ankara, in response, has refused to accept EU use of NATO bases and other assets in Turkey for its autonomous military operations and exercises, and to consent in principle to the use by the EU's ESDP operations of NATO assets even outside Turkey. In fact, it would be nearly impossible, in any case extremely difficult, more costly and risky to operate with European armed forces outside NATO in the Middle East or even in the Eastern Mediterranean. Only the US has the means to do that in an emergency. But even for US operations, a refusal of Turkey to allow the use of Turkish air space, territory or facilities in Anatolia for military operations, as in the 2003 war against Iraq, can be a considerable disadvantage. The denial by Turkey of transport and deployment of an expeditionary force and of air attacks against Iraq cost the US the planned second front for a two-tier offensive on Baghdad and valuable time during the campaign.

But beyond negative tactical-operational effects and even a frustrated military strategy in conflict, the absence of NATO ally Turkey from the "international coalition" in 2003 caused political damage for the US in the Middle East and also in Europe. The complex situation within NATO and the EU in 2002 before the show-down at the UN between the US and Britain, supported by the majority of the allies but against a strong Franco-German opposition, was compounded by the refusal of Paris and Berlin to allow alliance preparations for active support of Turkey in case of a counter-attack by Iraq against Turkish territory. The issue was hypothetical and such a contingency on NATO's and Europe's southeastern flank was highly improbable, but the risk had to be covered and NATO's Military Committee had asked the North Atlantic Council to authorize operational planning for force deployments and logistic support in time. The Franco-German opposition prevented this during several critical weeks and in fact paralyzed NATO's crisis response capability, thus reinforcing opposition in Turkey against the US policy. At the same time, it exposed the latent fragility of the European-Turkish relationship and of the bilateral American-Turkish alliance, which had happened before on several occasions: in the 1960s over Turkish threats with armed intervention in Cyprus and US arms embargos against Turkey; in 1973, when Ankara refused to let the US use the NATO bases and Turkish air space for re-supply of Israel with spare parts for its fighter-bombers during the defensive war against Syria and Egypt; in 1974, after the Turkish occupation of Northern Cyprus and in 1990-1991, when Turkey did not join the US-led international coalition against Iraq, but let the US use its air space and air bases to attack Iraq, which it did not permit in 2003. European-Turkish relations on all these occasions were ambivalent and subject to the pressure of political tensions over Turkish policy at varying degrees from Britain to France, Germany, Italy and Greece.

In every instance, the Turkish government of the time followed what Ankara understood as the national interest with only one limit: the minimum of co-operation with the US as the main ally and protector against Soviet Russia. European interests came not even always third after Turkish and American, since regional interests of Turkey vis-à-vis the Middle East usually intervened, in particular common ones with Iran and Iraq on the Kurdish issue. Since the 1990s, Turkey's relations with Israel, then improved, have come in-between as well. Turkey is no unconditional ally or partner. Ankara defines and pursues Turkish interests as a regional power in the Middle East. The question for dealing with the Middle East is, whether these interests could be "europeanized," under what conditions and at what political price for Europe.

Turkey has its own view on Central Asia as on the Gulf region and the Near East. It is indispensable for any effective European political or military strategy in the Eastern Mediterranean in an acute crisis as it is in the Middle East. Would there be a "European priority" for Turkey if immediate Turkish interests in the region were at stake? If American involvement was a given or were to become necessary for Turkey's security or energy supply, would Ankara choose Europe over

America, if there were no agreement between both, as in 2002-2003? In this alliance crisis, France and Germany with Belgium and Luxemburg in tow had held up procedures in NATO preparations for the crisis deployment of allied anti-air force components to Turkey in order to offer a shield against possible Iraqi air attacks, however unlikely such attacks may have been in the given circumstances. The time for decision lost in the critical weeks at the end of 2002 contributed to the Turkish refusal to consent to US troop landings in Anatolia and complicated the US-Turkish negotiations before the war. It also contributed to a loss of opportunity for US strategy to make in-depth preparations to deal with the post-campaign underground resistance in occupied Iraq and to the inability of US forces to control the Syrian and Iranian borders of Northern Iraq. Has this been to the political advantage of Europe and has it reinforced the position of the EU in the Middle East?

NATO has taken notice of the risks and challenges as of the options available to it, similar to the EU's "strategic partnership" approach to the region. The advantage of the new "Istanbul Cooperation Initiative" for the Middle East of the Atlantic alliance is America's and Turkey's full participation. The North Atlantic Council's Summit Declaration at Istanbul on June 29, 2004[17] on this initiative concentrates on military security, non-proliferation of WMD and counter-terrorism, similar to the EU "strategic partnership" concept in this regard, as does the EU-US Declaration supporting peace, progress and reform in the broader Middle East and the Mediterranean.[18]

Turkey is suited for both. In the meantime, NATO has suggested in its new partnership advance to the EU in 2005 that the extensive program of its "Istanbul Cooperation Initiative" for "a new set of relationships," including "interoperability" of military forces of each future partner in the region with the NATO countries as well as "in the multilateral dimension of the Mediterranean Dialogue," and using "mechanisms and tools derived from other NATO initiatives such as the partnership of peace (PfP)" in Europe and (former Soviet) Central Asia. NATO authorities speak of "complementary" patterns, but while

---

[17] The North Atlantic Council, "Istanbul Summit Communiqué," June 29, 2004, para. 37. Available at http://www.nato.int/docu/pr/2004/p04-096e.htm

[18] "EU-US Declaration Supporting Peace, Progress, and Reform in the Broader Middle East and the Mediterranean," reprinted in EUISS, *EU security and defence*, op. cit., p. 144-146.

this is obviously possible, there is the competitive element as well, as in all EU-NATO relations across the board, which is the main reason for a "strategic partnership" between NATO and the EU.

In considering an admission of Turkey, the Europe of the EU has to consider these and other questions about Turkey's position between Europe and the Orient. As far as Europe is concerned, the wider the Middle East is geopolitically defined, the more independent of Europe Turkey will become for its foreign relations in the pursuit of its strategic interests outside Europe, the more influential and critical its policies will be for, and eventually in the EU. The notion of a "strategic partnership" between the enlarged EU and the "Greater Middle East" can no longer be separated from relations between Turkey and its Oriental neighbors. Ankara is the capital with the best knowledge of the region and the most valuable experience in dealing with the main countries (which was demonstrated in 2002 when the Chief of the Turkish General Staff, General Hilmi Özkok warned the emissaries of the US Administration visiting Ankara against intervening with armed force in Iraq and against the likely political consequences in Iraq for the entire region).

The EU enlargement, hence, has the most valuable and the most critical strategic implications in the case of Turkey, not only for the "Greater Middle East," but in particular for the Eastern Mediterranean, the Gulf region and the Caucasus with the Caspian region—the new main theatre of strategic challenges to Europe's security, energy supply and global aspirations. The notion, expressed by the EU commissioner Günter Verheugen in a famous comment after the recent enlargement about the envisaged membership of Turkey and of "Europe, a World Power from the North Cap to the Caucasus," may be realistic or not. The idea may become true or vanish for the simple reason of strategic overextension and political overcommitment. But whatever happens, Turkey will be the key to success or failure of EU enlargement policy and strategic partnership in the "Greater Middle East."

The EU policies of enlargement and of active involvement in the Broader Middle East tend to move the outer boundaries of European security and economic-political strategy "east of Jordan" and east of Turkey into the Gulf region and beyond towards Central and Southwest Asia. This extension of the area of European responsibility for regional stability, orderly change by reform, consolidation of the nuclear non-proliferation treaty and, where needed, diplomatic mediation of conflict, puts the EU squarely into the center of the political problems of the Orient. This is an unprecedented situation since the end of the colonial era of the British and French empires in the Mediterranean and the wider Middle East.

The EU will sooner or later confront American, Russian, Iranian, Saudi Arabian and even Indian, Chinese and Pakistani competitors for energy supply, investment and political influence. Energy, development and conservation of natural resources, i.e. water, social welfare and health care for the populations of this large and diverse region form the foundation of political reform and stability; they are strategic factors. This fact has emerged in the present post-war crisis of Iraq, in the increase of social and political tensions in the two other key countries of the Gulf Saudi Arabia and Iran as well as in the former Soviet Central Asia in Turkmenistan, Uzbekistan, Tajikistan and Kyrgyzstan, where popular revolt, organized crime and social disorder are endemic. It may well emerge within the coming years in Kazakhstan, the largest country of the region, bordering in the east on China, in the northwest on Russia, and which still has a sizeable European (Russian/Ukrainian) population.

The enlarged EU's policies and economic activities would therefore have to take into account many possibly adverse interests and developments. The cultural-religious background of the region is not favorable to compromise and peaceful resolution of the conflict. The aftermath of the Afghan Civil War of the 1970s to the 1990s, the psychological and political repercussions of the three Gulf wars since 1980, the Shiite clerical revolution and dictatorship in Iran and the prevailing insecurity in Afghanistan and in the Pakistani border regions with the hidden presence of residual Al Qaida and Taliban groups in the tribal areas have created persistent hostility towards the West in general, which does include Europe in this Oriental perception of the non-Islamic outside world, i.e. the industrial economies and trading countries, seeking their advantage over the Muslim peoples.

By their stated objectives for Iraq and their presence in Afghanistan as associates of the US and members of NATO, the EU partners appear neither in a neutral nor in an independent role, even if they have their own policies and rely more on "soft" than on "hard" power.

Their ESDP activities have not yet unfolded and their stated objectives make it necessary of them to cooperate with the US, as much directly as indirectly within the political framework of the UN.

In Iraq the European allies of the US avoided a collective responsibility of security operations by either NATO or the EU since 2003. Yet the pressure to commit themselves in accordance with UN resolutions and their own as well as the US stability pact proposal has been steadily mounting. The Iraqi interim government has asked for an armed international security force in addition to the American and British forces and the smaller foreign troop contingents. The EU supports the plans for democratization of Iraq as it does for Afghanistan. If these processes were to advance and achieve positive results, the EU would have to take an active part in consolidation of peace, security, stability, public sanitation, welfare and economic investment in the modernization of infrastructure, transports, water and energy supply. Such tasks are precisely the "soft power" tools of the ESDP and the traditional instruments of EU development assistance and cooperation.

The appeal the EU seeks to inspire on the Broader Middle East and North Africa by peaceful cooperation and humanitarian assistance, the economic advantage and energy supply security it tries to gain by its activities will force a high political profile on the EU in this part of the world and make the enlarged economic community, which is still the hard core of the EU, look more like a political power in pursuit of its own interests.

This appearance of Europe as an organized political-economic force with a military arm and linked somehow to the US tends to lend plausibility to the perception of the EU as an expansive global player, advancing on the traces of the former European empires in the Orient. Again this is inevitable, if the enlarged EU is to advance its legitimate interests and to protect its economic investments in the region with its political demands on the regional governments.

In Afghanistan, the European allies and the EU partners are already fully exposed politically in and by the International Security Assistance Force (ISAF) under NATO command and control. In 2005, the allied objective is to coordinate ISAF and US military operations of "Enduring Freedom." The EU will therefore not be able to assume a truly independent position. The European interest in fighting the poppy crop of the peasants and the drug production by the clan chiefs and war lords does align EU policy with the US, although the European interests are authentic and formulated independently from the particular military objectives of the US.

These consequences are related to the ever-larger figure the EU strikes on the world scene by its simple geographical extension, even if the hard core of power is still lacking. In Oriental eyes the EU as well as NATO stretch from the Pillars of Hercules in the Strait of Gibraltar across the Mediterranean and the Gulf to the ruins of Alexander the Great's castles and cities in Pakistan. Enlargement and forward strategies, even without military forces, blend together in an image of a neo-imperial pose, even if the European countries have neither the intention nor the capabilities for political dominance in the Broader Middle East.

# The Larger EU and
# International Affairs

## Chapter 10

# EU Enlargement and Transatlantic Relations

Esther Brimmer

In May 2004, many decision-makers in Washington, D.C. celebrated the enlargement of the European Union. The further expansion of the European Union was another glittering star in the constellation of the transatlantic community. Including former Warsaw Pact countries in a leading western institution embodied the dramatic progress made towards a Europe whole and free. Although the enlargement brings in relatively poor and—with the exception of Poland—small countries, it could change the strategic dynamic in the Euro-Atlantic area affecting relations with the United States, the global superpower anchored in the region. The impact derives less from the size or wealth of the newcomers, but their number and the changes that the EU has to make to accommodate them. By growing from fifteen to twenty-five, the EU has passed an important tipping point. It can no longer think of itself as a largely western European organization, but more clearly becomes a continent-spanning entity of over 450 million people. It needs new internal mechanisms of governance, hence the effort to create a new Constitution for Europe.

The latest enlargement has fundamentally changed the nature of the European Union yet again. The EU has undergone changes before; an EU with the United Kingdom was a different entity than the continental Union of the original six. The again enlarged Union's external actions will change and will affect transatlantic affairs. This chapter argues that enlargement enables the EU to continue to realize its primary strategic goal of maintaining security in Europe and reconciling historic enemies, but makes it harder for the EU to accomplish a secondary strategic goal of being a sharply focused, international actor with a closely coordinated foreign policy and streamlined autonomous military capabilities, both shaped by a global outlook.

Enlargement makes the EU a more legitimate voice in foreign affairs comprising twenty-five countries and over 450 million people, but changes the mix of regional and global interests within the Union. The new members bring the border of the EU closer to unstable regions in Northern and Eastern Europe and the Middle East, intensifying the EU's interest in countries such as Russia, Ukraine, and Belarus, and areas including the Maghreb and the Levant. The enlarged EU is likely to refocus its international security attention on its neighborhood and away from larger global issues such as peacekeeping and sub-Saharan Africa. Yet, strategic use of development assistance is likely to increase. Thus, the most recent enlargement may strengthen the EU's traditional strategic approach of using economic and diplomatic instruments in foreign affairs, while weakening the EU's ability to be a global military player in peacekeeping and crisis management. If it wants to make a contribution in the area of military crisis management outside Europe, the EU will need to redouble its efforts to counter the centrifugal effects of enlargement.

Americans will still be able to work with the enlarged EU. Especially when addressing issues in the neighborhood east and south of the Union, the US will need to work with the EU even more closely. Enlargement makes the EU an even more important player in that region. However, transatlantic cooperation will still need to focus on global issues beyond the Euro-Atlantic region as well, even though the EU is less likely to be a global player on strategic peace and security issues across the globe. While this point could reduce some American's fears that the EU will be a global counterweight to the US, it would disappoint others searching for capable states to support peacekeeping and conflict prevention.

Despite this shift in strategic attention, the EU will remain an important factor internationally. With a large population, abundant resources, and EU citizens in lands from Portugal to Finland, the EU has the potential to act. Increasingly, the rest of the world will look the EU for its input on a wide range of concerns, but stretched thin by diverging regional interests, will the EU be willing to respond?

## American Visions of the EU as a Strategic Actor

For American leaders, the primary strategic mission of the European Union and its predecessors has been to provide security on the continent. Integration has been the framework for making another European war unthinkable by linking prosperity with interdependence. Enlargement continues that process by extending the zone of peace and stability to countries previously hidden behind the Iron Curtain.

Yet this fundamental objective is not the only mission the EU could pursue. While it is up to Europeans to choose the direction of their Union, it is legitimate for American leaders to have views on their choices because EU actions affect the US. Within the subset of American policy makers that can accept a positive role in international affairs for the EU, there are least two schools of thought. One sees the EU as a *sui generis* entity wielding "soft" power.[1] According to this view, by using its economic clout, substantial development assistance, and diplomatic connections forged over time, the EU has created a place for itself on the international scene.

The alternative school of thought sees the EU as somewhat more traditional international actor with "hard" military capabilities as well as soft power. Some Americans and some Europeans would like the EU to play a more significant role in managing global problems, especially those that require using military force. The effort to pledge military assets to a fledgling European Security and Defense Policy (ESDP) was part of realizing this vision. However, on this point European leaders have a nuanced—and potentially divergent—views ranging from neutral Sweden's preference for European crisis management to activist France's advocacy of autonomous European capacities, to the Atlanticist Netherlands' concern that EU mechanisms not undermine the cohesion of the NATO alliance. Indeed, during the European Convention and the negotiations on the European Constitution, the Netherlands and the United Kingdom defended the primacy of NATO in defense affairs.[2]

---

[1] Joseph Nye, *Soft Power: The Means to Success in World Politics* (New York: Public Affairs, 2004).

[2] Government of the Netherlands, "The Netherlands Approach to the IGC and the Constitutional Treaty," Government Memorandum on the Netherlands' approach to the IGC sent also to the Upper House of the Netherlands Parliament, September 16, 2003. Available at http://europa.eu.int/constitution/futurum/congov_en.htm

ESDP was born out of a European desire to be a more effective security actor in its own region. After the Balkan disasters of the 1980s, France and the United Kingdom led the effort to create ESDP with their 1998 St Malo declaration. Subsequent work by the EU Council and a series of pledges by Member States have put some muscle on the skeleton of the Headline Goals. The elaboration of ESDP opened the possibility for the EU to contribute militarily to peacekeeping. After all, ESDP was intended to accomplish the "Petersberg Tasks" which are largely of a peacekeeping nature. Advocates for multilateral security and conflict management saw ESDP as a way to harness capable western militaries to help UN and other peace operations.

Indeed, the EU itself has been accepting greater responsibility for "hard power" security. In 2003, the EU took over from the United Nations in Macedonia; and in 2004 took over military functions in Bosnia from NATO. Initially these operations looked like steps towards greater EU military engagement globally, but actually they reinforce the role of the EU in its region. The test question is would the EU launch another Operation Artemis in the near future?

In 2003, the EU deployed peace enforcement forces to eastern Congo in advance of the UN operation. It was seen as a new benchmark, but it may turn out to be the high water mark of EU military deployments outside its region. The French military provided the logistical backbone for the operation's rapid deployment. Meanwhile, some Europeans may have been willing to provide political support because they wanted to show Europe using might for right in contrast to the controversial American invasion of Iraq, which was occurring at the same time.

The newest EU members have less historical interest in sub-Saharan Africa and greater concern with their immediate region. After enlargement it would be harder to build EU-wide support for military deployment far from Europe. Yet the possibility of an EU contribution to international peace and security had been a reason for some in the US to support a stronger EU military presence. To the extent that enlargement makes the EU less likely to contribute material support to conflict management, the less likely the American peace and security community is to support EU military ambitions.

# The US, the EU, and the Neighborhood: ENP and NATO

The European Union has built an array of mechanisms for shaping policy in its region, of which the enlargement process itself is the most important example. The EU also funded Technical Assistance to the Commonwealth of Independent States (TACIS) and other aid for the Eurasian region. The latest component is the "European Neighborhood Policy" (ENP), which attempts to create a framework for countries geographically close to the European Union, but which are not candidates for membership. These programs tried project stability into regions beyond the scope of membership.

The latest enlargement is likely to amplify this role. The new members care deeply about containing instability and advancing democracy in nearby parts of Europe. Hence, it was not surprising that Poland, Lithuania and others took an active interest in the Orange Revolution in Ukraine. Each new member brings into the EU an active interest in the regions just beyond their own borders, pushing outward (and eastward) the EU's conception of its neighborhood.

The United States largely supports the EU's emphasis on projecting stability. Most Americans, whether liberal internationalists or neoconservatives, would like the EU to take greater responsibility for helping Eastern Europe and Central Asia. The EU's intensive, long-term, and rigorous *acquis communitaire* helped guide the reform in Central and Eastern Europe. If the neighborhood policy can provide effective incentives for reform despite lacking the allure of membership, it would perform a service and continue to enjoy American support.

Ironically sources of transatlantic tension in the EU neighborhood may not stem from too much Europe, but too little. One concern is that the ENP will not be attractive enough. Countries in Eastern Europe and North Africa may feel that they are being offered second-class status with onerous requirements but not the rewards desired. In coming years, the US may wish that the EU consider accepting as members certain countries slated for the ENP, not for membership. For example, the idea of Ukraine eventually becoming a member of key Euro-Atlantic organizations has been more warmly received in Washington than in parts of Europe. On April 21, 2005, during a NATO ministerial meeting, US Secretary of State Condoleezza Rice stated:

NATO has responded to a historic election in Ukraine by extending an invitation to Ukraine to begin an intensified dialogue on membership issues. During the meeting last month, President Bush assured President Yushchenko of our support for Ukraine's desire to integrate into Euro-Atlantic structures. NATO's offer today of an intensified dialogue on membership issues raises NATO's cooperation with Ukraine to a new level and underscores NATO's ongoing commitment to assist the people of Ukraine on their ambitious reform agenda.[3]

Speaking less than a week later, EU Commissioner for External Relations and European Neighborhood Policy Benita Ferrero-Waldner commented:

My own feeling is that membership distracts us from the real issue. Reform in Ukraine is now an urgent matter—necessary for membership, yes, but above all necessary for the welfare of Ukrainians. I believe we should expend our energies on supporting the reform process, not on idle speculation—and I believe the Ukrainian people agree. There are wounds to heal in Ukraine, and that will take time and effort. For now, even if our final destination has not been spelt out, the door is not shut and the general direction is clear—we want closer cooperation with Ukraine.[4]

Part of this divergence reflects the fundamentally different nature of membership in NATO and in the EU, but it also could presage a transatlantic difference in emphasis in policies towards Ukraine. The relationship between the EU and NATO in northeastern Europe could be a source of tension. When the EU and NATO enlarge in the same region there is concern that accepting a country into one organization (usually NATO) would pressure the other organization (the EU) to admit the given country. However, leaders in NATO and

---

[3] Condoleezza Rice, "Press Availability at the NATO Ministerial" (Vilnius, Lithuania, April 21, 2005). Available at http://www.state.gov/secretary/rm/2005/45017.htm

[4] Benita Ferrero-Waldner, "The EU and Ukraine—what lies beyond the horizon?" Speech at Mardi de L'Europe Luncheon, hosted by the Madariaga European Foundation and the EastWest Institute (Brussels, April 26, 2005). Available at http://www.europa.eu.int/comm/external_relations/news/ferrero/2005/sp05_257.htm

the EU have managed this problem before and are likely to be able to do so again.

The most dramatic example could be Turkey. Turkey has long been a member of NATO, but has only recently been ready to begin the long path to EU membership. In December 2004, the EU announced that accession talks would begin in October 2005. However, fear of admitting Turkey and the realization that the latest round of enlargement has changed the EU fueled opposition to the proposed European constitution in France, usually a driving force for deeper European integration. Enlarging to twenty-five changed the internal dynamics of the European Union. It is now much harder for the Franco-German engine to propel the Union, because having more members creates possibilities of new coalitions within the Union to advance issues that may not be on Paris' or Berlin's agendas. Admitting Turkey would have an even more profound impact on the EU. Thus, the accession of ten new countries has highlighted the costs of enlargement making Europeans more resistant to future expansion, especially the admission of Turkey. In contrast, the 2004 enlargement to Eastern Europe reminded many Americans of the contribution of the EU to regional stability. Therefore, ironically, Americans may want enlargement more just as Europeans want it less. This will be continuing source of tension in transatlantic affairs.

## Complement or counter-weight?

Enlargement raises a long-term strategic question: will a larger EU try to complement or counter-balance the United States in international affairs? This question underlies many of the debates about transatlantic political engagement, strategic dialogue, and military cooperation.

The question of counterbalance or counterweight presumes that enlargement enhances the EU's role as a strategic actor. However, enlargement creates a deeper irony. A larger EU has greater credibility to engage in international issues such as reform in Ukraine and the promotion of democracy generally. An enlarged EU also has capabilities to address non-conventional security threats. Yet, the expanded EU's very size means that it has lost some of the political cohesion that would enable it to be a decisive strategic actor. This change is not just a question of a divergence of views among elites. The enlarged EU has left many European citizens feeling even more distant from Brussels, and possibly less willing to support ambitious international action by the EU.

Two different scenarios are on the scales. The long-term strategic impact of the latest enlargement on transatlantic relations is likely to be determined by which way the scales tip. On one side is an EU that is strong enough to balance the US and on the other an EU that is too internally divided to be an effective international partner for the US. These two options are reflected in American opinion towards the enlargement. Even among those observers who think the European Union will be increasingly important, two schools of thought dominate analysis of transatlantic relations.

The first argues that the European Union and the United States not only share fundamental values, but can and should work together constructively on international issues. In this view, the European Union will often support US positions, or at most be an amicable rival. The EU would develop political and even military capacities that would enable it to work well with the US. Partners on both sides of the Atlantic could shape their programs ranging from development assistance to military engagement on the assumption that the transatlantic community would craft policies that complemented each other. The paradigm envisions continued US leadership, but with an ever stronger partner able to act internationally with the US or in ways acceptable to the US when Washington does not chose to engage directly.

The second school of thought sees the European Union as an alternative power within international affairs consciously balancing against the dominance of the United States. The US and the EU may share values, but differ so fundamentally on the means that the EU would be willing to oppose the US outright. In this analysis, the emergence of a more strategically coherent EU would challenge America's hegemony. The debate about cooperation between the EU and NATO resonates with this concern. For many in Europe and America, NATO's leadership is a manifestation of US dominance in the Euro-Atlantic arena. Thus, developing the EU's strategic capacity separate from NATO becomes a way to create a security framework based on European, but not transatlantic, foundations.

Proponents of these two contrasting schools of thought see European security through different lenses. For example, for the EU-as-complement school, the proposed solidarity clause in the draft constitution is beneficial. The text says, "Should a Member State fall victim to a terrorist attack or a natural or man-made disaster, the other Member States shall assist it at the request of its political authorities."[5] The phrase enables EU member states to draw on the mechanisms of the nascent European Security and Defense Policy (ESDP) to manage threats within the EU. Thus, EU members could use military assets to help each other fight terrorism, a form of mutual assistance beneficial to Europe, the United States, and the international community.

The solidarity clause enables the Euro-Atlantic community to enfold more states within the blanket of western security without obligating neutral states to violate their status. It also enables EU Member States to combine civilian and military assets in ways that could be particularly relevant to complex non-traditional threats such as terrorism. The mix of civilian and military resources could be particularly useful to the new Member States, which for the most part, have fewer domestic resources. In the EU-as-complement mode, the Member States would specialize in capabilities is areas where the US does not have a strategic comparative advantage such as peacekeeping, or combining light military and civilian assets in to respond to complex humanitarian emergencies.

Alternatively, the solidarity clause could be seen as a challenge to NATO. Under Article V of the North Atlantic Treaty, the twenty-six allies pledge to assist each other using "such action as deemed necessary, including the use of armed force" in the event of an armed attack.[6] NATO provides the bedrock for transatlantic defense. Thus, for some EU Member States the solidarity clause and emerging EU defense policy risked weakening the primacy of the NATO bond. Indeed the draft EU constitution acknowledged that many Member

---

[5] Conference of the Representatives of the Governments of the Member States, "Provisional consolidated version of the draft Treaty establishing a Constitution for Europe," Title V, Chapter III, Article III-231(1), CIG 86/04, (Brussels: June 25 2004), p. 252. Available at http://ue.eu.int/igcpdf/en/04/cg00/cg00086.en04.pdf

[6] North Atlantic Treaty Organization, "North Atlantic Treaty," Article 5, (Washington, DC: April 4, 1949). Available at http://www.nato.int/docu/basictxt/treaty.htm

States base their security on NATO first. As a compromise the constitution stated,

> The common security and defence policy shall include the progressive framing of a common Union defence policy. This will lead to a common defence, when the European Council, acting unanimously, so decides. It shall in that case recommend to the Member States the adoption of such a decision in accordance with their respective constitutional requirements.
>
> The policy of the Union in accordance with this Article shall not prejudice the specific character of the security and defence policy of certain Member States, it shall respect the obligations of certain Member States, which see their common defence realised in the North Atlantic Treaty Organisation, under the North Atlantic Treaty, and be compatible with the common security and defence policy established within that framework.[7]

Many in the US were concerned that European proponents of the solidarity clause intended to downplay the NATO link. Then head of the subcommittee on Europe in the House of Representative's Committee on International Relations, Congressman Douglas Bereuter wrote in an editorial for a French newspaper "...turning to other organizations to undertake collective defense would destroy the commitment at the heart of NATO and leave its member countries less secure." He continued stressing:

> But the European Union should not seek to usurp NATO's responsibility to defend its members' territories against outside threats, . . . In the event of an external attack against a member country, NATO must remain the primary vehicle for the allies to provide for their common defense.[8]

---

[7] Treaty Establishing a Constitution for Europe, "Specific provisions relating to the common security and defence policy," Chapter II, Article I-41 (2). Available at http://www.europa.eu.int/constitution/en/ptoc8_en.htm

[8] Douglas Bereuter, "Division of Labor: NATO, EU Can Separate Missions, Protect Unity," Editorial by NATO Parliamentary Assembly President Douglas Bereuter in *Defense News* and *Le Soir*, Available at http://www.nato-pa.int/Default.asp?SHORT-CUT=478

The virulent debate around the war in Iraq added fuel to the fire about counter-balancing the US. Many of the US' closest allies were shocked by the Bush Administration's willingness to split the transatlantic community by invading Iraq with the support of only some of its allies and over the vehement objections of others. Paris and Berlin found themselves agreeing with Moscow against Washington and London. Echoing earlier disputes, some in France and elsewhere argued that European institutions needed to be strengthened because the US could no longer be trusted with international leadership. The notion of creating an EU planning cell separate from NATO in the Brussels suburb of Tervuren gained prominence during this period. Planning within the EU is not inherently anti-American. The EU needs to conduct serious analysis to be a credible strategic actor, but how Member States undertake planning in the EU affects transatlantic affairs.

Ironically, the cool aftermath of the Iraq debate may prove even more conducive to the development of the EU as a security actor than the period of impassioned controversy. During the 2002-2003 transatlantic crisis, much of the decision-making occurred in capitals. European leaders did not turn to EU mechanisms to help them develop policy on Iraq. The efforts to create a Common Foreign and Security Policy (CFSP) melted in the white-hot heat of crisis. European leaders are looking to multilateral mechanisms to help them manage their engagement with the US on the subject of the on-going simmering conflict in Iraq. Acting in a multilateral framework can help deflect attention from national government's actions. NATO training missions and EU assistance enable European countries to help Iraq and Afghanistan without enraging their publics who are critical of the war.

An enlarged EU offers more scope for the complement/counter-weight controversy. New EU Member States, especially those from Central and Eastern Europe, tend to be more "Atlanticist" than some existing members. The new states know that many US leaders were more vocal opponents of Soviet dominance than were some of their western European counterparts. These countries appreciate the presence of the US as a counter-weight to powerful states within Europe. Enlargement brings countries like Poland into the EU fold along with long-time Atlanticists such as the United Kingdom and The Netherlands. Therefore, enlargement could decrease the influence of the EU-as-counter-weight argument among Member States.

## Transatlantic Strategic Dialogue

Even if the EU is not a formal counter-weight in a multipolar game of international politics, it need not always agree with the US In the business world we believe that competition leads to better ideas. This is true in the policy realm as well. By pointing out flaws in each other's approaches, the US and the EU can help each other improve. In a sense the EU can be an international "red team" playing a role akin to that of the in-house contrarian expert in US Department of Defense strategic planning exercises.[9]

However, most European leaders would hope for a more distinctive role. Increasingly, the EU has a voice in the transatlantic security debate. Traditionally, NATO was the venue for America's conversations with Europe about strategic issues. However, fighting terrorism, promoting human rights, advancing development, and containing contagious disease require a mix of resources many of which are lodged within the civilian assets of the EU rather than the largely military ones of NATO. Exactly which capacities should be housed where is basic question facing the transatlantic community today.

The EU joined the international strategic debate with its adoption of the European Security Strategy in December 2003. It outlined five key threats: terrorism, proliferation of weapons of mass destruction, regional conflicts, state failure, and organized crime.[10] The US would present a similar list. The United States needs to deepen is security dialogue with the European Union. This is complicated. The US is not a member of the EU and is used to having its transatlantic strategic conversations within NATO. Washington is learning to speak to both big international organizations in Brussels. During his February 2005 trip to Europe, President George W. Bush made a point of meeting with EU officials. In a 2004 speech commemorating fifty years of US-EU diplomacy, then Secretary of State Colin Powell noted:

---

[9] Office of the Under Secretary of Defense for Acquisitions, Technology, and Logistics, "Defense Science Board Task Force on Role and Status of DoD Red Teaming Activities," (Washington, D.C.: U.S. Department of Defense, September 2003). Available at http://www.fas.org/irp/agency/dod/dsb/redteam.pdf

[10] European Council, "A Secure Europe in a Better World: European Security Strategy," (Brussels: 12 December, 2003), pp. 3-4.

Now, what I've discovered over the last three years is that my horizon had to expand because it is not just the 26-nation NATO alliance that is so important, but just as important is the European Union. We're not a member of the European Union, but I'll tell you what, I spend more time with my European Union colleagues and working on issues that are in common between the United States and the European Union than I do with my NATO colleagues, even though I'm not a part of this.[11]

Engaging with the EU means addressing an entity where the US may have a voice, but no vote. The European Union is the most important organization of which the US is not a member. The US has to hone new diplomatic skills to encounter the EU, which is unlike any other body, both inter-governmental and supra-national, and both enlarging and fracturing into smaller circles of "enhanced cooperation."

## Transatlantic Strategic Action

From an American perspective, one of the most important concerns is whether enlargement will affect the EU's ability to be a global partner with the US Partnership includes working together across a range of activities that could engage civilian and military assets. If the EU is a larger player on soft power issues then we could expect to see greater EU engagement on transnational issues including development and human rights. One of the most difficult questions is to what extent will the EU be a military partner? With ESDP, the EU has outlined a program for peacekeeping and other military actions. In December 2004, the EU took over from NATO in Bosnia Herzegovina. Yet, as argued above, the EU may have less appetite for peacekeeping beyond its region.

While enlargement has refocused EU attention on its neighborhood away from hard security globally, it has also given the EU greater scope to engage in transnational issues. In particular, the

---

[11] Colin Powell, "Remarks at Reception in Honor of 50 Years of Formal U.S.-EU Relations and May 1 EU Accession," (Washington, D.C.: United States Department of State, May 6, 2004), available at http://www.state.gov/secretary/rm/32285pf.htm Also, the author attended the reception and heard these words.

enlarged EU is better partner for the US on homeland security anti-terrorism measures, because it can provide a way to engage more countries in standardized anti-terrorism measure. The EU has been active on adopting EU level measures from an EU-wide arrest warrant to creating a counter-terrorism coordinator. The continuing challenge is national implementation in Member States. Still, the EU provides one of the best mechanisms to spread these measures among European countries, which contributes to American security. Thus, EU enlargement can support the already existing transatlantic homeland security cooperation that has developed since September 11.

Enlargement also makes the EU more legitimate on norms-based transnational issues. When united, the EU can claim to speak for twenty-five democracies giving it credibility on issues such as human rights and development. Moreover, the Member States' willingness to cede sovereignty to Brussels makes them appreciate multilateral settings and skilled at managing them. Thus, on issues from reform of the UN Commission on Human Rights to consideration of the recommendations of the UN High-Level Panel, to addressing the Millennium Development Goals, the US is likely to find a more vocal and assertive EU. Enlargement helps the EU increase its visibility in international political venues to match its economic heft. The EU's economic strength and the authority of Brussels to represent all Members States on trade issues has given the EU strength in the World Trade Organization and international economic issues. American diplomats are already concerned that enlargement will increase the EU's influence in international political fora, even without foreign policy being centralized in an EU-level "competency." Just as the size of the Single Market makes companies want to comply with EU standards to be able to compete, the credibility of the enlarged EU, and the desire to benefit from EU aid, could encourage other countries to adopt the EU's approaches to economic, social and cultural rights or to development policies. Yet, while the US and the EU both value human rights and development, they differ on how to pursue these ideals. Thus, enlargement could exacerbate the already existing transatlantic differences on realizing international norms and global standards.

## Conclusion

Enlargement makes EU more credible on some issues, but even less able to act decisively. Ironically, just at the US accepts that the EU has a role in security, European publics may be less willing to support it; and EU leaders less able to expend political capital to advance it. Conceivably, in the short term, the internal political debates within the EU resulting from enlargement could persuade the US to turn back to NATO for transatlantic strategic conversations rather than pursue deeper US-EU strategic dialogue. Yet neither the EU nor NATO can address all transatlantic strategic issues effectively on their own; which, in the longer term, could lead to a renewed search for EU-NATO cooperation. With enlargement more countries are members of both organizations. If NATO-EU relations are badly coordinated more countries are affected, and there would be a greater waste of political effort. EU enlargement has increased the Union's strategic interest in its neighborhood. Developing effective EU-NATO cooperation in this region will be an important factor in transatlantic relations, especially after the 2004 enlargement of the European Union. Managing transatlantic cooperation after the latest enlargement will be complicated, but the EU's neighborhood may be a good place to start.

*Chapter 11*

# A Larger EU: A More Effective Actor in the United Nations?

Chantal de Jonge Oudraat

The 2004 European Union's (EU) enlargement was the fifth and largest enlargement since 1952.[1] By adding ten new members, the Union increased its population to over 455 million. Together, the twenty-five European Union states produce a Gross Domestic Product (GDP) of € 9.613 billion—28% of world GDP. In comparison, the United States has a population of over 293 million and a GDP of approximately € 8.439 billion.[2]

What impact will the 2004 enlargement have on the EU as an independent global political actor? More specifically, will it affect the EU's role and effectiveness in the United Nations (UN)?

There are two main schools of thought on these questions. One view—the Euro-optimist school—sees EU enlargement as an evolutionary step in the making of a prosperous Europe "whole and free."[3] For them successive enlargements are logical extensions of the post-

---

[1] The EU's founding members are Belgium, France, Germany, Italy, Luxembourg, and the Netherlands. Previous EU enlargements took place in: 1973 (Denmark, Ireland and the United Kingdom); 1981 (Greece); 1986 (Portugal and Spain); 1995 (Austria, Finland and Sweden); 2004 (Cyprus, Czech Republic, Estonia, Hungary, Latvia, Lithuania, Malta, Poland, Slovakia, and Slovenia). Bulgaria and Romania are expected to accede to the Union in 2007, and the EU will start accession talks with Turkey in 2005.

[2] Turkey's accession would increase the EU's population to some 550 million people. It is expected that Turkey's population will rise to 80 or 90 million by 2015—the date of possible accession for Turkey.

[3] Many institutionalists as well as the EU Commission and the EU High Representative subscribe to these views. See also Roy Ginsberg, *The Years of the European Union Foreign Policy: Baptism, Confirmation, Validation* (Berlin: Heinrich Boell Foundation, 2003); Alexandra Novosseloff, EU-UN Partnership in Crisis Management: Developments and Prospects (New York: International Peace Academy, June 2004); H. Wallace and W. Wallace, eds. *Policymaking in the European Union* (Oxford:Oxford University Press, 2000); and John van Oudenaren, *The Changing Face of Europe: EU Enlargement and Implications for Transatlantic Relations*, (Washington, DC: American Institute for Contemporary German Studies; AICGS Policy Report No. 6).

World War II European project. Optimists argue that the 2004 enlargement will change the relative weight of Europe in the world and will strengthen Europe's role as a global actor. They believe that a larger EU, because of its increased numbers, will automatically have more resources to bring to the table and thus be a more powerful actor within international institutions, particularly global institutions such as the United Nations. Optimists are therefore active proponents of enlargement.

The second school of thought—the Euro-pessimist view—stresses the challenges associated with enlargement.[4] Most proponents of this school of thought believe that it will be increasingly difficult to reconcile national interests with an ever-growing number of member states. They argue that the difference between small and big states and unequal economic development within the Union will lead to increasing friction. The result will be minimalist and incoherent EU policies. This, in turn, will diminish the role of the EU as a global actor and its role in global institutions such as the United Nations. Pessimists worry about collective action problems, and they consequently oppose enlargement efforts.

In this chapter, I make the case for an alternative third view—the Euro-pragmatic view. I believe that the push for successive EU enlargements is unstoppable and at the core of the European project. This project seeks to promote liberal democracy, "not as a monopoly of west Europeans but as [a] strongly to be preferred system to be defended against competing models in the immediate neighborhood."[5] That said, enlargement inevitably complicates decision-making processes and

---

[4] See, for example, Robert Lieber, *The European Union and the United States: Threats, Interests and Values*, (Washington, DC: ACES Working Paper, August 13, 2004). For a general discussion regarding the implications of enlargement see also Eberhard Rhein, *EU Enlargement: Short Term Costs—Long Term Benefits*, (Brussels: The European Policy Centre, January 21, 2002); Eberhard Rhein, *A Fresh Look at EU Common and Security Policy* (Brussels: The European Policy Centre, February 13, 2002); Lily Gardner, "The Implications of Enlargement for the EU as an International Political Actor: Opportunities and Risks," in *EU Enlargement and Transatlantic Relations: Background and Analyses* (Washington, DC: American Institute for Contemporary German Studies; AICGS Policy report No. 7), pp.85-110; and Andrew Moravcsik and Milada Anna Vachudova, *National Interests, State Power, and EU Enlargement* (Cambridge, Mass.: Center for European Studies, Harvard University, Working Paper No.97, 2002).

[5] H. Wallace and W. Wallace, "Introduction," in H. Wallace and W. Wallace, eds., *Policymaking in the European Union*, (Oxford: Oxford University Press, 2000), p.50.

raises collective action problems. Without strong leadership, these problems may become debilitating. The challenge is to make the best of an inevitable, inherently difficult, but potentially transformative situation.

I develop four main arguments in this chapter. First, EU enlargement *per se* does not make the EU a stronger international actor. Greater numbers do not necessarily translate into greater might. Second, EU enlargement does raise the level of expectations within the UN and around the world. According to the UN system of collective security, great powers have special responsibilities for the stability of the international system. Responding to this higher level of expectations will be difficult for the EU, but failure to meet these expectations, will undermine the EU's credibility and diminish its global role. Third, the EU's role as an independent global political actor—that is, an actor capable of developing and implementing a set of unified and coherent policies—depends on agreement and action by a limited number of European actors, most notably France, Germany, and the United Kingdom. Action by them under the EU umbrella strengthens the EU has a whole. New EU members may contribute to these efforts, but they are unlikely to be leaders of these efforts. Fourth, the EU and all EU member states frequently proclaim that strengthening the UN is a top priority. Yet, some EU action may actually undercut UN effectiveness. This is particularly true in peacekeeping operations. Indeed, military peace operations under an EU umbrella may have the unintended consequence of undercutting UN actions in this domain. Operations under the EU flag will reduce the already small pool of European soldiers available to serve in UN-led operations. The EU must be attentive to both the short term and long-term consequences of its interventions.

In this chapter, I analyze the impact of EU enlargement on the role and effectiveness of the EU within the United Nations and, more generally, the prospects for the EU's effectiveness as an independent global international actor. I will focus on the peace and security arena. I do four things. First, I begin by outlining the institutional responsibilities and competencies of both the EU and the UN in international peace and security affairs. Second, I discuss EU representation at the UN and examine EU contributions to the UN. Third, I examine the EU-UN relationship in the key policy area of conflict prevention and crisis management. I conclude with policy recommendations.

## Institutional Competencies and Responsibilities

EU statements routinely reiterate "that primary responsibility for the maintenance of international peace and security lies with the United Nations" and that the EU conflict prevention and crisis management capacity "aims to support the Security Council in carrying out its responsibilities under the UN Charter."[6] EU Presidencies frequently reiterate the EU's desire "to strengthen European Union collaboration with the United Nations in strategic sectors such as crisis management."[7] The EU Security Strategy adopted by the European Council in December 2003 states, "Strengthening the United Nations, equipping it to fulfill its responsibilities and to act effectively, is a European priority."[8]

Before examining whether and how the EU strengthens the UN system, it is important to discuss the EU and UN institutional mechanisms responsible for international peace and security.

### The European Union

Since the late 1990s, the EU has steadily developed its military and non-military capabilities and put into place dedicated institutional mechanisms within the European Council, the General Secretariat of the Council, and the Commission to deal with conflict prevention and crisis management.[9]

Within the EU, the main responsibility for security matters lies with the European Council. The appointment in 1999 of Javier Solana

---

[6] For example, see the statement by H.E. Mr. Ionanis Magriotis, Deputy Minister of Foreign Affairs of Greece on behalf of the European Union, on "The Security Council and Regional Organizations: Facing the New Challenges to Peace and Security," at the Security Council in New York on April 11, 2003. These statements did not prevent the Europeans from intervening in Kosovo without UN Security Council authorization.

[7] See the telephone conversation between the Italian Foreign Affairs Minister Franco Frattini and UN Secretary General Kofi Annan on August 5, 2003. Press Release, GAER, August 5, 2003.

[8] See *A Secure Europe in a Better World*. It may also be recalled that the EU General Affairs Council decided in June 2001 that UN-EU political cooperation would focus on three areas: (1) conflict prevention; (2) civilian and military aspects of crisis management; (3) the Western Balkans, the Middle East and Africa. The European Council in Göteborg endorsed this decision in June 2001.

[9] The principles of a more effective foreign and security policy for the European Union were defined in the Maastricht (1992), Amsterdam (1997) and Nice (2001) treaties and the European Union Constitution Treaty (2003).

as the Secretary General of the General Secretariat of the EU Council and as the EU High Representative for the Common Foreign and Security Policy (CFSP) of the Union was a big step forward. It provided the Union with an identifiable face. In addition, Solana occasionally develops autonomous policy initiatives and thus gives "voice to more than the simple sum of the EU parts."[10] Solana drafted the EU Security Strategy, which was adopted by the Council in 2003. It was another milestone in the development of CFSP in that it provided the Union with a foreign and security policy doctrine.[11]

The European Security and Defence Policy (ESDP) is the operational arm of the CFSP. The 1998 Anglo-French Declaration in St. Malo laid down the parameters of a European defense policy. The main objective of ESDP was the development of autonomous military capabilities for the Union to respond to international crises. The 1999 Helsinki European Council called for the creation of an EU Rapid Reaction Force (EURRF)—a 60,000-strong force capable of deploying within 60 days for at least one year. The EURRF was to be capable of carrying out tasks ranging from conflict prevention to the use of military force in peace enforcement operations. The military component was declared operational in May 2003, even though it was acknowledged that certain shortcomings persisted.

However, Nordic EU member states and Ireland insisted that ESDP should also have a civilian component. The civilian component of ESDP was defined at the Feira European Council in June 2000. The Council identified four priority areas and set targets for the deployment of police, rule of law experts, civilian administrators, and civil protection personnel. The Council also pledged to create a force

---

[10] See Antonio Missiroli, "ESDP-How it Works," in Nicole Gnesotto, ed., *EU Security and Defence Policy: The first five years* (1999-2004), (Paris: EU Institute for Security Studies, 2004), p. 63.

[11] The High Representative is supported in his daily work by a Policy Planning and Early Warning Unit. The Policy Unit is supported by a Joint Situation Centre (JCS) that has both civilian and military components. The High Representative can also appoint EU Special Representatives to help with crisis management and co-ordination of EU (Council) policy towards a region. In 2005 the EU had Special Representatives for: Moldova; the former republic of Macedonia; the Middle East Peace Process; the South Caucasus; Afghanistan; Bosnia and Herzegovina; the Stability Pact for Southern Europe; and the African Great Lakes region.

of 5,000 police officers, 1,000 of whom would be deployable within 30 days, and to develop a roster of 200 rule of law experts as well as 2,000 civil protection experts, 100 of whom would be deployable within 24 hours.[12] The civilian component became operational in November 2002.[13]

In 2004 the Council decided to create rapid reaction Battle Groups. These units are to be deployable within ten days and sustainable for at least 30 days (extendable to 120 days by rotation). These battalion-sized groups are comprised of up to 1,500 troops. In November 2004 it was decided to create up to thirteen Battle Groups with initial operational capability in 2005 and full capability in 2007.[14] Battle Groups could serve under—but not exclusively—a UN mandate and should be able to conduct missions in extremely hostile environments. Battle Groups could be deployed in two types of operations: (1) A Bridging Operation—that is, an operation that intervenes for a short period of time to allow an another organization such as the UN to mount a subsequent long-term peacekeeping operation; (2) A Stand-by Operation—that is, an operation that would be deployed in support of a UN operation and could be used to extract forces from hostile situations. Both models would require close coordination with the UN and fine-tuning on such issues as force generation. For example, the UN typically needs six months generate the necessary forces for its operations. This is a period much longer than the projected deployment of the Battle Groups.[15]

In 2004, France, Spain, Italy, the Netherlands and Portugal also committed to create a 3,000-strong European Gendarmerie Force

---

[12] The Nice Treaty (2001) added a Committee for Civilian Aspects of Crisis Management (CivCom) and a Policy Unit in the Secretariat. To plan and organize military operations, a Political and Security Committee (PSC, also known as COPS) and a European Military Committee (EUMC) was set up. It is supported by a European Military Staff (EUMS).

[13] For a critical analysis of the EU's civilian crisis management capacity, see Peter Viggo Jakobsen, *The Emerging EU Civilian Crisis Management Capacity-A "real added value" for the UN?* Background paper for the Copenhagen Seminar on Civilian Crisis Management arranged by the Royal Danish Ministry of Foreign Affairs, June 8-9, 2004.

[14] France, Italy and the UK are each responsible for one Battle Group to become operational in 2005. The other ten Battle Groups are collaborative ventures of several member states. See EU Military Capability Commitment Conference, Brussels, November 22, 2004.

[15] For a discussion of the Battle Groups and ESDP, see Fraser Cameron and Gerrard Quille, *ESDP: The State of Play* (Brussels: European Policy Centre, September 2004).

(EGF) to become operational in 2005 and deployable within 30 days. The EGF would have three main functions: conflict prevention; support for a military intervention; and post-conflict stabilization.[16]

While most foreign policy issues are the domain of the Council, the European Commission is responsible for a wide range of development and humanitarian issues—essential tools for conflict prevention or post-conflict stabilization and reconstruction.[17] The Conflict Prevention and Crisis Management Unit in the External Relations Directorate provides expertise and promotes conflict assessment methodologies within the Commission. In addition, the Commission's Humanitarian Aid Office (ECHO) is responsible for emergency assistance.[18] The Commission has also been very active in developing the civilian component of ESDP.[19] For example, in 2001 the Council created a Rapid Reaction Mechanism that allows the Commission to launch quick initiatives in peace building, reconstruction and development.

The European Parliament (EP) has less influence on EU foreign policy, although its influence has steadily increased. The European Parliament receives briefings by the Presidency, the High Representative and the Commission on CFSP and ESDP. Since 1999, the Council has also provided the EP with an annual report on the financial implications of CSFP for the general budget of the European communities. The EP has co-decision powers regarding the Community budget. In addition, in 2004 the EP's Committee on Foreign Affairs created a sub-committee on ESDP.

The EU Constitution streamlines responsibilities in the foreign and defence field by combining the roles, responsibilities and resources of

---

[16] For other civilian crisis management objectives see *Headline Goal 2010* endorsed by the European Council of June 17 and 18, 2004; *Action Plan for Civilian Aspects of ESDP*, European Council, June 2004; and *Civilian Capabilities Commitment Conference: Ministerial Declaration*, Brussels November 22, 2004. In June 2004 EU member states decided to increase capabilities in the areas of police, rule of law, civilian administration and civil protection. They also decided to establish a monitoring capability staffed with some 500 personnel.

[17] The Commission is the most integrated of EU institutions. It is the executive branch of the EU and can make legislative proposals to be approved by the Council and the European Parliament.

[18] In 2003 ECHO had a budget of 600 million Euros.

[19] The Political and Security Committee and the Directorate for Civilian Crisis Management are particularly important in this regard.

the High Representative for CFSP and the Commissioner for External Relations into a single EU Minister for Foreign Affairs.[20] The Constitution, if and when it is ratified by all EU member states, would also allow small groups of states to work together on policy initiatives that are not backed by all EU members. In the defence field, this procedure is called "structured cooperation."[21] Finally, the Constitution would create a legal personality for the EU, allowing it to sign treaties and become a legal observer to the United Nations.[22]

Although the draft EU constitution is an improvement over current EU arrangements, it does not resolve the problem of shared responsibilities between the Council and the Commission. This problem is especially pronounced in the areas of peacekeeping, humanitarian actions, terrorism and the fight against the proliferation of WMD—that is, situations that require a mix of both civilian and military responses. The military response is the responsibility of the Council—it remains squarely in the hands of government. The civilian response is mainly the responsibility of the Commission.[23]

---

[20] The Minister would be appointed by the Council and would be one of the Vice-Presidents of the European Commission. He would be accountable to the Council—member states—not the Commission. The Constitution would also get rid of the three-pillar structure. At present the Union is made up of three pillars. The first pillar covers economic, social and environmental policies and most decisions are made by qualified majority voting. The second pillar consists of CFSP and the third pillar is the Police and Judicial Co-operation in Criminal Matters (Justice and Home Affairs) pillar. Member states retain veto right over most decisions taken in each one of the latter two pillars. Similarly, the powers of the Commission with respect to the Council are restricted in the last two pillars. The new Constitution would give the Commission greater powers in Justice and Home Affairs.

[21] The Council would need to approve such initiatives by a majority vote. The idea of a select number of countries coming together for a specific policy initiative had already been introduced in the Amsterdam treaty. It was called enhanced cooperation. However, conditions were very strict and the procedure has never been used. Instead the EU has relied on negotiated op-outs from certain policies.

[22] The Union now has no legal personality The European Community (EC) has and is represented by the Commission. The EC was granted observer status at the UN in 1974.

[23] For more on the institutional architecture of the EU see *EU Crisis Response Capability Revisited* (Brussels: International Crisis Group, Europe Report No 160, January 2005). The Constitution would also establish an European Foreign Service see Giovanni Grevi and Fraser Cameron, *Towards an EU Foreign Service* (Brussels: European Policy Centre, Issue Paper 29, October 2004).

*The United Nations*

The UN has a broad and strong mandate for the prevention, management and resolution of violent conflict.[24] Indeed, the United Nations was established "to maintain international peace and security, and to that end: to take effective collective measures for the prevention and removal of threats to the peace (...)."[25] The UN Security Council (UNSC) was given primary responsibility for maintaining and restoring peace and security. Its decisions require the support of all five permanent members, and when taken under authority of Chapter VII of the UN Charter they are legally binding on all UN member states.[26]

The UNSC's ability to handle peace and security problems was severely constrained during—and by—the Cold War. However, since the end of the Cold War, the Council's level of activity in security affairs in general and in intra-state security problems in particular has increased dramatically. After the first Gulf War it established a body to oversee Iraqi disarmament—the UN Special Commission (UNSCOM). Since the early 1990s the UNSC has also been extremely active in the campaign against international terrorism. In 2001, it established a body to monitor implementation of its counter-terrorism decisions—the Counter-Terrorism Committee (CTC).[27] In 2004, the Council stepped up its counter-proliferation efforts and established a Committee (the 1540 Committee) to review and monitor efforts by states to prohibit and prevent nuclear materials from falling into the hands of non-state actors—that is, terrorist groups. In sum, since the end of the Cold War, the UNSC has increasingly asserted itself in the management of international peace and security issues by establishing specific subsidiary bodies tasked with the monitoring and verification of the implementation of its decisions.

---

[24] See also the UN Millennium Declaration A/Res/55/2 and the UN Security Council Resolution 1318 (2000) in which member states pledge to enhance the effectiveness of the United Nations in this field.

[25] See Charter of the United Nations, Article 1 (1).

[26] The five Permanent members of the Council are: China, France, Russia, the United Kingdom and the United States.

[27] See Chantal de Jonge Oudraat, "Combatting Terrorism," *Washington Quarterly*, Vol. 26, No.4, Autumn 2003, pp.163-176. In 2004, the Committee was enhanced by the creation of a small secretariat—the Counter Terrorism Executive Directorate (CTED).

Although the main locus of responsibility for conflict prevention and crisis management within the UN lies with the UNSC, many other UN bodies, departments and agencies also have responsibilities in this field.[28] For example, the General Assembly may discuss questions relating to the maintenance of international peace and security and make recommendations on these issues, even if problems that require action must be referred to the Security Council.[29] Within the Secretariat, the political and military operational aspects of conflict prevention and crisis management are dealt with by the UN Secretary-General, the Executive Committee on Peace and Security (ECPS), the Department for Peacekeeping (DPKO), the Department for Political Affairs (DPA), and the Department for Disarmament Affairs (DDA). The UN High Commissioner for Refugees (UNHCR) and the Office of the Coordination of Humanitarian Affairs (OCHA) are the main bodies responsible for the humanitarian aspects of conflict prevention and crisis management.

## The EU at the UN

All the major EU institutions—the European Council, including the EU High Representative for the Common Foreign and Security Policy (CFSP), the European Commission and the European Parliament—have called for an active commitment to "effective multilateralism" as a defining principle for the EU's external policy. They have pledged active support to the United Nations as the main pillar of the multilateral

---

[28] In his 2005 report *In Larger Freedom: Towards Development, Security and Human Rights for All* UN Secretary-General Kofi Annan also proposed the established of an intergovernmental Peacebuilding Commission and a Peacebuilding Support Office in the UN Secretariat. The main task of these bodies would be to safeguard countries from sliding back into war after peace agreements have been signed, by ensuring that there is a coordinated approach to all post-conflict activities.

[29] See Article 11 of the UN Charter. Article 12 of the Charter states that the General Assembly is not to make recommendations on problems under consideration by the Council. The predominance of the Council—and its often opaque decision making process, including the predominance of its permanent members, most notably the United States—has spurred much criticism in the corridors of the General Assembly. For recent efforts to reenergize UN General Assembly involvement in peace and security issues, see the high level retreat organized by the International Peace Academy in May 2003, *From Promise to Practice: Revitalizing the General Assembly for the New Millennium* at www.ipa.org.

system.[30] According to the European Commission, failure to support the United Nations would be "devastating."[31] The EU High Representative for Common Foreign and Security Policy stated in June 2003, "the fundamental framework for international relations is the United Nations Charter. Strengthening the United Nations, equipping it to fulfil its responsibilities and to act effectively, must be a European priority."[32]

The relationship between the EU and the UN is often examined under the broad umbrella of UN relations with regional organizations. This, however, is a perspective that fails to recognize the unique features of the EU. The European Union is more than a regional inter-governmental organization—a political association of states—in the traditional sense. The EU is a complex, evolving political entity that at times displays the characteristics of a unitary state and at times the characteristics of a traditional inter-governmental organization, where the lowest common denominator prevails. In addition, unlike many regional organizations, the EU is a major donor to UN programs.[33]

The relationship between the EU and the UN faces two types of problems. One is political and has to do with representation. The other is operational and is mostly a coordination problem.

*Representation*

Three issues arise with respect to the representation issue. The first has to do with the legal status of the EU and the question of who is entitled to speak for the Union in the UN. The second has to do with UN Security Council reform and the question of European representation at the Council. The third issue has to do with the organization of regional groups within the UN and over-representation of European states within UN bodies.

---

[30] See, the communication from the Commission to the Council and the European Parliament, *The European Union and the United Nations: The Choice of Multi-lateralism*, Brussels, 10.9,2003, COM (2003) 526, p.3.; *A Secure Europe in a Better World: European Security Strategy*, December 12, 2003, Council doc. CLO3-380 EN; The EU, *The Enlarging European Union and the United Nations: Making Multilateralism Matter*, (Brussels; The European Communities, April 2004).

[31] *The European Union and the United Nations.*

[32] Ibid., p.4.

[33] The EU, that is the Commission, contributes on average between € 300-400 million annually to various UN programs.

*Legal Status*

Pending the ratification of the EU Constitution, which would give the Union a legal personality and the potential to be formally represented at the UN, under current procedures the Union is represented by the state holding the Presidency of the EU Council.[34] EU visibility in the UN received an important boost in September 2000 when the EU leadership—past and current Presidents of the European Council (in this case France and Sweden), Chris Patten (the European Commissioner for External Relations) and Solana—met for the first time ever with the UN Secretary-General, Kofi Annan. Since that time, EU-UN meetings have been taking place at the ministerial level once or twice per year. The EU Presidency also makes statements on behalf of the EU in the open meetings of the UN Security Council.

On average, every six months some 20 statements are delivered at the UN Security Council on behalf of the EU. In January 2002, Solana addressed the UN Security Council for the first time.[35] He has subsequently addressed the Council on several other occasions.[36] These arrangements allow for greater EU visibility at the UN, but this does not necessarily translate into greater influence at the UN.

Under Article 19 of the European Union Treaty, member states shall coordinate their action in international organizations and at international conferences. The treaty also stipulates that member states will keep other member states informed of any common interests and that permanent members of the UN Security Council

---

[34] The Council established a small liaison office in New York in 1994 in the context of the Maastricht treaty. The EU Commission also has a delegation in New York and is the legal representative of the European Communities (EC).

[35] See his statement on January 29, 2002 at the UN Security Council public meeting on the situation in Africa.

[36] For example, see his statements on March 5, 2002 on the situation in Bosnia and Herzegovina and his statement on the DRC on July 18, 2003; or September 23, 2004 on Civilian Crisis Management. The High Representative has also addressed the UN Commission on Human Rights on March 19, 2002. The EU has also been active in the work of the UN Security Council Counter Terrorism Committee (CTC). The EU Presidency spoke on several occasions on behalf of the EU and submitted special EU reports on efforts undertaken at the European level to prevent and combat terrorism. See statements on April 23 2002 and the EU reports to the CTC S/2001/1297 dated December 28 2001 and S/2002/928 dated August 16 2002. See also the EU statements in the open UN Security Council debate of February 20 2003 and July 23 2003.

(France and the United Kingdom) will ensure the defense of the positions and interests of the Union. [37]

Efforts to keep EU member states informed of developments in the Security Council have improved since 2001. EU member states meet weekly in New York for the so-called Article 19 briefings.[38] That said, most of these briefings are post-facto actions. Sensitive political issues such as the war in Iraq or reform of the UN Security Council reform have not been raised.

Euro-pessimists argue that EU enlargement will increase divisiveness among EU members. They predict that consultation on politically sensitive issues will remain largely outside formal EU channels. They point to the fight over the Iraq war, the division between old and new Europe, and the situation with respect to Iran as examples of this problem. Euro-optimists believe that the emergence of EU policy statements and EU policy briefings is a huge step forward. This, it is said, will gradually create habits of cooperation. However, mere statements and briefings are not enough. Real progress must entail a willingness by EU member states to make a concerted effort to discuss sensitive political issues. Failure to take a position on sensitive issues, weakens the EU and ultimately the UN. The lack of a unified EU position on UN Security Council reform is particularly damaging, in this regard.

---

[37] The EU Constitutional Treaty has a similar provision. It stipulates in Article III-206: "(1) Member states shall coordinate their action in international organizations and at international conferences. They shall uphold the Union's positions in such fora. The Union Minister for Foreign Affairs shall organize this coordination. In international organizations and at international conferences where not all Member States participate, those, which do take part, shall uphold the Union's positions. (2) In accordance with Article I-15 (2), Member States represented in international organizations or international conferences where not all Member States participate shall keep the latter, as well as the Union Minister for Foreign Affairs, informed of any matter of common interest. Member States, which are also members of the United Nations Security Council, shall concert and keep the other Member States and the Union Minister for Foreign Affairs fully informed. Member States which are members of the Security Council will, in execution of their functions, defend the positions and the interests of the Union, without prejudice to their responsibilities under the United Nations Charter. When the Union has defined a position on a subject which is on the United Nations Security Council Agenda, those Member States which sit on the Security Council shall request that the Union Foreign Minister for Foreign Affairs be asked to present the Union's position.

[38] Article 19 briefings were established on the initiative of France and Spain during the Swedish Presidency. Germany was particularly instrumental in enhancing information to EU member states not member of the UN Security Council. Germany and Spain were both members of the UN Security Council in 2003 and 2004.

*UN Security Council Reform*

Reform of the UN Security Council has been on the UN agenda for over a decade. The Iraq war and the subsequent deep divisions among member states prompted UN Secretary-General Kofi Annan to call for far-reaching reforms, including UN Security Council reform.[39] He argued that if members states wanted "the Council's decisions to command greater respect" they needed to address the issue of its composition urgently.

Germany's active campaign in 2004 and 2005 to secure a permanent seat on the UN Security Council has been divisive among Europeans and Americans.[40] The main argument against a German Security Council is over-representation by European states on the Council. Some observers argue that if the aim of UN Security Council Reform is to make the Council more representative of the international community, then Europe should give up a seat instead of gaining another seat. Adding another European seat to the UN Security Council would actually make the Council less representative, particularly given the requirement under both the European Union Treaty and the European Constitution that European states should coordinate their positions in the UN. In addition, it is argued that given the increased importance of the European Common and

---

[39] See Kofi Annan's "Fork in the Road" speech to the General Assembly on September 23, 2003; and his report *In Larger Freedom.*

[40] In 2005 two models for UN Security Council expansion were on the table. Model A would increase the Council with six permanent members (without veto power) and three new two-year term non-permanent seats. In model A seats would be divided among four regions as follows: Africa: 2 permanent seats and 4 two-year term seats; Asia and the Pacific: 3 permanent seats and 3 two-year term seats; Europe: 4 permanent seats and 2 two-year term seats; Americas: 2 permanent seats and 4 two-year term seats. Model B provides for no new permanent seats but creates a new category of eight four-year renewable terms seats and one new two-year non-permanent and non-renewable seat. Seats would be divided among the four regional areas as follows: Africa: 2 four-year renewable seats and 4 two-year non-renewable seats; Asia and Pacific: 1 permanent seat; 2 four-year renewable seats and 3 two-year non-renewable seats; Europe: 3 permanent seats; 2 four-year renewable seats; and 1 two-year non-renewable seat; Americas: 1 permanent seat; 2 four-year renewable seats; and 3 two-year non-renewable seats. At present the Council has 15 members: five permanent members (China; France, Russia, the United Kingdom and the United States) and 10 non-permanent elected for two year non-renewable staggered terms. Each year five new members are elected. Non-permanent seats are allotted as follows: 5 for Africa and Asia; one for Eastern Europe; two for Latin America and two for Western Europe and other states.

Security Policy (CFSP) the Europeans should seek one EU seat in the UN Security Council.[41]

This argument fails to recognize political realities. Indeed, while the EU has made remarkable progress with respect to political integration, it is far from being a unitary state. The 2003 Iraq war demonstrated the existence of deep divisions amongst European states. National interests remain the main driving force of foreign policy decision making for most European states. European positions on issues before the UN Security are often not unified. Under these conditions, it is unrealistic to expect France and the United Kingdom to give up their permanent seats.

Italy, Spain, Poland and the Netherlands have all come out against a German seat on the Council and argued for an EU seat.[42] One of the arguments put forward is that a German seat in the UN Security Council would undermine attempts to further develop the CFSP. The logic of this argument is hard to follow. German membership of the Council would not alter either one of their country's national security interests nor obstruct the definition of a common European position. The public opposition of these countries seems to be more reflective of intra-European political bargaining processes.

In addition, opponents of a German permanent seat fail to recognize that, according to the founders of the United Nations, membership on the UN Security Council was to be based not on a logic of representation but on a logic of effectiveness. Article 23 of the UN Charter spells out the criteria for election to the UN Security Council. It stipulates "due regard being specifically paid, in the first instance to the contribution of Members of the United Nations to the maintenance of international peace and security and to the other purposes of the Organization (...)." Equitable geographical distribution is a secondary consideration. Membership of the Council confers special responsibilities and presupposes that members will make available their national resources for the common good.

---

[41] See, for example, John van Oudenaren, *AICGS Advisor*, April 7, 2005. In 2004 the European Parliament also spoke in favor of one EU seat to replace the current British and French seats.

[42] Opposition to a German seat on the Security Council is also strong in the United States, particularly after German opposition to the Iraq war and its subsequent unwillingness to deploy troops in Iraq.

**Table 1. Contributions to the UN General Budget and Peacekeeping Operations**

| | UN General Budget 2005 | | | | UN Peacekeeping 2005 | | | | |
|---|---|---|---|---|---|---|---|---|---|
| | $Millions | Share% | Top 20 | Share% | Civ.Pol | Milob | Troops | Total | Ranking |
| **United States** | **439.6** | **22** | | **26.5** | **332** | **20** | **11** | **363** | **30** |
| EU25 Total | 729.5 | 36.7 | | 38.5 | 1,006 | 328 | 3044 | 4,378 | |
| *EU-15* | *709.4* | *35.6* | | *38.1* | *835* | *266* | *2090* | *3191* | |
| Germany | 173.1 | 8.7 | 3 | 8.7 | 268 | 14 | 13 | 295 | 36 |
| UK | 122.4 | 6.1 | 4 | 7.4 | 99 | 16 | 284 | 399 | 29 |
| France | 120.5 | 6 | 5 | 7.3 | 162 | 34 | 403 | 599 | 21 |
| Italy | 97.6 | 4.9 | 6 | 4.9 | 66 | 20 | 108 | 194 | 44 |
| Spain | 50.4 | 2.5 | 8 | 2.5 | 45 | 7 | 203 | 255 | 38 |
| Netherlands | 33.8 | 1.7 | 12 | 1.7 | 6 | 16 | 2 | 24 | 76 |
| Belgium | 21.4 | 1.1 | 17 | 1.1 | | 11 | 7 | 18 | 81 |
| Sweden | 19.9 | 1 | 18 | 1 | 52 | 29 | 231 | 312 | 34 |
| Austria | 17.1 | 0.9 | 20 | 0.9 | 29 | 12 | 378 | 419 | 27 |
| Denmark | 14.3 | 0.7 | | 0.7 | 23 | 35 | 3 | 61 | 58 |
| Greece | 10.6 | 0.5 | | 0.5 | 17 | 9 | 26 | 73 | |
| Finland | 10.7 | 0.5 | | 0.5 | 7 | 29 | 8 | 44 | 66 |
| Portugal | 9.4 | 0.5 | | 0.5 | 42 | 8 | 11 | 61 | 57 |
| Ireland | 6.7 | 0.4 | | 0.3 | 19 | 26 | 439 | 484 | 24 |
| Luxembourg | 1.5 | 0.1 | | 0.1 | | | | | |
| *EU-10 (new)* | *20.1* | *1.1* | | *0.42* | *171* | *62* | *954* | *1187* | |
| Poland | 9.2 | 0.5 | | 0.1 | 124 | 23 | 574 | 721 | 20 |
| Czech Rep. | 3.7 | 0.2 | | 0.05 | 13 | 16 | | 29 | 72 |
| Hungary | 2.5 | 0.1 | | 0.1 | 12 | 16 | 82 | 110 | 51 |
| Slovenia | 1.6 | 0.1 | | 0.08 | 14 | 2 | | 16 | 84 |
| Slovakia | 1 | 0.1 | | 0.02 | | 3 | 298 | 301 | 35 |
| Cyprus | 0.8 | 0.04 | | 0.04 | | | | | |

(Continued on next page)

**Table 1. (Continued) Contributions to the UN General Budget and Peacekeeping Operations**

| | UN General Budget 2005 | | | UN Peacekeeping 2005 | | | | | |
|---|---|---|---|---|---|---|---|---|---|
| | $Millions | Share% | Top 20 | Share% | Civ.Pol | Milob | Troops | Total | Ranking |
| Lithuania | 0.5 | 0.02 | | 0.01 | 8 | | | 8 | 91 |
| Latvia | 0.3 | 0.02 | | 0.004 | | | | | |
| Malta | 0.3 | 0.01 | | 0.01 | | | | | |
| Estonia | 0.2 | 0.01 | | 0.01 | | 2 | | 2 | 102 |
| Japan | 389 | 19.5 | 2 | 19.3 | | | 30 | 30 | 71 |
| Canada | 56.2 | 2.8 | 7 | 2.5 | 109 | 13 | 205 | 327 | 32 |
| China | 41 | 2 | 9 | 1.9 | 192 | 60 | 790 | 1,042 | 16 |
| Mexico | 38 | 1.9 | 10 | 1.2 | | | | | |
| Rep. of Korea | 35.9 | 1.8 | 11 | 1.6 | 32 | 16 | 94 | 142 | 47 |
| Australia | 31.8 | 1.6 | 13 | 1.6 | | | | | |
| Brazil | 30.4 | 1.5 | 14 | 0.5 | 10 | 8 | 1,353 | 1,371 | 14 |
| Switzerland | 24 | 1.2 | 15 | | 12 | 17 | 2 | 31 | 70 |
| Russian Fed. | 22 | 1.1 | 16 | 1.5 | 135 | 99 | 116 | 350 | 31 |
| Argentina | 19 | 1 | 19 | 1 | 135 | 5 | 997 | 1,137 | 15 |
| TOTAL all UN member states | 1998.2 | 100 | | 100 | 6,466 | 2,113 | 58,571 | 67,150 | 103 |

Sources: Assessment of Member States' contributions to the UN Regular Budget for the Year 2005, December 23 2004, ST/ADM/SER.B/638; Implementation of General Assembly resolutions 55/235 and 55/236, Report of the secretary-General, A/58/157/Add.1, December 17 2003.

In July 2001 the General Assembly decided that the rates of assessment for peacekeeping operations should be based on the scale of assessments for the regular UN budget with a system of adjustments. It established ten levels of contributions. See A/Res/55/235 and A/Res/55/236 of December 23, 2000.

Data on Civilian Police (Civ.Pol), Military Observers (Milob) and Troops is current as of March 31 2005. See UN Department of Peacekeeping Operations website

Top 20 contributors to UN Peacekeeping Operations are: 1. Pakistan 9,903; 2. Bangladesh 7,978; 3. India 6,009; 4. Ethiopia 3,421; 5. Nepal 3,354; 6. Ghana 3,320; 7. Nigeria 3,041; 8. Jordan 2,701; 9. Uruguay 2,611; 10. South Africa 2,316; 11. Morocco 1,709; 12. Senegal 1,572; 13. Kenya 1,483; 14. Brazil 1,371; 15. Argentina 1,137; 16. China 1,042; 17. Namibia 880; 18. Sri Lanka 777; 19. Ukraine 755; 20. Poland 721.

Germany is the UN's third largest contributor to the UN budget. (See Table 1.) In addition, since the end of the Cold War, Germany has become increasingly active in UN-mandated military operations. Germany has amended its Constitution to allow for deployment of its troops in UN operations.

France and the UK have officially supported the German bid for a Council seat, but they have not been actively lobbying other EU members to come to a common EU position. They have shown little leadership on this issue.[43] They consequently missed an opportunity to make the UN a more effective organization. Security Council reform is an important part of the reform package presented to the UN member states by Kofi Annan in March 2005. Failure to follow up on Security Council reform could undermine other reform proposals and thus weaken the UN.

*Regional Groups*

UN member states are divided into five regional groups—Africa; Asia; Eastern Europe; Latin America; and Western Europe and other States. (See Table 2.) These regional groups are important mostly for electoral purposes—that is, election of non-permanent members to the UN Security Council, as well as other UN Committees with limited membership such as the Human Rights Commission, and the Economic and Social Council (ECOSOC).

With the end of the Cold War and more recent developments in EU enlargement, the continuing existence of the Eastern European group has been called into question by some observers. They argue that it gives EU members an advantage over other groups and leads to over-representation of European states in UN committees.[44]

The higher profile and greater cohesiveness of the EU is not always welcomed in the Western group. The United States and non-EU Western countries such as Australia and New Zealand feel that their ability to influence EU delegations is decreasing, and they are natu-

---

[43] Support by France and the United Kingdom for a German seat on the Council can also be explained because it helps to deflect from the discussion about France and the UK giving up their seats for one EU seat.

[44] See John van Oudenaren, *AICGS Advisor*, April 7, 2005.

rally frustrated by this situation. In addition, many non-EU states often adopt EU positions. As such the EU is often at the core of a powerful bloc, transcending the Western group.[45]

That said, the Iraq crisis in 2003 showed that unity and cohesiveness is far from assured, particularly when dealing with strategic international peace and security issues.[46] Moreover, the EU is not the only group that extends its influence beyond its regional group. Indeed, many other caucusing groups function in the United Nations. These groups are organized along particular interests. For example, many developing countries are part of the Group of 77 and the Non-Aligned Movement (NAM). The United States has been a strong proponent of the idea to organize a caucus of democratic states within the United Nations.[47]

A restructuring of the UN regional groups is certainly needed. That said, restructuring the regional groups is going to be a very sensitive and complex issue. It is interesting to note that the UN high-level panel established by Kofi Annan in 2003 did not tackle the restructuring of UN regional groups.[48]

## EU Contributions to the UN

EU member states are important contributors to UN programs and activities. EU member states have approximately 30,000 men and women working in UN and UN-mandated operations.[49] EU member states are the largest providers of official development assistance, accounting for approximately 50% of all development assistance world-

---

[45] Most new EU members also often aligned on EU positions. See Paul Luif, *EU Cohesion in the UN General Assembly* (Paris: European Union Institute for Security Studies, Occasional Papers No 49, December 2003).

[46] The Middle East is the exception in this regard. On EU Cohesiveness in the UN see Luif, *EU Cohesion in the UN General Assembly*.

[47] See, for example, Ivo Daalder and James Lindsay, "An Alliance of Democracies: Our Way or the Highway," *The Financial Times*, November 6, 2004.

[48] See the Report of the High-Level Panel on Threats, Challenges and Change, *A More Secure World: Our Shared Responsibility*, (New York, A/59/565, November 29, 2004) It may be noted that Germany in her bid for a Security Council seat has proposed to keep the Eastern European Group and allot this group one non-renewable two year seat on the Council.

[49] See the statement by Magriotis to the UN Security Council on April 11, 2003.

## Table 2.    UN Regional Groups, 2005

**African Group (53):** Algeria; Angola; Benin; Botswana; Burkina Faso; Burundi Cameroon; Cape Verde; Central African Republic; Chad; Comoros; Congo; Côte d'Ivoire; Democratic republic of the Congo; Djibouti; Egypt; Equatorial Guinea; Eritrea; Ethiopia; Gabon; Gambia; Ghana; Guinea; Guinea-Bissau; Kenya; Lesotho; Liberia; Libyan Arab Jamahiriya; Madagascar; Malawi; Mali; Mauritania; Mauritius; Morocco; Mozambique; Namibia; Niger; Nigeria; Rwanda; São Tomé and Principe; Senegal; Seychelles; Sierra Leone; Somalia; South Africa; Sudan; Swaziland; Togo; Tunisia; Uganda; United Republic of Tanzania; Zambia; Zimbabwe.

**Asian Group (52):** Afghanistan; Bahrain; Bangladesh; Bhutan; Brunei Darussalam; Cambodia; China; Cyprus; Democratic People's Republic of Korea; Fiji; India; Indonesia; Iran (Islamic Republic of); Iraq; Japan; Jordan; Kazakhstan; Kuwait; Kyrgyzstan; Lao People's Democratic Republic; Lebanon; Malaysia; Maldives; Marshall Islands; Micronesia (Federated States of); Mongolia; Myanmar; Nauru; Nepal; Oman; Pakistan; Papua New Guinea; Philippines; Qatar; Republic of Korea; Samoa; Saudi Arabia; Singapore; Solomon Islands; Sri Lanka; Syrian Arab Republic; Tajikistan; Thailand; Timor-Leste; Tonga; Turkmenistan; Tuvalu; United Arab Emirates; Uzbekistan; Vanuatu; Vietnam; Yemen.

**Eastern European Group (22):** Albania; Armenia; Azerbaijan; Belarus; Bosnia and Herzegovina; Bulgaria; Croatia; Czech Republic; Estonia; Georgia; Hungary; Latvia; Lithuania; Poland; Republic of Moldova; Romania; Russian Federation; Serbia and Montenegro; Slovakia; Slovenia; The former Yugoslav Republic of Macedonia; Ukraine.

**Latin American and Caribbean Group (33):** Antigua and Barbuda; Argentina; Bahamas; Barbados; Belize; Bolivia; Brazil; Chile; Colombia; Costa Rica; Cuba; Dominica; Dominican Republic; Ecuador; El Salvador; Grenada; Guatemala; Guyana; Haiti; Honduras; Jamaica; Mexico; Nicaragua; Panama; Paraguay; Peru; Saint Kitts and Nevis; Saint Lucia; Saint Vincent and the Grenadines; Suriname; Trinidad and Tobago; Uruguay; Venezuela (Bolivarian Republic of).

**Western European and Others Group (29):** Andorra; Australia; Austria; Belgium; Canada; Denmark; Finland; France; Germany; Greece; Iceland; Ireland; Israel; Italy; Liechtenstein; Luxembourg; Malta; Monaco; Netherlands; New Zealand; Norway; Portugal; San Marino; Spain; Sweden; Switzerland; Turkey*; United Kingdom; United States of America.

Note: Kiribati and Palau are not members of any regional group.

*Turkey, which is in the Western European Group for election purposes, is also a member of the Asian group.

**Total: 191 Member States**

wide. EU member states provide 37% of the general UN budget and close to 40% of the UN peacekeeping budget. (See Table 1.)

The European Commission is a major source of financial support for UN programs, agencies and funds in the development and humanitarian assistance area.[50] Relations between the EU Commission and the UN focus predominantly on economic development and humanitarian assistance issues—financial, technical and operational support.[51]

Talks between the EU Commission and the UN to arrive at more predictable and efficient Commission funding of UN activities culminated on 29 April 2003 in an updated and improved Financial and Administrative Framework Agreement.[52] This new Agreement, by focusing on the technical coherence of development undertakings by the two organizations, should: help bring down the transaction costs of joint EU-UN projects and programs; facilitate a move from project funding by the EU to more long-term program funding by the EU; strengthen the visibility of the EU as a donor; and clarify EU and UN rules of reporting. Annual meetings between officials of the EU Commission and the UN will be held to review implementation of the agreement.

As the Commission gets more involved in conflict prevention and post-conflict stabilization and reconstruction efforts and as it increasingly becomes a direct funder of UN-based programs, it will naturally want to have more say over how these programs are run. The Commission should nonetheless be careful to avoid becoming a micro-manager of the funds it disburses to the UN. Inter-EU coordi-

---

[50] On average the Commission contributes between € 300-400 million annually to various UN programs. The Commission has also contributed to the UN Trust Fund for Preventive Action. This fund was created in 1996 to strengthen the preventive capacity of the UN Secretary General. Other UN agencies such as UNHCR and UNRWA also receive direct contributions from the Commission.

[51] In the UN the Commission represents the European Community (EC) the legal entity that was granted official observer status in 1974. As an observer the EC has no voting rights but it is party to many international treaties and has obtained full participant status in a number of important UN conferences. See Communication from the Commission to the Council and the European Parliament, *Building an Effective Partnership with the United Nations in the Fields of Development and Humanitarian Affairs*, COM (2001) 231, Brussels, May 2, 2001.

[52] See Financial and Administrative Framework Agreement between the European Community, represented by the Commission of the European Communities and the United Nations, April 29, 2003. An earlier version of this agreement was signed in 1999.

nation between the Commission, on the one hand, and the Council, on the other, is also key.[53]

EU enlargement will have little effect on the EU Commission-UN relationship. The contributions of the new EU members are small compared to those of the EU-15. The new EU members contribute US $ 20 million to the regular UN budget. This is less than Belgium's contribution alone. The Netherlands alone contributes 50% more to the United Nations than all ten new members combined. In terms of troops, the new members do slightly better. They contribute approximately 27% of all EU troops to UN operations.

Poland with 721 troops is Europe's number one troop contributor to the United Nations. That said, the EU 25 contributes only 6,5% of troops to all UN peacekeeping operations. (See Table 1.)

## Conflict Prevention and Crisis Management

Conflict prevention efforts are policy actions designed to keep violence from breaking out. According to one leading scholar, conflict prevention "will always be challenging because disputes are an inherent part of political, economic, and social discourse (...)."[54] Within the UN and the EU as well as in academic circles, experts usually distinguish between long-term and short-term conflict prevention actions. Development policies and other cooperation programs are crucial elements in long-term conflict prevention. The EU also sees trade, arms control, human rights, environmental policies and political dialogues as crucial elements of long-term conflict prevention efforts.[55] Short-term conflict prevention actions are emergency efforts to keep conflicts from crossing the violence threshold. These efforts may involve cooperative policies as well as coercive actions. They may therefore involve both civilian and military actors.

---

[53] The Commission has a mission to the UN separate from the Council's liaison office. Until 2004 both delegations were housed in different buildings, which did not help with coordination of policies.

[54] See Michael E. Brown, "Introduction," in Michael E. Brown, ed., *The International Dimensions of Internal Conflict* (Cambridge: MIT Press, 1996), p. 28.

[55] See *EU Programme for the Prevention of Violent Conflicts* endorsed by the Göteborg European Council in June 2001. See also Communication from the Commission, *Conflict Prevention*, COM (2001) 211, Brussels, April 11, 2001; and *Report on the Commission Communication on Conflict Prevention* by Joost Lagendijk, Committee on Foreign Affairs, Human Rights, Common Security and Defence Policy, November 9, 2001, A5-0394/2001.

Crisis management activities may overlap with conflict prevention efforts, but they also include actions taken after violence has broken out. Crisis management goals include escalation control, de-escalation, and the protection of people and assets. Like conflict prevention, crisis management may also entail short-term and long-term efforts, cooperative and coercive policy instruments, and both civilian and military actors.

Both the UN and the EU are broad-based institutions with strong development and humanitarian programs. Therefore, they naturally engage in long-term conflict prevention efforts. Unfortunately, this has not eliminated the need for short-term conflict prevention and crisis management actions.

Crisis prevention and conflict management strategies involve many different policy instruments, ranging from humanitarian assistance to fact-finding, mediation, confidence building measures, and peace operations. They also employ coercive measures such as political and economic sanctions, including the imposition of arms embargoes. Finally, the UN has used and authorized the use of military force to quell violent conflict.

Since the end of the Cold War, the track record of the UN in these areas since the end of the Cold War has been mixed. Its failure to prevent the genocides in Bosnia (1992-1995) and Rwanda (1994) stand out. Similarly, the EU's conflict prevention and crisis management attempts in the early 1990s in the Balkans were not particularly effective. Conflict resolution efforts by the UN in Central America, and more recently in East Timor have been more successful.

The Panel on United Nations Peace Operations concluded in August 2000 that effective conflict prevention actions had been impeded in the 1990s because of a "gap between verbal postures and financial and political support for prevention."[56] In addition, it argued that conflict prevention and crisis management are bound to fail in the absence of "significant knowledge generating and analytical capacity."[57] In other words, political will, resources and intelligence are keys

---

[56] See the *Report of the Panel on United Nations Peace Operations* (*Brahimi Report*), A/55/305 and S/2000/809, August 21, 2000, para. 33.

[57] *Brahimi Report*, para. 67.

to effective conflict prevention and crisis management. Member states often failed to provide the UN with these critical assets in the 1990s.

In addition, many short-term conflict prevention and crisis management operations have been hampered by disagreements among UN and EU members over the use of military force.[58] Member states of both organizations have been hesitant to embrace the one overriding lesson learned in this area in the 1990s—namely, that short-term conflict prevention and crisis management actions need to be backed up by military capabilities and enforcement powers. Belligerent actors are deterred only by strong military action. The threat or use of military force is often a prerequisite to the effective use of other civilian policy instruments. Learning this central lesson is one of the keys to devising more effective conflict prevention and crisis management strategies in the 21st century.

The difficulty for the UN and the EU is that they have no independent military capabilities. They are consequently dependent on their member states to make military resources available. States will release military resources—and face the political risks of combat casualties—only when faced with overriding humanitarian imperatives or when national interests are engaged. This is the case the UN and the EU have to make if they want to engage in short-term conflict prevention and crisis management endeavors.

The development of a European Security and Defence Policy (ESDP), including a European Rapid Reaction Force (ERRF), should make the EU a more powerful and effective actor in the conflict prevention and crisis management arena. The deployment of a European Police Mission (EUPM) in Bosnia in January 2003 under the auspices of the ESDP was a first step.[59] But it was the launch of two ESDP military missions in March and June 2003 (Operation *Concordia* in Macedonia and Operation *Artemis* in the Democratic Republic of Congo) and the 2004 deployment of *EUFOR* in Bosnia and Herzegovina have led many to hope that the EU is taking steps to becoming a stabilizing force in conflict zones. (See Table 3.)

---

[58] This has also become an issue in the fight against terrorism.

[59] In July 2004 the Council launched preparations for a military operation in Bosnia and Herzegovina—*Althea*—to ensure a seamless transition from the NATO-led SFOR force to an EU-led EUFOR. EUFOR deployed at the end of 2004 with a force of 7,000 troops.

## Table 3.   ESDP Operations

| Name | Duration | Deployment Level | Budget |
|---|---|---|---|
| **Concordia** EU military operation in the former Yugoslav Republic of Macedonia | April 2003– December 2003 | 350 troops | € 6.2 million |
| **Artemis** EU military operation in the Democratic Republic of Congo | June 2003– September 2003 | 1,800 troops | |
| **EUFOR-Althea** EU military operation in Bosnia and Herzegovina | December 2004– | 7,000 troops | € 71.7 million common costs* |
| **EUPM** EU Police Mission in Bosnia and Herzegovina | January 2003– December 2005 | 530 police officers 400 support staff | € 38 million |
| **EUPOL Proxima** EU Police Mission in the former Yugoslav Republic of Macedonia | January 2004 | 200 police officers | |
| **EUJUST Themis** Rule of Law Mission in Georgia | July 2004 | 10 international law experts | |
| **EUPOL Kinshasa** EU Police Mission in The Democratic Republic of Congo | December 2004– December 2005 | 30 civilian police officers | € 4.3 million |
| **EUJUST Lex** Rule of Law Mission in Iraq (training) | July 2005– June 2006 | 24 (5 in Iraq) | € 10 million common costs |

Sources: EU Council website. See also European Security Review, ISIS Europe, No. 25, March 2005.

* Common costs exclude personnel costs. For details on the financing mechanism of EU ESDP operations see Council Decision 2004/197/CFSP of February 23, 2004.

However, caution is warranted. The Artemis operation provided a platform for strengthening EU-UN cooperation in peacekeeping and led to a joint declaration welcoming such cooperation in the Balkans and Africa.[60] European leaders reiterated their commitment to con-

---

[60] See Joint EU-UN Declaration of September 24, 2003.

tribute to the UN's objectives in crisis management, but their agreed areas of cooperation focused on the soft side of peacekeeping: planning, training, communication, and the exchange of information on best practices. It is far from certain that *Concordia* and *Artemis* will be precursors for more extensive EU-UN military operations in the future.[61]

First, these were small operations that were limited in time and scope. Concordia involved a force of some 350 troops and lasted from April to December 2003.[62] Artemis involved 1,800 troops, mostly French soldiers, and lasted from June to September 2003.[63] In addition, the Artemis operation, which intervened at the height of violent conflict, presupposed that some other organization—the UN—was capable of taking over. From a UN perspective this transition was not seamless. In particular, it was regrettable that none of the military officers deployed under Artemis remained in place for the UN operation.[64] Re-hatting has been extremely successful in the past—notably in Bosnia and Haiti—and would have sent an important message to local combatants.[65]

Second, despite formal appearances, the EU was and is not in charge of these operations. Although the EU declared ESDP and the ERRF operational in December 2001 and May 2003, respectively, the EU lacked the necessary planning and command capabilities necessary

---

[60] See Joint EU-UN Declaration of September 24, 2003.

[61] On EU-UN relations in this domain see Kennedy Graham, *Towards Effective Multilateralism-The EU and the UN: Partners in Crisis Management*, (Brussels: European Policy Centre, EPC Working Paper, November 2004); Alexandra Novosseloff, *EU-UN Partnership in Crisis Management: Development and Prospects* (New York, International Peace Academy, June 2004); Thierry Tardy, *Limits and Opportunities of UN-EU Relations in Peace Operations: Implications for DPKO* (New York, UN Peacekeeping Department, Best Practices Unit, September 2003).

[62] It was followed by an EU-run police operation Proxima, involving 200 police officers.

[63] Artemis handed over to the UN mission in the DRC. When Artemis deployed in Bunia, the UN Mission in the DRC (MONUC) had a strength of 4,386 troops—well below the authorized strength of 8,700 troops.

[64] See *Operation Artemis: The Lessons of the Interim Emergency Multinational Force* (New York, Department of Peacekeeping Operations, Peacekeeping Best Practices Unit, Military Division, October 2004).

[65] Artemis was a stopgap measure. On re-hatting in the past, see Donald C. F. Daniel, Bradd C. Hayes, and Chantal de Jonge Oudraat, *Coercive Inducement and the Containment of International Crises* (Washington DC: United States Institute of Peace Press, 1999).

for the deployment of robust peace operations. *Concordia* relied on NATO assets, and *Artemis* relied on French assets. Given the unlikelihood of significant increases in European defense budgets, it is difficult to see how the EU's capability problems can be solved. EU's military capabilities will remain marginal.

Third, while some individual member states such as France may have strong political incentives to use the EU umbrella, many other EU member states are more interested in the civilian components of ESDP—police, rule of law, civilian administration and civilian protection. At present, the EU has two police missions—*EUPM* in Bosnia and Herzegovina, involving 530 police officers, and *Proxima* in Macedonia, involving 200 police officers—and one rule of law mission in Georgia—*EUJUST Themis*, involving 10 international law experts. In sum, EU member states remain deeply divided over the final form and objectives of ESDP.

Fourth, coordination of the many CFSP/ESDP instruments across the three EU governing pillars is exceedingly complex because different pillars have different decision-making procedures and because the roles of EU agencies and member states in each of these pillars is different. While the split responsibilities might give some EU institutions incentives to push for military interventions, on the whole institutional confusion over the use of military and civilian policy instruments is debilitating: it keeps the EU from devising effective policy.[66] The draft EU Convention is an improvement over the current institutional arrangement, but it does not fully resolve the problem. In any event, decisions to deploy troops will remain in the hands of individual member states. Like the UN, the EU will have to rely on coalitions of the willing for the foreseeable future. Deployment of the EU Battle Groups or its Gendarmerie force is far from automatic and will have to be preceded in each case by political decisions of each participating country. EU enlargement will not change these fundamentals of CFSP and ESDP.

---

[66] This becomes even more difficult if we add the fight against terrorism or efforts to counter the proliferation of weapons of mass destruction to the mix.

## Conclusions and Recommendations

Conflict prevention and crisis management are essential policy activities in a dynamic and dangerous world. The EU has a wide array of conflict prevention and crisis management instruments at its disposal. These instruments include political dialogue, mediation, cooperation agreements, trade policy instruments, development assistance, economic and social policies, humanitarian and emergency relief, support for rehabilitation and reconstruction, as well as coercive measures such as the use of economic and political sanctions and military force.

EU enlargement raises the level of expectations within the UN and around the world. Responding to this higher level of expectations will be difficult for the EU. Indeed, the EU has both an institutional problem and an image problem. Its institutional problem derives from the fact that many European institutions have overlapping and shared responsibilities. It is consequently difficult to pinpoint responsibilities. At the same time, this affects its image problem—shared and complex lines of responsibilities make it hard to claim recognition for important contributions. This is particularly true within the United Nations.

New EU members will be able to enhance their presence in the UN. Indeed, EU membership allows new members to specialize and develop niche areas of interest and excellence, much in the same way they are developing niche military capabilities within NATO. This may increase their influence in the UN. EU membership also gives them greater insight in UN Security Council deliberations.[67] In general, small states—and most new EU members are small states—gain by being members of international clubs and the EU is among the most important ones.

That said, action by the EU within the UN will depend on agreement and action by a limited number of European actors, most notably France, Germany, and the United Kingdom. Action by them under the EU umbrella strengthens the EU as a whole. However, they

---

[67] Consultation and coordination among EU members will continue to develop. That said, this process of consultation and coordination is mostly of a re-active nature. Sensitive political questions that require more pro-active stances will remain largely outside the formal EU consultation process.

should be careful not to undercut UN actions. The UN Secretary-General has repeatedly stressed that UN peacekeeping operations are in dire need of highly trained and skilled soldiers. He has also deplored the fact that few soldiers from developed countries are available for UN peacekeeping operations. Operations under the EU flag will reduce the already small pool of European soldiers available to serve in UN-led operations. Short-term EU bridging operations, like the 2003 Operation Artemis in the Democratic Republic of Congo (DRC), should make sure that sufficient follow-on forces are available. Failure to do so will transform short-term success stories into long-term failures. The EU must be attentive to both the short term and long-term consequences of its interventions.

The EU and the UN are natural allies in the field of conflict prevention and crisis management. The UN has international legitimacy in taking actions to prevent or stop violent conflicts. It is also physically present in many parts of the world.

The following actions could be taken to enhance EU-UN cooperation and action in the future.

### Determine Conflict Prevention and Crisis Management Priorities

The EU and the UN both have a very broad conception of conflict prevention and crisis management. It is not a coincidence that both the EU and the UN need to define their priorities more effectively. The development of a European Security Strategy provides some general priorities for the EU, but these ideas will have to be operationalized in concrete programmatic initiatives. In doing so, the EU should involve UN officials at different levels of the UN bureaucracy. The EU and the European Commission should aim to develop a robust, cooperative relationship with the UN in the security arena. The UN's inter-agency dialogue with the European Commission is providing a valuable springboard for other inter-institution meetings. The European Parliament could also play an important role in this regard. The multilateralization of peace operations and counter-terrorism efforts, as well as the development of intelligence capabilities, should become priority areas.

*Multilateralize Peace Operations*

Both the UN and the EU have expressed interest in developing the role of regional organizations in the field of conflict prevention and crisis management. The EU has launched programs in Africa and Asia to support regional integration and regional organizations with a clear conflict prevention mandate. The UN has also engaged in dialogues on these issues, and it has engaged in joint operations with regional and sub-regional organizations in these regions. The EU and the UN should work together more closely and exchange information and lessons learned on their experiences in this field. This is especially important given the poor track record of regional organizations in conflict prevention and crisis management. Joint approaches to help regional organizations develop conflict prevention and crisis management capabilities should be developed. More attention should be devoted to peacekeeping, in particular. At present, a multitude of multilateral and bilateral peacekeeping training programs is under way in Africa and Asia. Greater coordination is needed between the EU and the UN as well as between individual EU members and other UN member states, particularly the United States.

*Build Intelligence Capabilities in the EU and the UN*

Intelligence and analytical capabilities are essential for effective conflict prevention and crisis management efforts. Unfortunately, intelligence capabilities are in short supply in most international organizations. States are wary of having international organizations manage intelligence information because they doubt the ability of the organization to preserve secrecy and because they fear that these organizations might become more independent. EU and UN officials should engage their member states on this issue and identify ways for member states to share more intelligence. Intelligence-sharing experiences in peacekeeping operations could provide useful precedents and guidelines. The experiences of organizations such as the Organization for the Prohibition of Chemical Weapons (OPCW), the International Atomic Energy Agency (IAEA), the UN agencies responsible for uncovering Iraqi weapons of mass destruction programs—UNSCOM and UNMOVIC—and international law enforcement agencies such as Interpol and Europol could be helpful in this regard. For example, experiences in these organizations suggest that intelligence is shared more easily if it is for a known and limited objective.

*Increase the Visibility of the EU at the UN*

The locus of responsibility for conflict prevention and crisis management within the EU lies with the European Council and the EU's High Representative. However, the Commissioner for External Affairs and the Commissioner for Development Cooperation also have responsibilities in this area. The EU Constitution streamlines the institutional framework for conflict prevention and crisis management, but it does not solve the tensions between the Commission and the European Council and the institutional complexity of EU decision-making in this area.

It is imperative for the EU to make EU policy-making procedures more transparent for UN officials. Many in the UN do not understand EU procedures. More contacts between UN officials and the EU would help galvanize relations. This needs to be done not just at the top, but at every level of the respective organizations. The European Commission and the European Council should consider expanding their presence at the UN, particularly their New York delegations.

*Produce Annual "EU at the UN International Peace and Security Reports"*

The European Parliament should request an annual report from the European Commission, the EU High Representative and the countries holding the Presidencies of the European Council on EU activities within the UN on international peace and security issues. This report should provide a comprehensive assessment of EU-UN conflict prevention and crisis management efforts. It should cover development and humanitarian relief as well as efforts in the arms control and disarmament field, efforts to deal with intra-state conflicts and failing states, and efforts to fight terrorism and other transnational security threats. These reports should set benchmarks for evaluating the effectiveness of EU-UN cooperative efforts. These reports would also help the EU increase its public profile in this arena.

*Strengthen the EU's Legal Identity and Presence at the UN*

The EU as an institution has a weak legal status in many UN bodies. The European Community has observer status in the UN General Assembly and as such can participate in the Assembly's debates. Once the EU attains a legal personality, this status would be transferred to the EU. Political realities within the EU make the possibility of an

EU seat on the UN Security Council remote, but greater visibility could be given to the High Representative or the future EU Foreign Minister. The EU Presidencies as well as the permanent and non-permanent members of the UN Security Council should be encouraged to allow the High Representative play a more active role at the UN Security Council on behalf of the EU.

## Prospects for the Future

The EU is committed to strengthening the role of the UN in maintaining and restoring international peace and security issues and making it a more effective organization. The EU is also committed to exchanging information, cooperating in fact-finding missions, coordinating with the UN in field training and more generally the planning and implementation of conflict prevention and crisis management missions. The development of the ESDP, the ERRF and the EU Battle Groups, and the EU Gendarmerie Force hold out the promise of providing the UN with more effective military capabilities. This could be the EU's most important contribution to the development of the UN in the years ahead. The development of ESDP and the deployment of troops face many political and material roadblocks, but progress on these central initiatives will be one of the keys to the strengthening not just of the EU—but also the United Nations and EU-UN relations. If new EU members contribute to these efforts, they will strengthen both the EU and the UN.

*Chapter 12*

# The Larger EU and the Global Economy

Daniel Gros and Leonor Coutinho

## Introduction

This chapter begins by providing some indicators of the change in the economic size of the EU 15-25 (in relation to the US and the global economy) showing that in terms of GDP and trade flows this enlargement did not drastically change the size of the EU. If measured at current exchange rates, the EU-25 economy (as that of the EU-15 before) is actually somewhat larger than the USA's and represents about a third of global economic activity.

Section two then turns to the main effect of EMU: namely, the emergence of a single European currency, the euro, as a competitor to the US dollar as the global currency. If the euro does partially replace the US dollar in some of its international functions, large portfolio shifts can be expected. However, although the portfolio shifts could be quite large in absolute terms (several hundred billions of euro), they should not have any major disruptive effects on exchange rates or capital flows because they will be distributed over time and because financial markets have become so sophisticated that the currency of denomination of international assets and liabilities can be changed quickly and at a low cost.

The impact of EMU, or for that matter of the EU, on global macroeconomic management, which is discussed in the third section, is also likely to remain limited. There is anyway, at least at present, little effective macroeconomic coordination. With the European Central Bank representing most of the EU in the monetary field, global cooperation in the monetary field has theoretically become easier to organize. However, as all major central banks have exclusively domestic objectives (explicit or implicit 'inflation targets') nothing is being done in reality. Cooperation in other fields remains also non-existent, and anyway be difficult to organize because EMU has not led to a real coordination of fiscal or structural policies in the EU.

Section four briefly summarizes the challenge posed by the main global imbalance, namely the US current account deficit, and how its resolution might affect the EU.

In most of this chapter we will jump between the EU and the euro area. Both present two faces of Europe: external trade policy is conducted at the level of the EU, whereas monetary policy is unified only for the twelve member countries of the euro area (with Denmark a 'non-voting' member and three smaller new member countries likely to join by 2007). This difference has one important implication: unlike the US, the EU's trade policy is not likely to be affected by developments in the foreign exchange markets. A stronger euro is unlikely to be accompanied by more protectionism.

## The EU in the World Economy

Before discussing the effects enlargement might have on the position of the EU in the world economy, it is useful to provide some basic data.

The two measures of economic size that are most often used are gross domestic product (GDP) and external trade. Table 1 therefore presents some data about GDP and international trade for the three major world economies (the EU, the USA and Japan). The data suggests that whether one considers the euro area, the EU-15 or the EU-25, Europe is large enough to affect the world economy. The external trade of the enlarged EU-25 accounts for roughly one-sixth of world trade and it accounts for 30 percent of world GDP.

The economy of the EU-25 member states combined is about the same size as that of the USA, both in terms of GDP (at current 2004 exchange rates) and trade flows if one uses the average of exports and imports. But the EU exports much more and imports somewhat less than the US. EU-25 exports to the rest of the world have over the last years typically exceeded US exports by about 25% (but imports have been 25% lower).

**Table 1.    The EU in the world economy**

| Panel a: GDP | | |
| --- | --- | --- |
| | € billions | % of World GDP |
| Eurozone | 7,243 | 22.5 |
| EU 15 | 9,288 | 28.8 |
| EU 25 | 9,720 | 30.2 |
| EU 29 | 10,027 | 31.1 |
| NMS | 432 | 1.3 |
| US | 9,641 | 29.9 |
| Japan | 3833 | 11.9 |

| Panel b: Trade (M+X)/2 | | | | | |
| --- | --- | --- | --- | --- | --- |
| | € billions | % of World trade[1] | % of World trade[2] | Exports | Imports |
| Eurozone | 1033.4 | | | 1082.9 | 983.9 |
| EU 15 | 993.2 | 19.5 | | 997.2 | 989.2 |
| EU 25 | 923.1 | | 18.4 | 903.6 | 942.6 |
| EU 29 | | | | | |
| NMS[3] | 177.8 | 3.5 | | 161.1 | 194.5 |
| US | 1002.1 | 19.7 | 20.0 | 733.0 | 1271.2 |
| Japan | 398.8 | 7.8 | 8.0 | 440.6 | 357.0 |

[1]Treating EU-15 as an entity, [2]Treating EU-25 as an entity, [3]Extra-New Member States (NMS),Trade is measured by (imports + exports)/2, excluding intra-EC exports and imports for the Community, goods only. Source: Eurostat

The euro area is somewhat smaller than the USA in terms of GDP but it is of a similar size if measured by trade flows and much larger in terms of exports. The euro area is larger than the Japanese economy in terms of both trade and GDP by a margin of about 50 per cent.

In terms of some financial indicators 'Europe' would be much bigger than the USA. But it all depends at what variables one looks. Table 2 shows that all twenty-five member countries together hold almost $400 billion in foreign exchange reserves, approximately as much as Japan, and several times more than the amount held by the USA ($68 billion).[1]

---

[1] The total reserves held by the EU 25, the US and Japan represent about 80 percent of the total reserves held by industrial countries, and about 30 percent of the total World reserves.

**Table 2    The EU in International Finance**

| | Foreign Exchange Reserves (end 2003)* | Percentage of Total |
|---|---|---|
| Euro Area | 247.0 | 26.9 |
| EU 15 | 303.5 | 33.0 |
| NMS | 86.0 | 9.4 |
| EU 25 | 389.4 | 42.4 |
| Japan | 461.2 | 50.2 |
| US | 68.0 | 7.4 |
| Total (EU25+Japan+US) | 918.6 | 100.0 |
| Industrial Countries | 1,103.7 | |
| World | 3,013.8 | |

Billions of USD
*Total Reserves minus Gold.
Source: IMF, International Financial Statistics

## The Euro in the Global Financial Markets

The most visible expression of European integration in financial terms is the euro. What role does it play on global financial markets? Has it been able to displace the US dollar, as many had hoped? At first sight the answer appears to be no. Table 3 below shows the role of the major international currencies in terms of foreign exchange market turnover. A comparison of the more recent data with pre-EMU ones shows little difference in that the share of the euro seems to be very close to that of the DM and the share of the dollar has increased compared to the early 1990s. However, one should be careful when comparing the euro with the deutschmark, because turnover data for the deutschmark includes bilateral trade with currencies that are now part of the euro and that should be excluded from the comparison. Only excluding the bilateral trade between the deutschmark and other euro area currencies would it be possible to infer about the true differential between the euro and its predecessor in terms of their international role.[2]

---

[2] Detken, Carsten, and Hartmann, Philipp "The Euro and International Capital Markets," European Central Bank Working Paper April 19, 2000.

**Table 3.  Currency distribution of reported foreign exchange market turnover for selected currencies**

(Percentage shares of average daily turnover in April)

|  | 1992 | 1995 | 1998 | 2001 | 2004 |
|---|---|---|---|---|---|
| US dollar | 82 | 83.3 | 87.3 | 90.3 | 88.7 |
| Euro (Deutsch mark before 1999) | 39.6 | 36.1 | 30.1 | 37.6 | 37.2 |
| Japanese yen | 23.4 | 24.1 | 20.2 | 22.7 | 20.3 |
| Pound sterling | 13.6 | 9.4 | 11 | 13.2 | 16.9 |
| Swiss franc | 8.4 | 7.3 | 7.1 | 6.1 | 6.1 |
| All currencies | 200 | 200 | 200 | 200 | 200 |

Notes: Because two currencies are involved in each transaction, the sum of the percentage shares of individual currencies totals 200% instead of 100%. The figures relate to reported "net-net" turnover, ie they are adjusted for both local and cross-border double-counting. For 1992-98, the data cover local home currency trading only.

Source: Triennial Central Bank Survey of Foreign Exchange and Derivatives Market Activity in April 2004

The situation is somewhat different in terms of securities markets. For example, in the bonds markets the total amount of bonds and notes in euro is similar to that outstanding in dollars (the exact proportions depend on the exchange rate) and in terms of new issuance the euro area is actually considerably larger.

**Table 4.  Bonds and Notes by Currency of Issue**

|  | Amount outstanding end 2003 | Net issuance during 2003 |
|---|---|---|
| Global total | 11,105.3 | 1397 |
| Euro | 4834.8 | 786.8 |
| Hong Kong dollar | 45.6 | 6.3 |
| Pound sterling | 778.9 | 86.3 |
| Swiss franc | 195.6 | 15.8 |
| US dollar | 4494.9 | 448.3 |
| Yen | 488.4 | 3.8 |

Source: Triennial Central Bank Survey of Foreign Exchange and Derivatives Market Activity in April 2004

As an aside it is also worthwhile to consider the importance of the world economy for the EU. This can be best measured by the weight of trade in GDP as shown in Table 5 below. It is apparent that the EU-25 is less open to trade than the EU-15, with the share of trade in

GDP going from 10.8 to 9.6% for the enlarged EU. The latter value is quite similar to that of the US, but significantly below that of the almost 15% for the euro zone, which is thus about 50% more open than either the EU-25 or the US. It is also interesting to note that the degree of openness for the US varies enormously depending on whether one considers exports or imports. Exports (of goods) amount to only 6.6% of US GDP, against over 15% for the euro zone and over 9% for the enlarged EU. But in terms of imports the shares are rather similar: 11.5% for the US against 13.8 and 9.8 for the Eurozone and the EU-25 respectively.

**Table 5.    Trade as % of GDP (2002)**

|  | (M+X)/2 | Exports | Imports |
|---|---|---|---|
| Eurozone | 14.6 | 15.3 | 13.9 |
| EU 15 | 10.8 | 10.9 | 10.8 |
| EU 25 | 9.6 | 9.4 | 9.8 |
| NMS* | 39.8 | 36.1 | 43.6 |
| US | 9.0 | 6.6 | 11.5 |
| Japan | 9.4 | 10.4 | 8.5 |

*Extra-NMS; Trade is measured by (imports + exports)/2, excluding intra-EC exports and imports for the Community, goods only. Source: Eurostat

Table 5 shows the large difference that exists between the new and the old member states. This difference is likely to impact the stance of the EU on trade and regulatory issues. A first point to note is that accession, and the adoption of the EU's Common External Tariff by new member states, has automatically led to a decline in "European" trade barriers, because the average tariffs of new members were in generals higher than the 3.6 percent average external tariff applied in the EU (data from the European Commission).[3] However, enlargement will also probably raise some challenges for transatlantic trade relations, in areas like regulatory convergence. In financial services, for example, the new member states will find it more difficult to accept and implement the increasingly sophisticated regulatory apparatus that is becoming the norm in the US and international financial

---

[3] In cases where exporters to new member states are worse off as a result of enlargement, due to an increase in tariffs, these can ask for compensation from the EU, according to agreements under the WTO.

centers. The representatives of the new member states that either sit directly around the table or behind the Commission will find it more difficult to accept US inspired regulatory norms than the old member states which are home to many firms with transatlantic roots and business.

## The Influence of Europe in the Management of the Global Economy

This chapter has so far argued that, in the short run, EMU will change the global monetary system much less than is often assumed. Experience and theoretical considerations suggest that the euro is unlikely to replace the US dollar as the pre-eminent global currency, although the domestic base for the euro is at least as strong as that of the dollar.

It remains to be seen whether EMU will lead to more exchange-rate stabilization at the global level. At the macroeconomic level, the difference between EMU and the present is actually minor since over two-thirds of the EU have had de facto fixed exchange rates since 1987 (with a brief interruption in late 1993).

However, the influence of Europe in the international financial institutions might change over time. The best example for this might be the so-called Bretton-Woods institutions, namely the World Bank and the IMF in which European representation is fragmented because it is exercised exclusively by member countries. But this might change over time. As the management structure of the World Bank and the IMF are very similar; it suffices to concentrate on the IMF as pars pro toto.

The sum of the weights of member countries in a number of international economic organizations (such as the International Monetary Fund (IMF), the Bank for International Settlements (BIS) and the World Bank) is larger than that of the USA if one just adds up the quotas of all individual member countries. For example, the sum of the national quotas of the twenty-five EU member states in the IMF is about 32.2 percent (just slightly above the 30 percent for the EU-15) compared to a US quota of below 18 percent and about 6 percent for Japan (see Table 6).

However, even after the introduction of the euro, individual member countries will wish to continue to be represented in these organizations, as any independent political entity is entitled to representation in the IMF and the World Bank regardless of arrangements for its currency. Full political union, not EMU, would therefore be a condition for the EU to participate as one entity in the management of the international economic institutions.

**Table 6.    IMF (and World Bank) quotas**

|  | Calculated quota | Actual quota | Votes | Excluding intra-EU25 trade | | |
| --- | --- | --- | --- | --- | --- | --- |
| Euro Area (12) | 29.61 | 23.20 | 22.94 | 17.89 | 13.80 | 11.52 |
| Total EU-15 | 36.8 | 30.11 | 29.77 | 22.56 | 18.27 | 14.29 |
| Total EU-25 | 38.44 | 32.18 | 31.92 | 23.38 | 19.34 | 19.34 |
| United States | 17.11 | 17.38 | 17.11 | 21.28 | 21.28 | 21.28 |
| Japan | 10.12 | 6.23 | 6.14 | 12.59 | 7.64 | 7.64 |
| Other | 35.95 | 46.28 | 46.98 | 42.75 | 51.74 | 51.74 |

Source: Bini Smaghi, Lorenzo "A Single EU Seat in the IMF?," Journal of Common Market Studies, June 2004, 42 (2), pp.229-48.

The present IMF quotas or voting rights of individual EU member countries are, however, based mostly on the size of their overall international trade and financial relations. With a common currency, a large part of the trade (whether in goods, services or capital) of participants should no longer be regarded as 'international', and the basis for assessing their quotas would be correspondingly smaller. In this sense EMU should imply a reduction of the voting rights of European countries not only in the IMF, but also some other international economic institutions, such as the World Bank, EBRD, OECD, WTO and the BIS. The data on the economic size presented above would imply that the entire EU-25 (and somewhat less the euro area) should have about the same weight as the USA, whereas its current aggregate quota in the IMF is almost twice as large (and about 50 per cent larger if one considers only the euro zone).

Viewed from a more general perspective the status quo limits the European influence also for two less tangible reasons:

*The 'small country syndrome.'* No individual member country on its own can hope to have a decisive influence on the global scene. There is therefore little incentive at the member country level to spend the resources required to make policy proposals or participate actively in the debate. Given the technical and analytical expertise that is required in this area an active participation in the policy process is possible only for countries that develop and maintain over long periods a highly qualified staff. This is especially the case for most new member countries.

*Dis-economies of scale.* As smaller member countries cannot have finance ministries of the same size as the US it is clear that their official cannot specialize to the same extent. The manpower employed in the international departments of the fifteen member states greatly exceeds that employed by the US Treasury, but the work of all these European officials is not coordinated and the often work at cross purposes, as they are driven by their domestic political and economic agendas.

Since most new member countries are very small and have no track record in participating actively in the management of the global economy enlargement can only reinforce these two handicaps.

However, the main obstacle to more macroeconomic coordination at the global level is not the lack of a unified European stance, but rather the nature of the priorities pursued by the thee big 'players' that are emerging from the ongoing trend towards regional arrangements.[4] The global economy is increasingly dominated by the three regional blocks centered around the EU, the USA and South East Asia (with Latin America left behind for the time being).[5]

Coordination is rendered difficult by the fact that these three regional groups have different priorities or 'reaction functions':

- The EU combines (implicit) inflation targeting with a passive fiscal policy.

- The US pursues a more activist, perhaps more Keynesian approach with both monetary and fiscal policy, but both geared towards internal balance.

---

[4] ICEPS "Adjusting to Leaner Times," 5th Annual Report of the Centre for European Policy Studies Macroeconomic Policy Group, July 2003.

[5] We are grateful to Angel Ubide for providing this idea.

- South East Asia has become 'mercantilist' and concentrates on maintaining export led growth (with only slight worries about reserve accumulation).

Thus, coordination becomes perhaps more important but more difficult at the same time because there is no shared economic philosophy. Monetary policies focus on domestic inflation in the major areas. But with increasing integration in global capital and goods markets this implies that, exchange rates become the key variable in the global adjustment to shocks. It follows that in principle there is a need for a more active foreign exchange management/coordination in this regional world. But this is impossible to achieve as long as monetary policy remains geared towards domestic objectives.

## The EU and Global Imbalances

What is the interest of the EU in the management of the global economy? That depends on what one considers to be the main problem. The era of emerging markets crisis seems to be over for the time being after the waves of speculative attacks which went around the globe starting with Mexico in 1995. There are few new targets left as most emerging markets have now swung into surplus (see Table 7). The main exception seems to be the Central and Eastern European region. However, the new EU member countries can rely on more stable FDI inflows. The EU's own external accounts are close to balance with a small surplus, whether one considers the euro area or the enlarged EU.

The key issue for the global economy is at present the mounting US current account deficit. The counterpart to the huge (increase in the) US current account deficit has not been the EU, but mostly emerging markets, whose economies swung from moderate deficits to large surpluses. The US deficit is now so large, and has persisted for so long already, that the build-up in foreign debt is reaching unchartered territory.

Table 7 details the dramatic swings in external balances that have taken place over the last decade. From 1998 to 2004 the US current account deficit increased by over $450 billion. The external balance of the EU also deteriorated slightly over this period. But this was partially offset by higher surpluses of some smaller OECD countries so that the deterioration for the grouping 'advanced economies' was only about

$363.4 billion. As the world's current account did not change over the period (both in 1998 and in 2004 the statistical discrepancy had about the same size) this implies that most of the counterpart of the increase of the US deficit must have come from surpluses in emerging markets.[6] The biggest swings seem to have taken place in the Middle East with about $138 billion (recovering from very low oil prices), followed by Latin America, where the shift amounted to about $106 billion and the Commonwealth of Independent States (CIS) (after the Russian crisis). By contrast the contribution of developing Asia is limited because its external adjustment of this region was almost complete by 1998. It is interesting to note that the Chinese surplus also did not change significantly over the period considered here.

**Table 7.   Summary of Payments Balances on Current Account**
($ billion)

| | 1998 | 2000 | 2003 | 2004 | Change 2004-1998 |
|---|---|---|---|---|---|
| Advanced economies | 35.8 | −250.9 | −231.9 | −327.8 | −363.6 |
| United States | −209.6 | −413.5 | −530.7 | −665.9 | −456.3 |
| Euro area | 64.3 | −28.5 | 25.8 | 35.6 | −28.7 |
| European Union | 48.9 | −73.0 | 3.0 | −6.0 | −54.9 |
| Japan | 119.1 | 119.6 | 136.2 | 171.8 | 52.7 |
| Other advanced economies | 62.0 | 71.4 | 136.7 | 130.7 | 68.7 |
| Other emerging market and developing countries | −115.1 | 88.2 | 149.1 | 246.6 | 361.7 |
| Excluding Asian countries in surplus3 | −172 | 43.6 | 78.5 | 149.7 | 321.7 |
| Regional groups Africa | −19.4 | 6.5 | −1.7 | 1.1 | 20.5 |
| Central and eastern Europe | −19.3 | −32.7 | −37.0 | −50.6 | −31.3 |
| Commonwealth of Independent States | −9.6 | 46.3 | 36.2 | 64.4 | 74.0 |
| Developing Asia | 49.3 | 46.3 | 85.8 | 103.3 | 54.0 |
| Middle East | −25.5 | 69.5 | 59.3 | 112.5 | 138.0 |
| Western Hemisphere | −90.5 | −47.8 | 6.6 | 15.9 | 106.4 |
| China | 31.6 | 20.5 | 45.9 | 70 | 38.4 |

Source: World Economic Outlook, IMF, April 2005

---

[6] The statistical discrepancy (the world's current account deficit) was equal to $79.3 billion in 1998 and—$81.2 billion in 2004 (World Economic Outlook, April 2005).

There is general agreement that the US deficit cannot go on for-ever, but little agreement as to what happens next. Indeed it is exceed-ingly difficult to predict what will happen if the US deficit has to be reduced. Part of the adjustment could be in the Middle East and Latin America, but only if capital flows again to the latter. It seems likely, however, that the EU would have to provide at least a partial counter-part to any US adjustment.

Despite the seemingly bystander position, Europe has not been completely insulated from the global shocks. Although the euro area current account has remained largely in balance, the euro exchange rate has suffered large fluctuations since 1999.

Figure 1 displays the behavior of euro exchange rates, both the bilateral rate against the dollar and the nominal effective exchange rate, together with the US dollar nominal effective exchange rate. It can be observed, that the euro has swung significantly since its incep-tion. Since October 2000, when it had lost about 26 percent of its initial value against the dollar, it has appreciated by about 45 percent on bilateral terms. In effective terms the pattern has been similar. The fact that changes in the value of the euro have reflected to a sig-nificant extent changes in the dollar-euro bilateral exchange rate suggests that other currencies have largely followed the movements of the dollar.[7]

Table 8 shows the variance-covariance matrix for the euro, the dol-lar, the yen and two other Asian currencies chosen to proxy the behav-ior of currencies in the region (the Korean won and the Singapore dollar). The results show that the euro has been the most volatile cur-rency in effective terms, and far more volatile than the dollar. The euro has also displayed a negative covariance with the Asian curren-cies, while the dollar has a positive covariance with both the Korean won and the Singapore dollar.

---

[7] The 2004 IMF Report shows an estimate for the exchange rates of the rest of the world (excluding the euro area and the US), calculated as a residual. The behavior of these series shows that world currencies (besides the euro) have moved largely in tandem with the US dollar. See IMF, "Euro Area Policies: Selected Issues," Country Report No. 04/235, Washington D.C., August 2004.

**Figure 1. Euro effective exchange rate and bilateral exchange rate against the dollar**

Source: IFS and ECB

There is evidence therefore that the euro is taking some of the burden of the adjustment, despite the fact that the euro zone has been broadly in external balance. The IMF 2004 Report on euro area policies shows how shocks originating in the US, namely an increase in US multifactor productivity, a decline in the risk premium on dollar assets and an increase in US fiscal spending, can produce the same type of asymmetric responses between the euro zone and the rest of the world, taking into account asymmetries between the euro zone and the rest of the world in terms of size, openness, pass-through behavior, and foreign asset substitutability.[8] The study considers that the rest of the world is more open and relatively larger than the euro zone. It also assumes that pass-though is lower in the euro zone and that the rest of the world is more willing to substitute domestic assets for US assets. According to their model the re-balancing of the external balance would require a maximum appreciation of the euro of about 20 percent.

[8] IMF, "Euro Area Policies: Selected Issues," Country Report No. 04/235, Washington D.C., August 2004.

**Table 8.    Variance-Covariance matrix of selected exchange rates 1999-2004 (Monthly data, Percentages)**

|  | Euro | US $ | Japanese Yen | Korean Won | Singapore $ |
|---|---|---|---|---|---|
| Euro | 0.39 | | | | |
| US $ | –0.18 | 0.17 | | | |
| Japanese Yen | –0.05 | –0.09 | 0.26 | | |
| Korean Won | –0.08 | 0.14 | –0.17 | 0.25 | |
| Singapore $ | –0.08 | 0.09 | –0.07 | 0.10 | 0.07 |

Source: ECB, FED, Central Bank of Japan and IFS

Obstfeld and Rogoff also provide an estimate of the potential size of the adjustment using a two country new open economy model, with tradable and non-tradable goods, and home bias in the consumption of tradable goods[9]. In their model, a dollar depreciation shifts demand towards United States exports, but these effects is mitigated to the extent that there is home bias in consumers' preferences over tradable goods. In addition, against the common perception that a boost in European productivity will help close the global imbalance, according to the model this would only be the case if the productivity increase were in the non-tradable sector (where productivity gains are more likely to show up last). Higher productivity in tradable goods productions outside the US would mean that US exports would be less competitive, and the current imbalance would widen further, at least in the short-run. According to their estimates, closing a US current account of about 5.4 percent of GDP would require a real dollar depreciation of about 15 to 25 percent (and possibly higher if military spending increases permanently).[10] This estimate, which is broadly in line with the estimate given by the IMF, represents a large dollar movement that could potentially have destabilizing effects in the global economy[11]. If Europe remains a relatively rigid economy, and enlargement

---

[9] Maurice Obstfeld, and Kenneth Rogoff, "The Unsustainable U.S. Current Account Position Revisited," prepared for the July 12-13, 2004 NBER pre-conference on "G7 Current Account Imbalances: Sustainability and Adjustment."

[10] This estimate could be lower if one considers the effects of valuation changes on debt accumulation (see Gourinchas and Rey, 2004, Lane and Milesi-Ferretti, 2001, and Tille, 2003), but Obstfeld and Rogoff (2004)'s estimates suggest that this effect is relatively small in this case.

[11] IMF, "Euro Area Policies: Selected Issues," Country Report No. 04/235, Washington D.C., August 2004.

does not seem to change the picture much, it will have a difficult time adjusting to a massive dollar depreciation.[12]

## Concluding Remarks

Overall the data presented in this chapter suggest that the enlarged EU constitutes an economic unit of about the same size as the USA. The euro area is somewhat smaller in terms of GDP, but larger in terms of its international trade (a large proportion of which, however, is with European partners).

However, it is doubtful whether enlargement (or the introduction of the euro) automatically will lead to an increase in the European influence in the management of the global economy, since it will take time before the representation of EU member countries in international organizations will be unified and by that time their size might be reduced as well. Unification of the EU (or even euro area) representation is likely to take time because it will be resisted by national central banks and finance ministries which want to retain their present areas of influence. Moreover, it will be difficult to organize an effective EU representation as long as some important member states stay out of EMU. Enlargement has made it even more difficult to change the status quo because the new member countries are even more strongly subject to the 'small country syndrome'.

A smooth global rebalancing may require increased flexibility in the enlarged EU product and labor markets, more than an increase in productivity growth.[13]

---

[12] For an analysis of labor market rigidity in the candidate countries see CEPS, "The Euro at 25," Special Report of the CEPS Macroeconomic Policy Group, November 2002.

[13] Other sources used were Gourinchas, Pierre-Olivier, and Helene Rey, 2004, "International Financial Adjustment." Photocopy, Berkeley and Princeton, July; IMF, 2004b, World Economic Outlook, Washington D.C., September; Lane, Philip R. and Gian Maria Milesi-Ferretti, "The External Wealth of Nations: Measures of Foreign Assets and Liabilities for Industrial and Developing Nations." *Journal of International Economics* 55, December 2001,pp. 263-94; Titte, Cedric, "Financial Integration and the Wealth Effect of Exchange Rate Flucuations," Federal Reserve Bank of New York, August 2004.

## Chapter 13

# Transatlantic Cooperation on Development Assistance: Implications of EU Enlargement

Patrick M. Cronin and Muriel Asseraf

## Introduction

An optimistic perspective of European enlargement would view it as an opportunity for the European Union (EU) and the US government to forge common and complementary approaches to manage problems stemming from poverty and underdevelopment around the world; the pessimistic perspective could assume just the opposite. At a time when the transatlantic rift has been growing, clearly there is a need to search for issues that can unite us rather than divide us. Whether this opportunity can be realized in the decade ahead, however, will depend on the ability of leaders in Washington, Brussels, and European Union member state capitals to bridge these significant gaps that exist in philosophical approaches, policy priorities, and structural and organizational biases. Indeed, these problems have hampered cooperation on a range of programs designed to help poor countries, quite separate from the issue of EU enlargement.

This chapter will examine the current state of EU-US cooperation on development assistance and then analyze the potential for future cooperation in light of EU enlargement from 15 to 25 countries. The challenge to greater aid effectiveness in addressing shared concerns in the developing world is far less one of money than it is of achieving better coherence, coordination, and complementarity. Of the $68.5 billion in Official Development Assistance (ODA) spent by the industrialized countries in 2003, the United States was the largest single absolute donor ($15.8 billion or 24%), even though it ranked last as a percentage of gross domestic product (0.14). Meanwhile, the then-15 members of the European Union provided a total of about $36.8 billion (or 57%) in development assistance, of which about $8 billion was managed by the Commission and mostly implemented through Europe Aid, whose mission it is to implement the external aid instruments of the European Commission. The bulk of EU official development assistance—to Africa, the Caribbean and Asia—continues to be managed through EU Member States' bilateral aid programs. Based on current commitments and projections, by 2010 global ODA may rise to about $100 billion, with the EU contributing some 62% and the United States some 22%.

In contrast to these healthy contributions of ODA, the level of political and programmatic cooperation between these two major donors remains relatively modest. An explicit question of this chapter is whether the European Union and the United States can expand their cooperation and find greater synergy from combined and complementary approaches to development assistance rather than going it alone; and whether the enlargement of the EU will be an asset in improving cooperation. At the same time that ODA is growing fairly rapidly, both the EU and the United States have begun a series of helpful reforms that may provide further room for a common approach to development. To address this question realistically, however, it is important to recognize the numerous constraints on cooperation.

## International Security Context in EU-US Development Cooperation

Development cooperation has never been a hallmark of EU-US relations. At least for the US government, cooperation has been particularly influenced by the international security environment, and issues such as integrating Russia, managing a rising China, and seeking peace in the Middle East are issues that largely transcend development assistance. Thus, one can look even briefly at how approaches have varied among the cold war period, the first decade of the post-cold war, and then everything that has followed September 11, 2001.

### The Cold War

A brief reprise of the past half-century might begin with the impediments to cooperation that grew out of the structural and historical asymmetries between the United States and Europe in the decades immediately following the Second World War. Europe was recovering (with the help of the Marshall Plan), the third world was decolonizing, and the United States saw itself locked in a global struggle with communism for the hearts and minds of people around the globe. In several instances, President Dwight D. Eisenhower sought to distance the United States from the developing world policies of "old Europe"—policies that were designed primarily to preserve influence in the face of burgeoning post-colonial independence movements and the growth of a nonaligned movement. In short, US early-cold war policies vis-à-vis the developing world were more value-laden and ideological as opposed to the relatively more pragmatic European policies. This basic philosophical gap has become rigidified over time and endures today in the debate between a 'foreign policy' versus 'development' approach to foreign aid.

At the onset of the 1960s, with the creation of the United States Agency for International Development (USAID) and the Peace Corps, US President John F. Kennedy began a concerted effort at expanding economic development in Latin America and other parts of the developing world. US-European economic asymmetry limited cooperation between the two partners. By the late 1960s, a transatlantic rift over relations with the developing world widened over the Vietnam War. While Western Europe and the United States remained staunch allies over the fundamental objective on containing Soviet military power, political and policy differences continued to hamper cooperation over relations with the developing world. President Jimmy Carter's stress on human rights and President Ronald Reagan's desire to rollback communism in Latin America were both at odds with Europe's more pragmatic attitude.

*Post-Cold War*

The Cold War's cessation made the developing world more important on its own terms, as opposed to an object of a superpower struggle. But many Europeans were now faced with tearing down the walls that had divided them, while simultaneously coping with civil war in the Balkans. The United States was hoping to find a "peace dividend" after the cold war and thereby reduce spending in defense and international affairs. The 1990s will be remembered for the biggest decline in official development assistance since the OECD Development

Assistance Committee started measuring it. Even so, the executive branch saw the wisdom in increasing assistance to the former Soviet Union and Warsaw Pact countries. By the dawn of the twenty-first century, the common challenges of poverty, disease and conflict emanating from the developing world heightened the importance of addressing global poverty; still to be realized, however, is the agenda for action that will forge significantly greater EU-US cooperation on foreign aid. In 2000, the Millennium Development Goals, which seek to make huge inroads in reducing poverty, decreasing child mortality, bringing about universal primary education and other goals by 2015, became consonant with an international consensus on development priorities. Unfortunately, Europe and the United States have chosen to place more emphasis on differences—mostly minor—rather than to declare heated agreement and forge a more concerted approach to dealing with the developing world. Part of the discord was created by the major terrorist strikes on the United States on September 11, 2001, and America's reaction to them. While this may have little to do with development per se, the differences continue to hamper the scope and depth of cooperation across a range of issues.

*Post-9/11*

Two major issues are dampening prospects for significantly increasing cooperation on development assistance. First, the tragic events of September 11, 2001 changed U.S. policies toward the developing world. As intimated above, the United States has tended to view the developing world through a prism of either humanitarian aid or strategic interest, whereas Europe has focused more narrowly on development. America's global war on terror has not produced a ready consensus on the objectives to be sought by countries on both sides of the Atlantic. If Afghan reconstruction garnered great cooperation, Iraq was far more divisive, and other goals in addressing the sources of terrorism in the broader Middle East and North Africa remain quite problematic. These priorities for Washington, however, invariably relegated most other areas of cooperation to a distant-second priority. Furthermore, the longer-term US perspective in the post-9/11 world has homed in on creating accountable government throughout the greater Middle East—a political emphasis that once again accentuates tensions across the Atlantic. Smaller European countries in particular tend to favor protecting poverty-reduction strategies, whereas some of the larger European countries that generally share more of the US concern about radical Islam in the wake of the September 11, 2001 and March 11, 2004 security environment, more readily see the merit in focusing on addressing the acute weaknesses of state institutions and civil society within Arab countries.

It is also arguable that the European approach to democracy building is far more realistic and effective than the recent rhetorical blandishments emerging from Washington with respect to the Middle East. As Anne-Marie Slaughter has argued, "the EU model of building democracy—through assistance, admonition and accession negotiations"[1] could well inform the U.S. approach to post-conflict reconstruction and general emphasis on good governance. For instance, a September 2004 USAID review of "Monitoring Country Progress in Eastern Europe and Eurasia," indicates how the Northern Tier of Eastern European counties (the Czech Republic, Hungary, Slovakia, Latvia, Estonia, Lithuania, Slovenia, and Poland) have made great strides in governance and economic reform. This study is reinforced by the World Bank's *Doing Business in 2005* report, which notes that seven of the top ten reformers in the world are in Eastern Europe and that clearly EU enlargement was the greatest impetus for making it possible to do business (enforcing contracts, starting and closing a business, and hiring and firing).

A second issue preventing greater cooperation has concerned the means rather than the ends of development. The Bush Administration's emphasis on assembling a coalition of the willing invariably clashed with Europe's preoccupation with broadening and deepening an interconnected European Community. The former implied new rules centered on the US preferences, whereas the latter worked on deepening existing multilateral institutions. In this context, some across the Atlantic chose to emphasize differences: e.g., over ODA, with many Europeans choosing to focus on the percentage of assistance relative to national gross domestic product (in which the United States scores last), or over the European focus on social needs even at the expense of sustainable development, which require, *inter alia*, poor countries to commit to open governance and anticorruption, expand trade, support private enterprise, enforce property rights and the rule of law.

---

[1] Anne-Marie Slaughter, "What is this 'European Union'?" in *International Herald Tribune*, October 19, 2004.

The most productive path ahead may be in the middle: whatever resources are forthcoming, and hopefully they should be greater than in recent years, donor investments in poor country need to take seriously the lessons of aid effectiveness and hence greater accountability on the part of recipient nations. Nonetheless, as the EU continues to gain in importance and resources, it seems essential for the transatlantic cooperation to extend a practical agenda of cooperation between the US and the EU. As the European Union enlarges, the divide over processes and means could further widen without concerted actions from leaders on both sides of the Atlantic. Favoring a more concerted agenda for transatlantic cooperation on development, however, is the fact that the industrialized countries face myriad challenges from underdeveloped regions, since in a globalizing world it is impossible to erect frontiers to keep out terrorism, poverty, disease, and conflict.

From a more European perspective, if a single one can be said to exist, this post 9/11 period, and indeed previous periods, might be better defined as a period of a widening gap between wealthy and poor countries and between wealthy and impoverished people within less developed countries. As former EU commissioner for Development and Humanitarian Aid Poul Nielson said repeatedly during his tenure, the European Commission focus is on poverty alleviation through the support for health, education, energy and water, as well as through an increased reliance upon direct budget support to recipient countries. This poverty alleviation paradigm is codified in internationally agreed goals on reducing poverty (namely, the Millennium Development Goals or MDGs). But a strict adherence to these goals—not to mention an ever-increasing price tag that sometimes accompanies the push to achieve them—can open up a chasm with other foreign policy objectives required to promote peace, accountable governments, and sustainable development. These, in short, are two ends of the philosophical divide that must be bridged if foreign aid and development policies are to be made more coherent and effective in the context of transatlantic relations. As suggested above, we believe the divide is greater in perception than in reality.

## Current Limits on Cooperation

The main barriers to cooperation relate to either structure or policy. Structural constraints may be more difficult to change, or at least to change rapidly, although recent organizational changes in Europe and the United States suggest further change is possible. Philosophical and policy preferences may be even more susceptible to finding a middle way toward more complementary and cooperative approaches. Indeed, we argue that the most constructive agenda for cooperation may be started by concentrating on basic objectives and issues rather than existing programs and aid delivery mechanisms. A clear identification of common issues and concerns can provide generic building blocks for assembling a joint and mutually reinforcing approach to foreign aid; a focus on structure, labels, and programs, however, invariably accentuates differences. Structural and or organizational changes may well be needed, but they will be easier to effect by agreement on a common cause or short list of common goals.

Structural and institutional differences center on organizational decision-making, budgeting, and aid delivery. Washington and Brussels operate distinctively with respect to policymaking, agenda setting, and diplomacy and negotiation. Washington focuses foreign and economic policy in bilateral capitals, while the EU and individual European countries have more direct control over policy decisions. The EU is especially comfortable with a US government inclined to work through a multilateral body. The culture in Brussels favors an internal European dialogue—and necessarily a multilateral one—attempting to forge a greater consensus among European members. But there is no single interlocutor in Washington or Brussels who can bridge these fundamental differences between the two decision-making centers. When the United States seeks multilateral cooperation, it generally prefers to look first at smaller, more agile institutions, including the North Atlantic Treaty Organization (NATO) or, especially on development, the Group of 8 (or G8) process. Thus, NATO has served an important role in the rebuilding of Afghanistan, while the G8 process has spawned a variety of development initiatives in recent years, ranging from greater food security in Africa to new efforts to reach out to Islamic countries throughout the broader Middle East and North Africa. There is a compelling need for change in both systems: in Europe, there is a need to break down the barrier between policy making (DG External Affairs) and programs and implementation (DG Development); similarly, in the United States, there is a great need for identifying a single locus of decision-making authority, whether through the creation of a cabinet-level department for development similar to that which exists in Britain or by a much sharper delineation of authority in the State Department with interagency oversight and a tightening of the relationship between State and USAID as the main implementer of US aid policy.

Another largely structural difference relates to the internal machinery of the EU and US development bureaucracies over budgeting, contracting, and aid delivery. These differences also make cooperation difficult, even when policy will is strong. The annual budget of the European Union is established within the limits of expenditures set by a five-to-seven year financial planning framework known as 'the financial perspective.' Its ceilings must be respected in the annual budgetary process. This structure focuses the annual budget debate on the actual level of expenditure beneath the ceilings and the specific budget lines determined by the financial perspectives. The EDF, which is the main instrument for Community aid to the African, Caribbean and Pacific states and to the Overseas Countries and Territories, currently does not come under the general community budget, but it is instead funded by member states, and participation to the EDF is voluntary. Some are discussing integrating the EDF inside the budget in order to "ensure democratic control" over this important part of the EU development policy, without prejudice to the overall volume of EU assistance to the poorest countries. Others oppose "budgetization" because it would give equal weight to all aid recipients and not simply neighboring states. There are other EU funding mechanisms that touch on development and foreign aid including: humanitarian and food aid, which is the responsibility of the European Community Humanitarian Office or ECHO; cooperation with Mediterranean third countries and the Middle East, and cooperation with partner countries in Eastern Europe and Central Asia and the Western Balkan countries. Pre-accession funding, which has been a dominant focus in recent years with EU enlargement, is now set to decline, although it remains in place for Romania, Bulgaria and Turkey.

In contrast, the United States follows annual appropriations, occasionally supplemented through emergency supplemental budgets. The

President sends a budget to Congress in late January with the expectation that the Congress will pass a budget for the fiscal year beginning October 1 of that year. Because even this annual budget is delayed, however, US development aid is mostly without knowing for sure whether funding will be available. The basic distinction is that the EU is set up to make long-term commitments and, once they are made, those commitments are difficult to change. The United States is better poised to make year-to-year shifts. Moreover, the current US budget process calls for USAID to submit its proposed budget to the State Department, whose front office ultimately determines the final recommendation to the White House Office of Management and Budget prior to a President's budget submission to Congress. In other words, there is far more scope for the White House and State Department to impose a foreign policy imprimatur on long-term development programs. Congress then plays a role in the process that effectively reduces executive flexibility through numerous earmarks that require various accounts to be spent on specific projects, programs, and areas. These budget politics not only hamper transatlantic cooperation—whether with respect to ODA or post-conflict pledging conferences that typically focus on multi-year pledges—but also cooperation with developing countries, whose weak state institutions are prevented from knowing next year's funding.

This structural difference is further compounded by the fact that most existing contracting in the EU reaches out to governments, whereas USAID concentrates less on building state institutions than on delivering assistance through many nongovernmental organizations (NGOs) and civil society. To be sure, recent EU deliberations have given increased attention to the valuable role played by civil society within a country's development. But the basic divide between a focus on state-institution building versus civil society and NGOs hampers closer bilateral cooperation in the field. In both cases, the actual expenditure of aid on the ground is most often complicated and slow. The "pipeline" of pledged but unspent monies pouring into a recipient country can frequently exceed the amount of money actually spent in the year it was intended.

Recently, the EU has significantly simplified and streamlined its approach to development assistance. In its joint declaration in November 2000, the Council and the Commission produced its first general statement on development policy, defining the main objective of the European Union development policy as being poverty reduction and, eventually, eradication. The statement identified six priority areas where assistance can bring about added value: trade and development, regional integration, macroeconomic support and access to social services, transport, food security and sustainable rural development, and institutional capacity building and good governance. These areas certainly provide ample room for cooperative approaches with other donors, especially the United States. As part of the reforms instituted since 2000, the EU has also created Europe Aid as its main arm for implementation, improved accountability and monitoring, and created country strategy papers. Further work needs to be done, but some of the opaque and cumbersome processes that characterized the EU development previously are no longer huge impediments to cooperation.

Other extant impediments to cooperation are more discretionary, stemming from philosophical policy choices. Up until recently, the EU has generally considered development assistance as an endeavor separate from foreign policy. It views development goals as long-term projects that cannot and should not be subordinated to political interests of any kind. While many if not most development professionals in the United States take a similarly dichotomous view of development and foreign policy as totally separate entities, US development policy is still usually subordinated to larger economic, foreign, and security policy objectives. While the EU considers recipient-country governance issues as increasingly important, it does so through the prism of poverty alleviation; US officials, in contrast, have increasingly placed emphasis on greater productivity (indeed, these are the explicit goals of the Millennium Challenge Corporation, which was authorized by Congress in early 2004 to focus on "good performing" poor countries). US officials also use development and foreign aid monies more often to address democracy promotion, human rights, and other more general foreign policy concerns (especially recent years in the Middle East and North Africa). The fissures that developed between some European countries and the United States and Iraq, have only served to heighten European suspicions that the United States wants to convert economic development assistance programs into strategic and political programs. And yet it is possible to note that Europe and the United States generally share major foreign and security objectives, even while there is a need to more tightly align development policies.

Much of the apparent philosophical differences are less substantive than they might appear. In reality, there is largely a shared and new consensus that economic growth and poverty reduction are inseparable, and that most of the MDGs are important and fair ways to measure poverty reduction. The debate is really over secondary issues such as how much emphasis to place on private sector growth or how to place the MDGs in the context of country strategies.

Some policy differences are rooted in geography. Propinquity makes a difference when it comes to foreign aid. The EU focuses on pan-Europe and its new neighboring countries while the United States increasingly directs its attention outside of Europe, as development spending on Eastern Europe, the Balkans and former Soviet states decline. During the last decade, the European Union has developed a European Neighborhood Policy, as a response to the new opportunities and challenges created by the physical enlargement of the EU, in order to "develop a zone of prosperity and a friendly neighborhood ... with which the European enjoys close, peaceful and cooperative relations"[2] to a number of countries in Eastern Europe and the Mediterranean region. The Barcelona process, or Euro-Mediterranean partnership, was launched in 1995, and it is a good example of the EU's focus on its southern neighbors. It is marked by greater bilateral, multilateral and regional cooperation between EU members and 12 Mediterranean countries.[3] This neighborhood policy has started to, and will continue to encompass countries on the Eastern borders of the EU, through "political dialogue and reform; trade and measures to preparing partners for gradually obtaining a stake in the EU's internal market; justice and home affairs; energy, transport, information society, environment and research and innovation; and social policy and people-to-people contacts."[4] This process has meant that EU accession criteria have in part supplanted other economic development policies

---

[2] *"Wider Europe—Neighborhood: a New Framework for Relations with out Eastern and Southern Neighbors,"* Communication of the European Union, (Brussels, European Commission, 2003), p25.

[3] The 12 Mediterranean Partners, situated in the Southern and Eastern Mediterranean are Morocco, Algeria, Tunisia (Maghreb); Egypt, Israel, Jordan, the Palestinian Authority, Lebanon, Syria (Mashrek); Turkey, Cyprus and Malta; Libya currently has observer status at certain meetings.

[4] *"European Neighborhood Policy,"* Commission of the European Communities (Brussels, European Commission, 2004), p3.

among those countries hoping to be admitted to the EU in future years. The total of funding for the period 2004-2006 under external assistance instruments is €255 million.


## Record of Cooperation

One of the most constant features of the EU-US cooperation has been the proliferation of rhetoric of diplomatic harmony, one which, in the domain of development aid, has in fact tended to obscure the real challenges and might very well have contributed to distracting both the United States and the EU from accomplishing the agenda they had set for themselves. In fact, every year, the EU-US summit is yet another occasion for harmonious blandishments; the EU and the United States inevitably walk out of these summits adopting joint statements, and agreeing on an agenda for further cooperation, one which rarely is acted upon. The joint declaration that was issued at the Dromoland Summit in June 2004 reiterated the commitment of the EU and the United States to a number of issues of interest to both, like the fight against HIV/AIDS or the support of reform and democratization in the Broader Middle East and North Africa: "In recognition of the extent of the crisis, the statement reads, and of our joint commitment to fighting HIV/AIDS and other communicable diseases, we are determined to further strengthen our cooperation." There have been gains, to be sure, but EU-US cooperation on these vital areas have been palpably challenging.

This is not to say that there is no successful cooperation or that good people on both sides are not striving to expand the level of cooperation. Notwithstanding the structural and situational differences in approaches to development assistance, the recent record of EU-US cooperation has been punctuated with a number of successes, especially in the area of humanitarian assistance—where cooperation between ECHO and U.S. bilateral humanitarian programs within State and USAID have been marked by true cooperation. In addition, there has been progress in post-conflict reconstruction, although this is an area where there might be an opportunity for further alignment and cooperation. A few specific success stories follow below.

*Cooperation in Afghanistan*

The United States and EU serve as donor Co-Chairs of the Afghanistan Reconstruction process, and have provided Afghanistan with significant pledges of assistance, as well as accelerated disbursements to address that country's immediate security needs and to help prepare for elections. The EU and United States together have provided the mainstay of the international reconstruction effort. "In the resolution of such conflicts we have brought to bear not just financial resources but also technical expertise, and crucially, a commitment to principles of democracy and freedom, the absence of which all too often has encouraged the spread of regional conflict."[5] Strong European support for the free elections in Afghanistan in October 2004 provided the pivotal support for advancing an Afghan government. Without the validation of a disputed election by the United Nations and the OSCE observers, the post-election period threatened to fuel a resurgent civil war.

In Tokyo, in 2002, the EU pledged €1 billion over five years in support for Afghanistan. The EU is committed to the implementation of the Bonn Agreement to restore stability in Afghanistan, to reduce poverty, to improve the availability and access to food, to help tackle key cross-cutting issues that are critical to Afghanistan's future including de-mining, the sustainable return of refugees, the role of women and reducing opium poppy production.

Through USAID, the United States is also committed to increasing food availability and incomes, to providing small and medium scale businesses with credit for production, input trade, processing and marketing enterprises, to helping the Back-to-School campaign, which included printing and distributing new textbooks, training for teachers, and school rehabilitation, to providing basic health services across the country, to encouraging domestic and foreign investment through a stable and transparent system of economic governance, and finally to helping the government develop a sound legal and political foundation. Since 2001, the US has provided $588 million to humanitarian assistance and reconstruction in Afghanistan.

---

[5] *"The EU's relations with the United States of America,"* European Commission for External Relations' website, available at http://europa.eu.int/comm/external_relations/us/intro/peace2.htm#pov2

*The Balkans*

The Balkans is another region where cooperation has been visible. "The EU financial assistance to the Western Balkans started with humanitarian aid during the war and has since shifted to reconstruction and now, increasingly, institution building. Since 1991, through its various aid programs, the European Union has provided more than € 7 billion in assistance to the countries of the Western Balkans. In 2000, all previous mechanisms of European Union assistance to the region were replaced by a single, new instrument: Community Assistance for Reconstruction, Development and Stabilization (CARDS), aimed at underpinning the EU's political objectives in the region. The full financial envelope for 2000-2006 is € 4.65 billion."[6] The United States has also played an important role in that region. "Beginning in 1991, the US provided $2 billion of assistance to nine of the ten new Member States which joined the EU on May 1st, 2004, helping to accelerate the transition to private sector-led market economies and pluralistic societies."[7] Although the Balkans continue to be marked by problems, as in Serbia, a large extent of the progress in the subregion can be tied to EU-US development cooperation.

*Food Security and Ethiopia*

Cooperation on food security, especially in Africa, is well illustrated by support for Ethiopia, which with a population of 66 million people is the third most populated country in Africa. During the 1980s and 1990s, protracted civil war and recurring drought left the economy in deep crisis. Ethiopia also has the third largest number of people living with HIV/AIDS of any country in the world. Between 1995 and 2002, Ethiopia went from being the world's fourth largest recipient of food to the largest recipient. As a new wave of famine threatened Ethiopians in the early years of the twenty-first century, USAID pledged approximately 878,790 metric tons or 57 percent of the emergency food aid requirements for Ethiopia. Ethiopia also occupies a special place in the development cooperation program among the

---

[6] "*The EU's relations with South Eastern Europe*," European Commission External Relations website, available at http://europa.eu.int/comm/external_relations/see/sum_06_03/index.htm

[7] "*US-EU cooperate on Humanitarian, Development Assistance*," Fact Sheet of the United States Mission to the European Union, Brussels, 2004.

EU's 70 Africa, Caribbean and Pacific countries: Ethiopia is the largest recipient of EC support. But simply giving the most food is not halting the vicious cycle of famine that Ethiopians keep facing. Can the EU and the United States take their humanitarian programs to a more proactive, sustainable level? After years of food aid programs, the United States and the European Union agreed at the G8 summit in 2004 on an action plan aimed at "ending the cycle of famine in the horn of Africa, raising agricultural productivity, and promoting rural development in food insecure countries," representing an important step in the transition from food aid to food security. Even so, this record of cooperation over food security has been marred by intense divisions over the political conditionality of aid to the government as well as over the specific but critical issue of whether to provide any genetically modified organisms. Given the machinations of agricultural lobbies, the Common Agricultural Policy and sputtering World Trade negotiations, this may be an area that continues to be complex.

## Limited Cooperation

Despite recent successes, EU-US cooperation is far less than espoused in official rhetoric, where the two powers share common interests but lack more substantial cooperation, as in the following areas:

### The Middle East

At present the G8 remains the preferred forum for advancing development and democracy in the Broader Middle East and North Africa initiative, a project that is rooted in the aspirations of many in the Arab world but advanced most forcefully by the Bush administration. European skepticism about an overtly political approach strikes many European officials as either counterproductive or risky, and they generally prefer a focus on issues of economic development and poverty alleviation. Meetings in 2004 advanced this common cause, but there are still lingering doubts, in particular expressed by smaller European countries that may not share the same sense of urgency as larger member states of the EU. Moreover, as mentioned above, the EU experience of enlarging to incorporate former Soviet states and transition countries in Eastern Europe has had a remarkable effect on reforms. Nonetheless, the challenges emanating from the Greater Middle East, where there is generally poor governance, a rising youth bulge in population, poorly performing economies, and rising Islamic radicalism, are of important on both sides of the Atlantic.

## HIV/AIDS

There is a great convergence of interest over the rising challenge of HIV/AIDS. At the same time, there seems to be more competition for leadership on dealing with this urgent health pandemic. The EU has chosen the multilateral route, contributing to the Global Funds against HIV/AIDS, and the US has invested far more heavily in a unilateral approach (the President's Emergency Plan for AIDS Relief, which pledges to spend some $15 billion on HIV/AIDS, tuberculosis and malaria over a five-year period). These different emphases can still be complementary, although the complexity of issues encompasses where to invest resources (the Global Fund is wide open, but the U.S. approach has selected fifteen high-prevalence countries in Africa, the Caribbean and Vietnam); what kind of assistance to provide (while prevention is important to both the United States and the EU, Washington and Brussels have different approaches to reproductive rights); and treatment programs inevitably have led to rancorous discussions about favoring pharmaceutical firms over cheaper generic drugs made in the developing world. Notwithstanding these differences, the fact is that both the United States and Europe seem likely to move forward to address this global pandemic.

As with the struggle over generic versus brand-name medicines, there are other very specific issues of disagreement and controversy that have forestalled greater cooperation. The critical issue of reducing agricultural subsidies is at least part of the ongoing World Trade Organization Doha process; the European anxiety over U.S. distribution of genetically modified food has been subject to countless debates without substantial progress; and discord over the priority accorded to environmental goals has certainly deteriorated since the United States walked away from the Kyoto Accord.

## The Future Agenda and EU Enlargement

It is still early to draw any clear-cut conclusion as to the impact of enlargement on EU development policies. Nonetheless, a number of observations can already be drawn from the tendencies that have emerged in the accession process and a number of questions have already emerged from recent developments inside the EU.

First of all, in the area of development policy, all EU member states are bound to adopt coherent and complementary development policies. A number of areas are binding. When they entered the EU on May 1, 2004, the ten new member states automatically became members of the Cotonou Agreements (formerly known as the Lomé Convention), which aim at reducing poverty through "political dialogue, development aid and closer economic and trade cooperation" in the countries of Africa, the Caribbean and the Pacific. Soon, the new member states will also have to take part in the European Development Fund, and given their lack of interest in the African continent, negotiations for the upcoming budget of the funds are expected to be tough, both on the political and on the financial front. Along those lines, the new member states have also entered into all the association agreements that the EU holds with other countries.

There is also an ongoing debate about "budgetization" of EU aid. At present, about three quarters of external aid is financed from the budget and one quarter from the EDF. The budget figures include aid to some pre-accession countries and sums for a variety of budget lines. They are governed by the overall financial perspectives for the EU as a whole. "EDF budgetization would bring all monies within the full purview of the political process with the parliament, which could help improve allocation to the poorest countries. [...] For accession countries, budgetization could reduce the total cost of participating in aid programs."[8]

Until May 2004, the ten new member states of the European Union were the first recipients of EU aid under the neighborhood policy. One of the questions that arose when they joined the EU was one concerning the distribution of EU financial resources. The new member states have neither the financial nor the institutional capacity to transition from their position of aid recipients to aid donor. New member states have very low levels of ODA which amount to one sixth to one sixteenth of the minimum target set in Monterrey for current EU Member states. Only Slovenia, Malta and Cyprus have the GNI per

---

[8] Simon Maxwell and Paul Engel, "*European Development Cooperation to 2010,*" (London: Overseas Development Institute Working Paper 219, 2003), p10.

capita levels necessary to be classified as donors.[9] In the coming years (period of the 9th EDF), the financial consequences of enlargement on development policies will probably be discreet, because the new member states are not required to contribute to the 9th EDF. In the short term, the financial consequences of enlargement might be "limited to an allocation of budget contributions among member states and a lowering of the average ODA/GNI ratio."[10] However, starting in 2007, the new member states will be required to contribute, and effects of enlargement may be more substantial, given the pressures of enlargement, especially in the agricultural and structural areas.

Though EU enlargement will undoubtedly have a financial impact on EU development policies, it is difficult to know today how the budget will be altered. How long will it take for the new EU members to catch up to ODA/GNI ratio levels required by the EU? How much will the 9th and subsequent EDF be affected by the contributions of the new members states?

In terms of policies, the new member states are also expected to adopt the Common Declaration of the European Community on Development Policy of November 2000, which states that, "The Treaty establishing the European Community provides that the Community and the Member states shall coordinate their development cooperation policies and consult each other on their aid programs, including in international organizations and during international conferences." The declaration also adds, "The main objective of the Community development policy is grounded on the principle of sustainable, equitable and participatory human and social development. Promotion of human rights, democracy, the rule of law and good governance are an integral part of it." The new member states are still far from agreeing on all these principles. They do not feel the need to pay for other countries' development, and neither does their general public. Most of the new member states' governments show little commitment to development assistance. A report conducted by the European Commission, Development Strategies in 2003 concluded that the main focus of development cooperation is precisely in those areas where their countries most suffered before 1989: democracy

---

[9] *"The Consequences of enlargement for Development Policy,"* Final Report, (Brussels: European Commission, Development6 Strategies, 2003), Volume 1.

[10] *"The Consequences of enlargement for Development Policy."*

and human rights and environment, rather than poverty reduction.[11] In the coming years, the trend of declining EC ODA towards the least developed countries might be reinforced, because it is consistent with the development policies pursued by new member states. It also reflects the growing focus, mentioned above, of EU development policies towards its Eastern and Southern neighbors.

How might EU enlargement affect the future of EU-US cooperation for development assistance? Indeed, demographics and poverty statistics show that there are growing needs in the developing world, and that the developing countries will increasingly put pressure on the developed world (conflicts spill-over, diseases, famines, HIV/AIDS, climate change, etc.). Will enlargement accentuate some of the existing differences: agreeing on the agenda, dealing through the structural impediments and importance of leadership or will enlargement facilitate cooperation on a number of issues?

From the perspective of the US government, there remains an expectation that EU enlargement will provide new leverage for Washington vis-à-vis Brussels because of the close ties between the United States and many new member states. But it remains far too early to tell whether this expectation will be realized.

Rather than simply seeking leverage, U.S. policymakers should join European leaders in a focused dialogue, which in turn can advance common understanding and joint action. And recently, there have been some hopeful signs of EU-US convergence for those looking for opportunities for cooperation. The EU has recently produced a new security policy concept that helps to bridge the gap between many European and American views about how to balance security with other needs in a post-9/11 world. The new European Security Strategy emphasizes the importance of the relations between international crime, terrorism, failed states and poverty.

"Development policy and other cooperation programs provide, without doubt, the most powerful instruments at the Community's disposal for treating the root causes of conflict. [...] If we are to be proactive in preventing future violent conflicts, then good governance, poverty

---

[11] *The Consequences of enlargement for Development Policy*," Final Report, (Brussels: European Commission, Development6 Strategies, 2003), Volume 1.

eradication, and the fights against [...] 'the dark side of globalization' —
environmental degradation, AIDS, terrorism and international crime—
must be placed at the center of our thinking on both security and
development."[12] In this address, if Chris Patten recognizes that the link
between peace and development is not new, he also emphasizes the shift
that the EU is making in integrating them in its external policy. "...The
scale of the problem and the appalling repercussions of recent conflicts
have made this a matter of self preservation. [...] We have no choice but
to make the promotion of sustainable development as much a part of
our fight for global security as the investment we make in sound multilateral institutions, fair international trade or even our armed forces."[13]
In fact, writes Gerrard Quille of the International Security Information
Service, Europe, "The US administration will be largely pleased with
the content of the ESS (European Security Strategy). The EU has
unambiguously re-calibrated its priorities to match those of the US and
the ESS places the responsibility on Europeans to support multilateralism on a constructive and 'results oriented' basis." This trend could
potentially be reinforced by the presence of the ten new member states,
which could in turn enhance EU-US cooperation on certain key issues
of development assistance.

However, not all member states of the EU are satisfied with this
new turn of events. The development ministers of Austria, Belgium,
Germany, Ireland, the Netherlands, Sweden and the United Kingdom
have signed a joint position paper on Development Cooperation in
the new Treaty for the European Union in May 2003, in which they
state that "International development cooperation is a vital and distinct element of the Union's external relations. It contributes both to
the Union's internal and external goals and is a clear expression of
Europe's wish to advance its values and foster peace and prosperity in
the wider world. The principal aim of the Union's development
efforts should be to eradicate world poverty."[14]

---

[12] *The Consequences of enlargement for Development Policy,*" Final Report, (Brussels: European Commission, Development Strategies, 2003), Volume 1.

[13] The Rt. Hon. Chris Patten, CH, *"Europe in the World: CFSP & its relation to development,"* (London: Overseas Development Institute, 2003), p2.

[14] Development Ministers of Austria, Belgium, Germany, Ireland, the Netherlands, Sweden and the United Kingdom *"Joint position paper on Development Cooperation in the new Treaty for the European Union,"* (Brussels, 2003), Available at europa.eu.int/futurum/documents/other/oth010503_en.pdf

The new member states are already pushing for a EU development policy that would be more directly in tune with the EU's interests. They argue that development policy should be subordinate to foreign policy, and based on national interests. (It is important to keep in mind that in development assistance, less than 20 percent of total EU aid comes from the Community budget, the remaining 80 percent being provided and managed by the member states. "Member states' diplomatic services and overseas embassies are far bigger than the network of delegations run from Brussels. Unless member states are fully with us and are prepared to join up forces with "Brussels," the EU will never achieve a 'sea change' in its external relations."[15]) Therefore, coherence, complementarity, and coordination between the EU and its member states will be crucial, and the more 'Americanized way' of viewing development assistance by the new member states represents an avenue for cooperation.

Another hopeful sign is the similitude between the EU accession process, and the Millennium Challenge Corporation. The Millennium Challenge Corporation, which was launched in 2002 by President Bush and "links greater contributions from developed nations to greater responsibility from developing nations," holds a lot of similarities with the EU accession process as a development strategy. In Eastern Europe, the European accession process forced the joining countries to implement reforms that would lead to improving democratic governance and economic liberalization in order to implement the *acquis communautaires*. The incentive for these reforms was EU accession. The Millennium Challenge Corporation uses the same underlying concept: candidate countries that want to qualify for MCC funding have to show their commitment to democratic rule and a market economy. For the first time, development has become a part of a strategy that integrates political and economic reforms on a large scale. The resemblance of these two concepts of aid conditionality or selectivity could point the way towards a healthy transatlantic dialogue on making development assistance more effective.

---

[15] Th Rt. Hon. Chris Patten, CH, *"Europe in the World: CFSP & its relation to development,"* (London: Overseas Development Institute, 2003).

## Policy Recommendations

In the wake of the 2004 national elections in the United States and the recent enlargement of the EU, there are a number of concrete steps that could be considered to advance EU-US cooperation on development aid. In particular, a focused, strategic dialogue could deepen a common understanding across the Atlantic and joint action in the developing world. This might best be achieved by the follow trio of steps.

*First, the EU and US should initiate a regular, high-level "strategic dialogue" on a few key areas in which more effective development policy and cooperation can make a tangible difference in the world.* Indeed, development cooperation may be just one of two or three areas of intensive dialogue and cooperation within an even larger strategic dialogue that reaffirms basic transatlantic relations. While officials will have to determine the precise agenda, they should agree to focus on three areas where the most gains need to be made or could most readily be made. As suggested below, some of those topics might be the Broader Middle East and North Africa initiative, post-conflict reconstruction, aid conditionality and criteria, and the nexus of trade, aid, and agriculture. A similar dialogue was initiated in 2002 to help advance specific areas of cooperation between the United States and Japan, and such a mechanism could be adapted to bolster EU-US cooperation. For this to become effective, both parties will have to improve their decision-making authority over development policy. Both DG RELEX and DG DEV would have to be jointly represented on the EU side, whereas the Under Secretary of State for Economics would be well placed to assume the lead role or the US Executive Branch.

*Second, the United States and the European Union should simultaneously launch a parliamentary dialogue on development aid.* A first step could be taken by the administration in Washington working closely with a bipartisan group of members of Congress who might be persuaded to go to Brussels with the express purpose of discussing concerns and opportunities with respect to development assistance. Such a process could then be perpetuated with reciprocal exchanges but focused on key issues of common concern.

*Third, the high-level official dialogue and parliamentary exchange should be complemented by a track-two approach in which the official process can be bolstered through a broader understanding of issues on both sides of the Atlantic.*

The future challenges as they pertain to development assistance and more specifically to the cooperation between the EU and the United States will have to be dealt with according to the stake and urgency they represent to both parties. In certain areas, cooperation should not, and cannot be hampered by structural or philosophical issues. In the next five to ten years, the United States and the European Union will be faced with a number of challenges emanating from the developing world, which they will have no choice but to confront. The question will be whether the EU and the United States will be able to face them together. As suggested above, some of these areas of interest are:

- The Greater Middle East;

- Post-conflict reconstruction and work in security sector reform;

- Aid conditionality of the kind hinted at by the Millennium Challenge Corporation's emphasis on objective criteria of good governance;

- and the nexus of trade, aid, and agriculture.

### Broader Middle East

For the sake of people in the Middle East, as well as for the sake of U.S. national security, and European political and security interests, the need for the promotion of reform in the broader Middle East is pressing and critical. In the United States, officials have been working on something akin to a Marshall Plan for the Muslim world, an initiative that began as the Middle East Partnership Initiative in late 2002 and evolved into the Broader Middle East and North Africa initiative by 2004. In Europe, leaders have been promoting reform in the Mediterranean basin for a decade, mainly through the Barcelona Process, which aims at promoting economic growth and political openness, but with very limited success. There is a growing consensus on the goals that must be reached, and on the importance of mobilizing resources to reach them. There is also an increasing recognition of the problem within many of these countries themselves. What is lacking, however, is a consensus on how to reach those goals. But in fact, as we think about specific structures for providing assistance, we should borrow from recent experience in establishing new entities such as the Global Fund for HIV/AIDS, Tuberculosis and Malaria and the Millennium Challenge Corporation, which both the EU and the United States might find ways to endorse. These models suggest a transparent, locally-owned, competitive, enterprise- and results-oriented assistance program around which a new consensus could be erected.

*Post-conflict Reconstruction*

A second area in which the United States and the EU should be focusing on expanded cooperation relates to post-conflict reconstruction. The lessons of the post-cold war era are clear: no country and no international body currently has sufficient capacity for leading and implementing expeditious and broad post-conflict rebuilding programs. Because the entire world has had the unfortunate opportunity to witness the dreadful consequences of letting fragile states become failed states, in certain parts of the world, the challenge of state-building is and should be a priority for both Washington and Brussels. In places like Afghanistan of course, the record of accomplishment is not trivial. But ongoing challenges in Sudan and Iraq, and future challenges around the developing world will test the capacity and readiness of these two huge donor communities to act in concert. In all these places, there is great need for security and development assistance, and the EU and the US could and should build a common capacity, and use the expertise that was gained in the Balkans. The CSIS post-conflict reconstruction project's four pillars of post-conflict reconstruction[16] could be the start of an entente between the EU and the United States. First, security is required before any reconstruction can be successful, although there is an acute need to address critical rebuilding programs even in an area of insurgency. Second, donors need to focus on building legitimate, effective political and administrative institutions and a participatory political process. Third, when the security is still being established, it is important to protect the population from starvation, disease, and the elements; as the situation stabilizes, attention shifts from humanitarian relief to long-term social and economic development. Fourth and finally, justice and reconciliation are critical to long-term success; an impartial and accountable legal system and ways to deal with past abuses are vital to successful post-conflict state building. These areas call for greater joint EU-US cooperation.

*Food Security*

A third pressing issue that might make officials' list of key areas for dialogue and action might be the need to move from famine reaction to famine prevention and food security. In the last decade famine devastated the Horn of Africa and the threat of famine looms today in Southern Africa. More than 80 million people in Africa are severely malnourished, while an additional 120 million live in extreme poverty, primarily in rural areas, and are threatened by famine and food insecurity. Agricultural productivity on the continent is low and has stagnated for decades. While natural disasters sometimes are a contributing factor, famines in Africa, as elsewhere, almost always have political roots. Dramatic increases in agricultural productivity are needed if Africa is to meet the goals of reducing by half by 2015 the number of hungry and malnourished Africans, and the number of Africans living in extreme poverty. As a promising start, at the last G8 summit in June 2004, the G8 countries have agreed to support the New Partnership for Africa's Development (NEPAD), and the principles and goals set out in the Comprehensive Africa Agriculture Development Program. Three initiatives have been agreed upon which aim at promoting broad based rural development and at raising agricultural productivity in food insecure area. The first one will be specifically directed towards breaking the cycle of famine in the Horn of Africa, and at increasing agricultural productivity. The second one will look at improving worldwide emergency assessment and response systems. The third one will aim at boosting agricultural productivity and rural development in food insecure countries, especially in Africa.

A fourth area, related to previous issue, would establish a serious dialogue to identify specific ways to improve foreign aid coherence in the realms of aid, trade and agriculture. A fifth area might consider the criteria donors use to determine where development aid is directed, especially in light of the Millennium Challenge Corporation's criteria of political and economic freedom. Other areas should, in the coming years, become the subject of a purposeful dialogue. As this essay has tried to show, there are still too many areas of common interest to both the US and the EU, and in which cooperation is hindered by what appear to be almost irreconcilable conceptions or policy choices. Such is the case with the fight against HIV/AIDS or the Millennium Development Goals. Both the United States and the European Union recognize the need to act to stop the spread of HIV/AIDS, malaria and tuberculosis, but the routes they have chosen differ. The question of poor performer countries is also an unresolved question. If the Millennium Development Goals have been developed and agreed upon to deal with good performers, no such framework is yet in place to deal with the countries that have not even really started to develop. What will be the common ground for dealing with those countries inside the development community, in the United States and in EU? There should be more concerted dialogue, and a deepened understanding on the approaches chosen on either side of the Atlantic.

*The Debate Over ODA Spending*

Finally, one way for the the United States to end the stale debate over whether major donors will ever reach (0.7% of GNI on development) would be to announce a commitment to a realistic percentage of ODA (e.g., between 22 and 25 percent of the global total). Much of this progress may be made with individual EU member states, whether with respect to bilateral or multilateral programs, and here we note that major donors often rely on bilateral discussions among a small group of EU Member States; on development issues, this often focuses on France, Germany, the UK, the Netherlands and Sweden).

## Chart 1.    Top Ten Recipients of ODA from European Community and United States

| Top Ten Recipients of EC Gross ODA/OA (USD Million) | | Top Ten Recipients of US Gross ODA/OA (USD Million) | |
|---|---|---|---|
| 1. Poland (OA) | 662 | 1. Egypt | 919 |
| 2. Romania(OA) | 511 | 2. Russia (OA) | 813 |
| 3. Hungary (OA) | 416 | 3. Israel (OA) | 529 |
| 4. Czech Republic (OA) | 355 | 4. Pakistan | 494 |
| 5. Ex-Yugoslavia Unsp. | 311 | 5. Serbia and Montenegro | 353 |
| 6. Serbia and Montenegro | 307 | 6. Colombia | 330 |
| 7. Turkey | 291 | 7. Ukraine (OA) | 257 |
| 8. Tunisia | 261 | 8. Jordan | 225 |
| 9. Morocco | 226 | 9. Peru | 188 |
| 10. South Africa | 187 | 10. Afghanistan | 188 |

Source: OECD

## Chart 2.    Net ODA from United States and European Community

| | Net ODA | 2001 | 2002 | Change 2001/02 |
|---|---|---|---|---|
| **USA** | Current (USD m) | 11,429 | 13,290 | 16.3% |
| | Constant (2001 USD m) | 11,429 | 13,140 | 15.0% |
| | ODA/GNI | 0.11% | 0.13% | |
| | Bilateral Share | 72% | 80% | |
| | Net Official Aid (OA) | | | |
| | Current (USD m) | 1,542 | 2,313 | 50.0% |
| **EC** | Current (USD m) | 5,961 | 6,561 | 10.1% |
| | Constant (2001 USD m) | 5,961 | 6,085 | 2.1% |
| | ODA/GNI | 6,656 | 6,962 | 4.6 |
| | Net Official Aid (OA) | | | |
| | Current (USD m) | 2,689 | 3,104 | 15.4% |

Source: OECD

**Chart 3.    Net Official Development Assistance in 2003**

**Preliminary data**

| | 2003 | | 2002 | | | |
|---|---|---|---|---|---|---|
| | ODA US$m current | ODA/ GNI % | ODA US$m current | ODA/ GNI % | 2003 ODA US$m[1] | Percent Change 2002 to 2003[1] |
| Australia | 1,237 | 0.25 | 989 | 0.26 | 1,008 | 1.9 |
| Austria | 503 | 0.20 | 520 | 0.26 | 412 | −20.7 |
| Belgium | 1,887 | 0.61 | 1,072 | 0.43 | 1,535 | 43.2 |
| Canada | 2,209 | 0.26 | 2,006 | 0.28 | 1,904 | −5.1 |
| Denmark | 1,747 | 0.84 | 1,643 | 0.96 | 1,433 | −12.8 |
| Finland | 556 | 0.34 | 462 | 0.35 | 461 | −0.2 |
| France | 7,337 | 0.41 | 5,486 | 0.38 | 6,030 | 9.9 |
| Germany | 6,694 | 0.28 | 5,324 | 0.27 | 5,530 | 3.9 |
| Greece | 356 | 0.21 | 276 | 0.21 | 287 | 4.0 |
| Ireland | 510 | 0.41 | 398 | 0.40 | 418 | 5.1 |
| Italy | 2,393 | 0.16 | 2,332 | 0.20 | 1,943 | −16.7 |
| Japan | 8,911 | 0.20 | 9,283 | 0.23 | 8,459 | −8.9 |
| Luxembourg | 189 | 0.80 | 147 | 0.77 | 155 | 5.6 |
| Netherlands | 4,059 | 0.81 | 3,338 | 0.81 | 3,296 | −1.3 |
| New Zealand | 169 | 0.23 | 122 | 0.22 | 133 | 9.3 |
| Norway | 2,043 | 0.92 | 1,696 | 0.89 | 1,776 | 4.7 |
| Portugal | 298 | 0.21 | 323 | 0.27 | 243 | −24.8 |
| Spain | 2,030 | 0.25 | 1,712 | 0.26 | 1,633 | −4.6 |
| Sweden | 2,100 | 0.70 | 1,991 | 0.83 | 1,710 | −14.1 |
| Switzerland | 1,297 | 0.38 | 939 | 0.32 | 1,122 | 19.5 |
| United Kingdom | 6,166 | 0.34 | 4,924 | 0.31 | 5,512 | 11.9 |
| **United States** | **15,791** | **0.14** | **13,290** | **0.13** | **15,541** | **16.9** |
| Total DAC | 68,483 | 0.25 | 58,274 | 0.23 | 60,540 | 3.9 |
| **Memo Items** | | | | | | |
| **EC** | **8,147** | | **6,561** | | **6,666** | 1.6 |
| **EU Countries combined** | **36,825** | 0.35 | **29,949** | 0.35 | **30,599** | 2.2 |
| G7 countries | 49,501 | 0.21 | 42,646 | 0.20 | 44,919 | 5.3 |
| Non-G7 countries | 18,982 | 0.46 | 15,627 | 0.47 | 15,622 | −0.0 |

[1]Taking account of both inflation and exchange rate movements.

Note: The data for 2003 are preliminary pending detailed final data to be published in December 2004. The data are standardised on a calendar year basis for all donors, and so may differ from fiscal year data available in countries' budget documents.

Source: OECD, 16 April 2004.

## Chapter 14

# Between EU and US: The Enlarged Union, Security and the Use of Force

Antonio Missiroli

In the new security environment created by 9/11, the European Union (EU) is expected (and claims) to be a major international actor. Long used to projecting itself externally as a primarily 'civilian power,' it is now confronted with challenges that require a much broader array of foreign and security policy instruments. In a way, it is now called to develop capabilities that have long been 'foreign' to its way of conducting international affairs as a collective entity (the European Community proper), although some of its members—most notably Britain and France—were much less reluctant to resort to them as individual international actors. However, much as it has made some progress in this direction lately, the EU still tends to define its common external action through trade, aid and, above all, its own geographical expansion.

Enlargement is, in fact, a peculiar 'security' policy. Peacefully extending the Union's norms, rules, opportunities and constraints to the applicants for EU membership has made, and will continue to make, instability and conflict in the wider European region less likely. Yet the enlargement that took place in spring 2004—the fifth (or sixth, counting German unification) since 1973—was a vastly more complicated exercise, fundamentally different in size, scope and character from the previous ones. As a result, it is likely to change radically the institutions, policies and even the nature of the Union.

The internal implications of these changes—especially regarding institutions—have been debated vigorously in the proceedings of the European Convention and the subsequent Intergovernmental Conference, leading up to a "Constitution" for the enlarged Union (the relevant Treaty was eventually signed in Rome on October 29, 2004). Financial issues are likely to take center stage in 2005-2006, with a view to delivering the EU budget for 2007-2013. But how will this enlargement affect the way in which the EU projects itself externally, politically and, now, also militarily? The answer to this question depends also on the specific contribution that the ten new member states will bring into the European foreign policy fold, and their overall impact on the Union's Common Foreign and Security Policy (CFSP) and European Security and Defense Policy (ESDP) proper.

## The record

### The military/operational dimension

For almost a decade, the eight central European states that were admitted to the EU in May 2004—plus Bulgaria and Romania—have been engaged in peace-support operations, mainly in the Balkans. Starting in 1996, all ten sent forces to Bosnia as part of IFOR or its successor, SFOR. Romania and Slovenia participated in the Italian-led operation 'Alba' to stabilize Albania after its 1997 meltdown. After the 1999 Kosovo war, all EU applicants except Latvia and Romania have contributed troops to the KFOR peacekeeping mission in Kosovo. As a rule, the central Europeans have provided these forces as components of bigger multinational units and under foreign command. The troops have been limited in numbers and restricted in function, but they have proved the willingness and ability of the applicants to perform in Article 17-type peace support operations, which may encompass "humanitarian and rescue tasks, peace-keeping tasks and tasks of combat forces in crisis management, including peacemaking."[1]

After committing forces and equipment to the "Headline Goal–plus" and adding a few more at the Capabilities Improvement Conference held in November 2001,[2] the EU candidates also pledged

---

[1] Such operations, enshrined in Art.17 of the Treaty on European Union (TEU), are still currently known as "Petersberg tasks": they were first articulated at a Ministerial Council of the Western European Union (WEU) in June 1992 at the Petersberg, near Bonn. In 1997, on a joint proposal made by Sweden and Finland, they were unanimously incorporated in the EU Treaty. The term "peacemaking" actually means "peace-enforcement"—a language that the German WEU delegation considered too strong when the "tasks" were originally formulated [cf. Willem F. van Eekelen, *Debating European Security 1948-1998* (The Hague: Sdu Publishers, 1998)]—and covers operations under Chapter VII of the UN Charter.

[2] For some figures on their "voluntary" contributions cf. Antonio Missiroli, "EU Enlargement and CFDP/ESDP," *European Integration*, no.25 (2003), pp.1-16.

to contribute to NATO's Response Force as well as, more recently, to the EU's so-called "battle-groups" for UN-mandated missions.[3] As is the case with other EU members, these forces are mostly 'double-hatted,' that is, they are committed to both NATO and the EU, which makes them less available in reality than on paper. Finally, virtually all EU candidates (bar Malta and Cyprus) participated in the first EU-led military operation ('Concordia'), which took place in the former Yugoslav Republic of Macedonia (FYROM) between March and December 2003, in cooperation with NATO. The newcomers' commitments are much less significant as regards the EU Civilian Headline Goal, most notably the pool of 5,000 policemen to be deployed in third countries for peace-building purposes. This may also be due, however, to the substantial absence of *gendarmerie*-type agencies in the central European countries, although some border control services of this kind are now being set up to combat cross-border crime and illegal immigration more effectively.[4]

Participation in NATO-led (mostly) and now also EU-led missions has helped drive most of the central Europeans towards some sort of role specialization. Such specialization, of course, is about making virtue out of necessity: scarce financial, technical and human resources have to be channeled towards viable objectives.[5] The Czechs, for example, have focused on developing nuclear, biological and chemical decontamination units; the Hungarians on engineering squads; the Romanians on mountain light infantry. Such specialization is all the

---

[3] Launched in February 2004 on a Franco-British proposal backed by Germany, the so-called "battle-groups" are battalion-size units meant to be deployable within a few days and to sustain peace-enforcement operations for one month or more in any theatre. They can be national or multi-national (normally built around a "framework nation") and are expected to be operational by 2007, although a few might be so earlier. At the Military Capabilities Conference held in Brussels on 22 November 2004, up to 13 such "battle-groups" were offered by the EU member states (the initial target was seven to nine): four national (respectively by Britain, France, Italy and Spain) and nine multi-national, i.a. one formed by Germany, Austria and the Czech Republic, one by Italy, Hungary and Slovenia, and one by Poland, Germany, Slovakia, Latvia and Lithuania. Lithuania has also offered a water purification unit and Cyprus a medical unit, while Estonia is expected to join the scheme shortly.

[4] See Derek Lutterbeck, "Between Police and Military: The New Security Agenda and the Rise of Gendarmeries," *Cooperation and Conflict*, 39, no.1 (2004), pp.45-68.

[5] For a partial overview see Timo Behr, Albane Siwiecki, *EU Enlargement and Armaments: Defence Industries and Markets of the Visegrad Countries*, edited by Burkard Schmitt, Occasional Paper no.54 (Paris: EU Institute for Security Studies, 2004). Available at www.iss-eu.org.

more important since the new EU members (plus Bulgaria and Romania) are in the process of overhauling and modernizing their military forces. Some—Bulgaria, Romania and, to a lesser extent, Slovakia—had to get rid of over-manned and top-heavy force structures inherited from Warsaw Pact times. Slovenia and the Baltic states, with a more recent record of national independence, had to set up credible forces almost from scratch. Not unlike the older EU members, most of the new ones are also gradually moving away from conscription towards professional armies. Of the central European then EU applicants, in 2003 only the Czech Republic, Bulgaria and Romania met the target set by NATO of 2 percent of GDP for expenditure on defense. Poland, Lithuania and Slovakia almost attained it (and would do so eventually in 2004), while Hungary and Slovenia were the laggards, but all pledged to increase spending in the years to come. In this, of course, the central Europeans are quite similar to—if not more performing than—the older EU member states, among which only a tiny minority (notably Greece, France, Britain and Portugal) actually meets the NATO target.[6]

*The political/institutional dimension*

Since CFSP is mainly declaratory and does not entail a proper legal *acquis* to be incorporated into national law by the applicants, negotiating the relevant chapters in the accession negotiations did not raise significant problems for the new members.[7] The only relatively controversial issues—apart from the division of Cyprus, to be addressed separately in the UN framework—concerned pending border disputes with third countries (especially Russia) and those problems that would arise only if some applicants would be taken in before others. In the end, however, the EU went for the 'Big Bang' and admitted up to ten new members in one go, while the border settlements remain to be ratified by the Russian side.

---

[6] For the latest figures cf. International Institute for Strategic Studies, *The Military Balance 2004-2005* (Oxford: Oxford University Press, 2004).

[7] See Pal Dunay, *Boxes: Why CFSP and ESDP Do Not Matter Much to EU Candidate Countries*, Robert Schuman Centre Policy Paper n.01/5 (S.Domenico di Fiesole: European University Institute, 2001).

By contrast, ESDP was seen as potentially more demanding. The applicants reacted late and defensively to its launch in 1999: they hardly understood its rationale and feared that it would undermine NATO's internal cohesion and/or drive the Americans out of Europe. For all—both those who were already in the Alliance and those who were queuing up to join it—the key issue was the establishment of a clearly defined relationship between ESDP and NATO—one in which NATO would be the leading institution and ESDP would be acceptable only within or under the supervision of NATO. Over time, however, their attitudes evolved towards a warmer acceptance of the EU efforts in this field, and "Atlanticist" reservations (such as Poland's) were toned down also in order to display the required political commitment. Whilst the signature of bilateral agreements on cooperation and consultation in crisis management between NATO and the EU—in December 2002 ('Berlin plus') and December 2003—made it easier for them to do so, some residual ambivalence over the implications of ESDP would remain and resurface dramatically during the Iraq crisis in early 2003.

On the wider EU front, representatives of the ten acceding countries were first involved in the 2002–2003 proceedings of the Convention on the Future of Europe as "observers." In the ensuing EU Intergovernmental Conference (IGC), which started a few months before their actual accession, they were endowed with full voting rights. In both fora, one of their main concerns was to be involved on an equal footing. Their worries over a "two-tier" EU were probably made more acute by a series of initiatives taken by some older member states, such as the push for "enhanced cooperation" on defense and military matters. This proposal, which the current EU treaty prohibits, would entail the possibility for selected groups of member states to carry out certain policies—in the fields of armaments, operations, possibly even common defense—on behalf of the whole Union. Central Europeans and other smaller EU members were also unhappy about the proposed abolition of the Union's rotating presidency, and Poland, in particular, was critical of both the alleged Franco-German attempt to shape the Constitutional Treaty to suit their own interests and objectives—Warsaw resented its exclusion from the Convention's Secretariat (the Presidency opted for a Slovenian to represent the candidate countries) as well as the way in which issues of the utmost importance to the newcomers were dealt with inside the forum—but also of the repeated display of 'Big Three'-type political clubbing, that also included the United Kingdom. On the latter point, however, Poland was certainly not alone in the EU: Italy and Spain, to name just two, expressed similar concerns.

In the end, at any rate, a generally satisfactory compromise was reached at the IGC: according to the draft Constitutional Treaty, a) "enhanced cooperation" proper is just a generally enabling provision, which may be used only "as a last resort" and on certain conditions; b) "a group of member states" may indeed be entrusted with "the implementation of a task" under the authority and supervision of the whole Council, but selective participation to operations is already a fact in both the EU and NATO; c) what is called "structured permanent cooperation" on defense concerns, in principle, all member states, and the accession criteria look sufficiently flexible to allow for a large set of participants; d) both the mutual defense clause (Art.I-41) and the solidarity clause (Art.I-43) apply to all EU members and, in principle, do not threaten the role of NATO; e) the rotational presidency remains in place, if slightly modified, for all policy areas but foreign and defense policy, where the task of representing and coordinating the EU is assigned to the newly created "Union Minister for Foreign Affairs," combining the roles currently played by the Commissioner for External Relations and the Council's High Representative for CFSP.[8] For the newcomers, however, the issue of equal treatment inside common institutions and equal opportunities to join common policies is bound to remain on the front burner long after enlargement.

*The geo-strategic dimension*

With the exception of sizable and often very vocal ethnic communities in the United States, none of the central European newcomers to the EU has significant overseas interests, let alone a colonial past. Nor do they have a commercial and diplomatic outreach comparable to that of most older member states. In contrast to previous enlargements, therefore, the forthcoming one will not entail a significant widening of the geographical horizons of the Union's external policies.

---

[8] For a more detailed overview cf. Antonio Missiroli, "Mind the Gaps: The Constitutional Treaty and Beyond," in *EU Security and Defence Policy—The First Five Years (1999-2004)*, edited by Nicole Gnesotto (Paris: EU Institute for Security Studies, 2004), pp.145-154, available at www.iss-eu.org.

The newcomers and the remaining applicants do, however, have a strong interest in the formulation of those external policies of the enlarged Union that might affect their immediate vicinity. Some of them are the new external frontier of the EU. The permeability and safety of the eastern borders and all common "neighborhood" policies will become vital interests and will, presumably, shape their behavior inside the EU, and not only regarding CFSP proper.[9] The condition of national minorities, cross-border trade, visa regulations, energy and environmental issues, Balkan stability and the region's eventual integration into the EU, relations with Belarus, Ukraine (a central Polish, but also Slovakian and Hungarian worry), Moldova (a key Romanian priority) and, of course, Russia are likely to become more immediate concerns of the EU as a whole, or at least to be put more decisively on the EU agenda.

In this respect, the interests and sensitivities of the newcomers may not automatically coincide with those of the older member states—nor among themselves, for that matter—be it on the permeability of external borders, the most appropriate response to Russian policies, or even the prospect of Turkish membership of the EU.[10] About the latter, in particular, the central Europeans—though certainly not Cyprus—look much more open than most of the EU-15, out of a combination of gratitude vis-à-vis Ankara (for having supported their NATO entry), reciprocity (EU enlargement must remain an open process), and strategic calculations. Support for Turkey's bid is strongest in Bulgaria, possibly the only friendly neighbor of Ankara's. In Poland, backing Turkey's application is seen also as instrumental to opening eventual EU accession for Ukraine and, in perspective, even Belarus—both considered as ultimately more "European" than

---

[9] The notion of a new "neighbourhood" of the enlarged EU, requiring a specific common policy, was first formulated in a Communication of the European Commission in March 2003. In principle, it encompasses both the Eastern and the Southern "neighbours" of the EU, irrespective of their eligibility for eventual EU membership. The new European Commission that took office in November 2004, however, separates competence over enlargement (including Turkey and the Western Balkans) from "neighbourhood" policy, that falls under the external relations portfolio (Relex). For a first analysis cf. Judy Batt et al., *Partners and Neighbours: A CFSP for a Wider Europe*, Chaillot Paper no.64 (Paris: EU Institute for Security Studies, 2003), available at www.iss-eu.org.

[10] See e.g. Judy Dempsey, "Expansion Brings EU to Foreign Policy Void," *International Herald Tribune*, October 8, 2004.

Turkey.[11] Yet it cannot be ruled out that, at a later stage, popular worries about i.a. the financial support that the EU is bound to give to Turkey—to the detriment of the current new member states—end up changing the attitudes of local political elites.

On other matters, the new members may rather be mainly passive and reactive, aligning themselves with the prevailing consensus among old members on matters of arguably secondary importance, and/or looking at ways to increase their bargaining power in matters that they consider more vital. An early case in point was last year's EU-led peace support operation 'Artemis' in the Democratic Republic of Congo. Most newcomers—then still "acceding" but already "fully associated" to CFSP and ESDP—regarded it as not particularly relevant and possibly even risky, including the political danger of dragging the entire Union into a colonial-type crisis. Furthermore, NATO was not involved. Yet they eventually decided to give it the green light, provided no contribution in men or money was expected from them.[12]

*The American/Russian dimension*

A likely exception to this general pattern is the matter of NATO and transatlantic relations. As discussed above, all ten candidates from central Europe have pushed for a clear understanding and a more or less explicit hierarchy between the Alliance and the Union: they do not want to be forced to choose between Washington and Brussels on security matters. This explains why they welcomed with warmth and also relief the so-called "Berlin-plus" agreement as well as the deal on planning for crisis management mentioned above: taken together, these set both the general framework and the specific procedures for strategic consultation and operational cooperation between the two organization in the Euro-Atlantic area, bringing to a provisional end

---

[11] Cf. Judy Dempsey, "Poland's Vision of EU—Pressing for Turkey and Ukraine to Join," *International Herald Tribune*, September 2, 2004.

[12] The operation was the first fully autonomous UN Chapter VII-type military operation conducted by the EU. It was carried out between June and September 2003, upon a direct request by UN Secretary-General Kofi Annan, and was led by a French battalion-size force (with France acting as "framework nation") backed by a limited contingent of Swedish special forces and logistical support by some other EU members, plus a handful of third countries including, South Africa and Brazil. For an overall assessment of this and other ESDP operations cf. Gustav Lindstrom, "On the Ground: ESDP Operations," in *EU Security and Defence Policy ...quot.,* pp.131-144, available at www.iss-eu.org.

almost a decade of political tensions and sometimes petty disputes. Whilst the markedly 'Atlanticist' orientation of the EU newcomers will add next to nothing, per se, to the overall spectrum of existing positions among the current EU members, it may slightly tip the Union's internal balance. Actual membership, however, may change the perception of national interests and shape new loyalties. Also, there are various shades of 'Atlanticism' among the EU newcomers, with Poland and the Baltic States on top, Hungary, the Czech Republic and Slovakia somewhere in the middle, and Slovenia at the bottom. These shades appear in both official statements and popular attitudes, as reflected also in innumerable opinion polls.

Interestingly, such shades often match the spread and intensity of residual anti-Russian sentiments: the warmer the support for Washington, the stronger the hostility to Moscow. In this respect, central European 'Atlanticism' differs from the kind that can be found in London or Rome or The Hague, and may entail major EU-internal divergences over how to deal, notably, with Russia. In fact, tensions within the EU-25—especially between most newcomers and the main Western European capitals—have emerged already over how to negotiate with Moscow on transit to and from Kaliningrad (autumn 2002); on the extension of the Partnership and Cooperation Agreement between the EU and Russia to the new members (spring 2004); and, more recently, on the position to adopt about the Beslan massacre in North Ossetia (September 2004) and President Putin's role in the presidential elections in Ukraine (November-December 2004). On arguably all these occasions, the attitude of the central European newcomers was markedly more critical of Russian behavior than that of not only Paris and Berlin, but also London and Rome.[13] Needless to

---

[13] On Kaliningrad, some older member states—most notably France, Italy and Spain—seemed much more forthcoming with Moscow's demands than the candidates involved (and the European Commission itself), thus forcing a compromise that left some grudge especially in Lithuania and Poland. On the PCA, the Commission found itself in a stronger position due to its competence on trade and managed to rein in all the member states and present Russia with a united EU front, thus forcing it to accept the terms on offer. On Beslan, most reactions in Central Europe pointed critically to the responsibilities of the Russian special forces—while Western European capitals expressed almost exclusively their solidarity against the terrorist action—and, later on, to the domestic implications of the administrative reforms planned by President Putin. Finally, on the contested elections in Ukraine, nuances became apparent in that especially Poland and Slovakia were actively engaged in denouncing irregularities and also mediating between the opposing fronts in Kiev, while Rome, Paris, London and especially Berlin kept a much lower profile in order not to irritate Moscow.

say, neither Malta nor Cyprus fit into this pattern. In fact, they rather lie at the very opposite end of the spectrum and, while their overall impact on CFSP decisions is negligible, their non-membership of NATO's Partnership for Peace Program and, in particular, the still unsolved issue of Cyprus' reunification (with all its reverberations on relations with Turkey) create problems for ESDP. At any rate, and whatever the reasons for that, the EU at 25 is finding it more compli-cated to maintain a smooth relationship with Russia, as proved i.a. by the little diplomatic incident over Beslan (Moscow overreacted to a statement made by the Dutch EU presidency asking for "explana-tions" on the precise circumstances of the massacre), the persistent tensions over Moldova and the Caucasus,[14] Moscow's mistrust of the Union's "neighborhood" policy (insofar as it overlaps and contrasts with Russia's interests in its "near abroad") and its criticism of the OSCE, where it feels in a political minority now. The customary bian-nual bilateral summit scheduled for November 2004 was repeatedly postponed; when it eventually took place, both sides "agreed to dis-agree" over the crisis in Ukraine. During the latter, in particular, the central Europeans' distinctive attitude manifested itself in the active and decisive role played by the Polish and Lithuanian Presidents Aleksander Kwasniewski and Viktor Adamkus, alongside the High Representative for CFSP Javier Solana, in preventing a violent con-frontation as well as facilitating a peaceful solution and a relatively smooth transition in Kiev.

All this said, the central European newcomers' 'Atlanticism' does not always translate into automatic support for each and every American action or position on the international scene. A significant case in point—apart from the Kyoto Protocol—has been the contro-versy over the International Criminal Court (ICC). Signed in July 1998, the Treaty establishing the ICC entered into force in July 2002, despite the late withdrawal of the US (which, under the Clinton administration, had initially subscribed to it). Almost all the central European countries signed up to it between 1998 and 1999, and most

---

[14] Although not as active and present as the US, the EU now has a "special representative" for the South Caucasus region—the Finnish diplomat Heikki Talvitie—and is carrying out a very small "rule of law" operation (Eujust "Themis") in Georgia, in order to assist the new government led by President Mikhail Saakashvili in reforming the judicial and admin-istrative system. The operation was strongly pushed forward by the Baltic states, who are also active on the ground with own officials.

of them have subsequently ratified it, in compliance also with a specific EU common position. Ratification was fastest and smoothest in Hungary, Poland and Slovenia, probably also because it occurred in late 2001, that is, *before* the Bush administration decided to quit. It was more difficult in Slovakia and the Baltic states, also because it occurred *after* the US started putting pressure on the signatories: but the EU argument—especially on the eve of the enlargement decision in late 2002—did eventually prevail, although ratification is still stuck in the Czech Parliament, waiting for the required constitutional change. Indeed, diplomatic pressure from Washington aiming at signing bilateral immunity agreements via Article 98 of the ICC Statute, and entailing such measures as suppression of military assistance or financial aid, put the newcomers' governments under considerable political strain. At the end of the day, however, it has reaped modest results: of all the past and current EU applicants, only Romania has given in to the US while, despite the reduction in military assistance, Malta and Croatia have not.[15]

Finally, but no less interestingly, the newcomers' own historical experience with authoritarian rule has recently influenced their attitude towards CFSP also beyond (and independently from) American pressures and preferences. Between December 2004 and January 2005, in fact, the Foreign Ministers of the EU-25 came to the decision temporarily to suspend diplomatic measures that the Union had taken in June 2003 against Fidel Castro's regime in protest at the arrest of 75 Cuban dissidents. Some of those prisoners had been freed since, so the Council—on Spain's initiative—reconsidered the measures. At the request of the Czech Republic and Poland, however, their lifting became only "temporary," partially left to the discretion of the member states, and linked to strict conditions concerning the respect of human rights.[16]

---

[15] For an overview see Maguy Day, "CPI: l'autre offensive americaine," *Le Monde-2*, no.32, September 25, 2004, pp.24-25.

[16] Cf. *Bulletin Quotidien Europe* (English edition), no.8878, February 1, 2005, p.6. For an assessment of the newcomers' growing assertiveness in CFSP, seen also as a boost both to their own standing within the EU and their commitment to it, see Marc Champion, "Poland Makes Its Mark on EU Policy," *Wall Street Journal Europe*, February 17, 2005, p.1.

*The Iraq dimension*

By contrast, in the transatlantic and intra-European dispute over Iraq, all the central European countries basically sided with the US against what they considered as a Franco-German attempt to rally the EU against the Americans and, thereby, to split NATO. To make things even worse in their eyes, all that was being done with the active support of Russia. Although their publics appeared more skeptical of the reasons for waging war on Iraq, the heads of state and government of the EU newcomers joined in the exercise of "op-ed diplomacy" that displayed European divisions in the international press. On January 30, 2003, Vaclav Havel (in his last act as Czech President), along with Hungarian Prime Minister Peter Medgyessy and his Polish colleague Leszek Miller co-signed an open letter of support to the US with the Prime Ministers of Britain, Italy, Spain, Portugal and Denmark. A few days later their colleagues from the so-called "Vilnius Ten" group of candidates for NATO accession released a joint statement along even more blunt pro-American lines. All of this prompted US Defense Secretary Donald Rumsfeld to feel that he could dismiss the opposition of what he derided as "old Europe." For his part, the French President Jacques Chirac only confirmed the Central Europeans' perception when he grossly complained that the new EU members should rather have "remained silent."

Europeans appeared divided also within the UN Security Council: Germany sided with France (and Russia), Spain (and Bulgaria) with Britain. This dramatic split was followed by Poland's decision to participate in the Iraq war as the only other actual European "belligerent" country alongside Britain (technically, Denmark was one too, but its contribution was political rather than military). Once the war was over, a 2,500-strong Polish contingent took direct military control of a limited region in south-central Iraq, albeit with some assistance from NATO's Supreme Headquarters Allied Powers Europe (SHAPE) and financial support from Washington. Bulgarian (500) and Ukrainian (1,600) troops, too, served under Polish command within a 8,000-strong multinational force, while small contingents of Czech, Slovak, Romanian, Hungarian and Baltic troops also joined in the post-war coalition alongside Italy, Spain and the Netherlands. Finally, most of the acceding countries criticized (albeit not too vocally) the joint initiative by France, Germany, Belgium and Luxembourg to set up separate military headquarters for EU-led operations—the so-called

"Tervuren" blueprint—that further animated the transatlantic debate between April and September 2003.

Since then, the intra-European rift has been somewhat mended. The EU and its central European members and applicants continue to work well together in the Balkans. There has been also a more constructive spirit among Western Europeans proper, as proven by the deals jointly drafted by France, Germany and Britain on ESDP (the headquarters for EU-led operations, the initial set-up of the EU Defense Agency, the above mentioned compromise on the Constitutional Treaty), and mostly welcomed by all the acceding countries. Paradoxically, however, the signing of the framework agreements on security and military cooperation between the EU and NATO ahead of the two parallel enlargements may have deprived the central European newcomers of a crucial strategic asset in the internal EU game. Indeed, there could now be less political capital to make from adopting a staunchly pro-American stance inside the Union.

Meanwhile, some disillusionment over Iraq seems to have emerged even in the central European countries, in particular, since the spring of 2004, in conjunction with the revelations over the Abu Ghraib prison and the US Congressional Report. In March 2004 the Polish President Aleksander Kwasniewski complained openly about having been "deceived" over the threat of weapons of mass destruction (WMD).[17] More lately the government in Warsaw—disappointed by the Spanish withdrawal (Madrid was expected to take over command in the area), the still intangible benefits (no single tender won for Iraqi reconstruction), and the very tangible costs of the operation (roughly US $280 million in 2004)—has even started thinking aloud about a possible withdrawal from Iraq by the end of 2005. For its part, Hungary announced already in autumn 2004 that it would withdraw its 300 men right after the Iraqi elections—as would the Netherlands—while Romania and Bulgaria are still thinking about it, as is Ukraine. Whilst the number of casualties has remained low (almost 20 for the Poles, a few less for the Bulgarians), the number of troops on the ground has hardly increased since summer 2003. Even

---

[17] See Thomas Fuller, "President of Poland 'deceived' on Iraq," *International Herald Tribune*, March 19, 2004. In an interview to *Gazeta Wiborcza* published on April 30, 2004, however, Kwasniewski acknowledged that he should have rather said "badly informed"—and not by American and British allies, but just by "intelligence services."

the promising turnout and outcome of the Iraqi elections in late January 2005 has not fundamentally changed the picture. And the central Europeans' repeated call for NATO to be comprehensively involved on the ground in Iraq, too, can be read both ways: as just more evidence of their deep-rooted 'Atlanticism,' but also as an indirect demand for a less unilateral approach to post-war reconstruction and peace-building in the region.

## Trends and prospects

### The political/cultural dimension

Indeed, the long-term impact of Iraq on transatlantic relations in general and the central Europeans' special brand of 'Atlanticism' in specific may turn out to be quite complex. Broadly speaking, the moral debt vis-à-vis Washington is still felt in central Europe. Yet the idea of 'regime change' by military force, though initially accepted by sections of Polish public opinion in the run-up to the war, is now a major source of rethinking in most parts of central Europe—all the more so after peaceful 'regime change' has succeeded elsewhere, from Georgia (January 2004) to Ukraine (December 2004), thanks to converging efforts from the US and the EU.

In this respect, a series of broadly based opinion polls taken recently shows some interesting developments. It is once again in Poland—arguably the key player in foreign and defense policy among the newcomers[18]—that some shift is discernible. Firstly, as compared to 2003, feelings are warmer vis-à-vis the EU and less warm vis-à-vis the US. Secondly, people appear now torn between a more independent approach from Washington and the traditional drive to get ever closer to it (which instead was the overwhelming view until 2003). Thirdly, 77 percent of Polish interviewees—topping the EU chart—believe that Europe should acquire more military power to be able to protect its interests separately from the US, and 68 percent want a more powerful EU in order to cooperate more effectively with the US. Fourthly, Polish support for keeping own troops in Afghanistan and Iraq has fallen sharply and is among the lowest in Europe. Finally,

---

[18] See e.g. Marcin Zaborowski, David H.Dunn, eds., *Poland: A New Power in Transatlantic Security* (London: Frank Cass, 2003).

while pursuing the national interest is seen as more important than getting UN approval (arguably a Polish exception within Europe), support for "war" as a necessary means to obtain justice is relatively low: still higher than in "old" Europe, but significantly lower than in the UK, Turkey or, a bit surprisingly, the Netherlands.[19]

If this is the picture concerning the new members, what is likely to be the overall configuration for the enlarged EU? The same opinion polls (taken in June 2004) show a similar, at times even more pronounced shift in the major Western European countries. Support for US global leadership has declined everywhere since 2003, and 64 percent of Europeans believe that "Europe" should acquire more military power to be able to protect its interests separately from the US, although the preference is for doing so in order to cooperate more effectively (rather than compete) with Washington. Interestingly, however, only 22 percent of Europeans believe that their governments should be spending more on defense, which clearly displays a lingering in-built contradiction. Furthermore, despite controversy over American foreign policy, 65 percent of all European interviewees believe that Europe and the US have grown closer or remained about the same in recent years: only minorities in every country believe that they have grown further apart.

Finally, and perhaps most importantly, Europeans more or less share the American perception of the threat posed by international terrorism, a terrorist attack using WMD, conflict between Israel and its Arab neighbors, the global spread of pandemics, a major economic downturn, Islamic fundamentalism, and large immigrant and refugee flows. Americans, however, are comparatively more supportive of the use of force to prevent a terrorist attack, stop nuclear proliferation, defend a NATO ally, and remove a government that abuses human rights. Europeans, by contrast, are more supportive of using military force when meeting such challenges as providing relief (food and medical assistance) to victims of conflict, stopping fighting in a civil war, and deploying peacekeeping troops after a conflict has ended. On the average, Europeans are also keener on obtaining a UN mandate for the use

---

[19] Incidentally, even less US-friendly results were recorded in Slovakia: cf. The German Marshall Fund of the United States, *Transatlantic Trends*, Available at www.transatlantic-trends.org. See also Daniel Dombey, "Americans are from Mars, Europeans from Venus, say surveys on world view," *Financial Times*, September 9, 2004.

of force and less keen on considering military strength as the best way to ensure peace. Interestingly, majorities even in such countries as France (63 percent), Germany (57) and Spain (66) would support deploying their own soldiers to Iraq if the United Nations approved a multilateral force to assist with security and reconstruction.[20]

However limited in scope, these polls only confirm that, whilst the threat perception is not dissimilar across the Atlantic, there remain differences as to how to respond (or pre-empt) possible threats and, in particular, over the conditions for the use of military force. This is, incidentally, the same conclusion one can reach by comparing—with all the necessary distinctions—the US National Security Strategy from September 2002 and the European Security Strategy (ESS) from December 2003.[21]

In this respect, however, some nuances exist also across Europe itself, although the latest enlargement has not added significant new ones to the overall spectrum. In fact, some European countries are more inclined than others to resort to military force in the defense of non-vital national interests (however defined). More often than not, such countries have an important colonial past and still have significant overseas interests: they normally have also domestic institutional arrangements that confer a certain primacy to the executive (over the legislative) in deciding over military action abroad. Some European countries may be more prone than others to use force even without a UN mandate, but only very few seem ready to go it alone (or with the US only) if need be. Comparatively, many more European countries are ready to resort to military force if this happens within a multilateral framework (NATO and, now, the EU) and with some international legitimacy: that is, as all EU documents state, "in accordance

---

[20] Ibid, *Transatlantic Trends*.

[21] See Jean-Yves Haine, "Idealism and Power: The EU Security Strategy," *Current History*, 103, no.671 (2004), pp.107-111; and Alyson J.K. Bailes, "The European Security Strategy: An Evolutionary History," Policy paper no.10, SIPRI, Stockholm, February 2005. For direct comparisons cf. Alyson J.K. Bailes, "US and EU Strategy Concepts: A Mirror for Partnership and Difference?," *The International Spectator*, 39, no.1 (2004), pp.19-33; and Simon Duke, "The European Security Strategy in a Comparative Framework: Does It Make for Secure Alliances in a Better World?," *European Foreign Affairs Review*, 9, no.4 (2004), pp.459-482.

with the principles of the UN Charter."[22] While the experience of the Kosovo war in 1999 prevented the EU member states from mentioning a UN Security Council resolution as an indispensable precondition for the collective use of force, the experience of the Iraq war has somewhat tipped the balance in the opposite direction, but without altering the overall picture significantly. Finally, almost all EU countries remain still quite reluctant to adopt 'coercive diplomacy'—at least in the way the US conceives and practices it—as their preferred modality of common external action. There is no shortage of examples to prove this point: to date, the European Union as a whole has rarely agreed to resort to negative diplomacy, even less to military deterrence, vis-à-vis third countries on its own. The 'average' EU member, so to speak, tends rather to subscribe to the formulation enshrined in the ESS whereby "none of the new threats is purely military, nor can any be tackled by purely military means. Each requires a mixture of instruments": and this applies as much to the fight against terrorism as to failing states and regional conflicts. In other words, the use of force per se (actual or even potential) is almost never considered as the best or principal way to deal with crises. More often than not, it is seen as a last resort and conditioned to some form of international legitimacy.

*The operational/strategic dimension*

The same ESS, however, also invites the Union at large to become "more active" in pursuing its strategic objectives, and "to develop a strategic culture that fosters early, rapid, and, when necessary, *robust* intervention"—thus implying that such a culture is still missing. All ESDP operations to date, in fact, have mostly been relatively small, short and low-intensity (only 'Artemis' had fairly robust rules of engagement), or of a mainly civilian nature, thus never putting to real test the Union's "strategic culture." Right at the end of 2004, however, the EU members embarked on their first sizeable and truly demanding Art.17-type mission, namely Operation 'Althea' in Bosnia-Herzegovina, taking over from NATO's SFOR. Almost all member states (22, old and new) and all EU applicants bar Croatia (for understandable reasons) are on board, as are such diverse third countries as

---

[22] For a first overview see Adrian Hyde-Price, "European Security, Strategic Culture, and the Use of Force," *European Security*, 13, no.4/II (2004), pp.323-343.

Albania, Argentina, Canada, Chile, Morocco, New Zealand, Norway and Switzerland. The 7,000-strong, quintessentially UN Chapter VII operation has a specific UN mandate (UNSC resolutions 1551 and 1575) and is conducted in cooperation with NATO under the "Berlin plus" agreement. Operational commander, in fact, is D-SACEUR General John Reith, force commander on the ground is Major General David Leakey, with Britain de facto acting as the "framework nation." This will probably be the crucial testing ground for European ambitions and overall capabilities—given that the EU has also conducted a police operation (EUPM) in Bosnia-Herzegovina since 2003–and for a gradual "devolution" of certain tasks from the Alliance to the Union in the traditional Euro-Atlantic area.

This said, it can still be expected that, if and when a major crisis erupts in the new "neighborhood" of the enlarged EU (especially if Russia is somehow involved in it), the first reflex for all Europeans will still be to consult Washington and, if "robust intervention" is required, check things out with NATO. A certain measure of transatlantic consultation and cooperation, in other words, remains vital for effective crisis management in and around Europe and especially for dealing with Russia, although the development of ESDP and the growing engagement of the EU as a security actor now offer a wider set of policy options. Developments in Georgia, Ukraine and, at least in part, also Moldova are good cases in point. They also prove that the geographical scope of CFSP and ESDP has broadened considerably in recent times, thus overcoming the original "planning assumption" made in 2000 of a maximum radius of 4,000 Km (10,000 for purely humanitarian operations) from Brussels.

A possible special case is, arguably, sub-Saharan Africa. Here the Union can build on the experience made with 'Artemis' in 2003, and can do so well beyond the small follow-up operation (Eupol Kinshasa) launched in 2004 and tasked with training local police forces. The whole concept of EU "battle-groups," in fact, is geared to framing the capabilities required for UN-mandated interventions in that area. The December 2003 EU Presidency document on NATO/EU consultation, planning and operations states that "where NATO as a whole is not engaged, the EU, in undertaking an operation, will choose whether or not to have recourse to NATO assets and capabilities, taking into account in particular the Alliance's role, capacities and involvement *in the region in question*" (italics added).[23] This is a further loophole that opens up the possibility of a special EU role—at least by default—in that region. In fact, NATO is unlikely—especially now that it is getting increasingly involved "out of area," in Afghanistan and possibly Iraq— to launch or take over peacekeeping operations in that part of the world, although this does not rule out specifically US regional involvement and engagement. In turn, some EU countries (most notably Britain and France) have a tradition to that effect, and also have the means to live up to the foreseeable operational challenges. However, such a tradition—that includes the use of military force and the occasional bypassing of the UN—is national rather than European, as also the recent examples of Sierra Leone and Ivory Coast have shown. As a result, several member states still appear reluctant to give *carte blanche* to London or Paris for missions in sub-Saharan Africa to be conducted under a EU flag. This does not apply only to the newcomers: it is worth recalling former German Defense Minister Volker Ruhe's famous remark that "the Eurocorps is no Afrika Korps," as much as the general reluctance among the EU-15 fully to accept the WEU operational concept of 'lead nation' (*nation-pilote*), whereby a single country is collectively mandated to carry out a military mission on behalf of the whole organization. Consequently, EU-led peace support operations in the region are likely to materialize only if the UN explicitly endorses them and if local actors and regional organizations are adequately involved. The experience made with Iraq has only strengthened the caution with which "robust intervention" in delicate areas is dealt. This explains also the hesitation shown by most EU countries throughout 2004 vis-à-vis the humanitarian crisis in Darfur (Sudan)—a hesitation which, combined with the relative inability to intervene by the African Union, has so far led to inaction.

*The institutional/historical dimension*

The actual challenge of 'Althea' and the potential challenge of building peace in sub-Saharan Africa raise, in turn, the issue of the necessary capabilities and leadership. The latest enlargement adds

---

[23] The document can be found in Antonio Missiroli, comp., *From Copenhagen to Brussels— European Defence: Core Documents*, 4, Chaillot Paper no.67 (Paris: EU Institute for Security Studies, 2003), pp.322-323, Available at www.iss-eu.org.

very little to the existing picture, as will do the future accession of Bulgaria and Romania, expected for 2007 (or 2008 at the latest). Whilst overall capabilities are still inadequate, leadership is not always welcome, especially if and when it is presented as a *fait accompli*, a restricted and exclusive club, or just a claim. On top of that, the sheer numerical size of the enlarged Union may occasionally make taking decisions marginally or occasionally more complicated: in this domain, in fact, unanimity is required (and maintained in the "Constitution") but it is also the simple 'shaping' of common positions that is becoming trickier in overcrowded rooms and time-consuming *tours de table* at 25-plus.

In this respect, the new EU Constitutional Treaty may help find some workable solutions. First of all, the appointment of a "Union Minister for Foreign Affairs" is expected to foster policy and institutional coherence, concentrate the right of initiative, and establish a single line of command in external action, all of which is crucial to crisis management. Secondly, the new provisions on "permanent structured cooperation" are meant to set demanding but flexible benchmarks for the enhancement of national and common military capabilities, along with a specific institutional framework for further pooling and interoperability among EU members. Accordingly, leadership would be based primarily on performance and compliance, and the resulting group of countries would presumably come to represent the first address to turn to in the EU for peace support operations implying the use of military force.

Both the "Minister" and the "permanent structured cooperation" scheme, however, will be put in place only when (and if) the "Constitution" is ratified and enters into force. And, presently at least, there still is a big question mark over the whole ratification process. Interestingly, the first member states to have completed it are three newcomers, namely Lithuania (November 2004), Hungary (December 2004) and Slovenia (February 2005), where ratification followed a simple parliamentary procedure. Yet the popular referenda that are planned in several EU countries may well cast a long shadow over the fate of the new Treaty, to the extent that contingency plans have already begun to be drafted and discussed. And, interestingly once again, the outcome will be equally uncertain in the old and the new member states: in Britain or France as much as in the Czech

Republic or Poland. In this respect, too, the enlarged EU is set to be very much like the smaller, older one.

Last but not least, with the recent and the current enlargement (involving Bulgaria and Romania), which have basically dealt with the legacy of the Soviet Empire, an entire cycle is coming to an end. The use of enlargement as a security policy 'by other means' is reaching its climax and, and the same time, its possible limits. From 2007 onwards, in fact, the continuing enlargement of the EU will become an entirely new ball game, involving countries (from the Western Balkans to Turkey to the Eastern "neighborhood" itself) with completely different and highly complex historical and political legacies, namely those of the Ottoman and Russian Empires. Also, the overall level of acceptance of further enlargements inside the current EU is expected to go down significantly, thus raising the stakes—especially if more popular referenda are called, e.g. on Turkey's eventual accession—and forcing the enlarged Union to think more strategically in terms of both its ultimate external borders and its foreign and security policy proper.

*Chapter 15*

# EU Enlargement and the EU's Common Agricultural Policy (CAP): Strategic Implications[1]

Peter Wehrheim

## Introduction

Agricultural policy is one of the policy areas in the European Union (EU) in which the transfer of policy-making power from the national to the supra-national level has evolved furthest. Furthermore, the Common Agricultural Policy (CAP) is the essential instrument for addressing environmental, social, and economic challenges of the EU's rural areas which comprises about 90% of the EU's total territory. In terms of the share of the total EU budget allocated to this policy area—in 2004 45.8%—the CAP has been one of the EU's important policy areas. At the same time the CAP has been a matter of many debates in the previous and in the on-going round on international trade negotiations under the auspices of the GATT and the WTO. Therefore agricultural policy implications of the current round of EU enlargement—similarly to previous rounds—have received special attention and are particularly relevant for US-EU relations. Consequently, the question how and under which conditions the CAP of the EU could be adopted by the new Member States in the course of the most recent enlargement has been under close scrutiny by the international community in general and the US in particular.[2] Additionally, the extension of the CAP to ten additional

---

[1] This paper represents solely the views of its authors and can not in any circumstances be regarded as the official position of the Commission. The author gratefully acknowledges comments on earlier drafts given by various colleagues but the sole responsibility for the contents is his.

[2] See for instance, Economic Research Service/US Department of Agriculture, Briefing Room at: www.ers.usda.gov.briefing/EuropeanUnion/IssuesEnlargement.htm

countries has been a much discussed issue because of the relatively great significance of agriculture in the acceding countries. Given this importance of the CAP in the EU and of the agricultural sector in the candidate countries, strategic implications in general and significant effects on international agricultural markets were to be expected.

In this paper, however, we argue that the extension of the CAP to the new Member States was a relatively smooth process and not a "big bang." Neither any distortions of international markets nor any significant new trade disputes have arisen in the context of agriculture and this enlargement round. We argue that this is mainly the result of the latest reform of the CAP prior to enlargement and a carefully designed pre-accession strategy as regards the agricultural sector. In view of the manifold challenges associated with the structural transition of agriculture in the new Member States this should be considered as a major achievement of this enlargement round as such. Against this background the objective of this paper is neither to discuss all implications of extending the CAP, nor to elaborate on all of its effects on the agricultural markets within the new Member States. Instead, the focus of this discussion will be on strategic aspects and particularly those which have an international dimension.

The paper is structured as follows: in the next section we will provide an overview of agriculture in the new Member States and the challenges which had to be dealt with when transferring the CAP to these countries. The third section contains a brief description of the CAP and its most recent reforms. The fourth section outlines the major elements which were part of the accession strategy as regards agricultural policy. In the following section we discuss the most important strategic implications related to agriculture and enlargement. In the final section we look ahead and discuss some potential implications of the most recent round of enlargement for the extension of the CAP to additional candidate countries. Because of the relative size of the agricultural sector we will focus this outlook on the enlargement to Romania and Bulgaria (who are expected to become members in 2007) and on the potential enlargement by Turkey with which the European Council has decided to open accession negotiations in October 2005.

## The Challenge

Because of the significant size of agriculture and various structural deficiencies of the agricultural sector in the acceding countries the transfer of the Common Agricultural Policy to the new Member States has been one of the major challenges of this latest round of EU enlargement.[3] In fact, European Commissioners Fischler, Verheugen and Byrne stated at the Council of Agricultural Ministers in 2002 in Bruxelles "… that the restructuring of the agricultural sector in the candidate countries was the most important theme in the enlargement context." In the following chapter we will describe some of the structural features of agriculture in the new Member States in a comparative way which will indicate the magnitude of the task.

Regarding agricultural issues the ten countries which became new members of the EU as of May 1, 2004, may be grouped in two categories: On the one hand there are eight Central and Eastern European Countries (CEEC). On the other hand there are the two Mediterranean countries, Cyprus and Malta. The latter are rather small islands and have specific agricultural production conditions: arable land and water is relatively scarce and the mild climate of the Mediterranean Sea allows for intensive agricultural production of special crops (e.g. vegetable, fruits, wine etc.). In contrast, agriculture in the CEECs is much different. Production structures are still much determined by the legacy of the socialist era. For instance, after World War II, farms in most CEECs were collectivised because of which a significant number of large farms can be observed. In some countries parts of the farmland has been restituted after the collapse of socialism. However, in others this was not possible anymore because it was difficult to identify the former owners or because the legal basis did not foresee restitution to all former owners. At the same time there were some exceptions such as Poland and Slovenia where, in addition to collective farms, many small farms remained in private hands. In fact, to differing degrees, the following conditions characterise agricultural production in most of the CEECs: a significant share of agricultural production still comes from very small, semi-subsistence oriented small scale farms which are weakly linked with commercial

---

[3] EU Press release of March 18, 2002, No. 02/68.

markets.[4] These farms were and in some rural areas still are important buffers against falling poor. Therefore, to date in most CEECs the farm sector still has a dual structure consisting of relatively large-scale farms and a big number of very small, semi-subsistence farms.

Due to the latest round of EU enlargement the importance of rural areas and the agricultural sector has increased again. The additional weight of agriculture in the new Member States and the three candidate countries in comparison to the average of "old" Member States (EU-15) is revealed by two indicators in Figure 1: agricultural land and the agricultural work force are shown in relation to the level in the EU-15 in 2003. Enlargement by the ten new Member States increased the agricultural area by 27% from about 133 million ha (EU-15) to about 169 million ha (EU-25). The agricultural work force increased by about 52% from 6.836 million (EU-15) to 10.375 million (EU-25). The accession of Romania and Bulgaria will add another 15% of agricultural area but even 49% of the agricultural workforce to the one in the EU-15 in 2003. Thinking ahead further the potential enlargement by Turkey would add another 29% of agricultural land and almost double (plus 97%) the agricultural work force in comparison to the EU-15 in 2003! Obviously significant structural change might occur by the time of a potential accession of Turkey.[5] Nevertheless the challenge would be significant given the absolute size of this sector in Turkey compared to the EU-15.

In the former socialist countries the significant number of farm workers is mainly due to a legacy from the socialist period when hidden unemployment was a typical feature both for the large-scale former collective farms as well as for the semi-subsistence oriented small farms. Particularly where the small-scale farms still prevail the share of the total workforce that is still employed in agriculture continues to be high. With the exception of Malta, this share is higher in all new

---

[4] For further information of the extent and the effects of the phenomenon see for instance: S. Abele, and K. Frohberg, (eds.) *"Subsistence Agriculture in Central and Eastern Europe: How to Break the Vicious Circle?"* Vauk Academic Publishers, 2003.

[5] The EU's budget is planned on the basis of multi-annual inter-institutional agreements on budgetary discipline to give stability to annual budgets and better support to EU priorities. The costs for an accession of Turkey have not been taken into account in the "Financial Perspectives for 2007-13," because of which the earliest possible date for an accession would be 2014.

**Figure 1.  Agricultural land and people employed in agriculture, forestry and fishery in the new Member States, Bulgaria and Romania, and Turkey in relation to the EU-15 in 2002**

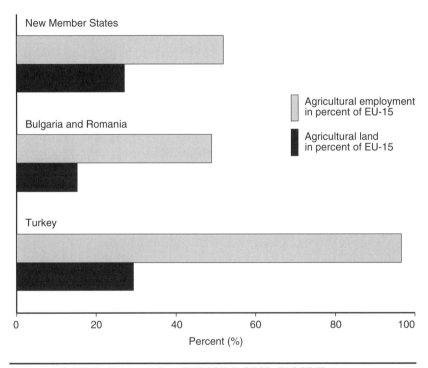

Sources: DG AGRI, official data from EUROSTAT, OECD, FAOSTAT etc

Member States than the respective average share in the "old" Member States (see Figure 2). Compared to the average in the EU-15 the share of the work force employed in agriculture is also very high in the candidate countries Romania and Bulgaria. Apart from other problems such as macro-economic and administrative weaknesses, the high share of agriculture in total employment in the case of Romania but also in Bulgaria and the associated structural deficiencies related to agriculture may have contributed to the delay in the accession process in the case of these two countries. Similarly the fact that agricultural employment constitutes about one third of the total work force in Turkey may indicate that specific policy measures would be required to complement structural change in agriculture prior to and following a potential accession of Turkey to the EU.

**Figure 2.    Share of total work force employed in agriculture in the new Member States and some of the Candidate Countries in comparison to the EU-15 average, 2003**

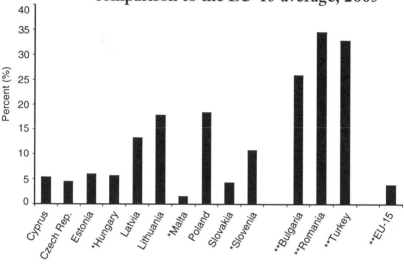

Notes: * = 2002; ** = estimate
Sources: DG AGRI, official data from EUROSTAT, OECD, FAOSTAT etc.

The relative importance of agriculture in the economy as indicated by the sector's contribution to total national value added is in all accession countries and all candidate countries higher than on average in the EU-15 (see Figure 3). However, in the Czech Republic, Malta, Poland, and Slovenia, the sector's contribution is less than twice as high as for the EU-15. In the case of the Slovak Republic, Cyprus, and Hungary the share is about twice as high as in the EU-15. Particularly, the latter two have a comparative advantage in the production of various agricultural speciality crops. Furthermore, the graph indicates that in the three candidate countries considered here the contribution of agriculture to total value added is between 5 to 6 times higher than in the EU-15 indicating that this sector plays a far more important overall role in these economies and underpins the strategic importance of agricultural policy issues in the accession negotiations with these countries.

**Figure 3.  Share of total value added produced in agriculture in the new Member States and some of the Candidate Countries in comparison to the EU-15 average, 2003**

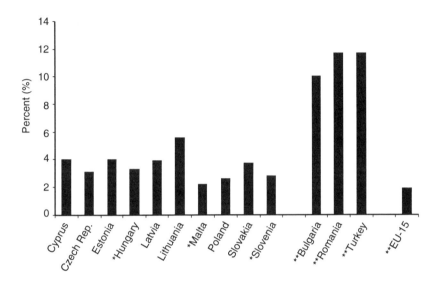

Notes: * = 2002; ** = estimate
Sources: DG AGRI, official data from EUROSTAT, OECD, FAOSTAT etc.

Finally, the comparison of Figure 2 and 3 reveals another feature which has significant implications: The share of the total work force employed in agriculture in the accession and candidate countries but also in the EU-15 is in almost all cases higher than the sector's contribution to total national value added. The only exception is Malta, where 1.6% of the island's workforce produced 2.2% of total national value added. Again there are marked differences in the degree to which the share of employment exceeds the share in value added. In the case of the EU-15 and some of the new Member States the employment rate is moderately larger going up to a factor of 2 (e.g. Cyprus, Czech Republic, Estonia, Hungary, Slovakia). However, in the case of some countries the share of people employed in agriculture exceeds the share of the sector's contribution to national value added by a factor of between 2 and 3 (Latvia, Lithuania, Slovenia, Bulgaria, Romania, and Turkey) or even close to 6 in the case of Poland. In this context it is also important to note that significant variation regarding both indicators shown in Figures 2 and 3 is hidden behind the relatively low average for the EU-15. For instance, agriculture's share in total employment varies in the EU-15 also between 0.9% and 18.4% for the UK and for Portugal, respectively. Therefore the averages should not obscure one from keeping the absolute figures in mind. In that respect Poland is by far the largest agricultural player among the new Member States as revealed by both indicators. The utilized agricultural land in Poland, for instance, is—in area—similar to that of Germany (in 2003: 16,891 and 16,971 thousand ha, respectively) and the number of people employed in the Polish agricultural sector was with 2,505,000 people about as high as the aggregate number of people employed in the agricultural sector of Austria, France, and Germany combined. Hence, the integration of the Polish agricultural sector into the CAP is one of the major challenges faced in this round of enlargement. The second challenge revealed by the comparison of Figures 2 and 3 is the observation that agriculture in many of the new Member States but also in the candidate countries is a comparatively inefficient sector that has significant and inherent structural problems.

In addition to these supply side factors, for which the accession countries and the "old" Member States differ, there are also some additional profound differences relating to income and demand side factors. For instance, the average GDP per capita in terms of Purchasing Power Parity for 2003 was in all new Member States below the average of the EU and varied between 41 and 78% (for Cyprus and Latvia, respectively). This income gap was associated with higher expenditure shares for food in the accession countries: in 2001 the average share of household income spent on food was 28.3% in the ten new Member States compared with 16.2% for the EU-15. In 2001, in Bulgaria and Romania this share reached 31.8 and 39.9%, respectively and was even higher in Turkey with 51.0%.[6] Generally, the income in rural areas is even lower than the national average and poverty is a severe issue in some rural areas of the CEECs and even more so in some regions of Turkey. These few indicators reveal that on top of structural support in favour of rural areas the implementation of the CAP is also crucial as regards the income situation of consumers because the CAP's price policy is a two-edged sword: any price

---

[6] EUROSTAT, Statistical Yearbook on Agriculture, 2003, Luxembourg.

increases in favor of agricultural producers would at the same time be detrimental for consumers. As a consequence of higher food prices and relatively low elasticities for food demand consumers would have to increase their expenditures for food. Consequently price increases for agricultural commodities that may have been welcomed by farmers in the CEECs would at the same time have been perceived negatively by consumers and thereby have weakened the reputation of the CAP and the EU in the new Member States.

The conclusion of this review of selected structural indicators is that the most recent round of enlargement has increased the diversity of Member States in the EU as regards the agricultural sector as will the upcoming rounds of enlargement. To meet the challenge of great diversity which also is associated with income disparities, redistribution policies will at least remain as important as they are today, if not even become more important. In this context and given the significant economic, environmental, and social importance of agriculture and rural development in the new Member States the importance and relevance of the CAP has increased rather than decreased. The instruments and the quality of the CAP, however, with which needed support is being offered to "old" and new Member States has changed substantially.[7] This will be elaborated further in the next section.

## The Reform of the Common Agricultural Policy

The CAP is based on the Treaty of Rome and, until recently, important elements of it dated back to the 1960s and 1970s. By the end of the 1970s the CAP had been successful in encouraging higher productivity of agriculture and assuring that consumers had stable supply of affordable food. However, in the 1980s the EU had to deal with permanent surpluses of major farm commodities that were associated with high budgetary costs, distortions of world markets, and which did not always serve the interests of farmers, taxpayers, and consumers best. Hence, in the early 1990s pressure to reform the CAP increased. One could argue that the expectation of the enlargement of

---

[7] The central role of the CAP in this context is highlighted in the context of preparing the next programming period of the CAP, i.e. for the years 2007-13. For instance, the Commission is currently preparing a EU strategy document related to the rural development policies in which the relevance and importance of the CAP in the context of enlargement will be explained. See : http://europa.eu.int/comm/agriculture/

the EU by the new Member States from Central and Eastern Europe in the early 1990s has contributed to this pressure.[8]

In fact, a first set of CAP reform was launched in 1992 when direct payments for individual production sectors were introduced and when the lowering of administered producers prices, i.e. reducing of market price support, started. Production limits helped further to reduce trade surpluses and a new emphasis was placed on environmentally sound farming. Additional rural development measures were introduced to accompany the restructuring of the agricultural sector and to respond to the public's changing priorities. The next step in this reform process was taken with the so-called AGENDA 2000 which reinforced the reliance of farmers on the market and further encouraged environmentally sound production. For a first time the AGENDA 2000 reform merged the individual development measures into a comprehensive policy framework. Thereby, starting with the AGENDA 2000, all agricultural policies were structured in two "pillars": pillar 1 represents the traditional market regulations for major agricultural commodities such as cereals, dairy, beef, sugar beet etc.[9] And pillar 2 pertains to policy measures which relate to rural development in a broader sense: alongside the market measures and the elements of a competitive European agriculture, this policy tool acknowledges the varied needs of the rural world and meets the expectations of European society as regards quality of agricultural products, animal welfare and environmental requirements.[10] As an essential part of the European agricultural model, it aims to put in place a consistent and lasting framework for guaranteeing the future of rural areas and promoting the maintenance and creation of employment in all European rural areas. Hence, the policy measures under pillar 2 are designed to strengthen the agricultural and forestry sector, to improve the socio-economic conditions in rural areas, thereby improve their competitiveness, as well as to preserve the environment and the rural heritage.

---

[8] See DG AGRI, The Common Agricultural Policy explained, http://europa.eu.int/comm/agriculture/publi/index_en.htm

[9] More details on the EU's agricultural market policies are to be found on http://europa.eu.int/comm/agriculture /markets/index_en.htm

[10] European Commission (2001), The new rural development policy and its principles, Bruxelles, http://europa.eu.int/comm/agriculture/rur/

Then in June 2003 a further fundamental CAP Reform was agreed. It entailed a major policy change as regards the choice of instruments: the CAP Reform decoupled the direct payments granted to farmers from production. As of 2005 farmers in the EU-15 get direct support as a "single farm payment" which is based on the average amount of subsidies received between 2000 and 2002, which is unrelated to current production decisions and which is therefore "decoupled." Farmers who are granted the single farm payments have to comply with and meet certain standards for which the European public has a high demand (e.g. certain environmental, public health, and animal welfare legislation) as of January 1, 2005, and in some countries as of January 2007. Direct payments of more than €5000 per farm are subject to reductions of 3, 4, and 5% in the years 2005, 2006, and 2007, respectively. These funds will be transferred to pillar 2 of the CAP—what is called "modulation"—whereby rural development policies are further strengthened. Furthermore, at the Council of the Agricultural Ministers of the EU at Luxemburg on April 22, 2004, the "second wave" of the recent CAP Reform was agreed upon. Building on the same principles as the first part of these reforms additional individual market orders were revised and modernized (i.e. sectors for tobacco, hops, olive oil and cotton). The major part of this second reform wave will come into effect in January 2006. The reforms were complemented by the strengthening of rural development measures to assist producers to adapt to the structural change, "… achieved by reorienting the CAP measures to reward healthy, high-quality products and practices, and developing alternative sources of income and economic activity."[11]

The new orientation of the CAP is also one of the reasons why the EU wants non-trade concerns relating to these standards to be addressed in the ongoing Doha round of WTO talks.[12] Hence, these reforms entailed general regime changes from price-based subsidies to direct income support of farmers.[13] The rationale behind the reforms is that the departure from price support will make farmers more

---

[11] European Commission, Directorate-General for Agriculture (2004), The Second Wave of CAP Reforms. Newsletter, May, special edition. Bruxelles, http://europa.eu.int/comm/agriculture/

[12] European Commission, EU agriculture and the WTO, September 2001. http://europa.eu.int/comm/agriculture/

[13] Rodriguez, José Silva, in an interview given to the Delegation of the EU in Japan, July 2003.

responsive to market signals, discourage over-production and thereby reduce the need to rely on export subsidies. In fact, this switch in the policy regime may be the culmination of a long running controversy with significant international implications, as the new direct payment schemes are far less trade distorting than previous policy regimes. This has an effect on the judgment of the CAP by international trade partners and on the ongoing WTO negotiations on agriculture because these "Fully decoupled payments could see a large part of EU farm payments shift from the WTO Blue box (trade distorting, allowed within limits) to the Green box (non-trade distorting)."[14] As such these direct payments would not be subject to cuts in future agreements on liberalizing agricultural trade. Because these payments are decoupled they are expected not to affect negatively farmers in the countries of other big agricultural exporters such as Australia, Canada, or the USA, nor those in developing countries. Therefore, this CAP reform is also considered to be a significant contribution of the EU to the on-going WTO round in general and a recognition of the concerns of the developing countries in particular.[15] However, trade partners from the Cairns Group, for instance, would like to develop stricter Green Box criteria or even establish a spending ceiling for the decoupled green box payments as well.[16]

Generally, international agricultural trade partners of the EU acknowledged that the reform of the CAP under Agenda 2000 was an important step in making the transfer of the CAP to the new Member States acceptable. For instance, Economic Research Service (ERS) of the US Department of Agriculture, argues in a policy brief on "EU Enlargement" that clearly it would have been very costly for the EU to extend CAP price support mechanisms existing in the early 1990s to the candidate countries: the EU would have had difficulties in meeting many of its WTO commitments. ERS argues further that these factors, among others, spurred the EU to adopt the CAP reforms. Canada argues similarly: "The impact [of enlargement] on

---

[14] Foreign Agricultural Service, Mission to the EU (2005), CAP-Reform, http://www.useu.be/agri/cap.html

[15] European Commission, Directroate General for Agriculture (2003), Overview of CAP-Reforms, Newsletter, July, special edition, Bruxelles, http://europa.eu.int/comm/agriculture/

[16] International Centre for Trade and Sustainable Development (ICTSD), Newsletter Bridges June 2003, (www.ictsd.org).

world cereal, oilseed and livestock markets in the short-to-medium-term is expected to be minimal, due in part to agricultural policy reforms introduced in the EU-15."[17] Also EU's trade partners from developing countries acknowledge that the CAP reform was a major step forward. For instance, Minister of Agriculture from Mauritius, Praving Jugnauth, argued in a July 2003 speech that the CAP-reform has been a qualitative departure from the past and came at a time when extension of the CAP to the new Member States was at stake.[18]

Hence, one could argue that the reform of the CAP over the last decade was in itself a strategic prerequisite to making the accession process in the agricultural sector as smooth as possible. Furthermore, it is noteworthy that enlargement thereby has also pushed the EU to pursuit a consistent reform approach. In contrast to other big players in agricultural markets such as the US, the removal of these policy instruments which were distorting international agricultural trade most has been continuous and linear over the past decade.

## The EU's strategy for transferring the CAP to the new Member States

The EU prepared accession of the ten new Member States with a carefully designed strategy starting with pre-accession partnerships which were negotiated in the first half of the 1990s. Given the above mentioned size and structural problems of the agricultural sector in the acceding countries it is obvious that these bilateral strategies also contained elements which intended to support a smooth transition from national to the EU's common agricultural policy scheme. Some of the components which were particularly important for the agricultural sector were the so-called Phare program which started in 1989, the Sapard (i.e. Special Accession Programme for Agriculture and Rural Development), and the ISPA program (i.e. Instrument for Structural Policies for Pre-Accession) which effectively started in 2001.[19] The

---

[17] Agriculture and Agri-Food Canada, Bi-weekly newsletter, May 2002.

[18] Speech of the Agricultural Minister of Mauritius at the 8th Special ACP Ministerial Conference on Sugar, July 2003.

[19] ISPA was established by Council Regulation No. 1267/1999 in June 1999 on the basis of a Commission proposal in Agenda 2000 to enhance economic and social cohesion in the applicant countries of Central and Eastern Europe for the period 2000-2006. For further info see: http://europa.eu.int/comm/enlargement/pas/ispa.htm

Phare program was originally designed as a tool to aid Poland and Hungary in economic transition and later on was extended to other candidate countries.[20] With this program a total sum of € 11 billion was made available for the period 2000-2006 for co-financing of respective projects in the CEECs. Under the umbrella of Phare, the Twining program gave support to preparing the administration in the new Member States to adopt the EU's *acquis communautaire*, the complete legal body that constitutes the legal base for the EU's rule of law.[21]

As regards agricultural trade relations the so-called Europe Agreements were important. These bilateral treaties agreed upon by individual CEECs and the EU effectively liberalized trade bilaterally, i.e. between the individual candidate countries and the EU-15 but not among the candidate countries, to a significant extent prior to enlargement. Trade liberalization as regards agriculture was done in consecutive steps in order to avoid market distortions due to sudden removal of trade barriers in individual sectors. In a first step the Europe Agreements implemented tariff-rate quotas at reduced or zero tariff rates. These were later on complemented by the so-called "double-zero" and "double-profit" protocols which effectively eliminated import tariffs and export subsidies for bilateral trade with agricultural products. Furthermore, complementary bilateral agreements between the EU and individual CEECs allowed partial mobility of labor in the agricultural sector. In the case of Poland a specific quota of seasonal workers was allowed to seek employment in specific sectors of the EU-15, i.e. for people working in the tourism sector (e.g. waiters and people working in room services) and in primary agricultural production.

As a result of this pre-accession strategy the EU-25 had achieved a high level of integration of markets and policies prior to enlargement. On average 65 % of all agricultural exports of the new Member States and 69% of all imports went to or originated from EU-destinations over the period of 1999-2003. Moreover, agricultural policies in the candidate countries and the EU-15 were brought into alignment over

---

[20] Originally created in 1989 to assist Poland and Hungary, the PHARE programme later on provided support to all new Member States from Central and Eastern Europe. For further info see: http://europa.eu.int/comm/enlargement/pas/phare/

[21] The Twinings program focused on two forms of support: on the one hand the creation of administrative structures mandatory to adopt the *acquis commmunautaire* and on the other hand on strengthening the administrative capacity by supporting training measures.

the last decade. Therefore, many of the gains expected from extending a customs union and from extending the CAP to the new Member States was already realized prior to enlargement.[22] One important effect of extending the EU's customs union territory to the ten new Member States, however, is materializing only now after enlargement took effect: Prior to enlargement bilateral trade *among* the candidate countries was often restricted by the numerous trade barriers in place. Even though the candidate countries had concluded various regional trade agreements, e.g. the Central European Free Trade Area/ CEFTA, agricultural trade was in most cases excluded from liberalization. Therefore, agricultural trade barriers between the candidate countries were not removed until accession took effect which is now creating the ground for substantial trade creation between the new Member States.

As of May 1, 2004, the CAP was transferred to the new Member States and replaced the respective national agricultural policies in place prior to enlargement. Thereby, the nation-states transferred an important and integral part of their national legislative power to the supra-national level, i.e. to the level of the EU. In this respect, the major benefits for the new Member States, which were associated to the adaptation of the CAP, were the integration into the common agricultural market of the EU and the EU's support schemes, the adaptation of the EU's common agricultural trade regime, and the access to structural aid for rural areas. Furthermore, the reforms of the CAP and particularly the continuous reduction of internal agricultural support prices, since 1992 have helped to keep the effects on consumers in the acceding countries limited in spite of the high food expenditure shares in these countries: the reduction in guaranteed agricultural commodity prices has helped to limit the degree of price increases for food commodities in the accession countries.

Given the fact that agriculture accounted for about 45% of the total EU budget prior to this reform, it was essential to complement these reforms with a new financial discipline which effectively introduced an upper bound for the expenditures for the farm budget in

---

[22] European Commission, Directorate-General for Agriculture, Prospects for Agricultural Markets and Income 2004-2011 for EU 25, Dec. 2004, http://europa.eu.int/comm/agriculture/publi/caprep/prospects2004b/

general and for the direct payments in particular. The respective financial mechanism that was agreed upon by the Brussels European Council of October 2002 ensures that the upper limit for agricultural market and income support for the years 2007-2013 is fixed. Additionally, the task was to guarantee that the extension of direct payments to the new Member States would not be detrimental for the mandatory structural change. Likewise, the extension of the direct farm payments was not to pose a threat of further increases of the expenditures for the EU's agricultural policies. Therefore, it was agreed to phase in gradually the newly designed direct payments in the new Member States between 2004 (starting with 25% of the level granted in the EU-15) and 2013 (when direct payments will be fully aligned with those of the EU-15). In order to facilitate implementation a simplified "single area payment" scheme was introduced in the new Member States, except Slovenia and Malta. Based on this scheme, farmers receive direct payments in accordance with uniform, regionally determined support levels. In Malta and Slovenia the classical national payment scheme will be applied until 2007 when the "single payment scheme" will be introduced directly. Additionally, the new Member States were granted the option to pay so-called top-ups to the direct payments, using parts of rural development funds. One argument against transferring the full level of direct payments to the new Member States was revealed by an economic impact study by the Commission in 2002. The immediate introduction of the full EU-15 level of direct aid in the candidate States would have a negative effect on the restructuring of the sector.

Furthermore, the rural development measures under pillar 2 of the CAP are perceived as useful tools to meet some of the specific restructuring needs in the new Member States. Rural areas have a significantly lower income than urban areas; primary agricultural production is often relatively inefficient; rural population is characterized by an over-proportional share of old people; and the rural economy reveals a significant dependence on one sector, i.e. the primary sector (see also section 2 above).[23] Therefore the new Member States were eligible to the whole range of rural development measures directly following accession. To further increase the usefulness of this policy tool, as of

---

[23] European Commission (2004) Fact Sheet: New Perspectives for EU Rural Development, Bruxelles, http://europa.eu.int/comm/agriculture/

May 1, 2004, additional instruments were implemented, for which exclusively the new Member States are eligible. These measures were designed for the transition period 2004-06 and include, for instance, support schemes for improving food safety and quality, for the setting up of agricultural producer organisations, and for semi-subsistence farms.

Summing up, the pre-accession strategy effectively allowed many farmers in the new Member States to taste the benefits of membership in advance of enlargement.[24] After integration into the EU the new Member States acquired access to the single agricultural market of the EU, direct income support measures, and a broad set of rural development measures some of which are fine-tuned to meet the specific demands of the rural areas in the new Member States. The international gains of the accession strategy as regards agriculture should be a smooth integration of the new Member States into the international agricultural trade regime.

## Strategic implications

Trade and trade negotiations. As a consequence of the EU accession the new Member States were obliged to remove their previous national trade regimes and to replace them with the EU's external tariff schedule. Formally this constitutes an expansion of a customs union. Given the relatively high levels of external protection originating from the CAP in the past, one major strategic question related to the agricultural sector discussed in the context of the most recent rounds of EU enlargement was how world agricultural markets would be affected by expanding the EU's agricultural tariff regimes to additional countries. The extent of these effects generally depends on the level of agricultural market protection before and after adopting the CAP. In the case of the southern enlargement of the EU—which then was the European Community (EC)—in the mid-80s to Spain and Portugal the price levels for various agricultural products increased in these countries after accession. In contrast, price levels for some commodities decreased in the case of other former enlargement rounds (e.g. the enlargement to Sweden, Finland and Austria in 1995) at least

---

[24] EU Commission, Directorate Generale for Agriculture and Rural Development, Enlargement and Agriculture, http://europa.eu.int/comm/agriculture/eu25/index_en.htm

in some sub-sectors. Generally, the effects of enlargement depend on the difference between the pre- and the post-enlargement price levels in individual commodity markets. The changes in the external protection through tariffs and the associated price changes have two major trade effects: trade creation and trade diversion. Trade creation occurs if production is relocated due to enlargement from the more costly domestic producers to the new partner country where producers are more efficient. A hypothetical example may illustrate the point. Country A (e.g. a new member state) produces fruits more efficiently than country B (old customs union). After the enlargement of the customs union a non-discriminatory tariff would be removed because of which fruits from country A would become more competitive in country B. In consequence, exports from country A to country B would replace domestic production in the latter: trade has been created. However, this theoretical argument holds only when the respective products are homogenous and when consumers have the same preferences for the product independent from where it is produced. In the case of EU enlargement by Austria it was expected that milk would be imported from new partners within the EU after enlargement. However, due to strong preferences of Austrian consumers for milk from their own region, this expectation did not materialize.

Trade diversion occurs if a product that prior to enlargement (given a non-discriminatory tariff-level) has been imported from the lowest cost producer from a third country is—after enlargement—replaced with imports from a partner country which becomes more competitive due to the preferential trade within the enlarged customs union. While trade creation makes production more efficient and therefore is normally positive to all parties involved, trade diversion tends to make production less rationale which is a disadvantage. It particularly may subtract from the welfare of trade partners, which are not part of the customs union. In fact, trade partners from third countries whose market shares is expected to decline due to the enlargement of an existing customs union may therefore lose from such a bilateral policy change. Therefore, the EU's major trade partners in agricultural markets have been concerned about the potential of trade diversion in former rounds of enlargement given the high importance of the EU both in world agricultural export and import markets. Based on the GATT Treaty (particularly Article XXIV:6) those partners who are members of the WTO have the right to seek compensation for (agricultural) trade losses incurred because of higher overall trade protection following the conclusion of a bilateral trade agreement.

A case in point was the southern EU enlargement to Spain, when trade diversion was substantial in the case of feed maize (corn). Before EC accession Spain imported substantial amounts of maize as poultry feed from the US. Following accession protection levels for maize imports to Spain from the US rose because of which Spain imported maize from the lowest-cost producer within the Union, which at the time was France. In this case the US claimed compensation based on the GATT treaty and, in fact, was granted an import quota for maize at lower tariff levels than the standard one applied by the EC for maize after accession of Spain.

Another related issue is that the enlarged EU—"old" and new Member States alike—has to satisfy their existing WTO obligations. In agriculture these obligations are based on the Agreement on Agriculture which was the final result of the Uruguay Round of trade negotiations. The EU and all new Member States have signed this agreement and obligated themselves to implement specific policy changes as regards their agricultural sector contributing to a liberalization of the respective sector policies. They are associated with specific obligations to reduce subsidies and protection levels in the agricultural sector in three areas: domestic support, import protection and market access, and export subsidies. Prior to enlargement various studies attempted to quantify the extent to which these commitments of the "old" and the new Member States of the EU to reduce agricultural trade protection may be violated after extending the CAP to the new Member States. Some studies estimated that there would be a considerable potential for upper bounds of import protection, domestic support and export subsidies being exceeded after accession. This would have provided the grounds for trade partners to demand significant compensations, for instance in the form of tariff quotas.[25] Others argued that due to more moderate world market price projections and

---

[25] For instance, K. Frohberg, M. Hartmann, P. Weingarten, and E. Winter, "Auswirkungen der EU-Osterweiterung auf die Beitrittsländer—Analyse unter Berücksichtigung bestehender bi- und multilateraler Verpflichtungen," in: M. Brockmeier, F. Isermeyer, and S. von Cramon-Taubadel, (Hrsg.), *"Liberalisierung des Weltagrarhandels—Strategien und Konsequenzen, Schriften der Gesellschaft für Wirtschafts—und Sozialwissenschaften des Landbaues,"* Bd. 37, Münster-Hiltrup, S. 183-193, 2002.

the introduction of production limiting policies (e.g. quotas) in the new Member States after accession in some of the key agricultural sectors, problems with keeping commitments in the area of subsidized exports may actually be less severe.[26]

However, most of these ex ante studies did not or not fully take into account the final reform package associated with the most recent CAP Reform. As indicated above, the major element of these reforms is to reduce market price support for various core agricultural commodities while direct income support will be decoupled from production and combined into single farm payments. In contrast to the pre-reform period, this implies that farmers get the major share of their income support out of the EU's budget and independent of their production decisions. Thus, EU farmers are now much more flexible to respond to market signals. Because these direct payments do provide no direct production incentives they are not distorting trade and therefore are more widely accepted in the context of WTO negotiations. Therefore, these reforms were an important step to help the "old" but also the new Member States to meet their WTO commitments. Furthermore, because producer prices in the new Member States have risen only for some agricultural sub-sectors—and for these at moderate rates—the negative effects on world markets were very limited, if not positive, as a consequence of the positive growth effects partially resulting from the enlargement process. If the administered and guaranteed producer prices which became effective in the new Member States after accession had been significantly higher than prior to it or significantly above prevailing world market prices this would have stimulated over-production in the new Member States. In the absence of very significant growth of domestic food demand the disposal of the resulting excess supply on world markets would have necessitated export subsidies or other costly intervention schemes.

In October 2004 the European Commission released details on compensation demands made by the EU's trading partners. Main trading partners such as the US, China, and Japan submitted compensation demands mainly for agricultural products. However, the scope

---

[26] Kuhn, A, and P. Wehrheim, Agricultural Trade Diversion due to Eastern Enlargement—A Quantitative Analysis based on a Partial Equilibrium World Trade Model (WATSIM), In: Ahrens, H., Grings, M. and Petersen, V. (eds.), *Perspektiven der europäischen Agrar—und Ernährungswirtschaft nach der Osterweiterung der EU*. Halle/Saale, (2003).

of the claims was limited to only a few products such as bananas, rice, poultry and sugar. Furthermore, the extent of the compensation claims was also moderate. The (bilateral) negotiations over these claims were still on-going at the time of writing this chapter. However, particularly regarding the agricultural sector it should be clear that extending the CAP to the new Member States will also benefit the EU's trading partners. Even though these advantages are likely to be of a more qualitative nature, they may easily outweigh potential negative effects in individual commodity markets: Access to the agricultural markets of all ten new Member States is standardized according to the rules set forth by the CAP with a single tariff and a single set of administrative procedures. This should significantly reduce transaction costs of the EU's trade partners and enhance their access to the markets in the new Member States.

Another strategic implication in this context is that the weight of the EU within the WTO has been strengthened given the inclusion of the votes of ten new Member States. This may also result in some of the EU's proposals for further liberalization of the agricultural sector in the on-going round of trade negotiations—the Doha-Round—being backed by a more forceful coalition. In a Policy Brief on "EU Agriculture and the WTO" (2004) former EU Commissioner for Agriculture and Fisheries Franz Fischler stated that it is clear that the EU says "yes" to further rounds of liberalization of the agricultural sector provided that all countries, including the developing countries and the EU can benefit from it. This view is supported by the new Commissioner for Agriculture and Rural Development Mariann Fischer Boel who stated that reaching a deal on the modalities for agriculture within the WTO as part of an overall package for the WTO ministerial meeting in Hong Kong in December 2005 is one of DG Agri's top priorities for 2005. Support in these WTO negotiations for specific elements of the new and reformed CAP may be particularly strong for policies which are of pivotal importance for the new Member States such as rural development policies.

Summing up, the extent to which the EU's international trade obligations have been challenged due to the extension of the CAP to the new Member States has been rather limited. Hence, one may conclude that negative (trade) effects of extending the CAP to the new Member States on international agricultural markets have been widely avoided.

**Impact of enlargement since May 2004.** Generally, despite some regional difficulties or those of specific sectors, developments since accession indicate overwhelmingly positive effects of EU membership on agriculture. In general investments in agriculture have significantly increased alongside income perspectives in most new Member States and, in some rural areas, have even induced a small boom.[27] Furthermore, production effects during the first months after accession have been very moderate which complies with what has been predicted in many ex-ante studies.[28] Hence the relative weight of the new Member States in total agricultural production of the EU is not expected to change rapidly: The new Member States together contribute in 2004 about 20% of the EU-25 cereals production, 10% to 17% of the EU-25 meat production and 15% of the milk production in the EU-25.[29] While limited expansion of agricultural supply in the new Member States is also the result of relatively low short run supply elasticities in agriculture, model estimates document that these effects will be similarly moderate in the medium and long run. Nevertheless some notable changes are expected.[30] Accession is expected to foster a restructuring of intra-EU agricultural trade. For instance, pork production is expected to continue to have a comparative advantage in the "old" Member States such as Denmark as regards low fat content or feed use efficiency. In contrast new Member States have significantly increased competitiveness in some sectors as for example in poultry production mainly because of substantial foreign direct investments in production and processing but also lower labor and energy

---

[27] European Commission, Directorate-General for Agriculture, Prospects for Agricultural Markets and Income 2004-2011 for EU 25, Dec. 2004, http://europa.eu.int/comm/agriculture/publi/caprep/prospects2004b/

[28] See, for instance, M. Banse, W. Muench and S. Tangermann Eastern Enlargement of the European Union: A General and Partial Equilibrium Analysis, In: G.H. Peters, and P. Pingali (eds.), *Tomorrow's Agriculture: Incentives, Institutions, Infrastructure and Innovations,* August 2000. pp. 488-497; or: K. Frohberg, M. Hartmann, P. Weingarten, and E. Winter, "Auswirkungen der Osterweiterung auf die Beitrittsländer," In: M. Brockmeier, F. Isermeyer, and S. von Cramon-Taubadel, (eds.) *Liberalisierung des Weltagrarhandels,* Göttingen, 2002.

[29] European Commission, Directorate-General for Agriculture, Prospects for Agricultural Markets and Income 2004-2011 for EU 25, Dec. 2004, http://europa.eu.int/comm/agriculture/publi/caprep/prospects2004b/

[30] See speech presented by DG Agriculture's Deputy Director-General Ahner at a conference in Sofia on Agriculture and EU enlargement.

costs. In other sectors, such as dairy products, subsistence production in the new Member States is still substantial with almost 20% of total output. As long as such high rates of subsistence production continue to prevail, the competitiveness of such sub-sectors will be dampened.

DG Agriculture's Deputy Director-General Ahner concluded in early 2004, that medium-term perspectives for agriculture in the new Member States generally seem to be quite positive. Production will become more efficient, food quality standards are increasing and agritrade will be redirected towards the comparative advantage of individual Member States further. The expectations of such positive agricultural sector developments are confirmed by first statistical evidence on the development of sector income in 2004. For instance, first estimates of agricultural incomes in the EU for 2004 by the EU's statistical office revealed a year-to-year increase of 53.8% in the new Member States.[31] This indicates the generally positive effects of implementing the CAP in the new Member States. The rise in income can be explained by two factors: first, more favorable market conditions accounting for about 60% of the rise, and second, the granting of mostly decoupled public support accounting for the remaining 40%. In comparison to 2003, agricultural incomes increased particularly much in Poland (+74%) and even more so in the Czech Republic (+108%). Additionally, first reviews of the individual agricultural markets also showed that at least in 2004 no major distortions occurred.

**The future evolution of the EU's Common Agricultural Policy.** One may also ask how the enlargement will affect the political economy of shaping the CAP in the future. As indicated above, the reforms of the first pillar of the CAP have proceeded relatively far already and the major elements of these reform packages are likely to remain in place for a long time because political agreement on financing this policy area until 2013 already has been reached. At the same time the second pillar of the CAP—the rural development policy—is currently being prepared for the next programming period. In the light of the structural problems in agriculture, the Commission pro-

---

[31] EUROSTAT, Accession boosts farm income in new Member States, Dec., Press release, http://www.eurostat.cec.eu.int/, Luxembourg.

posal for this policy area is to further strengthen it in the next programming period (2007-2013).

Given the most recent reform packages few major additional policy changes are to be expected in the nearby future, but rather a consolidation and continuation of the reform-packages which already have been initiated. The largest remaining challenge is probably the reform of the sugar sector for which the market regime remained untouched for the last 40 years. Although everyone agrees that it needs reforming, DG Agri's Commissioner Mariann Fischer Boel acknowledges that there is a wide range of interests involved. She intends to bring forward proposals on this issue in June 2005.

However, it is noteworthy that the latest enlargement round may also have effects on the future reforms and the respective debates in this area of policy-making. The distribution of votes in the relevant EU institutions has changed. First, more Member States may imply that the opinions raised in favor and against certain policy proposals will become more complex and it may make the forging of coalitions more difficult. Second, it may also imply that the relative weight of the big Member States such as Germany and France who have played a very active role in the past in shaping the CAP will decrease while the voice of the new Member States may be heard more strongly. Third, the manifold structural problems of rural areas in the new Member States sketched out above may imply, that in the future, the second pillar of the CAP will become more important. This may again have an impact on the willingness of the big countries to finance the CAP and the structural measures associated with it. In fact, at the end of 2004 the question how and to which extent the second pillar of the CAP will be financed in the next programming period was not settled yet. The major issue in this debate at the end of 2004 was at which level the budget of the EU would be capped. While the Commission proposed a level of 1.14 percent of Gross National Product, a group of countries which are net contributors to the budget, including France and Germany, proposed to introduce an upper ceiling of 1.0 percent. As long as the EU's agricultural policies remain as important in budgetary terms as they are today, public choice theory suggests that Member States with a relatively large agricultural sector will be more in favor of maintaining high levels of budgetary support for this sector than countries in which the importance of agriculture has diminished more significantly (i.e. the 'restaurant table argument'[32]). Furthermore, it is worth mentioning that an acceptance of the European Constitution would also increase the weight of the European Parliament in the EU's policy making including agricultural policies.

## Outlook: Potential implications of future rounds of enlargement and conclusions

The two potential future enlargement rounds discussed in this chapter may pose similar challenges related to the agricultural sector again and therefore may also have a strategic dimension again. On the one hand the enlargement by Romania and Bulgaria will be significant as regards agriculture given the size of this sector in both countries (see above). However, the accession of these two countries has been anticipated for long and, similar to the integration of the new Member States in 2004, the preparation of transferring the CAP to these additional countries is well under way. This is reflected in the accession negotiations with both countries in which specific conditions for the adaptation to the CAP have been agreed upon. The accession negotiations with both countries were concluded in late 2004. Therefore the conditions for extending the CAP to Romania and Bulgaria are fixed already. Hence, the integration of the agricultural sectors of these two countries was partially taken into account in the preparation of the financial perspectives for the coming programming and budgeting period, i.e. the years 2007-2013. By introducing ceilings to some of the expenditures related to agricultural policies, most notably direct payments, the total level of agricultural expenditures associated with extending the CAP to the new Member States has been limited to an acceptable degree.

---

[32] This arguments states that supra-national financing of certain policy areas (e.g. of agricultural policies) may pose a problem because it may divorce a country's financial decision from financial responsibility and may encourage countries to lobby for higher expenditures (e.g. through the EU) in order to maximize the country's net receipts (or "of eating in a restaurant") or minimize the country's net contributions to the costs of the common policy area (or "the share of the bill"). See J. Pokricak, H. de Gorter, and J.F. Swinnen, "Does there exist a 'Restaurant Table Effect' in the CAP?," Discussion Paper, University of Leuven, 2002.

This will also be one of the big issues in the negotiations with Turkey, which were scheduled to start in October 2005. Costs of a potential accession of Turkey differ substantially depending on which conditions will be agreed upon in the negotiations for the adaptation of the CAP. Some academics have taken the accession of the CEECs as a blueprint for their *ex ante* calculations. The new Member States will be granted the direct payments for farmers but during a transitional period the level of direct payments will be lower than the one in the "old" Member States. A study by the University of Wageningen indicates that granting direct payments to farmers in Turkey after a potential enlargement in 2015 would result in total expenditures for direct payments of about €3.6 billion (at the value of the 2004 euro).[33] Rural development expenditure would be about €1.6 billion. Additionally, and under 2004 policy conditions, Turkey could be eligible for about €9.5 billion to €16.6 billion (in 2004 values) for structural aid while its estimated contribution to the EU budget would be € 5.4 billion. In contrast to these estimates, in mid-2004 former EU Commissioner Franz Fischler presented estimates which were much higher. In a letter to other Commissioners of the EU he warned that extending the CAP to Turkey would create additional budgetary outlays of € 11.3 billion.[34] At the other end of the scale ranges a study of the Humboldt University in Berlin/Germany which estimated the net transfers of extending the CAP to Turkey to be about € 1.6 billion. [35] Hence it should be taken into account that the estimated costs of applying the CAP to Turkey vary significantly. Regardless of the eventual size of budgetary outlays these studies indicate substantial costs and thus renewed substantial effects on the complete system of the EU's budget financing. Hence, one of the central issues in the context of the potential accession of Turkey to the EU will be to settle early on the direct costs that will be associated with transferring the CAP and the EU's structural policies. One possible solution to this challenge may be a tool which has often been used in previous rounds of enlargement: certain agricultural policy measures are phased in during

---

[33] Cf. Turkey in the EU, Wageningen University, Oskam et al. 2004.

[34] The letter and the respective estimates of the costs for expanding the CAP to Turkey were cited, for instance, in the *Financial Times* on September 10, 2004.

[35] Grethe 2004, Turkey's Accession to the EU. http://www.agrar.hu-berlin.de/wisola/va/wp70.pdf

transitional periods. This could help to limit the pressure on the EU budget as well as on Turkey's agricultural sector which in many production areas lags behind in terms of competitiveness.

Summing up, we argue that the strategic and international implications of this round of EU enlargement as regards agriculture were quite moderate. The extension of the CAP to the new Member States was a relatively smooth process and not a "big bang." Neither any distortions of international markets nor any new trade disputes have arisen in the context of this enlargement round. This is mainly the result of two factors. First, reforms of the CAP prior to and in anticipation of enlargement, which were associated with far-reaching decoupling of agricultural support schemes. These reforms made the CAP more transparent and more compatible with the EU's international agricultural trade commitments. Second, the carefully designed pre-accession strategy for the agricultural sector helped to smoothen the adoption of the CAP in the new Member States. In view of the manifold challenges associated with the structural transition of agriculture in the new Member States this should be considered as a major achievement of this enlargement round as such. The related international benefits are evident. For the new Member States from Central and Eastern Europe, extension of the CAP helped in pushing forward the transition process from "plan to market" in the agricultural sector, while facilitating integration into the international agricultural markets for all new Member States.

Looking ahead, it should be acknowledged that the extension of the CAP to additional candidate countries will not be easy. While agreement has been reached already over the terms of extending the CAP to Bulgaria and Romania, this task will be a far greater challenge for Turkey. To assist these candidate countries to carry out the mandatory reforms a carefully designed pre-accession strategy is needed to make this process similarly smooth as the extension of the CAP to the new Member States. The mandatory support schemes for this process are provided by the Union via its Pre-Accession Strategy.[36]

---

[36] For further information, see http://europa.eu.int/comm/enlargement/financial_assistance.htm

# Chapter 16

# EU Enlargement and the Global Environment

David Michel

Over the past fifty years, environmental policy in the European Union has grown from an ad hoc collection of incidental measures to the creation of an explicit multi-level environmental governance system.[1] The EU now occupies a pivotal position at the intersection of domestic and international environmental politics. Among its member states, the EU develops and enacts its own environmental policies and programs. Today, the EU's internal environmental legislation includes some 450 regulations and directives covering air and water pollution, waste management, biodiversity, chemical safety, noise, energy, industrial risks, and more.[2] In the international arena, the EU negotiates multilateral policy agreements on a widening range of regional and global environmental issues. Alongside national governments, the Union is a party or signatory to 76 international environmental accords.[3] From furnishing a loose institutional framework for harmonizing national laws within the common market, the EU has come to exercise significant supranational competences and capacities, both shaping European environmental policy and increasingly influencing international environmental action.

---

[1] Philipp M. Hildebrand, "The European Community's Environmental Policy, 1957 to '1992': From Incidental Measures to an International Regime?" *Journal of Environmental Politics* 1 (4) 1993; Regina S. Axelrod, Norman J. Vig, and Miranda A. Schreurs, "The European Union as an Environmental Governance System," in *The Global Environment: Institutions, Law, and Policy*, 2nd ed., eds. Regina S. Axelrod, David Leonard Downie, and Norman J. Vig (Washington, DC: CQ Press, 2005).

[2] Any attempt to quantify the EU's environmental legislation depends in part on how wide the "environment" net is cast. The number offered here was derived by consulting the EU's "EUR-Lex" database, available at http://www.europa.int , and searching the "Environment" classification for directives and regulations in force.

[3] From the Environmental Treaties and Resource Indicators (ENTRI) database maintained by Columbia University's Center for International Earth Science Information Network (CIESIN) at http://sedac.ciesin.columbia.edu/entri/

The EU's eastward expansion raises opportunities and serious challenges alike for the European and the global environment. Enlargement extends the ambit of one of the world's most ambitious systems of environmental protection. Since May 2004, EU environmental policy encompasses economies and ecosystems from the Arctic Circle to the Adriatic Sea, the Carpathian Mountains to the Canary Islands. Enlargement also brings ten new states into the EU's commitment to promoting global sustainable development and international environmental cooperation. Yet the "green accession" will be no bed of roses. The entrants must adopt and apply the whole of the EU's regulatory regime to the polities and problems of eight Central and Eastern European societies still emerging from the Communist legacy and the very different environmental issues and resources of two small island nations.[4] The EU, for its part, must accommodate ten additional members into its already complex environmental policy-making processes, integrating their inputs and reconciling their disparate interests in Brussels and at the international bargaining table.

This chapter examines enlargement's consequences for EU and international environmental policy. It proceeds in four stages. The first section sets out the principles and objectives of EU environmental policy that has continued to evolve even as the Eastern aspirants first envisaged and subsequently negotiated their adhesion to the European club. The next portion briefly describes the Union's policy-making institutions and its distinct character as an international environmental actor, both regulating its member states and representing common EU positions in the wider world. With accession, the new entrants take on the EU's goals and join its institutions. Their preferences, politics, and publics become part of EU decision-making. A third section, then, discusses the environmental and institutional challenges the accession states confront in the ongoing process of importing and implementing EU policy. The last section explores some of enlargement's potential implications for the future of EU and global environmental affairs.

---

[4] This chapter focuses on the eight Central and East European accession countries (CEECs): the Czech Republic, Estonia, Hungary, Latvia, Lithuania, Poland, Slovakia, and Slovenia. Two more CEECs, Bulgaria and Romania, are expected to join the EU in 2007. Though Malta and Cyprus do not suffer from the Communist environmental and political legacy, their accession raises many of the same institutional and financial issues as for the CEECs.

## The European Union and Environmental Governance

From the launch of the common market to the most recent round of expansion, environmental issues have ascended "from silence to salience" on the EU's political agenda.[5] Early EU legislation arose not from any concerted effort to preserve the environment but as practical health and safety related measures intended to reduce distortions in the internal market. With rising popular awareness of environmental problems, however, the EU faced mounting pressures to broaden its policy purview. The transboundary nature of many environmental threats, such as acid rain and marine pollution, rendered them largely impervious to purely national remedies, highlighting the necessity for supranational solutions. The global scope of other risks, like climate change and ozone depletion, underlined the need for coordinated European strategy towards crafting international responses. Drawn from above by international negotiations and driven from below by member state publics and governments, the EU has progressively assumed an ever-greater role in environmental policy, while at the same time moving to more fully incorporate environmental considerations into all of its decision-making.[6]

### The EU's Expanding Environmental Remit

The 1957 Treaty of Rome founding the European Economic Community (EEC) made no explicit mention of the environment.[7] It formulated no environmental policies and established no environmental institutions. Promoting economic growth then stood foremost among the six original members' objectives. The EU's early environ-

---

[5] Albert Weale, "Environmental Rules and Rule-Making in the European Union," *Journal of European Public Policy* 3 (4) 1996, p.595. For the historical development of EU environmental policy, see e.g. Hildebrand, "The European Community's Environmental Policy"; Pamela M. Barnes and Ian G. Barnes, *Environmental Policy in the European Union* (Cheltenham, UK: Edward Elgar, 1999).

[6] Alberta Sbragia, "Institution-Building from Below and Above: The European Community in Global Environmental Politics," in *European Integration and Supranational Governance*, eds. Wayne Sandholtz and Alec Stone Sweet (Oxford: Oxford University Press, 1998).

[7] The European Union formally came into being in November 1993, following the 1992 Maastricht Treaty of European Union. The EU subsumed but did not supersede the European Economic Community, officially known since Maastricht simply as the European Community (EC). The EU's environmental competences reside within the EC. For the sake of convenience, in common parlance the term EU is now used also when referring generally to events and policies prior to 1993.

mental initiatives were few in number and narrowly tailored, conceived as addressing specific barriers to trade in the internal market. Only in 1967 did it pass its first "environmental" directive on classifying, labeling, and packaging dangerous substances, approving just eight more directives and one regulation in its first fifteen years.

By the early 1970s, however, global concern over modern society's adverse environmental impacts was building rapidly, fueled by a string of popular and academic works cataloguing humanity's numerous witting and unwitting insults to the natural world.[8] It was increasingly evident that many environmental dangers lay beyond individual states' ability to control. Swedish scientists, for example, traced acidification of Swedish lakes and soils to wind-borne contaminants from sources across Europe. Sweden's experience enduring others' pollutants led it in December 1967 to propose a UN conference specially devoted to the environment.[9]

The UN Conference on the Human Environment, convened in Stockholm in June 1972, marked a watershed in global recognition of environmental degradation as a worldwide problem requiring cooperative solutions. Attended by delegations from 114 nations, it gave new impetus and legitimacy to national and international environmental policy efforts. One early 1973 poll found EU citizens cited pollution as the member states' single most important problem, above unemployment, poverty, or inflation.[10] Heightened public attention mobi-

---

[8] Among the popular works were Rachel Carson, *Silent Spring*, (Boston: Houghton Mifflin, 1962); Jean Dorst, *Before Nature Dies* [Avant que nature meure] trans. Constance D. Sherman (Boston: Houghton Mifflin, 1970 [France 1965]); Rolf Edberg, *On the Shred of a Cloud* [Spillran av ett moln] trans. Sven Åhman (Tuscaloosa, AL: University of Alabama Press, 1969 [Sweden 1966]); Richard A. Falk, *This Endangered Planet: Prospects and Proposals for Human Survival*, (New York: Random House, 1971). Among the expert assessments were President's Science Advisory Committee, *Restoring the Quality of Our Environment: Report of the Environmental Pollution Panel*, (Washington, DC: The White House, 1965); Study of Critical Environmental Problems, *Man's Impact on the Global Environment: Assessments and Recommendations for Action* (Cambridge: MIT Press, 1970); Donella H. Meadows et al., *The Limits to Growth: A Report for the Club of Rome's Project on the Predicament of Mankind* (New York: Universe Books, 1972).

[9] See Annica Kronsell, "Sweden: Setting a Good Example," in *European Environmental Policy: The Pioneers*, eds. Mikael Skou Andersen and Duncan Liefferink (Manchester: Manchester University Press, 1997).

[10] Cited in Angela Liberatore, "Problems of Transnational Policymaking: Environmental Policy in the European Community," *European Journal of Political Research* (19) 1991, p.287.

lized public policy. Gathered in Paris in October 1972 in the wake of the Stockholm conference, the EU heads of state requested that the European Commission draft a formal environmental policy for the Community.

The European Council of Ministers approved the EU's First Environmental Action Program (EAP) in November 1973.[11] The EAP affirmed in its Preamble that the "harmonious development of economic activities and a continued and balanced expansion . . . cannot now be imagined in the absence of an effective campaign to combat pollution . . . and an improvement in the . . . quality of the environment." To that end, it elaborated a set of objectives, priorities, and measures for the period 1973-1976. It also put forward a suite of guiding principles for EU policy. Pollution prevention should be preferred over post hoc remediation. Polluters should bear the costs of reducing pollutants or repairing damages they cause. Policy-making in all areas of EU activity—agriculture, industry, energy, etc.—should take environmental protection and improvement into account. In an early statement of the "subsidiarity" principle, the EAP asserted shared policy responsibility between the EU and its members; decision-making should reside at the appropriate level for taking effective measures given the type of pollution and its geographic scope. And announcing the Union's international vocation, the EAP urged the EU to play a greater role supporting international environmental action. Revised, refined, and reiterated in additional EAPs over the subsequent decades, these principles remain at the core of EU environmental policy.

Having ridden a rising tide of concern into the 1970s, the global wave of environmental mobilization receded somewhat in the face of the economic difficulties of the following years. With the decade's two oil crises, industrialized economies softened and resistance in many quarters to stricter environmental regulation hardened.[12] The EU's Second (1977-1982) and Third (1982-1987) EAPs evinced this down-

---

[11] Declaration of the Council of the European Communities and of the Representatives of the Governments of the Member States Meeting in the Council of 22 November 1973 on the Programme of Action of the European Communities on the Environment, *Official Journal of the European Communities* 15 (C112) 20 December 1973.

[12] See Andersen and Liefferink eds., *European Environmental Policy*; Miranda A. Schreurs, *Environmental Politics in Japan, Germany, and the United States* (Cambridge: Cambridge University Press, 2002).

shift in political momentum, serving largely as extensions of the first.[13] As Europe weathered an economic slump, Brussels' primordial preoccupation that environmental regulations not impede trade gave way to worry they not constrain growth. Indeed, securing the compatibility of environmental protection with economic progress would become the lodestar of European and global environmental policy.

*From Environmental Protection to Ecological Modernization and Beyond*

The late 1980s witnessed a resurgence of international environmental activity. Scientific and public apprehensions over acid rain, biodiversity loss, deforestation, ozone layer depletion, and climate change, were growing. Global threats previously unsuspected or only dimly perceived now seemed to call out for cooperative international responses.[14] At the same time, the UN's World Commission on Environment and Development prominently recast the debate pitting economic growth versus environmental protection. Its 1987 report on *Our Common Future* put the case for "sustainable development" that "meets the needs of the present without compromising the ability of future generations to meet their own needs."[15] In Europe, Green parties, having first entered national legislatures in the early 1980's, garnered increasing electoral success and political influence. The 1989 EU elections saw Green parties treble their share of the popular vote, more than doubling their Parliamentary contingent. By 1992, polls

---

[13] Resolution of the Council on the Continuation of the Implementation of the European Community Policy and Action Programme on the Environment (Second EAP), *Official Journal of the European Communities* 20 (139) 13 June 1977; Resolution of the Council on the Continuation of the Implementation of the European Community Policy and Action Programme on the Environment (Third EAP), *Official Journal of the European Communities* 26 (C46) 7 February 1983.

[14] See Gareth Porter, Janet Welsh Brown, and Pamela S. Chasek, *Global Environmental Politics*, 3rd ed. (Boulder, CO: Westview Press, 2000); The Social Learning Group, *Learning to Manage Global Environmental Risks: A Comparative History of Social Responses to Climate Change, Ozone Depletion, and Acid Rain, Vol.1* (Cambridge: MIT Press, 2001).

[15] WCED, *Our Common Future* (Oxford: Oxford University Press, 1987), p.43. Commonly known as the "Bruntland Report" after the Commission's chair, Norwegian Prime Minister Gro Harlem Brundtland, the publication became an international best seller, reprinted five times in 1987 and seven times in 1988-1990. While sustainable development gained particular credence from the WCED, the idea predates the Commission report. See Peter J. Hammond, "Is There Anything New in the Concept of Sustainable Development?" in *The Environment After Rio: International Law and Economics*, eds. Luigi Campiglio et al. (London: Graham & Trotman, 1994) for a brief economic genealogy.

found 85% of EU country citizens thought environmental protection "an immediate and urgent problem" and up to 91% supported a common EU environmental policy.[16]

Equally importantly, a generation after and six new members on from its inception, the EU had embarked upon a revitalization of the European project. The resultant reforms signally enhanced the Union's environmental authority. Previously, EU environmental regulation stood on uncertain footing, relying on a generous reading of the power to harmonize national policies impacting the internal market.[17] The 1987 Single European Act planted environmental policy on solid legal ground and committed EU environmental law to a "high level of protection." It inserted a specific Environment Title in the EEC Treaty, incorporating elements contained in the EAPs such as polluter pays, prevention at source, and adherence to subsidiarity. The 1992 Maastricht Treaty stipulated environmental policy should be based on the precautionary principle, emphasizing preventive action to counter prospective risks. The 1997 Amsterdam Treaty fixed sustainable development among the EU's fundamental aims and mandated environmental protection be integrated into the definition and implementation of Community policies and activities.[18]

The EU's Fourth (1987-1992) and Fifth EAPs (1992-2000) reflected these developments.[19] The Fifth program in particular capped the Union's evolution from viewing environmental protection

---

[16] Cited in Elizabeth Bomberg, *Green Parties and Politics in the European Union* (London: Routledge, 1998), pp.94, 13.

[17] For discussion of the evolving legal basis for EU environment policy, see Ludwig Krämer, *E.C. Treaty and Environmental Law*, 2nd ed. (London: Sweet & Maxwell, 1995) by a former Head of Legal Matters in the European Commission's Environment Directorate; Andreas R. Ziegler, *Trade and Environmental Law in the European Community* (Oxford: Clarendon Press, 1996).

[18] See David Wilkinson, "Maastricht and the Environment: The Implications for the EC's Environment Policy of the Treaty on European Union," *Journal of Environmental Law* 4 (2) 1992; Andrew Jordan, "Step Change or Stasis? EC Environmental Policy After the Amsterdam Treaty," *Journal of Environmental Politics* 7 (1) 1998.

[19] Resolution of the Council on the Continuation of the Implementation of the European Community Policy and Action Programme on the Environment (Fourth EAP), *Official Journal of the European Communities* 328, 7 December 1987; Towards Sustainability: A Community Programme of Policy and Action in Relation to the Environment and Sustainable Development (Fifth EAP), *Official Journal of the European Communities* C 138, 17 May 1993.

as subsidiary to the common market imperative to improving environmental quality as a primary goal in its own right. The Fifth EAP embraced sustainable development, declaring, "it is essential to view environmental quality and economic growth as mutually dependent."[20] Within the EU, it held, sound environmental and economic management can complement each other. Policies encouraging resource efficiency, for instance, can foster innovation in environmentally beneficial clean technologies. These technologies can in turn create new industries and jobs and boost the EU's global competitiveness, a policy rationale dubbed "ecological modernization."[21] Beyond the EU, the program stressed that many environmental threats ignore borders and called the Union to exercise its moral, economic, and political authority to support collaborative solutions to international environmental problems. The current Sixth EAP (2001-2010) cements this transition. It summons the EU to "work towards strengthening international environmental governance" through multilateral cooperation, conventions, and institutions, and act as "a leading partner in the protection of the global environment and in the pursuit of a sustainable development."[22]

The EU now considers environmental sustainability integral to its future prosperity and crucial to long-term global stability. Persuaded the Union faces "a quantum shift resulting from globalisation . . . requir[ing] a radical transformation of the European economy," the EU heads of state, meeting in Lisbon in March 2000, proclaimed the "strategic goal for the next decade: to become the most competitive and dynamic knowledge-based economy in the world, capable of sustainable economic growth." The market, investment, and employment opportunities environmental policies can create, the EU believes, hold

---

[20] Towards Sustainability, p.28.

[21] See European Commission, *Growth, Competitiveness and Employment: the Challenges and Ways Forward Into the 21ˢᵗ Century—White Paper*, COM(93)700 final, Brussels, 5 December 1993; European Commission, *Communication on Environment and Employment (Building a Sustainable Europe)*, COM(97) 592 final, Brussels, 18 November 1997. On ecological modernization, see e.g., Arthur P.J. Mol and David A. Sonnenfeld eds., *Ecological Modernization Around the World: Perspectives and Critical Debates* (London: Frank Cass, 2000).

[22] Decision No 1600/2002/EC of the European Parliament and of the Council Laying the Sixth Community Environment Action Programme, *Official Journal of the European Communities* L 242, 10 August 2002, pp.14, 4.

one of the keys to realizing the "Lisbon Strategy."[23] Sustainability is also an important international objective. Environmental degradation counts among the emergent threats EU External Relations Commissioner Chris Patten branded "'the dark side of globalisation.' . . . [It] must be placed at the centre of our thinking on both security and development." Left unaddressed, deteriorating environmental conditions can hamper poverty reduction, exacerbate competition for natural resources, and provoke population displacements, political turbulence, even violent conflict. "Put simply, we have no choice but to make the promotion of sustainable development as much a part of our fight for global security as . . . even our armed forces."[24] From an ancillary amenity in the original common market, environmental protection and global sustainability have become an avowed priority of EU policy in the twenty-first century.

## The EU as an International Environmental Actor

The EU holds a unique, Janus-faced place in international environmental politics. The Union and the member states share joint environmental policy-making competence in the EU's internal policies and external relations. The division of powers and responsibilities between them is overlapping and "non-zero sum."[25] As such, the EU is both a political arena and a policy agent. It provides the institutional forum in which the member countries collectively forge EU policies. At the same time, the EU is itself a player in the policy process, raising

---

[23] European Council, "Presidency Conclusions," Lisbon European Council, 23 and 24 March 2000, at http://ue.eu.int/ueDocs/cms_Data/docs/pressData/en/ec/00100-r1.en0.htm ; see also European Council, "Presidency Conclusions," Göteborg European Council, 15 and 16 June 2001, at http://ue.eu.int/ueDocs/cms_Data/docs/pressData/en/ec/00200-r1.en1.pdf ; European Commission, *Facing the Challenge: The Lisbon Strategy for Growth and Employment*, Report from the High Level Group chaired by Wim Kok (Luxembourg: Office for Official Publications of the European Communities, 2004), pp.35-38.

[24] Rt. Hon. Chris Patten, External Relations Commissioner, "Europe in the World: CFSP and its Relation to Development," Overseas Development Institute, 7 November 2003, at http://europa.eu.int/comm/external_relations/news/patten/sp07_11_03.htm See also European Commission, *A Sustainable Europe for a Better World: A European Union Strategy for Sustainable Development*, COM(2001)264 final, Brussels, 15 May 2001; European Council, *A Secure Europe in a Better World: European Security Strategy*, Brussels, 12 December 2003, at http://www.iss-eu.org/solana/solanae.pdf

[25] See Fritz W. Scharpf, "The Joint-Decision Trap: Lessons from German Federalism and European Integration," *Public Administration* 66 (3) 1988.

issues, advancing positions, engaging and engaged by governments and interest groups.[26] The marble-cake intermingling of authority continues beyond policy elaboration to the execution and enforcement of EU "directives" and "regulations." Directives define a framework for national measures. They mandate a binding result but leave the form and method of meeting their obligations to the member states. Regulations are directly applicable to the member states, automatically entering national law. In both cases, national and local authorities effectively implement EU legislation in practice, while remaining answerable to European institutions in principle.[27]

*Environmental Policy-Making in the EU*

EU environmental policy-making is a "multi-layered" process.[28] Several EU institutions as well as the national governments play important roles. Atop the EU's policy-making apparatus sits the European Council, composed of the member country heads of state and or government plus the President of the European Commission. The EU's paramount decision-making authority, the Council works by consensus, only very exceptionally resorting to a vote. Though the European Council rarely takes up specific environmental matters, it provides strategic direction and political guidance. Its "Presidency Conclusions" often frame the issues for environmental policy-making, as when the March 2000 summit launched the "Lisbon Strategy."

At the core of all EU policy-making stands the European Commission, a combination of multinational civil service and international secretariat exercising a mixture of supranational administrative

---

[26] See Wayne Sandholtz and Alec Stone Sweet eds., *European Integration and Supranational Governance* (Oxford: Oxford University Press, 1998); Albert Weale et al., *Environmental Governance in Europe: An Ever Closer Ecological Union?* (Oxford: Oxford University Press, 2000).

[27] See Krämer, *E.C. Treaty and Environmental Law*, pp.131-144; Wyn Grant, Duncan Matthews, and Peter Newell, *The Effectiveness of European Union Environmental Policy* (London: MacMillan Press, 2000), pp.66-88.

[28] Alberta Sbragia, "Environmental Policy: The 'Push-Pull' of Policy-Making," in *Policy Making in the European Union*, 3rd ed., eds. Helen Wallace and William Wallace (Oxford: Oxford University Press, 1996), p.236. For thorough treatments of the EU institutions, see Desmond Dinan, *Ever Closer Union: An Introduction to European Integration*, 2nd ed. (Boulder, CO: Lynne Rienner, 1999); Neill Nugent, *The Government and Politics of the European Union*, 5th ed. (Durham, NC: Duke University Press, 2003).

and executive functions. Only the Commission may initiate Community legislation. The Directorate-General (DG) Environment, created in 1981, manages environmental policy. It develops policy proposals for legislative approval and oversees their execution, wielding substantial authority to formulate the detailed secondary rules necessary to implement EU environmental regulation.

The Council of Ministers comprises the member state ministers for given policy areas. The Council of Environment Ministers is the primary forum for explicitly intergovernmental input into EU environmental actions. While it cannot initiate environmental legislation, it can request submissions from the Commission. It also frequently issues resolutions and recommendations to spark or shape Commission policy proposals. The Council of Environment Ministers negotiates final agreement on and must pass all environmental legislation. Decisions take place by qualified majority voting, a procedure weighting each member country's vote in rough proportion to its population.

The European Parliament (EP) shares legislative duties with the Council of Ministers. Considered the EU's most pro-environment body, the EP cannot initiate legislation, but it may ask the Commission for proposals. Like the Council of Ministers, the Parliament's Environment committee has effectively used independently prepared "own-initiative" reports pro-actively to prod the Commission's environmental agenda.[29] By far Parliament's most significant powers are its rights to amend and veto EU law. Under the "co-decision" procedure, extended by the Maastricht and Amsterdam Treaties to include environmental affairs, the EP may propose amendments to legislation before the Council of Ministers. If, after three rounds of consultations, either body declines to approve a common text, the measure does not pass.

The European Court of Justice interprets and applies Community law; assures its consistent application; and ensures EU and member state actions and international treaties remain compatible with its provisions. It hears cases brought by member governments, EU institutions, and—under certain circumstances—by local authorities, interest groups, or individuals, ruling by simple majority. Court decisions are binding on member states and it can impose financial penalties for

---

[29] See David Judge, "'Predestined to Save the Earth': The Environment Committee of the European Parliament," *Journal of Environmental Politics* 1 (4) 1992.

non-compliance. Despite the initial lack of a clear treaty basis for environment policy, the Court has long upheld a broad reading of the EU's legislative competence in this field.[30]

### The EU in International Environmental Policy-Making

The same considerations that initially motivated the EU's internal environmental policies also underlay its early approach to external environmental relations. Varying national adhesions to and implementation of international environmental accords could impinge upon the free movement of goods within the European market. Yet while the Treaty of Rome specifically empowered the EU to conduct external commercial relations, it said nothing of the environment. Then in 1971 the European Court judged in its European Road Transport Agreement decision that wherever the EU has enacted common rules internally, there too it implicitly acquires authority to assume international commitments towards the same ends. Subsequent Court opinions augmented the EU's external powers, allowing it to enter international agreements deemed necessary to obtain Union objectives even in the absence of internal legislation. The EU soon joined member states in negotiating several accords, such as the 1974 Paris Convention on Marine Pollution and the 1979 Geneva Convention on Long Range Transboundary Air Pollution.

When the 1987 Single European Act formally incorporated the environment into the EEC Treaty, it also expressly established the EU's authority to co-operate with third countries and international organizations within its areas of competence. Critically, actual EU and member state competences vary across environmental issues. In a few fields, fisheries are one, the EU exercises sole authority. Most international environmental matters entail shared competences, with the EU negotiating alongside its members towards "mixed agreements" to be ratified by both the Union and national governments. In fact, the members have carefully guarded their prerogatives in this domain, never ceding exclusive powers for environmental agreements to the EU.[31]

---

[30] See Ida J. Koppen, "The Role of the European Court of Justice," in *European Integration and Environmental Policy*, eds. J.D. Liefferink, P.D. Lowe, and A.P.J. Mol (New York: Belhaven Press, 1993);

[31] See Krämer, *E.C. Treaty and Environmental Law*, pp.84-86; Ziegler, *Trade and Environmental Law in the European Community*, pp.199-208.

Even where the EU enjoys internal authority to undertake environmental diplomacy, it has had to earn international acceptance of this Community competence. It is not a member of many environmental negotiating fora, such as the United Nations Environment Program or the International Maritime Organization, and has only observer status at the UN General Assembly. Consequently, the EU must usually obtain the right to attend treaty conferences held under their auspices on a case-by-case basis. The individual EU countries are UN members and do attempt to co-ordinate their stances on questions relevant to the Union. But with the rising salience of transboundary issues, the EU increasingly sought recognition as a distinct participant in conventions involving its competences and to be accorded more robust standing—giving it "speaking" rights and the ability to submit proposals—than the observer rank typically granted international organizations.[32] Many negotiations now make formal allowance for the participation of Regional Economic Integration Organizations, a novel legal class of which the EU is the unique current example. By this means the EU may take full part in the agreements, even casting the collective votes of its members in its areas of competence, though not holding a separate vote of its own.

EU delegations arrive at the bargaining table directed by a mandate from the Council of Ministers. In those areas of the negotiation that involve Community competence, the Commission formulates this "common platform." Normally DG Environment prepares the draft mandate, but the complex nature of many environmental issues frequently necessitates contributions from several sectors. Crafting policy for the UN Framework Convention on Climate Change, for example, originally involved ten Directorates.[33] The final Council mandate, in most cases agreed by qualified majority voting, distributes authority between the Union and the members, defining the EU's role in the proceedings. Where the EU maintains exclusive authority, the Commission negotiates for the Union and the member states. Where the EU shares competence with its members, "dual representation"

---

[32] See e.g., European Commission, *Relations Between the European Community and International Organizations* (Luxembourg: Office for Official Publications of the European Communities, 1989).

[33] Jon B. Skjærseth, "The Climate Policy of the EC: Too Hot to Handle?" *Journal of Common Market Studies* 32 (1) 1994.

obtains. The Commission then represents the former and the country occupying the Council Presidency represents the latter, each stepping forward in turn depending on the question at hand. Where the states retain exclusive competence, they speak for themselves. Co-ordination meetings between the states and Commission endeavor to attune national and EU positions across the various issues arising during negotiations.[34] Conventions concluded by the Commission must be approved by the Council of Ministers with the assent of the Parliament, whence they become binding on all EU countries. Member states may ratify individually, as part of the EU, or both.

Just as Community environmental policy gradually grew beyond harmonizing regulations across the common market, so the EU's international agenda has expanded beyond negotiating particular conventions to the preservation of the global commons. EU policy now aims at "the integration of environmental concerns and objectives into all aspects of the Community's external relations," and to promote the environment among the concerns and objectives of the international community.[35] Environmental protection figures in formulating and implementing the EU's programs of international cooperation, development aid, and technical assistance in every region of the globe. In Europe and abroad, the EU advocates incorporating environmental considerations into all areas of policy-making in pursuit of sustainable development.[36]

## From Fifteen to Twenty-Five

By the close of the twentieth century, the EU had constructed one of the world's strongest and most extensive systems of environmental protection. Its neighbors to the East, in contrast, had suffered enormous environmental damage over the preceding decades. As membership negotiations with the Central and Eastern European countries

---

[34] See Sbragia, "Institution-Building from Below and Above"; John Vogler, "The External Environmental Policy of the European Union," in *Yearbook of International Co-operation on Environment and Development 2003/2004*, eds. Olav Schram Stokke and Øystein B. Thommessen (London: Earthscan, 2003).

[35] Sixth EAP Art.2(6).

[36] See, Sixth EAP Art. 9; European Commission, *A Sustainable Europe for a Better World*; European Commission, *Towards a Global Partnership for Sustainable Development*, COM(2002) 82 final, Brussels, 13 February 2002.

(CEECs) began, the EU recognized that "Enlargement is the biggest challenge ever for EU Environmental Policy and one of the ultimate tests for it."[37] The entrants face sizable environmental and institutional hurdles integrating the Union's regulatory regime. Yet the EU also envisages enlargement as offering important opportunities to enhance environmental quality in the accession states, reduce their transboundary environmental impacts, and catalyze their sustainable economic modernization.[38]

*The Environment in the Accession States*

To many observers looking over the fallen Iron Curtain, it seemed a "Green Curtain" had divided Europe as well.[39] An emphasis on heavy industry and centrally planned production targets drove the Communist regimes' command economies. They paid little heed to conservation or pollution prevention. After forty years of state socialism's equal insensitivity to economic incentives and environmental externalities, severe pollution plagued the CEECs. One 1990 study examined seventeen issues, from waste disposal to habitat destruction, for each of six countries, so generating 102 evaluations. Of these, one was judged "catastrophic," sixteen "major," thirty-two "serious," and thirty-eight "significant." Just fifteen appeared either effectively managed or negligible problems.[40]

Energy policy typified the system's economic inefficiencies and environmental indifference. State subsidies held energy prices well below production costs. Ineffectual or nonexistent price signals prevailed up

---

[37] Domingo Jimenez-Beltran, Executive Director of the European Environment Agency, quoting EU Environment Commissioner Ritt Bjerregaard, in "Environment in the European Union—Situation and Prospects," European Parliament Public Hearing, Brussels, 20 April 1999, at http://reports.eea.eu.int/SPE19990420/en/page001.html

[38] See e.g., "Interview: Commissioner Bjerregaard," *Enlarging the Environment: Newsletter from the European Commission on Environmental Approximation*, no.5, July 1997.

[39] I borrow the expression from Christopher Williams, "From Iron Curtain into Green Curtain: The Environmental Crisis in Central and Eastern Europe and the Emerging Green Movements/Parties, 1989-91," paper presented at the Conference on New Perspectives for Social Democracy in Central and Eastern Europe," Brussels, October 1991, cited in Volkmar Lauber, "The Political Infrastructure of Environmental Politics in Western and Eastern Europe," in *Environmental Cooperation in Europe: the Political Dimension*, ed. Otmar Höll (Boulder, CO: Westview Press, 1994), p.262 note 28.

[40] Jeremy Russell, *Environmental Issues in Eastern Europe: Setting an Agenda* (London: Royal Institute for International Affairs/World Conservation Union, 1990), pp.2-3.

to the international level. Bulk pipeline deliveries of natural gas from Russia to Lithuania, for example, went un-metered at the border. Absent real cost constraints on consumption, energy use per unit of economic output was three times or more the Western European average, with the attendant environmental consequences.[41] Given the weight of energy intensive industries in their economies, the importance of coal in their fuel mix, and their outdated technologies, the CEECs generated air pollutants like particulates, sulfur dioxide ($SO_2$) and nitrogen oxides ($NO_x$)—responsible for acid rain and smog formation—as well as the greenhouse culprits carbon dioxide and methane all at levels multiples above EU emissions relative to GDP.[42]

Serious liquid and solid waste pollution also afflicted the region. Factories, farms, and cities commonly discharged untreated industrial effluents, agricultural run-off, and raw municipal sewage straight into rivers and lakes. In the late 1980's, one-third of Latvia's wastewater and two-fifths of sewage in Czechoslovakia, Lithuania, and Poland was not treated at all.[43] Solid waste disposal presented another widespread problem, as improper incineration and landfill dumping released heavy metals and other toxic substances. CEEC nations produced 520 million metric tons of industrial waste annually in the late 1980's, compared to 330 million metric tons for all of OECD Europe. Most of these wastes ended in landfills, often without proper regulatory controls. Two-fifths of Poland's hazardous materials dumps, for instance, operated without legal safeguards.[44]

---

[41] David Stanners and Philippe Bourdeau eds., *Europe's Environment: The Dobří? Assessment* (Copenhagen: European Environment Agency, 1995), pp.408, 313.

[42] Russell, *Environmental Issues in Eastern Europe*, pp.9, 13, 15; Stanners and Bourdeau eds., *Europe's Environment*, p.401; World Resources Institute, *World Resources 1990-1991* (New York: Oxford University Press, 1990), pp.19, 346-349. For economic and emissions time series data from 1980-2000 for individual EU countries and CEECs, see OECD, *OECD Environmental Data Compendium 2002* (Paris: OECD, 2002) at http://www.oecd.org/document/21/0,2340,en_2649_34303_2516565_1_1_1_1,00.html

[43] Russell, *Environmental Issues in Eastern Europe*, pp.16-18; Stanners and Bourdeau eds., *Europe's Environment*, pp.337-339; F.W. Carter, "Poland," in *Environmental Problems in Eastern Europe*, 2nd ed., F.W. Carter and David Turnock eds. (London: Routledge, 1996), p.113; Juris Dreifelds, "The Environmental Impact of Estonia, Latvia and Lithuania on the Baltic Sea Region," in *Environmental Security and Quality after Communism: Eastern Europe and the Soviet Successor States*, eds. Joan DeBardeleben and John Hannigan (Boulder, CO: Westview Press, 1995), p.161.

[44] Stanners and Bourdeau eds., *Europe's Environment*, pp. 163, 349, 577-579; F.W. Carter and David Turnock, "A Review of Environmental Issues in the Light of the Transition," in Carter and Turnock eds., *Environmental Problems in Eastern Europe*, p.214.

The environmental impacts of these accumulated affronts were considerable. Dense smog frequently shrouded urban and industrial regions. Yearly average air pollutant concentrations in parts of the Czech Republic and Poland reached levels tenfold those in Western Europe. Daily values for $SO_2$ and particulates in some areas could exceed World Health Organization guidelines by a factor of four. Acid deposition levels across much of Poland, Czechoslovakia, and Hungary ranked among Europe's worst. Acidification exceeded critical loads in certain ecosystems by twenty times or more.[45] As dire as the threats to air and land were those to water. In the Czech Republic in the 1980s, just 17% of river waters qualified as potable after disinfection (Class I), and 34% were still unfit to drink after both physical and chemical treatment (Class III). Only 4% of Polish rivers and 1% of lakes attained Class I quality, while 40% of rivers were unclassed, their waters unsuitable even for industrial uses.[46]

Such environmental depredation imposed tremendous costs. Annual economic losses to the CEECs from health effects, lowered productivity, damages to assets and resources, etc., have been figured at 2% to 10% of GDP.[47] Most sobering is the human toll. Environmental pollution is a factor in a host of health problems. Exposures to various contaminants at the levels CEEC citizens experienced are associated with increased incidences of respiratory, cardiovascular, and blood diseases; cancers; nervous system and developmental disorders; and waterborne infectious diseases.[48] In 1988, the Polish Academy of Sciences found environmental conditions in twenty-seven areas, covering a tenth of the nation's land and a third of its population, were hazardous to human health. That same year, Hungary's National Institute of Public Health estimated one in twenty-four disabilities and one in every seventeen deaths in the country could be attributed to air pollution. In Czechoslovakia, the smog

---

[45] See Stanners and Bourdeau eds., *Europe's Environment*, pp.36-47.

[46] Russell, *Environmental Issues in Eastern Europe*, pp.16-17; Carter, "Poland," p.113; Cf. Stanners and Bourdeau eds., *Europe's Environment*, pp.82ff.

[47] World Bank, *Environmental Action Plan for Central and Eastern Europe: Setting Priorities*, Abridged Version of the Document Endorsed by the Ministerial Conference, Lucerne, Switzerland, 28-30 April 1993 (Washington, DC: World Bank, 1998), p.6.

[48] See WHO European Centre for Environmental Health, *Concern for Europe's Tomorrow: Health and the Environment in the WHO European Region* (Stuttgart: World Health Organization, 1995), pp.444-518.

and particulate concentrations occurring in the 1980s and early 1990s were linked to spikes of up to nearly 10% in daily mortality rates.[49] Throughout Central and Eastern Europe, environmental pollution still contributes to lower life expectancy and higher disease and mortality burdens than in the EU-15.[50]

The repercussions of environmental neglect in the accession states were not confined within their borders. Even less than the Iron Curtain did the Green Curtain ultimately seal East from West. On the contrary. When in 1993 a dozen European nations and the EU identified 132 "hot spots" for remediation to combat Baltic Sea pollution, 77 sites— including 39 of 47 "priority" targets—lay in the CEECs.[51] Some 50% to 75% of the $SO_2$ and an estimated 80% to 90% of the particulates liable for Western European smog episodes in the 1980s originated in Eastern Europe.[52] And the continued operation in the Czech Republic, Hungary, Lithuania, and Slovakia of fourteen Soviet-designed nuclear reactors particularly troubled the EU post-Chernobyl.[53]

Yet to characterize EU expansion as a Green Giant taking in a uniformly Dirty Dozen would be mistaken. It would obscure both enlargement's environmental complexity and the entrants' diversity. Though the CEECs suffer many common woes, significant variations

---

[49] Carter, "Poland," p.109; Carter and Turnock, "A Review of Environmental Issues," pp.222; Don Hinrichsen and Istvan Láng, "Hungary," in Carter and Turnock eds., *Environmental Problems in Eastern Europe*, p.90; Annette Peters et al., "Associations between Mortality and Air Pollution in Central Europe," *Environmental Health Perspectives* 108 (4) 2000; Jitka Jelänkoväj and Martin Braniåj, "Mortality During Winter Smog Episodes 1982, 1985, 1987, 1993 in the Czech Republic," *International Archives of Occupational and Environmental Health* 74 (8) 2001.

[50] See WHO, *Concern for Europe's Tomorrow*; R.E. Little, "Public Health in Central and Eastern Europe and the Role of Environmental Pollution," *Annual Review of Public Health* (19) 1998; WHO, *The World Health Report 2002* (Geneva: World Health Organization, 2002), pp.67-73.

[51] Twenty-one hot spots, including the eight remaining "priority" sites, were located in Belarus, Russia, and Ukraine. Denmark, Germany, Finland and Sweden, the EU littoral states, were home to the other thirty-four hot spots. See HELCOM [Helsinki Commission], *The Baltic Sea Joint Comprehensive Action Programme*, Baltic Sea Environmental Proceedings no.48 (Helsinki: Government Printing Centre, 1993).

[52] Stanners and Bourdeau eds., *Europe's Environment*, p. 41.

[53] European Commission, *Agenda 2000: Communication for a Wider and Stronger Europe*, DOC/97/6, Strasbourg, 15 July 1997, pp.65-66; European Parliament, *Nuclear Safety in the Applicant Countries of Central and Eastern Europe*, Briefing Note 40, Strasbourg, 22 March 1999. Bulgaria operates another six Soviet reactors. Romania has one Canadian-built reactor and Slovenia two US-built reactors.

of degree and kind exist between and within countries. So, pollution stemming from energy use bedevils every state in the region. But Poland derives 74% of its primary energy production from hard coal, Lithuania 75% from nuclear, and Estonia 78% from oil shale, each fuel creating distinct production and waste issues.[54] Many analyses note the CEECs present a patchwork of environmental blight, hot spots like Poland's 27 hazardous zones juxtaposed with largely unaffected areas.[55] But perhaps a kaleidoscope provides a better metaphor. With each turn of the lens focusing on a different pollutant—lead, $SO_2$—in a different medium—water, air—at a different scale, a different pattern of impacts emerges. Acid rain falling on farm fields degrades the soil; in forests it defoliates trees, and in cities corrodes facades.

*The Challenges of Accession*

Accession requires candidate countries assume the *acquis commu-nautaire*, the collected commitments and responsibilities contained in the EU's treaties, legislation, and international accords.[56] Approximation, as the process is known in EU parlance, demands applicants fulfill three duties upon entry: transposition, implementation, and enforcement. Transposition enjoins entrants to fully integrate the mandates of EU law into their national legislation and procedures. Implementation entails the practical application of the *acquis*, including providing the infrastructure and resources necessary for the competent authorities to carry out their duties. Enforcement calls for the establishment of appropriate measures to effect compliance with EU law. By the same token, approximation also imposes three challenges: financial, institutional, and political.

To realize their accession obligations, the new members will incur appreciable expense to install and operate environmental facilities,

---

[54] Figures for 2002. Derived from Eurostat, *Energy: Yearly Statistics Data 2002* (Luxembourg: Office for Official Publications of the European Communities, 2004).

[55] Russell, *Environmental Issues in Eastern Europe*, p.29; REC, *Strategic Environmental Issues in Central and Eastern Europe: Regional Report Vol.1* (Budapest: Regional Environmental Center, August 1994), p.10.

[56] See European Commission, *Guide to the Approximation of European Union Environmental Legislation*, SEC(7) 1608, Brussels, 25 August 1997, revised and updated January 1998. Of the EU's vast catalog of environmental law, the Commission determined the entrants would effectively have to adopt and apply some 70 directives and 21 regulations.

pollution control, and waste management systems.[57] Total outlays have been tallied at €80 billion to €110 billion for the ten CEEC enlargement states. Projected costs vary widely country to country, from €1.5 billion to €2.4 billion in Latvia to €22 billion to €43 billion in Poland. So too does the estimated economic burden, from 2% of GDP annually for the Czech Republic up to 11% for Bulgaria. On average, the EU figures compliance with the environmental *acquis* will demand 2% to 3% of entrants' GDP for several years. In 2000, however, combined public and private environmental spending ranged from 0.5% of GDP in Latvia to 2.2% in Hungary, averaging 1.6% of GDP across the CEEC ten. Though comparable to EU country spending in GDP terms, this amounted to just €37 per capita given the CEECs' smaller economies, compared to €243 in the UK and €272 in Germany. Overall, the CEECs' environmental investments for 1996-2000 covered only 16% of their estimated needs.[58]

In addition to physical infrastructure, adopting the environmental *acquis* requires adapting the entrants' institutional infrastructure. The CEECs were not regulatory *tabula rasa* prior to enlargement. Many established environment ministries at the same time as the West. Many possessed strict legislation. Yet the Communist environmental commitment was mostly rhetorical. Environmental agencies were deliberately feeble. Enforcement of environmental statutes was negligible, adherence nominal. Czechoslovakia's Water Act contained some 2400 exemptions, including one for all of Prague.[59] Emerging from

---

[57] The EU has made several forms of financial assistance available. Its PHARE, SAPARD, and ISPA programs provided €2.5 billion annually to the ten CEE countries in the pre-accession period to support their transition, including environmental projects. DG Environment's LIFE Financial Instrument for the Environment added €640 million per year in co-financing for various initiatives. With their accession in 2004, the entrants gain access to the EU's Structural and Cohesion Funds, budgeted at €21.7 billion for 2004-2006. All along, however, the EU has emphasized that 90% of the necessary environmental financing would have to come form the new members' own sources. See European Parliament, *The Enlargement Process of the EU: Consequences in the Field of the Environment*, Working Paper, ENVI 106 EN, Luxembourg, April 2003, pp.15-23.

[58] EDC Ltd./EPE absl, *Compliance Costing for Approximation of EU Environmental Legislation in the CEEC*, Dublin/Brussels, April 1997; European Commission, *The Challenge of Environmental Financing in the Candidate Countries*, COM(2001) 304 final, Brussels, 8 June 2001; Eurostat, *Environmental Protection Expenditure in Accession Countries Data 1996-2000* (Luxembourg: Office for Official Publications of the European Communities, 2002).

[59] Andrew Tickle and Joseph Vavrou?ek, "Environmental Politics in the Former Czechoslovakia," in *Environment and Society in Eastern Europe*, eds. Ian Welsh and Andrew Tickle (New York: Longman, 1998), p.120.

Communist rule, the new governments undertook sweeping reforms in many areas, the environment being just one, enacting new laws and creating new institutions. Environmental accession, then, is no matter of simply slotting EU ordnances into open spaces in the entrants' legal code. It entails meshing the ends and obligations of often complex EU regulation into the practices and performance of domestic institutions still in the midst of great political and socio-economic change.[60]

Applying the *acquis* will sorely tax the CEECs' administrative capacities. Environmental ministries remain politically weak compared to other government offices. Negotiations between the Finance and Interior Ministries determine budgeting for the Czech Environmental Ministry, for instance. Next door, Slovakia's Energy and Agriculture Ministries routinely develop policy without consulting the Environment Ministry. Environmental agencies often struggle to marshal the financial, technical, and human resources necessary to implement and enforce EU legislation. Especially at the regional and local levels often charged with much environmental management, authorities frequently lack sufficient personnel, training, and equipment. In its comprehensive assessments of the candidates' progress six months before accession, the EU found five of the CEECs still only partially satisfying the legislative and administrative prerequisites of membership on many environmental issues. All displayed shortcomings in various areas, from transposing regulations to staffing offices.[61]

Mirroring these domestic difficulties, the same lack of institutional resources will likely hamper the CEECs initial participation in

---

[60] See e.g., Ladislav Miko, "The Czech Republic on the Way to Accession: Problems in the Environmental Field"; Tomasz Zylicz and Katharina Holzinger, "Environmental Policy in Poland and the Consequences of Approximation to the European Union"; and R?ta Ba?kyt? and Ar?nas Kundrotas, "Environmental Policy in Lithuania and the Acquis Communautaire," all in *Environmental Policy in a European Union of Variable Geometry? The Challenge of the Next Enlargement*, eds. Katharina Holzinger and Peter Knoepfel (Basel: Helbing & Lichtenhahn, 2000).

[61] ECOTEC Research and Consulting, *Administrative Capacity for Implementation and Enforcement of EU Environmental Policy in the 13 Candidate Countries*, DGENV Contract: Environment Policy in the Applicant Countries and Their Preparations for Accession, Final Report, Brussels, 2001; European Commission, *Comprehensive Monitoring Report on the State of Preparedness for EU Membership of the Czech Republic, Estonia, Cyprus, Hungary, Latvia, Lithuania, Malta, Poland, Slovenia, and Slovakia*, Brussels, October 2003. See also the individual country monitoring reports, available at http://www.europa.eu.int/comm/enlargement/report_2003/

Brussels' complex policy-making structures. A crucial challenge to future environmental policy in the enlarged EU resides not in the rigor of Community legislation but in the adaptability of CEEC institutions.[62] The EU's environmental *acquis* embodies both particular administrative procedures and a particular administrative culture in its aptitudes, attitude, and outlook. How rapidly and effectively can CEEC institutions adjust their performance to the EU's regulatory style? How well will they be able to identify and reproduce their successes, rectify and learn from their mistakes, participate in the EU's conclaves, contribute to its policy debates? These feats cannot be taken for granted. As the eminent Polish parliamentarian and historian Bronislaw Geremek has cautioned, "institutions can be established rather quickly, but political mentalities change very slowly."[63]

The EU foresaw many of these financial and institutional challenges and guided the applicants to develop plans for meeting them.[64] But some observers hold the EU's own actions precipitate a third test tied to the strains of the first two. As in earlier enlargements, the EU precluded any possibility entrants might partially adopt the *aquis* on the grounds that differential adhesion to Union law opens the door to its dilution. Instead, the EU agreed to limited temporary derogations, allowing the new members additional time after accession to phase in certain legislation.[65] Some candidates protested having to apply the *acquis* before being assured entrance to the club. But the enlargement negotiations' political dynamic left them little bargaining leverage to press a different course. After once intimating it might postpone accession if the EU refused compromise on compliance deadlines, Poland rapidly retreated, unwilling to purchase lesser obligations at

---

[62] See Phedon Nicolaides, *Enlargement of the EU and Effective Implementation of Community Rules: An Integration-Based Approach*, Working Paper 99/W/04 (Maastricht: European Institute of Public Administration, 1999).

[63] Bronislaw Geremek, cited in Peter Hardi, "East Central European Policy Making: The Case of the Environment," in Höll ed., *Environmental Cooperation in Europe*, p.190; see also Susan Baker and Petr Jehliâka, "Dilemmas of Transition: the Environment, Democracy and Economic Reform in East Central Europe—An Introduction," *Environmental Politics*, special issue 7 (1) 1998.

[64] European Commission, *Agenda 2000*; European Commission, *Accession Strategies for Environment: Meeting the Challenge of Enlargement with the Candidate Countries in Central and Eastern Europe*, COM(98) 294, Brussels, 20 May 1998.

[65] See European Commission, *Agenda 2000*, p.57; European Parliament, *The Enlargement Process of the EU*, pp.2-3.

the price of later admission to the Union.[66] Consequently, some analysts consider the CEECs may see accession's environmental criteria as a unilateral imposition, undermining their legitimacy. When observing those rules inevitably bumps up against other political and economic priorities, the CEECs' determination to implement the more difficult commitments may falter.[67]

## The Enlarged EU and International Environmental Politics

Since May 2004, the questions surrounding environmental enlargement take on a new cast. With the transition from applicants to members of the Union, the challenges EU environmental policy previously posed to the CEECs from without become challenges the CEECs pose to EU environmental policy from within. Enlargement's ramifications extend far beyond the EU's borders. Accession brings EU policies to bear on the CEECs' considerable environmental problems. It also brings the CEECs' politics and preferences to bear on the EU's environmental policy in Europe and in the world. At home, the EU will have the interests of twenty-five states before it. Abroad it will have the interests of twenty-five states behind it.

*Environmental Policy in the Enlarged EU*

In light of their manifest environmental and institutional burdens, many analysts anticipate the accession countries will exert a marked drag on EU environmental policy.[68] By the EU's own admission, the

---

[66] John M. Kramer, "EU Enlargement and the Environment: Six Challenges," *Environmental Politics* 13 (1) 2004, pp.294-295. See also Joanne Caddy, "Harmonisation and Asymmetry: Environmental Policy Co-ordination Between the European Union and Central Europe," *Journal of European Public Policy* 4 (3) 1997.

[67] Susan Baker and Ian Welsh, "Differentiating Western Influences on Transition Societies in Eastern Europe: A Preliminary Exploration," *Journal of European Area Studies* 8 (1) 2000, pp.94ff; Kerstin Tews, "EU Enlargement and Environment," in *Problems and Chances in the East Enlargement of the EU*, ed. Ilja Srubar (Hamburg: Reinhold Krämer Verlag, 2003).

[68] See e.g., Susan Baker, "Between the Devil and the Deep Blue Sea: International Obligations, Enlargement and the Promotion of Sustainable Development in the European Union," *Journal of Environment and Planning* (2) 2000; CEPS, *The Environment in European Enlargement*, Report of a CEPS Working Party (Brussels: Centre for European Policy Studies, 2000); David Wilkinson, Claire Monkhouse, and David Baldock, *The Future of EU Environment Policy: Challenges and Opportunities*, A Special Report for the All-Party Parliamentary Environment Group (London/Brussels: Institute for European Environmental Policy, December 2004).

entrants' "full compliance with the environmental *acquis* will probably only be achievable in the long term."[69] In negotiating forty-three transition periods, variously granting the CEECs from 2005 to 2015 to carry out certain directives, the EU averted inaugurating enlargement under a cloud of non-compliance. Yet it also refused or reduced a score of requested delays, and many of the deadlines appear unrealistically short.[70] The derogations the EU did accord aptly but awkwardly cover the very investment intensive, administratively arduous obligations most vulnerable to disruption by the CEECs' financial, institutional, and political difficulties. By deferring, rather than differentially tailoring or dispensing with the more onerous environmental requisites, the EU may have opened lasting, potentially insidious implementation gaps between the new members and the EU-15. Some analyses suggest the European Court could furnish a safety valve, using its discretion to manage infringement proceedings to moderate the impacts of an Eastern implementation deficit. The necessarily ad hoc nature of such case-by-case enforcement, however, has engendered concerns about the dangers of developing an excessively litigious approach to EU regulatory compliance. The environmental sector already accounts for over a third of all actions brought for breach of EU law, with annual new complaints jumping from 161 in 1996 to over 500 in 2003.[71] Chronic compliance problems in the CEECs, even unintentional, could weaken the regime's continuing credibility.

While much work remains before the CEECs fulfill their existing responsibilities, the entrants must also grapple with myriad other

---

[69] European Commission, *Accession Strategies for Environment*, p.1.

[70] DANCEE, *The Environmental Challenge of EU Enlargement in Central and Eastern Europe* (Copenhagen: Danish Cooperation for Environment in Eastern Europe/Ministry of Environment, 2001), pp.11-12; WRR, *Towards a Pan-European Union*, Reports to the Government 59 (The Hague: Netherlands Scientific Council for Government Policy, 2001), pp.167-168. Compare the requested transition periods in DANCEE, Table 3.1, and WRR, Table 4.14, with the agreed transition periods in European Parliament, *The Enlargement Process of the EU*, Table, p.2.

[71] See Charalampos Koutalakis, "Environmental Harmonization in Central Eastern Europe: Lessons from the Southern Enlargement," The Hellenic Observatory, London School of Economics and Political Science, London, July 2004, at http://www.lse.ac.uk/collections/hellenicObservatory/pdf/HO_e_papers/Koutalakis_Paper_0704.pdf ; R. Daniel Kelemen, *The Rules of Federalism: Institutions and Regulatory Politics in the EU and Beyond* (Cambridge: Harvard University Press, 2004); European Commission, *Fifth Annual Survey on the Implementation and Enforcement of Community Environmental Law—2003* (Luxembourg: Office for Official Publications of the European Communities, 2004), p.6.

pressing claims on their limited political and economic resources. Indeed, though environmental movements played an important part in the 1989 revolutions, environmental issues have since slipped down the public agenda. Green parties have struggled to gain traction and domestic NGOs remain weak. CEEC civil society seemingly provides poor foundations for strengthening environmental standards beyond the demands of accession.[72] Now that membership gives them a hand in shaping Community actions, many share the European Parliament's concern that the enlargement countries "may not have an equivalent commitment to ensure a high level of environmental protection, and could form a blocking minority that might resist measures to firm up future EU requirements."[73]

If so, their choices could weigh heavily on EU policy. In the consensus driven European Council, even without assuming a descent into least-common-denominator decision-making, objections from the CEECs could demote or dilute environmental priorities. Under the representation arrangements agreed in preparation for enlargement by the 2001 Treaty of Nice, the CEECs seat 151 of 732 Members of Parliament. In the Council of Ministers, qualified majority voting requires legislation pass by 72.3% of the votes and be approved by either a majority or two-thirds of the member states, according to the case. Here, the eight CEECs hold 77 of 321 votes, or 24%.[74] Were they to close ranks with Belgium, Ireland, and the Southern European states, widely—if not always entirely accurately—considered the Union's environmental "laggards," EU policy could conceivably take a more conservative turn.[75]

---

[72] Andreas Beckman, "Pushing on the Door: the Role of East European NGOs in Enlarging the EU," in *EU Enlargement and Environmental Quality: Central and Eastern Europe and Beyond*, eds. Sabina A-M. Crisen and JoAnn Carmin (Washington, DC: Woodrow Wilson International Center for Scholars, August 2002); David L. Ellison, "Politics and the Environment in Central Europe," paper prepared for the 2004 Conference of Europeanists, Chicago, 11-13 March 2004, at http://www.europanet.org/conference2004/papers/G6_Ellison_revised.pdf

[73] European Parliament, *The Enlargement Process of the EU*, p.62.

[74] Treaty of Nice, *Official Journal of the European Communities* C 80/81, 10 March 2001. Transitional arrangements apply until 2007, when, assuming they accede, Bulgaria and Romania will hold 17 and 33 seats respectively in the EP, and add 10 and 14 votes respectively to the Council.

[75] On the leader-laggard dynamic in EU environmental policy, see Sbragia, "Environmental Policy: The 'Push-Pull' of Policy-Making." Cf. Tanja A. Borzel, "Why There is No 'Southern Problem'. On Environmental Leaders and Laggards in the European Union," *Journal of European Public Policy* 7 (1) 2000.

Enduring implementation failures or persistent political opposition from the CEECs could convince some members that the EU can no longer achieve ambitious policies collectively. Some observers evoke the possibility the EU could then split into different environmental camps. Provided new regulations conform to the EU treaties, EU policy permits members to enact national legislation where no EU law exists or, in certain circumstances, where members judge Union standards insufficiently rigorous. Alternatively, under circumscribed conditions, the Enhanced Cooperation procedures introduced by the Amsterdam and Nice Treaties allow a minimum of eight members to work through EU institutions to adopt regulations stricter than those applied by the Union as a whole. Should the CEEC entrants consistently thwart strong EU policy, environmental "leader" states may eventually turn to these tools where they can.[76]

There is reason to question, though, whether the new members will prove systematically hostile to progressive EU policies. In fact, CEEC states rapidly looked to engage the EU on environmental issues after Communism's collapse. A 1991 Czech initiative created the ongoing "Environment for Europe" process, launching regular pan-European ministerial conferences and establishing a first international institutional framework for addressing regional environmental issues.[77] Decided to revamp their inadequate environmental regulations, the CEECs mostly enacted standards comparable to and in some cases surpassing EU legislation.[78] Some are pioneering innovative instruments such as environmental funds to finance environmen-

---

[76] Ingmar von Homeyer, Alexander Carius, and Stefani Bär, "Flexibility or Renationalization: Effects of Enlargement on EC Environmental Policy," in *The State of the European Union: Risks, Reform, Resistance, and Revival, Vol.5*, eds. Maria Green Cowles and Michael Smith (Oxford: Oxford University Press, 2000); Stefani Bär, Ingmar von Homeyer, and Anneke Klasing, "Overcoming Deadlock? Enhanced Co-operation and European Environmental Policy After Nice," in *Yearbook of European Environmental Law, Vol.2*, ed. Han Somsen (Oxford: Oxford University Press, 2002).

[77] See Brian Slocock, "'Whatever Happened to the Environment?': Environmental Issues in the Eastern Enlargement of the European Union," in *Back to Europe: Central and Eastern Europe and the European Union*, ed. Karen Henderson (London: UCL Press, 1999), pp. 154-157.

[78] See e.g., Miko, "The Czech Republic on the Way to Accession"; Zylicz and Holzinger, "Environmental Policy in Poland"; Baškytė and Kundrotas, "Environmental Policy in Lithuania," in Holzinger and Knoepfel eds., *Environmental Policy in a European Union of Variable Geometry?*

tal protection and investments.[79] And the environmental priorities the candidates conveyed to the Commission prior to accession parallel those of the EU.[80] Today, CEEC decision-makers claim the EU policy model and its sustainable development goals as their own. Rather than banding to frustrate future measures, CEEC experts dismiss prospective coalitions with the EU's environmental laggards, pointing instead to more attractive alliances with their neighbors and green role models, Austria and Germany.[81]

Perhaps such professions are only politic from accession state officials at present. But environment ministries are not the lone CEEC constituency for the EU's commitment to a "high level of environmental protection." Much of the new members' hypothesized antagonism to stringent regulation stems from the imputed costs. To be sure, CEEC governments, firms, and taxpayers will scrutinize the price of environmental policies. But they will also consider the benefits. Here, cross-national polling data show CEEC citizens no less willing than their EU compatriots to accept increased taxes or dedicate a portion of their incomes for the purpose of pollution prevention.[82] Key sectors of the CEEC business community support adopting EU environmental standards. The EU is the region's primary trading partner, representing more than half its imports and exports, and is its leading source of foreign direct investment. For multinationals and export-oriented enterprises in particular, meeting EU regulations assures access to the EU market. It is often a precondition for subcontracting to EU firms, reduces transaction costs, avoids accusations of ecological dumping, and may open "green" commercial opportunities.[83]

---

[79] Neil Hawke and Pamela Hargreaves, "Financing Environmental Improvement: the Use of Environmental Funds in EU and CEE Countries," *European Environmental Law Review* (April) 2003.

[80] REC, *Applicant Countries' Contribution to the 6th Environmental Action Programme*, Final Draft, Compiled for European Commission DG Environment (Szentendre, Hungary: Regional Environmental Center, 9 October 2000).

[81] Petr Jehli?ka and Andrew Tickle, "Environmental Implications of Eastern Enlargement: The End of Progressive EU Environmental Policy?" *Environmental Politics* 13 (1) 2004, pp.86-92.

[82] Ronald Inglehart et al. eds., *Human Beliefs and Values: A Cross-Cultural Sourcebook Based on the 1999-2002 Values Surveys* (Mexico City: Siglo Veintiuno Editores, 2004), Tables B001, B002.

[83] See Liliana B. Andonova, *Transnational Politics of the Environment: The European Union and Environmental Policy in Central and Eastern Europe* (Cambridge: MIT Press, 2004).

All told, the advantages for the CEECs of joining the EU environmental regime will almost certainly outweigh the costs. The gains from fully applying the *acquis*, from improved public health, avoided pollution damages, increased economic efficiency, etc., are substantial. They have been calculated at €102 billion to €531 billion net present value for the ten CEECs over the period 1999-2020, equivalent to €9.3 billion to €54 billion annually. Lower to upper-bound estimates for expected annual benefits equal 4.8% to 14.5% of GDP in the Czech Republic, 2.2% to 15.6% in Hungary, 2.9% to 14.8% in Poland, and 3.9% to 19.0% of GDP in Slovakia. For the eight CEEC entrants, the *lowest* estimate of benefits (€87.3 billion) is 10% greater than the *highest* figure (€79.3 billion) for environmental accession's costs.[84] Should experience confirm these projections, the argument that strong standards can increase both the economic and environmental commonweal would likely influence CEEC politicians and publics pondering future EU measures as well.

Over time, the Eastern entrants will undoubtedly alter the arc of EU environmental policy. Collective decision-making will be both more varied and more cumbersome in a Union of twenty-five than of fifteen. The CEECs as a group, however, are unlikely to prove either overwhelmingly favorable or unremittingly resistant to progressive EU environmental policies. Accession obliged the applicants to accept the Union's regulatory regime at once and as a whole. As EU members, the CEECs will influence, evaluate, and respond to each new policy proposal individually. Measure to measure and state to state, the CEECs' preferences and positions will naturally differ.

EU policy-making itself could reinforce this tendency. Each enlargement raises anew the question of ensuring policy cohesion in a Union embracing more diverse national circumstances. In response, the 1997 Amsterdam Treaty reaffirms subsidiarity, instructing Brussels to favor regulating by broad framework directives "leav[ing] to the national authorities the choice of forms and methods" of implementa-

---

[84] ECOTEC Research and Consulting, *The Benefits of Compliance with the Environmental Acquis for the Candidate Countries*, DGENV Contract: Environment Policy in the Applicant Countries and Their Preparations for Accession, Final Report, Birmingham/Brussels, July 2001; European Commission, *The Challenge of Environmental Financing in the Candidate Countries*.

tion.[85] But the very space EU legislation increasingly leaves to national administrative discretion opens the field to sharpened domestic political debate. Competing interests can fare very differently under contrasting applications of the law. In Poland, World Bank cost estimates for environmental accession vary from $22 billion to $43 billion. Diverging interpretations of EU requirements largely account for the difference.[86] Precisely because disparate conditions prevail among the CEECs, differing constructions of the issues will likely muster different domestic coalitions in each country, differentially shaping their respective behavior in Brussels.

Ultimately, environmental policy in the enlarged EU will more resemble Gulliver's travails than Sisyphus'. Rather than struggling against a single rock of CEEC opposition, it will labor under multiple constraints—political resistance, conflicting economic priorities, capacity limitations, implementation shortfalls—some looser here, others binding more tightly there, and originating not only in the East but from all points of the compass. Unlike Gulliver, EU environmental policy cannot hope to escape all such restraints. But unlike Sisyphus, it will yet progress.

## The Enlarged EU and the World Environment

The European Union now covers 3.9 million square kilometers and counts 454 million inhabitants producing an annual GDP of €10 trillion.[87] On one indicator of environmental pressure, the economy's demand for raw materials, the EU every year requires 16.5 tonnes (metric tons) per capita of Direct Material Input—fossil fuels, minerals, biomass—in the EU-15 and 11.5 tonnes in the accession states.[88]

---

[85] Treaty of Amsterdam, Protocol on the Application of the Principles of Subsidiarity and Proportionality [Art.6], *Official Journal of the European Communities* C 340, 7 November 1997.

[86] Gordon Hughes and Julia Bucknall, *Poland: Complying with EU Environmental Legislation*, World Bank Technical Paper No.454 (Washington, DC: World Bank, February 2000), pp.ix passim.

[87] Eurostat, *Key Facts and Figures About the European Union* (Luxembourg: Office for Official Publications of the European Communities, 2004), pp.8, 69; Eurostat, *Eurostat Yearbook 2004* (Luxembourg: Office for Official Publications of the European Communities, 2004), pp.40, 120.

[88] EEA, *Europe's Environment: The Third Assessment* (Copenhagen: European Environment Agency, 2003), p.19.

The Union's twenty-five member countries annually consume 1.69 billion tonnes oil equivalent in energy and emit 5.07 billion tonnes $CO_2$ equivalent of greenhouse gases.[89] Their cities, towns, industry, and infrastructure yearly increase the EU's built-up surface area by 1.5% and their citizens each generate over 500 kg of municipal waste. Their fleets land 6.7 million tonnes of fish and their foresters fell 350 million cubic meters of trees a year.[90] By any measure, the EU looms very large in the Earth's ecology.

The EU aspires to tread more lightly on the planet's environment and to carry greater weight leading international environmental policy-making. The Union's own impacts on the world's atmosphere, oceans, and land underscore the considerable pressures threatening the shared global commons and the need for concerted action to preserve them. Its integration into the international economy, its reliance on the world's natural resources for food, fuels, and raw materials, and its concerns that rising environmental stresses exacerbate poverty and political instability underlie the EU's interests in global sustainable development.[91] "Interdependence is the defining characteristic of the modern world," avers British Prime Minister Tony Blair. "What we lack at present is the common agenda that is broad and just and global institutions to execute it. That is the real task of statesmanship today."[92] To the nations of the world striving to construct an international architecture for governing the global environment, the EU holds out its own system of collective deliberation and pooled sovereignty as a template. "A cooperative, multilateral approach is vital, . . . [that] seeks to strengthen international environmental law and the authority of multilateral organizations," Commission President Romano Prodi recently argued. "I cannot think of a greater challenge.

---

[89] Gross inland energy consumption and greenhouse gas emissions in 2001. Eurostat, *Energy: Yearly Statistics Data 2002*, p.9; EEA, *Analysis of Greenhouse Gas Emissions Trends and Projections in Europe 2003* (Copenhagen: European Environment Agency, 2004), pp.4, 10.

[90] Eurostat, *Eurostat Yearbook 2004*, pp.172, 246, 248; Eurostat, *A Selection of Environmental Pressure Indicators for the EU and Acceding Countries* (Luxembourg: Office for Official Publications of the European Communities, 2003), p.14. Built up land data for 13 of the EU-25.

[91] Robert Madelin et al., *Report of Working Group "Strengthening Europe's Contribution to World Governance,"* White Paper on Governance, Working Group No.5, An EU Contribution to Better Governance Beyond Our Borders, Brussels, May 2001.

[92] Tony Blair, "Prime Minister's Speech on Sustainable Development," London, 24 February 2003, at http://www.number-10.gov.uk/output/Page3073.asp

But Europe can draw on 50 years of European integration for all the instruments it needs to propose a new development model."[93]

Expansion might then be expected to enhance the EU's global standing as exemplar and as exponent of sustainable development and international environmental collaboration. The entry of ten new members extends the sphere of its environmental laws and adds heft to its environmental statecraft. Yet many of the same questions accession raises within the Union recur in its external relations. The attraction of the EU example will wax or wane not with enlargement's reach but with its success. And just where the CEECs' preferences fall on particular issues could either fortify or water down the EU's international stance. Indeed, even as it offers its model of environmental cooperation to the international community, the EU has drafted a new Constitution for Europe, compelled in part by the complexities of multilateral governance in an ever-larger Union.[94]

Climate change diplomacy illustrates the challenges confronting the EU's leadership ambitions. With accession, the EU gathers twenty-three of the thirty-eight countries whose greenhouse emissions the 1997 Kyoto Protocol limits.[95] The ability to speak for so many parties lends the EU the strength of numbers in the international forum. Yet greater numbers could render such potentially potent EU consensus harder to gain, more difficult to maintain, and ponderous to maneuver in fluid multilateral negotiations. Already, prior to enlargement, critics complained the EU devoted more time to internal coordination meetings than to international bargaining. Having laboriously forged a common position, the EU often seems unprepared with alternative strategies when its interlocutors parry

---

[93] Romano Prodi, President of the European Commission, "Climate Change—The Real Threat to Global Peace," San Rossore, 15 July 2004. See also Robert O. Keohane "Ironies of Sovereignty: The European Union and the United States," *Journal of Common Market Studies* 40 (4) 2002; Fraser Cameron, "The European Union and Global Governance," EPC Working Paper (Brussels: European Policy Centre, November 2003).

[94] Fully discussing the Constitution lies beyond the scope of the present chapter. It appears, however, that some of the Constitutional reforms intended to streamline the EU's internal dynamic and strengthen its external action could work to reduce the environment's place in Community policy. See Peter Beyer et al., "The Draft Constitution for Europe and the Environment—the Impact of Institutional Changes, the Reform of the Instruments and the Principle of Subsidiarity," *European Environmental Law Review* (July) 2004.

[95] Malta and Cyprus have no emissions obligations.

Union proposals or proffer their own initiatives.[96] During one crucial 2000 climate conference in The Hague, the US and UK appeared to have engineered a last-minute transatlantic accommodation, only to see negotiations collapse into public recriminations when the Union's full complement could not coalesce around Britain's mediation.[97]

Enlargement also intersects with specific elements of the evolving climate regime in ways that could undercut EU leadership efforts. In Kyoto, the EU-15 pledged to trim their total greenhouse gas emissions 8% below 1990 levels by 2008-2012. Under this collective cap, known as the EU "bubble," the Union elaborated a burden-sharing agreement whereby some members' deeper cuts (e.g., −21% in Denmark and Germany, −12.5% in the UK) allow emissions to grow in the Cohesion countries (e.g., +25% in Greece, +27% in Portugal). Meanwhile, independently of the EU, the CEECs promised to clip greenhouse gas production by 6-8%. But because their emissions had already tumbled precipitously as their economies contracted after 1989, these targets in fact leave them substantial headroom they are unlikely to need. Kyoto's rules in turn let the CEECs sell unused portions of their allowances to other countries who may then count them as credits against their own emissions limits. Denounced as trafficking in "hot air," these phantom reductions have generated considerable controversy. Buyer and seller could meet their Kyoto obligations on paper without eliminating any real emissions at all.[98]

With the Protocol's entry into force in February 2005, negotiations will soon turn to hammering out greenhouse policy beyond Kyoto. As Kyoto's avowed champion, the EU will come under considerable pressure to bolster the regime's forward momentum by pushing for additional emissions reductions. Enlargement may complicate the enterprise. The CEECs will be loath to surrender much of the copi-

---

[96] See Farhana Yamin, "The Role of the EU in Climate Negotiations," in *Climate Change and European Leadership: A Sustainable Role for Europe?* eds. Joyeeta Gupta and Michael Grubb (Dordrecht: Kluwer Academic Publishers, 2000).

[97] "Summary of the Sixth Conference of the Parties to the Framework Convention on Climate Change, 13-25 November 2000," *Earth Negotiations Bulletin* 12 (163) 27 November 2000; Michael Grubb and Farhana Yamin, "Climatic Collapse at The Hague: What Happened, Why, and Where Do We Go From Here?" *International Affairs* 77 (2) 2001.

[98] See Michael Grubb, Christiaan Vrolijk, and Duncan Brack, *The Kyoto Protocol: A Guide and Assessment* (London: Royal Institute of International Affairs, 1999).

ous (marketable) quotas Kyoto provided them and will doubtless argue from the Cohesion countries' example to be permitted significant emissions growth. Importing Eastern hot air into the EU bubble, however, would invite accusations of environmental hypocrisy and set a lax precedent for urging emissions cuts on other parties. No EU negotiating strategy that appears to significantly pad the Union's collective post-Kyoto commitment with spurious CEEC reductions will likely prove politically saleable in the international arena. But holding the CEECs to less inflated targets—while still leaving room for their economic development—risks requiring potentially untenable exertions from the remaining EU members. Despite their present policies and planned future measures, the EU-15 are projected to miss their Kyoto target, let alone a stricter post-Kyoto limit.[99] No EU negotiating strategy that appears to rely on significantly deeper reductions from the EU-15 will likely prove politically credible in the international arena. If it is to lead the international community to shoulder further climate commitments, the EU will have to demonstrate how the European Community will do so as well.

Promoting international cooperation forms only one facet of the EU's wider sustainable development agenda and negotiating formal conventions only one avenue of its influence. (After all, of some 1200 international environmental agreements concluded since 1972, the EU participates in fewer than 80.)[100] Enlargement itself represents an important vehicle for the Union's global environmental goals. Accession's environmental obligations, the EU believes, afford the new members "the opportunity to make progress towards an economic development that is sustainable and avoids the type or scale of environmental problems now faced in Western Europe."[101] In the EU's sustainable development strategy, "Acting at home will provide international leadership."[102]

---

[99] EEA, *Greenhouse Gas Emissions Trends and Projections in Europe 2004* (Copenhagen: European Environment Agency, 2004). Nine of the EU-15 are also projected to fall short of their EU burden-sharing obligations.

[100] See Ronald B. Mitchell, "International Environmental Agreements: A Survey of Their Features, Formation, and Effects," *Annual Review of Environment and Resources* (28) 2003.

[101] European Commission, *Communication: On the Sixth Environment Action Programme of the European Community—"Environment 2010: Our Future Our Choice,"* COM(2001) 31 final, Brussels, 24 January 2001, p.5.

[102] European Commission, *A Sustainable Europe for a Better World*, p.5.

Early signals show some degree of success. To be sure, accession is barely a year old, approximation is not complete, and many implementation issues remain. Much recent progress in the CEECs reflects "clean-up by default" as pollution levels dropped with their economic downturn and restructuring.[103] Even so, as the Eastern economies recover, available evidence suggests their efforts to introduce EU standards are bearing fruit. Water quality in the CEECs displays marked improvement. EU policies have contributed to decreased discharges from agricultural, industrial, and municipal sources, lowering pollutant concentrations in rivers, lakes, and coastal waters.[104] The accession states have also dramatically curbed air pollution. From 1990-2000, they cut particulate matter emissions by 35%; $NO_x$ diminished 31%; $SO_2$ dropped 60%; and the heavy metals cadmium and lead fell by 47% and 60%. Analyses into the influences of various emissions drivers— population and GDP growth, fuel mix, etc.—indicate abatement measures prompted by EU legislation weigh heavily in these trends.[105]

For several reasons, the enlargement experience could reverberate outside the EU. First, such accomplishments demonstrate the Union fulfilling its environmental rhetoric and leading by example. As it strives "to promote international action to protect the environment," the EU is keenly aware the "[Community's] credibility . . . will be commensurate with the extent to which it puts its own house in order."[106] Second, the pollution reductions realized by the CEECs result in good measure from installing new environmental plant and equipment. Enlargement expands market possibilities for Europe's rapidly growing environmental technologies sector, providing a commercial complement to leverage the EU's pursuit of policy clout.[107] By the same token, enlargement expands the EU market overall, increasing the incentive to exporters everywhere to meet its regulatory

---

[103] Petr Pavlínek and John Pickles, "Environmental Pasts/Environmental Futures in Post-Socialist Europe," *Environmental Politics* 13 (1) 2004, p.243.

[104] EEA, *Europe's Environment: The Third Assessment*, pp.165ff.

[105] EEA, *Air Pollution in Europe 1990-2000* (Copenhagen: European Environment Agency, 2004).

[106] (Fifth EAP) *Towards Sustainability*, p.12.

[107] Pawel Kaźmierczyk ed. *The Environmental Technology Market in Central and Eastern Europe: An Overview of the Czech Republic, Hungary, Poland, Slovakia, and Slovenia* (Szentendre, Hungary: Regional Environmental Center, December 1997); ECOTEC Research and Consulting, *Analysis of the EU Eco-Industries, Their Employment and Export Potential*, Study for the European Commission DG Environment, Brussels, 2002.

requirements. (It is for this reason that EU—or US—product standards frequently become the de facto international standard.) Finally, the green accession essentially conducts an enormous public field trial of EU environmental policies. National decision-makers seeking environmental solutions frequently look to other countries' experiences, drawing on approaches tested elsewhere rather than developing new measures *ex nihilo*. International organizations from the World Bank and OECD to the International Network of Green Planners increasingly endeavor to facilitate and propagate such policy learning. Europe's other transition economies and many newly industrializing nations suffer environmental stresses similar to the CEECs. And their levels of economic and institutional development are generally closer to the new members than the EU-15, making the accession states appear a more pertinent potential model. The enlargement countries' example could provide an indirect fillip to the EU's international influence through the cross-national diffusion of best practices and emulation of successful policy instruments.[108]

Nevertheless, the EU's often pronounced lack of progress in many other areas tempers the appeal of enlargement's green example. Waste production in the entrant states is rising. EU policies may even have discouraged some successful pre-existing recycling and waste management policies. Extending the EU's Common Agricultural Policy seems destined to intensify agricultural practices in the accession countries. Without measures to the contrary, expanded production could increase soil erosion, pollution from pesticide and fertilizer use, and biodiversity and habitat loss. And the CEECs appear well on their way to adopting the EU's unsustainable car dependency and road transport patterns, abetted by EU infrastructure development programs and investments.[109]

---

[108] See Kristine Kern, Helge Jörgens, and Martin Jänicke, "The Diffusion of Environmental Policy Innovations: A Contribution to the Globalisation of Environmental Policy," Discussion Paper FS II 01-302, Wissenschaftszentrum Berlin für Sozialforschung, Berlin, 2001; Helge Jörgens, "Governance by Diffusion: Implementing Global Norms Through Cross-National Imitation and Learning," FFU Report 07-2003, Environmental Policy Research Center, Freie Universität Berlin, 2003; Kerstin Tews, Per-Olof Busch, and Helge Jörgens, "The Diffusion of New Environmental Policy Instruments," *European Journal of Political Research* (42) 2003.

[109] EEA, *Europe's Environment: The Third Assessment*; Zsuzsa Gille, "Europeanising Hungarian Waste Policies: Progression or Regression?" *Environmental Politics* 13 (1) 2004; EEA, *Agriculture and the Environment in the EU Accession Countries: Implications of Applying the EU Common Agricultural Policy* (Copenhagen: European Environment Agency, 2004); EEA, *Paving the Way for EU Enlargement: Indicators of Transport and Environment Integration—TERM 2002* (Copenhagen: European Environment Agency, 2002).

Achieving the Union's sustainable development objectives demands more than cumulating disparate environmental improvements. It will require coordinating policies at multiple levels, across sectors and across borders, in a coherent long-term framework. EU exhortations will not suffice. Implementing such environmental integration depends largely on member state actions. EU climate policy goals, for instance, hinge on energy policy tools that remain the preserve of national governments. Laying the ground for more holistic approaches, the 1998 Cardiff European Council urged the sectoral Council formations to craft environmental integration strategies.[110] The EU's Strategy for Sustainable Development flatly states, "Sustainable development should become the central objective of all sectors and policies."[111] Yet that degree of policy cohesion will elude the enlarged EU for some time. Institutional rivalries, fragmented responsibilities, and poor co-ordination between relevant authorities dog much of the CEEC policy apparatus. Community environmental integration efforts have flagged as well. Commission reviews openly acknowledge the need for "Revitalising the Cardiff process" and "A new start for the Lisbon strategy."[112] The EU's new members pose a critical first test to these new beginnings.

Over the three decades since the EU's first environmental initiatives, environmental policy has become both an essential element of European integration and a central component of the Union's engagement with the world. Eastern enlargement challenges these developments. Managing the Union's increasing domestic diversity demands according to members an indispensable degree of national policy discretion. Ensuring the Union's sustainable environmental future demands requiring from members an indispensable degree of international policy coordination. Indeed, this, in a nutshell, is the fundamental challenge confronting global environmental governance. Where the EU must reconcile subsidiarity with policy integration, the world community must reconcile national sovereignty with international

---

[110] European Council, "Presidency Conclusions," Cardiff European Council, 15 and 16 June 1998, at [http://ue.eu.int/ueDocs/cms_Data/docs/pressData/en/ec/54315.pdf].

[111] European Commission, *A Sustainable Europe for a Better World*, p.6.

[112] European Commission, *Integrating Environmental Considerations Into Other Policy Areas—A Stocktaking of the Cardiff Process*, COM(2004) 394 final, Brussels, 1 June 2004, p.33; European Commission, *Working Together for Growth and Jobs—A New Start for the Lisbon Strategy*, COM(2005) 24, Brussels, 2 February 2005.

interdependence. "Europe can be a beacon of economic, social, and environmental progress to the rest of the world," so the EU proclaims.[113] How well the Union of twenty-five nations will succeed in merging the sometimes diverging claims of subsidiarity and sustainability will tell whether that beacon will show the way to possible greater global cooperation or illuminate instead a cautionary tale.[114]

---

[113] European Commission, *A New Start for the Lisbon Strategy*, p.3

[114] The author thanks Anne Bergenfelt, Anne Burrill, Ian Clark, and Rob Donkers for very helpful discussions, and the project editors and participants for their comments on an earlier draft.

# About the Authors

**Muriel Asseraf** was a Research Assistant at the Center for Strategic and International Studies. She holds a Master of International Affairs from Columbia University's School of International and Public Affairs where she focused on International Security Policy, exploring in particular tools of preventive security. Before that, Ms. Asseraf was a broadcast journalist in Paris, France. She holds a B.A. in French Modern Literature and Linguistics from the University of Paris III-La Sorbonne Nouvelle.

**Henri J. Barkey** is the Bernard L. and Bertha F. Cohen Professor in International Relations and International Relations Department Chair at Lehigh University. He served as a member of the U.S. State Department Policy Planning Staff (1998-2000). He has authored, co-authored and edited four books, the most recent being *Turkey's Kurdish Question* (with Graham Fuller). Most recently he has written "The Endless Pursuit: Improving U.S.-Turkish Relations," in Morton Abramowitz (ed.) *Friends in Need: Turkey and the United States after September 11*, "Cyprus: The Predictable Crisis," *The National Interest* with Philip H. Gordon, and a forthcoming U.S. Institute of Peace Special Report, "Turkey and Iraq: The Perils (and Prospects) of Proximity."

**Timofei V. Bordachev** is Deputy Editor-in-Chief of "Russia in Global Affairs" and Director of Studies of the Council on Foreign and Defense Policy (SVOP). From 1998 to 2003, he was Assistant Editor at Carnegie Moscow Center and held the position of Researcher then Senior Researcher at Russian Academy of Science (Institute of USA and Canada, Institute of Europe) where he developed research programs on conflict resolution and Russia – EU affairs. Timofei Bordachev studied modern history at Saint-Petersburg State University (Department of History). He then obtained a degree of Master of Arts in European Politics and Administration at College of Europe (Bruges, 1997) and a degree of Candidate of Science at Saint-Petersburg State University (Institute of International Relations, 1998).

**Esther Brimmer** is Deputy Director and Director of Research at the Center for Transatlantic Relations at the Paul H. Nitze School of

Advanced International Studies at The Johns Hopkins University. From 1999-2001 she was a Member of the Office of Policy Planning at the U.S. Department of State. She also served as a Senior Associate at the Carnegie Commission on Preventing Deadly Conflict and as a Special Assistant to the Under Secretary of State for Political Affairs. She has worked for the Democratic Study Group in the U.S. House of Representatives and for the management consultancy firm McKinsey & Company. She received her D.Phil. and master's degrees in international relations from the University of Oxford. She wrote a monograph on "The United States, the European Union and International Human Rights Issues" and edited two other volumes, *The European Union Constitutional Treaty: A Guide for Americans* and *The EU's Search for a Strategic Role: ESDP and Its Implications for Transatlantic Relations.*

**Leonor Coutinho**  is currently a Research Fellow of the Portuguese Science Foundation (FCT), visiting the Economics Department at Georgetown University, in Washington D.C. Her current research interests are in the area of open economy macroeconomics, policy coordination, and the external implications of European economic integration. She was previously a Marie Currie Research Fellow at the Centre the Centre for European Policy Studies, in the area of macroeconomic policies and EU-US economic relations. She has also worked as a consultant for the World Bank on several occasions, in the area of international finance. She has obtained a Ph.D. in Economics, from the European University Institute in Florence.

**Patrick M. Cronin**  is Senior Vice President and Director of Studies at the Center for Strategic and International Studies (CSIS) in Washington, D.C. Dr. Cronin is also Executive Director of the Hills Program on Governance. Previously, he served as Assistant Administrator for Policy and Program Coordination at the U.S. Agency for International Development (USAID). Prior to that, Dr. Cronin served as Director of Research and Studies at the U.S. Institute of Peace. From 1990 until 1997, he held various positions at the National Defense University's Institute for National Strategic Studies, including head of Asian studies, director of research, and deputy director of the Institute. At the same time, he helped create *Joint Force Quarterly* and was the journal's first executive editor. He had also taught at the Paul H. Nitze School of Advanced International Studies (SAIS) at Johns Hopkins University and at the University of

Virginia. He was a commissioned officer in the U.S. Naval Reserve (intelligence) from 1987 until 2000. Dr. Cronin attended Oxford University, where he earned both D.Phil. and M.Phil. degrees in international relations, and the University of Florida, Dr. Cronin's publications include *The United States and Coercive Diplomacy, 2015: Power and Progress*, and *From Globalism to Regionalism: New Perspectives on U.S. Foreign and Defense Policies.*

**Chantal de Jonge Oudraat** is Senior Fellow and Research Program Coordinator at the Center for Transatlantic Relations, Paul H. Nitze School of International Studies, Johns Hopkins University. She is also an Adjunct Professor at the Edmund A. Walsh School of Foreign Service, Georgetown University and Vice-President of Women in International Security (WIIS). In 2002 she was a Robert Bosch Foundation Research Scholar at the American Institute for Contemporary German Studies (AICGS), Johns Hopkins University. Previously she served as co-director of the Managing Global Issues project at the Carnegie Endowment for International Peace in Washington D. C (1998-2002), Research Affiliate at the Belfer Center for Science and International Affairs, Harvard University (1994-1998), and Senior Research Associate at the United Nations Institute for Disarmament Research (UNIDIR) in Geneva (1981-1994). She was the co-editor of *Managing Global Issues: Lessons Learned* (2001) and the author of many book chapters and articles. Dr. de Jonge Oudraat received her Ph.D. in Political Science from the University of Paris II (Panthéon).

**Stefan Fröhlich** is Professor of International Politics at the University Erlangen-Nürnberg, Germany. From 2002 to 2003 he was Visiting Professor at the Johns Hopkins University's Center for Transatlantic Relations in Washington D.C. From 1998-2002 Prof. Fröhlich was Director of the postgraduate "European Studies Program" at the Center for European Integration Studies in Bonn and Teaching Professor at the Department of Political Sciences at Bonn University. He served as a Research Assistant in the German Bundestag (1985-1999) and at the Department of Political Sciences in Bonn (1998-1994). 1997 he was Senior Fellow at the Deutsche Gesellschaft für Auswärtige Politik (German Council on Foreign Relations). He studied of Political Sciences, English, and Spanish in Bonn, Paris, Washington, and Philadelphia (MA) and obtained his Ph.D. (1989) and Dr.habil. (1996) from Bonn University. He has published numerous books and articles in national and international anthologies and journals on European integration issues, transatlantic relations, and U.S. and German foreign policy.

**Daniel Gros** is the Director of the Centre for European Policy Studies, a leading think tank on European affairs. He has served on the staff of the IMF, as an advisor at the European Commission, and as visiting professor at the Catholic University of Leuven and the University of Frankfurt. He has advised the governments of Russia, Ukraine and other Central and Eastern European countries on trade and exchange rate matters and their relations with the EU. He is currently advisor to the European Parliament and member of the Conseil Economique de la Nation (2003-2005); from 2001-2003 he was a member of the Conseil d'Analyse Economique (advisory bodies to French Prime Minister and Finance Minister). Since April 2005 he is President of San Paolo IMI Asset Management. He has published widely in international academic and policy oriented journals. He authored numerous monographs and four books.

**Ulrike Guérot** is a Senior Transatlantic Research Fellow in the Berlin office of the German Marshall Fund, where she focuses on a broad range of issues dealing with European integration and transatlantic relations. Her previous positions include the German Council on Foreign Relations (DGAP), Berlin, where she headed the European Union Unit. Prior to DGAP, Dr. Guérot has been an Assistant Professor at the European Studies Department of The Paul N. Nitze School for Advanced International Studies (SAIS), Johns Hopkins University, in Washington, D.C.; a Senior Research Fellow at the Paris-based think-tank Groupement d'Etudes et de Recherches 'Notre Europe' under the guidance of President Jacques Delors; and a staff member on the German Bundestag's Committee on Foreign Relations. Her work has been widely published, and she is a frequent commentator on European affairs for European and American newspapers, radio and TV stations.

**Nicolae Idu** is Jean Monnet professor and president of the Romanian European Community Studies Association. Dr. Idu is also director general of the European Institute of Romania and director of the Romanian Journal of European Affairs; former secretary of state (vice-minister) for European Integration with the Romanian Government.

**László J. Kiss** is Professor of International Policy at Corvinus University and at Andrássy German-speaking University both of which are in Budapest. He is also Director of the Teleki Institute Centre for Foreign Policy Studies. He has published extensively on Hungarian, German and Austrian foreign policy. His most recent books are *Europe of 25: National and European Interests in Europe* and *Globalization and Foreign Policy: International System and Theory at the Turn of Millennium*. He is President of the Editorial Board of the Hungarian periodical *Foreign Policy Review*.

**Anne-Marie Le Gloannec** is a Senior Research Fellow at CERI, National Foundation for Political Sciences, Paris. From 1997 until 2001 she was Deputy Director of the Centre Marc Bloch, Berlin. She has been teaching at various institutions including Viadrina, Frankfurt an der Oder ; Freie Universität, Berlin ; IEP, Lille ; IEP, Paris ; and the Johns Hopkins School of Advanced International Studies, Bologna. She has written on Germany, German foreign policy, and European foreign policy. Her latest publications include "Partial Decoupling, Limited Linkages and Possible Spill-overs : Greek-Turkish Relations in a Wider Context," in Mariso R. Lino ed. : *Greek-Turkish Relations: A Key to Stability in the Eastern Mediterranean* (2005); coeditor with Aleksander Smolar the volume *De Kant à Kosovo : mélanges en l'honneur de Pierre Hassner* (2003); and editor of *Der Staat in Deutschland* (2002).

**Michael Leigh** is the Deputy Director General in the European Commission's Directorate General for External Relations, responsible for European Neighbourhood Policy, relations with Eastern Europe, Southern Caucasus and Central Asia, Middle East and South Mediterranean. Before joining DG External Relations, he was Director in DG Enlargement responsible for Turkey as well as Bulgaria, Cyprus, Malta, Romania. He was an advisor to Commissioners Hans van den Broek, Frans Andriessen and Lord Cockfield. He has held a number of other positions in the Commission and the General Secretariat of the Council for over twenty years. Dr. Leigh's background is in political science; he holds a BA from Oxford University, a PhD from M.I.T., and has published and lectured on European integration, foreign policy and international relations at Wellesley College, the University of Sussex, and Johns Hopkins School of Advanced International Studies in Bologna.

**David Michel** is Senior Associate at the Center for Transatlantic Relations at The Johns Hopkins University's Paul H. Nitze School of Advanced International Studies. He is also Program Coordinator of the Center's Transatlantic Dialogue on Climate Change, a study group engaging a broad range of stakeholders and opinion leaders from both sides of the Atlantic to examine issues facing the US and the EU as they seek to address the ongoing challenge of global climate change. He has written on issues of capacity building, intergenerational equity, and international justice in climate policy, and has consulted with several NGOs participating in the climate regime negotiating process. Educated at Yale University, the École des Hautes Études en Sciences Sociales, Paris, and The Johns Hopkins University, his current research focuses on transatlantic relations, the politics of complex multilateral negotiations, and international environmental cooperation.

**Antonio Missiroli** is Senior Research Fellow at the EU Institute for Security Studies in Paris. His most recent publications are "Central Europe between the EU and NATO" (*Survival*, Winter 2004-05), the chapter on "Italy: what change, what continuity" in *La defence en Europe*, edited by Patrice Buffotot (2005). Also, he edited a Chaillot Paper on *Disasters, Diseases, Disruptions: A new D-Drive for the EU* . From July 2005 he will be Chief Policy Analyst at the European Policy Centre in Brussels.

**Hanna Ojanen** is Senior Researcher at the Finnish Institute of International Affairs (Helsinki). She obtained her Doctorate of Political and Social Sciences at the European University Institute in Florence. Her previous positions include Professor in international politics, Department of Political Science, University of Helsinki (2002) and Visiting Fellow, WEU Institute for Security Studies, Paris (1999). She is a member of the editorial committees of several journals, among which the *Journal of Peace Research and Cooperation and Conflict*. Her publications include "If in 'Europe,' then in its 'core'? Finland," in Kaiser, Wolfram & Jürgen Elvert (eds.) *European Union Enlargements: A Comparative History* (2004); "EU defence policy and relations with NATO: some competition may be welcome," *The Yearbook of Finnish Foreign Policy 2004*; "La Finlande dans l'Union Européenne: quelle européanisation?" in *Nordiques*, vol. 1 (2/2003); together with Nina Græger and Henrik Larsen," The ESDP and the

Nordic countries: Four variations on a theme. Programme on the Northern Dimension of the CFSP" (2002), and "The EU and its 'Northern Dimension' - an actor in search of a policy, or a policy in search of an actor?" *European Foreign Affairs Review*, vol. 5 (3/2000).

**Kristi Raik** is a researcher in the Finnish Institute of International Affairs. Dr. Raik's recent publications include "EU Accession of Central and Eastern European Countries: Democracy and Integration as Conflicting Logics'," *East European Politics and Societies* 18:4 (2004), 567-594; (with Teemu Palosaari), "It's the Taking Part that Counts: The new Member States adapt to EU foreign and security policy", *FIIA Report* (10/2004); and *Democratic Politics or the Implementation of Inevitabilities? - Estonia's Democracy and Integration into the European Union.* (2003).

**Lothar Rühl** is former State Secretary in the German Defense Ministry (1982-1989). He studied law and history in Bonn and Paris, was Deputy Editor-in-chief of *Die Welt* from 1969-1983, correspondent for the "ZDF" in Brussels 1973-1980, and since 1993 Professor for International Politics at the University Cologne. His publications include *Rußlands Weg zur Weltmacht* (Russia's way to a world power) 1981; *Zeitenwende in Europa* (Turning points in Europe) 1990; *Aufstieg und Fall des Russischen Reiches* (Rise and fall of the Russian Empire) 1992; *Deutschland als Europäische Macht* (Germany as a European power) 1996; *Can the CSCE be a Role-Model to Frame the Political Processes of the Greater Middle East with Europe and the US?* 2004; *Das Reich des Guten. Machtpolitik und globale Strategie Amerikas* (The benign empire: Power Politics and global Strategy of the US) 2005.

**Peter Wehrheim** works for the European Commission in the Directorate General for Agriculture and Rural Development. Until 2004 he was an Assistant Professor and Research Fellow at the Faculty of Agriculture, University of Bonn, Germany. Between 2002 and 2003 he was a visiting scholar at the Department of Economics, University of Maryland. His has a background in agricultural, resource, and transition economics as well as in quantitative policy analysis. Among the research projects he was in charge of were various related to Russia's transition process, others dealt with aspects of EU enlargement and resource management in Central Asia. In 1994 he received his Ph.D. from the University of Giessen, Germany, with a dissertation on "Agricultural Sector Effects of EU Enlargement by the EFTA

Member States – a Quantitative Analysis". He has been a consultant to the European Commission, the World Bank, the Food and Agricultural Organisation (FAO) of the United Nations and national organizations in Germany.